Trinity

Gender in English Society, 1650–1850

THEMES IN BRITISH SOCIAL HISTORY

edited by John Stevenson

This series covers the most important aspects of British social history from the Renaissance to the present day. Topics include education, poverty, health, religion, leisure, crime and popular protest, some of which are treated in more than one volume. The books are written for undergraduates, postgraduates and the general reader, and each volume combines a general approach to the subject with the primary research of the author.

Currently available

Gender in English Society, 1650–1850

The emergence of separate spheres?

ROBERT B. SHOEMAKER

Longman
London and New York

Addison Wesley Longman Limited
Edinburgh Gate,
Harlow, Essex CM20 2JE,
United Kingdom
and Associated Companies throughout the world

*Published in the United States of America
by Addison Wesley Longman Inc., New York*

© Addison Wesley Longman Limited 1998

First published 1998

ISBN 0 582 103150 PPR
ISBN 0 582 103169 CSD

British Library Cataloguing in Publication Data
A catalogue record for this book is
available from the British Library

Library of Congress Cataloging-in-Publication Data
Shoemaker, Robert Brink.
    Gender in English society, 1650-1850: the emergence of separate
spheres / Robert B. Shoemaker.
    p.   cm. – (Themes in British social history)
    Includes bibliographical references and index.
    ISBN 0-582-10315-0 (ppr). – ISBN 0-582-10316-9 (csd)
    1. Sex role–England–History–17th century. 2. Sex role–England–
History–18th century. 3. Sex role–England–History–19th century.
4. England–Social conditions–17th century. 5. England–Social conditions–
18th century. 6. England–Social conditions–19th century.   I. Title.
II Series.
HQ1075.5.G7S56   1998
305.3'0942–dc21
                                                                97-38879
                                                                CIP

Set by 7 in 10/12 Baskerville
Produced by Longman Singapore Publishers (Pte) Ltd
Printed in Singapore

Contents

For Wendy and Roland

Acknowledgements

Gender is a relatively new subject in English history, but given the number of books and articles which have now been published it is arguably time to take stock and assess what the 'big picture' might look like. To attempt such a broad overview one must depend very much on the research of others, and I would here like to thank all those historians whose published work made this book possible to write. The writings of Leonore Davidoff, Catherine Hall, and Amanda Vickery posed the central problem addressed in these pages. The works of Maxine Berg, Anna Clark, Patricia Crawford, Peter Earle, Amy Erickson, Anthony Fletcher, Edward Higgs, Bridget Hill, Margaret Hunt, Thomas Laqueur, Phyllis Mack, Clare Midgley, Jane Rendall, Randolph Trumbach, and Deborah Valenze were also especially valuable. A number of other scholars generously allowed me to consult, and in some cases cite, their work in progress: John Beattie, Lisa Cody, Tim Hitchcock, Tim Meldrum, John Tosh, and Martin Wiener.

Much of the book was written during a very pleasant stint as a Visiting Scholar at the Institute for Research on Women and Gender at Stanford University. I am grateful to the staff and fellows of the Institute for their hospitality and for the opportunity to present an early draft of Chapter 5 to the scholars' seminar. The Institute was an exceptionally stimulating place in which to work and I would especially like to thank Susan Bell, Edith Gelles, Karen Offen, and Stephanie McCurry for many lively discussions.

Portions of the work in progress were read by Lisa Cody, Ludmilla Jordonova, and Mary Vincent and I am grateful for their helpful comments. In numerous conversations, Faramerz Dabhoiwala made many useful suggestions. Wendy Bracewell, Anthony Fletcher, Tim Hitchcock, Margaret Hunt, John Stevenson, and John Tosh read drafts of the entire manuscript and gave valuable advice and encouragement. Special thanks go to Tim Hitchcock, who has been a constant source of ideas and references over many years, and Margaret Hunt, whose careful reading and insightful criticisms saved me from numerous errors and forced me to clarify my thoughts. No doubt none of these gender historians will agree with everything that follows, but this book has benefited enormously from their un-stinting generosity.

On a personal note, I would like to thank Clara Shoemaker and the late David Shoemaker for showing me, from an early age, that there is more than one way to be a good mother and father. This book is dedicated to Wendy and Roland, without whom it would have been written much faster, but it would have been much less re-warding to write.

R.B.S.
Sheffield, April 1997

CHAPTER ONE

Introduction

Gender as a category of historical analysis first appeared in the writings of American feminists in the 1970s. By the 1980s the term was being used by historians of England, and by the mid-1990s books and articles with the word 'gender' in the title were appearing virtually every month. But what does the term mean? For some, it has become little more than a synonym for women, as a form of political correctness (as in the expression 'women and gender'). For others, it is a synonym for sex: even in scientific literature, 'gender' is now used in discussions of the behaviour of plants and insects. But the term's most powerful use is as an *alternative* to sex as a way of characterising the differences between men and women in history. Whereas the term 'sex' implies that these are based on biological differences, which are by implication unchanging, the term 'gender' is used to make the point that dissimilarities between the sexes are socially, culturally, and politically constructed, and are therefore subject to change. This is not to deny the importance of the biological distinctions between the sexes, but to argue that these can be interpreted in various ways and that therefore biological facts, by themselves, cannot explain the historically variable differences between men's and women's lives. Gender is thus 'a social category, imposed on a sexed body'.[1]

Gender history was also adopted as a means of introducing a relational notion into women's history. Since men and women are usually defined in terms of what the other is not, it is impossible to study one without needing to know about the other. Women's history had not always excluded men, but where masculinity was dis-

Place of publication is London unless otherwise stated.

1 Joan Scott, 'Gender: a useful category of historical analysis', *American Historical Review* 91 (5) (Dec. 1986), p. 1056.

cussed it tended to be depicted, unrealistically, as unchanging. Indeed, this was one of the criticisms levelled at feminist historians' use of the concept of patriarchy: it suggested that male dominance and oppression were constant in history.[2] As Natalie Davis argued in 1975, 'it seems to me that we should be interested in the history of both women and men, that we should not be working only on the subjected sex any more than an historian of class can focus entirely on peasants. Our goal is to understand the significance of the *sexes*, of gender groups in the historical past.'[3] Thus it became necessary to reconceptualise the history of both women and men. Although arguably most history until the blossoming of women's history in the 1970s had been solely about men, historians had failed to analyse masculinity *per se*, in the sense that they had failed to identify the ways in which definitions of suitable behaviour for men, as men, had changed over time. Stimulated by the men's movement of the late 1970s and early 1980s, in which it was argued that modern men were imprisoned by the patriarchal roles which society had cast for them, historians looked to the past, hoping to identify alternative conceptions of masculinity.[4]

Initially, however, gender history grew out of the insights and accomplishments of women's history and feminism. The substantial work on women's history in the past forty years, building on the pioneering work of Alice Clark and Ivy Pinchbeck in the first half of the twentieth century and stimulated by the postwar growth in social history and the feminist movement, shed considerable light on the history of concepts of femininity and other forces which shaped women's social roles (and, by implication, those of men). Nonetheless, gender history was also in a sense a critique of earlier women's history. By the early 1980s, women's or feminist history had been subject to a number of criticisms by historians, both from within women's history and the feminist movement and from without. There was concern that it had failed to have much of an impact on traditional history, in part because it had been too concerned with 'reclamation' – adding the women who had been left out of traditional historical accounts, without examining critically the whole framework of history. Women were now recognised to the extent that an extra chapter might be devoted to them in a textbook, or an

2 Sheila Rowbotham, 'The trouble with patriarchy', *New Statesman* (Dec. 1979).

3 N. Z. Davis, 'Women's history in transition: the European case', *Feminist Studies* 3 (1975–6), p. 90.

4 M. Roper and J. Tosh (eds), 'Introduction', in *Manful Assertions: Masculinities in Britain since 1800* (1991), p. 6.

extra lecture in a course, but this was essentially tokenism. Men remained the unanalysed norm, women the exception which merited specific mention. Symptomatic of this is the fact that while 'women' became an entry in the indexes to many books, few historians felt the need for a separate index entry for men. To most historians, what women's history had demonstrated was that some women in history had played important roles, in politics, religion, work, or culture, but that was all; their inclusion in historical writing did not change the fundamental male-centred narratives of history. Moreover, women had too often been presented as victims of an ever-present patriarchal system, who lacked agency to shape their own lives. Finally, women's history, it was argued, had presented women, as well as men, as a homogeneous and unchanging historical category, and thus had failed to take into account the very real differences in the historical experiences of women depending on their class, race, and other factors, as well as the fact that the category of 'women' itself was historically constructed. It was hoped that a new approach using gender would address these issues.

How historians would use gender as a new analytical tool was in a sense a wide-open question, since the major bodies of social theory used by historians (such as those of Marx or Weber) were developed in the nineteenth and early twentieth centuries and did not include gender as an analytical concept. Consequently, historians of gender have been particularly open to the influence of contemporary historiographical trends. Like much women's history written in the 1970s, early work on gender was influenced by the general efflorescence of social history of the time, and thus sought to document the historically different material situations of men and women, inserting gender into analyses of social systems alongside class and race. Given the political links between the socialist and feminist movements, it is not surprising that the British Marxist historical tradition was particularly influential, with its interest in the origins and development of class consciousness. Thus, two important early works covering the period of this study investigated the relationship between gender identities and class formation: Susan Amussen's study of how the hierarchies of class and gender in early modern England were reflected in political theory, and Leonore Davidoff and Catherine Hall's study of the role of gender in the formation of the English middle class between 1780 and 1850.[5]

5 S. Amussen, *An Ordered Society: Gender and Class in Early Modern England* (Oxford, 1988); L. Davidoff and C. Hall, *Family Fortunes: Men and Women of the English Middle Class, 1780–1850* (1987).

But as the theoretical interests of some historians changed in the 1980s, the history of gender changed as well. With the growing influence of literary theory, psychoanalysis, and post-modernism, historians began to focus on language and symbols as the keys to understanding how gender identities are created and maintained. As the grammatical origins of the term suggest, the pervasive binary oppositions in the English language appeared to be a key force in constructing or reinforcing gender identities. Focusing on definitions of sexual differences rather than their cause, gender came to be seen as a system of meanings which could be identified from close readings of texts. This approach has been particularly influential among literary and cultural historians, where a vast body of research has been published, but it has also influenced historians of politics and society. In her influential manifesto for gender history, Joan Scott argued that because gender distinctions are frequently used to express hierarchies of power, the study of the gendered language of society and politics provides keys to understanding how inequalities of both gender and power are constructed. Thus, Denise Riley's exploration of the interrelated development of the categories of 'women' and 'the social' in nineteenth-century discourse shed new light not only on nineteenth-century understandings of femininity, but also on the social reform movements of the time.[6] Discourse analysis, therefore, has begun to demonstrate that ideas about gender are both pervasive and influential in virtually all areas of history.

The linguistic and post-modernist turn in gender history has not been without its critics, however. Some feminists have argued that post-modernism is politically damaging, since in bypassing questions of causation it offers no programme for change. Hence the title of a recent critique is 'Gender as a postmodernist category of paralysis'. By focusing on the multiple meanings of masculinity and the ways in which men are constrained by discourses, it is argued, post-modernists de-emphasise the central facts of male power and privilege.[7] Others have criticised the focus on written discourse on other grounds: the reliance on language and texts as source materials makes it difficult to write about historically subordinate groups, such as women, who have written far fewer texts than men; it can lead historians to ignore non-written sources such as artefacts or

---

6 Scott, 'Gender', p. 1070; Denise Riley, *'Am I that Name?' Feminism and the Category of 'Women' in History* (1988), pp. 44–51.

7 Joan Hoff, 'Gender as a postmodernist category of paralysis', *Women's History Review* 3 (1994), pp. 149–68.

body language; and too much attention has been paid to dominant discourses at the expense of alternative viewpoints. More fundamentally, historians using this approach have often neglected to examine the relationship between systems of meaning and their historical context, often assuming that prescriptive literature constitutes a reliable picture of historical reality. As Jane Rendall has argued, identifying constructions of masculinity and femininity is only half the battle; historians then need to 'ask questions about the location, and extent, of those constructions ... as they change over time and place'.[8]

The approach adopted in this book, as part of a series on 'Themes in British Social History', is that of a social historian. Returning to the roots of gender analysis in sociological history, the book sets out to describe the ways in which male and female patterns of behaviour differed (or not) in important areas of private and public life over the period 1650–1850. Recognising the theoretical advances of recent years and the importance of language to the construction of gender roles, however, attention will be paid to the role played by ideas and ideologies in shaping such patterns of behaviour, and in constructing the records historians use. Thus the first substantive chapter is on ways of thinking about gender at the time, and throughout the book attention is paid to cultural expectations of proper masculine or feminine behaviour, as well as evidence of actual behaviour, in order to show how gender roles as lived were a product of the interaction between ways of thinking about gender and a combination of social, economic and political forces.

GENDER IN THE 'LONG EIGHTEENTH CENTURY'

The two centuries between 1650 and 1850 constitute a period of immense social, economic, political, and cultural change in England. Yet given the fact that gender roles often change very slowly, one often needs to look at such long and turbulent periods of time in order to detect significant changes. This period experienced industrialisation and considerable population growth; the emergence of a class society, with an increasingly prominent middle class; the breakdown of the religious monopoly held by the Church of England; the emergence of popular participation as a significant feature in political life, and a major reduction in the powers of the monarchy; and

8 Jane Rendall, 'Uneven developments: women's history, feminist history, and gender history in Great Britain', in K. Offen et al. (eds), *Writing Women's History: International Perspectives* (1991), p. 52.

the advent of mass literacy and widespread access to printed books, pamphlets, and periodicals. As will become evident, each of these developments had implications for gender roles.

Indeed, many historians have identified this as a crucial period of change in the history of gender roles, though the precise timing of the change depends on the perspective of the historian and the precise aspect of society which is being investigated. Despite differences in approach, a common argument is evident in the work of most historians of gender who have studied this period: that there was an increasing separation of spheres, a sharpening of the differences between male and female social roles. Thus, historians argue that this was the period in which the pattern of gender roles which dominated modern life until very recently was formed. The most important and influential of these arguments is that of Davidoff and Hall, whose book *Family Fortunes: Men and Women of the English Middle Class, 1780–1850* (1987), made the argument that this period witnessed the emergence of separate spheres in England, as an integral part of the process of the formation of a middle class with a distinctive identity and lifestyle: they argued that this was the period when middle-class women became excluded from public life and concentrated their attention on their domestic responsibilities, which were increasingly viewed as moral duties. Although *Family Fortunes* was perhaps the most sophisticated and influential of the arguments for the emergence of separate spheres, there are a number of other theories about changes in gender roles in this period which implicitly or explicitly involve a similar approach.

The earliest articulations of this approach came in the history of women's work, in books first published between the first and second world wars: Alice Clark's *Working Life of Women in the Seventeenth Century* (1919; despite the title the book covered the preindustrial period generally) and Ivy Pinchbeck's *Women Workers and the Industrial Revolution* (1930). Although the books addressed different time periods, they made similar arguments about a decline in women's work opportunities caused by fundamental changes in the structure of the economy. Both argued that, due to 'the triumph of capitalistic organisation' in Clark's case and the industrial revolution in Pinchbeck's case, employment became separated from the home in a way which led to significantly reduced employment opportunities for women and turned most women into homemakers. These arguments are still influential: Bridget Hill's survey of women's work in the eighteenth century, published in 1989, followed Pinchbeck's argument quite closely. More recently, Deborah Valenze has added an ideological dimension to this argument by ascribing women's exclusion from many industrial jobs in this period to the growing importance of the values of productivity and rationality which marginalised women, but the narrative of women's exclusion from work remains unchanged.[9]

As (allegedly) women began to spend more time with their families, it is argued that the family became more sharply differentiated from public life. A number of intellectual and literary historians have argued that the late-seventeenth and early eighteenth centuries witnessed the demarcation of family life as private and sentimental, and defined as feminine, in opposition to the masculine world of public affairs. Susan Amussen and others, for example, have pointed to the importance of John Locke's contractual theory of politics, which broke the previously assumed link between hierarchical theories of power in the family and within the state. Thus, the (feminine) family lost its political, and public, importance. Other historians have argued that the expanding realm of literature came increasingly to prescribe women's place as in the home. Kathryn Shevelow, for example, suggests that the first periodicals in the early eighteenth century enclosed women 'within the private sphere of the home' with their prescriptions of 'an increasingly narrow and restrictive model of femininity', and similar arguments have been made about late-seventeenth-century drama and the eighteenth-century novel. Women in literature were increasingly depicted and defined in sentimental, domestic, and maternal terms. Thus, Ruth Perry has argued that the celebrations of maternity in late-eighteenth-century novels led to the 'cultural appropriation of women's bodies for reproductive purposes'.[10]

Historians who have studied actual patterns of family life in this period have detected different changes: the two most influential works, by Lawrence Stone and Randolph Trumbach, argue that the patriarchal families of the seventeenth century gave way to more egalitarian marriages in the eighteenth, as family relationships be-

9 Bridget Hill, *Women, Work and Sexual Politics in Eighteenth-Century England* (Oxford, 1989); Deborah Valenze, *The First Industrial Woman* (Oxford, 1995). The historiography of women's work is reviewed in more detail in Chapter 4 (pp. 145–8).

10 Amussen, *An Ordered Society*; Susan M. Okin, 'Women and the making of the sentimental family', *Philosophy and Public Affairs* 11 (1981), pp. 65–88; Kathryn Shevelow, *Women and Print Culture: The Construction of Femininity in the Early Periodical* (London and New York, 1989), p. 1; Catherine Belsey, *The Subject of Tragedy: Identity and Difference in Renaissance Drama* (1985); Ruth Perry, 'Colonizing the breast: sexuality and maternity in eighteenth-century England', *Journal of the History of Sexuality* 2 (1991), p. 234.

came dominated by sentiment and affect. While egalitarian marriages might be seen to undermine gender difference, even these
historians have tried to fit their arguments into a model of emerging separate spheres. Stone has argued that the breakdown of patriarchy contributed to greater individualism and autonomy which
allowed for the development of separate spheres of activity for each
sex, with women spending their time on domestic duties and leisure
activities, and Trumbach has argued that egalitarian marriages actually led to more differentiated gender roles, since men felt that
equality might make them effeminate and therefore they felt the
need to assert their masculine identity outside the home, for
example by avoiding and disapproving of homosexual behaviour.
While Stone and Trumbach's work focused largely on the elite
classes, Anna Clark has charted the adoption of separate spheres by
the working class in the early nineteenth century in response to
growing domestic tensions resulting from changes in the sexual division of labour caused by industrialisation, and a political need to
demonstrate respectability to their social superiors.[11]

As women's lives were increasingly defined by their family responsibilities and became more sharply differentiated from those of
men, it is argued, greater emphasis was placed on women's distinctive features: their alleged greater religiosity and distinctive sexuality. A number of historians have suggested that this period
witnessed a 'feminisation of religion', in which women acquired a
more prominent religious role as a result of the growth of movements of religious enthusiasm and evangelicalism, which gave prominence to what were seen to be the feminine characteristics of
feeling, benevolence, and moral purity.[12] Concurrently, a considerable amount of recent work suggests that there were a number of
changes in both the ideology and practice of male and female sexuality. Thomas Laqueur has argued that there was a fundamental
change in ways of thinking about the body: while in the early modern period female bodies were seen as essentially similar to men's,
but less fully developed, in the eighteenth century there developed

11 Lawrence Stone, *The Family, Sex and Marriage in England 1500–1800* (1977),
esp. pp. 656–7 (it should be noted that Stone suggests that patriarchal marriages
reemerged after 1800); Randolph Trumbach, *The Rise of the Egalitarian Family:
Aristocratic Kinship and Domestic Relations in Eighteenth-Century England* (1978); idem, 'Sex,
gender and sexual identity in modern culture: male sodomy and female prostitution in
Enlightenment London', *Journal of the History of Sexuality* 2 (1991), p. 193; Anna Clark,
The Struggle for the Breeches: Gender and the Making of the British Working Class (1995).

12 Ruth Bloch, 'Untangling the roots of modern sex roles: a survey of four
centuries of change', *Signs* 4 (1978), pp. 245–52; see below, Chapter 6 (pp. 210–11,
216–17).

a 'two-sex' model of understanding the body, in which women's bodies were seen as completely different. At the same time women's sexuality was given a new and more distinctive definition. The early modern view that lust was a fundamentally (though not exclusively) feminine vice was transferred to men, and women were increasingly seen as sexually passive, as reflected in the belief in the early nineteenth century, not yet supported by medical evidence, that women did not need to experience an orgasm in order to conceive. Changes in actual sexual practice are difficult to study, but a recent argument posits a parallel change: Henry Abelove and Tim Hitchcock have argued that over the eighteenth century heterosexual intercourse came to focus exclusively on vaginal penetration, excluding previous practices of fondling and mutual masturbation. Concurrently, sexual practices such as homosexuality and masturbation were increasingly condemned.[13] In sum, recent arguments suggest that the role of men and women in sexual intercourse became increasingly differentiated and fixed, with men playing the active role and women the passive. Women were considered too morally pure to be attracted to sex, and were instead expected to concentrate on motherhood.

Both in the realm of ways of thinking about gender, and in terms of social practice, a number of similar arguments about changes in gender roles in this period have thus been made which fit within the separation of spheres paradigm. Despite these powerful arguments and the considerable amount of evidence marshalled in support of them, there have been some voices of dissent. A number of historians of work have pointed to long-term continuities in the basic structure of women's work, calling into question arguments that women's employment opportunities were crucially constricted by the development of capitalism or industrialisation. Recent research suggests that women's work was already low skilled, low status, low paid, and narrowly confined to a small number of sectors of the economy prior to these economic changes.[14] In an important article, Amanda Vickery has taken the argument for continuity further by arguing that a basic separation of spheres, in which 'women were associated with home and children, while men controlled pub-

---

13 Thomas Laqueur, *Making Sex: The Body and Gender from the Greeks to Freud* (1990); Henry Abelove, 'Some speculations on the history of "sexual intercourse" during the "long eighteenth century" in England', *Genders* 6 (1989); Tim Hitchcock, 'Redefining sex in eighteenth-century England', *History Workshop Journal* 41 (1996), pp. 73–90.
14 This historiography is reviewed in the introduction to Chapter 5.

lic institutions', was not a creation of this period, but 'could be applied to almost any century or any culture': arguments for a process
of separation of spheres by gender during this period are based on
the erroneous presumption that there was a significant degree of
overlap between the two sexes in previous centuries. Evidence from
the prescriptive literature, family life, and the sexual division of labour all suggest that such an overlap did not exist in the seventeenth century. Davidoff and Hall's argument tying the evolution of
separate spheres to the formation of the middle class in the early
nineteenth century is undermined by this evidence, as well as by the
fact that there was a similar separation of gender roles among a
broader spectrum of social groups, notably the gentry. The theme
of continuity is also evident in Anthony Fletcher's recent survey of
gender roles over the period 1500 to 1800, in which he emphasises
the continuity of patriarchal control over women's lives, despite its
changing foundations: 'it was not the programme and content of
gender training which changed between 1500 and 1800', Fletcher
argues, 'but merely its mechanism'.[15] In light of these comments it
is clearly necessary to pay more attention to the continuities in gender difference which persisted throughout this period.

   Following the lead of these recent critics, this book reexamines
the cumulative pattern of arguments that the period from roughly
1650 to 1850 witnessed the emergence of a separate spheres regime
of gender roles in which women were increasingly confined to the
home. It will be argued that there are far more continuities in gender roles over this long period than most historians suggest; that the
changes which did occur were less restrictive for women than is suggested by the term 'separate spheres'; that a degree of overlap in
the activities of the two sexes was always maintained; and that those
changes which did occur were the result of gender roles being
forced to adapt not only to ideological shifts, but also to broader social changes. In contrast to Vickery this book does not argue that no
important changes took place. As is evident from an analysis of conduct books and literary representations in Chapter 2, prevailing
ideas about gender difference *were* more sharply divided at the end
of our period than the beginning, and there were also fundamental
changes in ways of thinking of the body and sexuality, as discussed
in Chapter 3. Yet analysis of social practice will suggest that, al-

   15 Amanda Vickery, 'Golden age to separate spheres? A review of the categories
and chronology of English women's history', *Historical Journal* 36 (1993), quote
from p. 413; Anthony Fletcher, *Gender, Sex and Subordination in England 1500–1800*
(1995), p. 407.

though these new ideas could be influential, for example in shaping the types of employment available to men and women (Chapter 5), their impact on social practice was far less dramatic, especially in the 'private sphere' of sexual behaviour and family life (addressed in Chapters 3 and 4). Other, more important, changes in gender roles in this period resulted less from ideological changes than from the broader social and political changes which transformed English society by dramatically expanding both men's and women's opportunities in the 'public sphere' (Chapters 6 and 7). In questioning arguments about separate spheres we will thus question not only the extent of change which took place during this period (whether such a pattern of gender difference actually emerged in this period), but also the suitability of this metaphor for describing gender relations at any time during the period, and the role that ideological developments played in shaping such changes in gender roles as actually occurred.

Recent work also points to the need to extend the study of this topic back into the seventeenth century. While most research on separate spheres has focused on the period from 1750 to 1850, Vickery argues for important continuities from the seventeenth century to the nineteenth century. Taking a different tack, the key period in Fletcher's argument for the reformulation of patriarchy was between 1660 and 1800. Indeed, the important intellectual, cultural, and economic changes which are often seen as influential in shaping gender roles all started in the century before 1750. Not only, as is increasingly being argued, did this earlier period witness dramatic economic growth (in commerce, agriculture, and protoindustry) and social change (notably in urban areas, and among the middle class), but, as is demonstrated in Chapters 2 and 6, the ideological foundations of gender were seriously undermined by the events of the 1650s. The collapse of religious and political authority during the Interregnum led to new claims for women's fundamental spiritual equality with men, claims which would prove influential in shaping subsequent developments in feminist thought and religious and political practice. Any assessment of the changes in gender roles which took place between preindustrial and industrial England must thus start with the dramatic upheavals of the Interregnum.

Finally, the implications of recent work by a number of historians that the ideas and practice of separate spheres were not limited to the middle class suggest that arguments linking changes in gender roles specifically to a narrative of class development, arguments

which were common during the period when feminist history and
Marxist history were closely linked, may be difficult to sustain. While
social differences are frequently important when identifying patterns of gender conduct, it is clearly necessary to recognise that gender roles also cross social divides; class is therefore not the best
principle along which to organise a study of gender. Although there
is little material here on the aristocracy, the intention otherwise is
to examine gender roles throughout English society, paying attention to differences in patterns of male and female behaviour wherever they are significant.

PROBLEMS OF EVIDENCE

The historian of gender must confront significant evidential problems, though those raised by the history of masculinity and the history of femininity are very different. Historians of women have long
faced the difficulties associated with writing the history of the less
powerful, with sources either thin on the ground or created from
the point of view of men. For much of this period the majority of
women were illiterate, and thus we have no records of their own
thoughts (we should note, of course, that a significant, if always
smaller, proportion of men were also illiterate). Even where women
were able to write, cultural constraints which dictated that it was im-
modest to write for anything other than a private audience often
dissuaded them from doing so, or led to their writings not being
preserved. Thus the records of women's activities were generally
kept by men, and reflect the biases of a male-dominated society.
Where women are identified at all in the records, they are usually
identified by their marital status rather than social status or occupation, which makes it very difficult to analyse the social and economic position of women. Women's activities are also hidden by the
fact that households and married couples were very often recorded
under the name of the husband only. Thus the extent of married
women's membership in voluntary societies, for example, is impossible to measure. More fundamentally, the very categories of
thought and activities in the records were defined with the interests
of men in mind and do not reflect the realities of women's lives,
which frequently involved informal activities in work or politics
which tend not to get recorded. The very concept of an 'occupation', for example, was designed for men; women tended to work in
a number of different tasks, often combining a variety of forms of
paid labour with their domestic duties. Thus even when contempo-

raries did attempt to identify women by their economic activities, there was not an obvious occupational label which they could claim. Similarly, women's lack of formal rights meant that their political activities tended to be informal and behind the scenes and there-fore rarely recorded.

While the sources for the history of women are severely limited, those for the history of men are in a sense too plentiful. Whereas women tend not to be given an occupational label men always are, which often gives a misleading sense of occupational identity, since men, too, often worked in more than one job. Similarly, while men might be described as the heads of charitable societies in the nine-teenth century, it was sometimes the women behind the scenes who actually ran such organisations. A second problem with the history of men and masculinity concerns the secondary sources. Far too little work has so far been done by historians on this subject, for al-though most works of history have been about men, in most cases historians have failed to analyse such material with a view to com-paring and differentiating men's and women's activities, and par-ticularly to identifying changing definitions of masculinity and patterns of male behaviour. Because men are presumed to be the norm, their history is not differentiated from the general narrative of historical change. Paradoxically, it is far more straightforward to present an overview of the history of women over this period than a history of men, since the secondary literature on the former is so much richer than the latter. Consequently, this book often focuses disproportionately on the changing experiences of women, al-though every attempt has been made to identify important changes and continuities in male gender roles wherever they have been documented.

Further problems result from the fact that any study of gender roles raises questions about men's and women's private lives which, in centuries when such activity was thought to be unproblematic and therefore went unrecorded, can rarely be answered from the available evidence. Did husbands or wives have more informal power in the day-to-day conduct of marriages? Which partner in-itiated sexual intercourse, and how was it conducted? How did men and women perceive their respective roles at home and in the wider world? In an understandable rush to answer these questions, histo-rians have sometimes been too quick to formulate arguments based on limited evidence. More than most historians, in writing the his-tory of gender roles we need to be attentive to the limitations of the sources. Yet by drawing on the insights of post-modernism, we can

also learn from these limitations. By being alert to the ways in which
the categories of records are cultural constructions, we can see that
they themselves are often indicative of gendered attitudes. Through
an awareness of the ways ideologies and practices of gender roles
intersect, it is possible, with caution, to write a new history of gender
roles in the 'long eighteenth century'.

CHAPTER TWO

Ideas about Gender

In the contemporary western world, arguments that women and men naturally possess distinct and separate characteristics are often treated sceptically, but this is a phenomenon of the late twentieth century. People in the seventeenth, eighteenth, and nineteenth centuries had no hesitations in doing this. Heavily reliant on the ideas of Aristotle and the story of Genesis, medieval and early-modern European thought was based on fixed concepts of the masculine and the feminine. In this chapter we will explore what those ideas were, ask whether they changed over this period under the influence of broader intellectual changes, and look at the views of those who dissented from the widely held traditional concepts of gender roles. This chapter sets out the parameters of debate, the limits of thinking in pre-modern England on the nature and social functions of each sex. This begs the question, of course, of how men and women actually lived their lives, whether they acted in the ways prescribed by the authors discussed in this chapter. That is the subject of the remainder of the book. Before looking at social practice, however, it is best to consider how people actually thought about gender in this period.

Because gender roles were perceived as relatively fixed and had been so for centuries, there was little overt discussion of this issue at the time (with some notable exceptions) and this presents a problem of sources. The focus in this chapter is on printed literature, which arguably became more important than oral communication (such as sermons or songs) as a means of shaping popular opinion during this period; in any case, ideas disseminated orally frequently were derived from, or found their way into, print. Most printed material from the period is imbued with *implicit* ideas about gender, but the sources which address this issue explicitly are limited. This

chapter will commence with prescriptive sources, focusing on religious ideas, the assumptions about gender evident in medical writings, and conduct books. Turning to other forms of printed
literature which reveal implicit ideas about gender, we will then
examine periodicals, popular ballads and chapbooks, and novels.
Although such genres account for only a fraction of the possible
printed sources one could examine, their analysis allows us to consider ideas about gender which reached a far broader audience
than the prescriptive literature and which were arguably more influential in shaping gender roles. While the focus in the first two
sections will be largely on widely accepted mainstream views, in the
final section we will turn to the growth of feminism, which over the
course of this period greatly widened the parameters of public debate on gender roles.

PRESCRIPTIVE ROLES

Conceptions of gender difference in the seventeenth century were
fundamentally based on two premises: the biblical story of the creation of the two sexes and medical understandings of the biological
differences between men and women. The Christian view of gender
is clear from the story of Genesis. God created Adam first, and subsequently said, ' "it is not good that the man should be alone; I will
make him a helper fit for him." . . . So the Lord God caused a deep
sleep to fall upon the man, and while he slept took one of his ribs
and . . . made [it] into a woman and brought her to the man'
(Gen. 2: 18–22). One can read this part of the story as providing evidence that even before the fall, God defined women as inferior to
men. With the fall, in which Eve, by tasting the forbidden fruit and
offering it to Adam, was the primary actor, however, women's subordination was made clearer. Her punishment was to experience the
pain of childbearing, and to be subject to the rule of her husband
(Gen. 3: 16). The subjection of wives was more clearly spelled out in
the New Testament, where Paul states, in his letter to the Ephesians,
'as the church is subject to Christ, so let wives also be subject in
everything to their husbands' (Eph. 5: 24). Nonetheless, according
to Peter, husbands were expected to honour their wives and treat
them considerately, due to their vulnerable position as 'the weaker
vessel' (1 Pet. 3: 7).

    Medieval and early-modern Christians found several justifications
for women's inferiority in the story of Genesis and the New Testament: 1) woman was created after man, and from man, and there-

fore man must be more perfect; 2) Eve's role in the fall suggests pride (she thought that by tasting the fruit she could achieve equality with God), that she was governed by the passions, and that women's beauty and sexuality made them potential corrupters of men; 3) women were clearly expected to be subservient to their husbands; and 4) as the 'weaker vessel', women possessed not only less physical, but less mental strength than men. Nonetheless, defenders of women could point out that women and men were equal in their souls; both were created in the image of God and were thought to possess a rational soul. Although a misreading of Genesis by some medieval scholars suggested that even in terms of their souls women were only created in the image of man, not the image of God, this was a minority viewpoint, since it was difficult to ignore the last phrase of Gen. 1: 27: 'So God created man in his own image, in the image of God he created him; male and female he created them'.[1]

The position of women in Christianity was thus ambiguous: it was possible to emphasise either their fundamental inferiority dating from creation or their equality with men in the most important thing one can possess, the soul. How the Bible was interpreted on this issue varied over time. The reintroduction of Aristotelian thought, with its hierarchical view of gender roles, and its synthesis with Christian thought by Thomas Aquinas in the thirteenth century, led to greater emphasis being placed on female inferiority. Yet about the same time there developed a greater veneration of the Virgin Mary, who was seen to represent the positive female virtues of purity, innocence, and humility. The position of women in Christian thought was to a degree further improved by the Renaissance and Reformation, in which greater attention was paid to what women could achieve through education, and the equality of male and female souls was heightened by Luther's belief in the 'priesthood of all believers' and the Protestant reformers' focus on personal relationships with God. Nonetheless, the importance Protestants accorded to marriage and to the scriptures also led them to emphasise the subordination of women to their husbands and the inherent sinfulness of women as revealed in the Garden of Eden. In sum, the medieval notion of female inferiority was not dramatically altered by Renaissance scholars or Reformation theologi-

1 E. C. McLaughlin, 'Equality of souls, inequality of sexes: woman in medieval theology', in *Religion and Sexism: Images of Woman in the Jewish and Christian Traditions*, ed. Rosemary Ruether (New York, 1974), pp. 218–19; M. C. Horowitz, 'The image of God in man – is woman included?' *Harvard Theological Review* 72 (1979).

ans.[2] By the early modern period the Christian tradition incorporated a number of views on women, but the dominant view ascribed inferior qualities to women and placed them in direct subordination to men. Even where positive virtues were assigned to women, such as humility, they only served to highlight women's alleged inferiority.

As Anthony Fletcher has argued, over the course of the seventeenth and eighteenth centuries these scriptural arguments were undermined by the new cosmology which resulted from the scientific revolution, and they were increasingly supplemented by medical explanations of women's inferiority (though both arguments continued to be influential into the nineteenth century).[3] Early-modern medicine, based on the humoral theories of Aristotle and Galen, posited a hierarchical view of the sexes. Under the humoral theory, which viewed the body as composed of four different types of fluids, men were believed to be more perfect and more completely formed because they were hotter and drier than women. (As less perfect beings, women had an innate desire to achieve perfection by coupling with men.) Sexual difference was thus not based on the reproductive organs, which were perceived to be basically identical, except for the fact that female genitalia failed to emerge externally, due to insufficient heat, and remained inverted inside the body.

That such theories had little basis in biological reality is beside the point. As Thomas Laqueur has argued, conceptions of anatomy in this period were based not on sexual difference, but on cultural theories of gender roles: anatomy was a 'representational strategy' in which perceptions about gender differences were imposed on notions of the body.[4] Contemporaries, of course, saw things the other way around: social and cultural definitions of gender were justified by grounding them in perceived biological differences. As cooler and moister beings, women were seen to be weak and passive, and more suited than men to a sedentary lifestyle. (Menstruation, which was necessary because women possessed insufficient heat to purify the blood, further justified their concentration on domestic matters.) With a lower body temperature, women consumed food more slowly, thereby allowing them to store fat and blood for a foetus. Since women lacked the heat to drive sufficient

2 Ian Maclean, *The Renaissance Notion of Woman* (Cambridge, 1980), p. 27.

3 Anthony Fletcher, *Gender, Sex and Subordination in England 1500–1800* (1995), ch. 14. See also pp. 61–4, below.

4 Thomas Laqueur, *Making Sex: The Body and Gender from the Greeks to Freud* (Cambridge, Mass., 1990), pp. 34–5.

blood to the head, they had larger hips, smaller shoulders, and weaker brains than men.[5] Even Margaret Cavendish, the prolific writer of scientific and philosophical treatises and defender of women, wrote that women's brains were too 'soft' and 'cold' for rigorous thought.[6] Women were thus liable to mental inconstancy and deceptiveness. Rather than being governed by their brains, women were governed by their lower parts, and were susceptible to the irrational influence of their uterus, where, of course, they had an excess of blood. By the seventeenth century the uterus was no longer felt to have independent powers, but it was still thought to be sufficiently powerful to cause hysteria, loquaciousness, lust, and irrational behaviour. Men, of course, had everything that women lacked: their hot, dry humours made them active and gave them a general hardness of body and spirit, which gave them intelligence and led them to bravery and honour.[7]

Thomas Laqueur has characterised this understanding of the body as based on a 'one-sex' model of sexual difference, since differences between men and women were perceived as relative rather than qualitative: men were hotter, and although men and women had potentially the same reproductive organs, women's were less perfectly formed. Despite a considerable amount of anatomical research and increasing scepticism of Aristotelian ideas, these theories remained influential into the seventeenth century. Thus, William Harvey, the discoverer of the circulation of the blood, retained the belief that men were hotter, and he thought that it was this heat, rather than their hearts, which increased the supply of blood to their brains, thereby accounting for their larger size.[8] Nonetheless, over the seventeenth and eighteenth centuries the one-sex model came increasingly to be replaced by understandings which stressed the physical differences between the sexes, what Laqueur labels the 'two-sex' model. Female sexual organs, for example, were no longer viewed as imperfect versions of the male, but as perfectly formed for the job they were intended to do. (This was aided by the 'discovery' of the clitoris in 1561, viewed as a female penis, which meant that it became difficult to portray the vagina as an inverted and less fully developed version of the male penis, as it had been.[9])

5 Maclean, *Renaissance Notion of Woman*, pp. 34–5.
6 Quoted by Londa Schiebinger, *The Mind Has No Sex? Women and the Origins of Modern Science* (1989), p. 2.
7 Maclean, *Renaissance Notion of Woman*, p. 41; Laqueur, *Making Sex*, p. 108.
8 Schiebinger, *The Mind Has No Sex?*, p. 187.
9 Laqueur, *Making Sex*; Fletcher, *Gender, Sex and Subordination*, pp. 34–43.

From the late seventeenth century humoral understandings of gender difference were replaced by a new emphasis on sensational psychology based on the nerves. In the eighteenth century both medical writers and authors of fiction came to represent women as possessing thinner, finer, and more delicate nerves than men, thus making them more sensitive to external sensations than men. The new attention to nerves led to greater attention to sexual differences in the brain and differences in the physical structures of male and female bodies. This is reflected in the fact that, for the first time, medical textbooks provided separate illustrations of male and female skeletons. Significantly, however, the new medical theories were still used to justify female inferiority. In 1744, for example, Eliza Haywood reported in *The Female Spectator* that anatomists studying the brain had found that women were physiologically incapable of deep thought. Similarly, in the nineteenth century, evidence that women have larger skulls was used to argue that women's physical development had been arrested at a lower stage of evolution than men, and that their bodies were more similar to children than to men. In addition, the idea that women had finer nerves led to the theory that they were more susceptible to nervous disorders and mental instability, which could arise out of physical changes they experienced in their bodies. Victorian doctors paid considerable attention to the supposed disabilities (mental instability, hysteria, insanity) women suffered due to puberty, menstruation, pregnancy, childbirth, lactation, and menopause (while male puberty and sexuality were not seen as a problem).[10] Thus, despite the shift from a theory of gender hierarchy based on degrees of heat and moisture to theories of distinct gender difference based on nerves and anatomy, medical theories continued throughout this period to be used to justify restrictions on women's capabilities and therefore their opportunities in society. Indeed, the dichotomy of culture versus nature embodied in the new scientific and medical approaches was often perceived as a male/female dichotomy, with women represented as irrational, backwards, and limited by their physical bodies

10 G. J. Barker-Benfield, *The Culture of Sensibility: Sex and Society in Eighteenth-Century Britain* (1992), ch. 1; Schiebinger, *Mind Has No Sex?*, pp. 190–210; Eliza Haywood, *The Female Spectator* 2 (1744), pp. 240–1, cited by Londa Schiebinger, 'Skeletons in the closet: the first illustrations of the female skeleton in eighteenth-century anatomy', in C. Gallagher and T. Laqueur (eds), *The Making of the Modern Body: Sexuality and Society in the Nineteenth Century* (1987), p. 71; Anne Digby, 'Women's biological straitjacket', in *Sexuality and Subordination: Interdisciplinary Studies of Gender in the Nineteenth Century*, ed. Susan Mendus and Jane Rendall (1989), esp. p. 214.

while men were rational and civilised.[11] Throughout this period, men's bodies were never seen as an obstacle: the physical qualities men were believed to possess (such as strength and intelligence) only gave them capabilities.

Conduct Books

Historians of medicine have demonstrated that popular health texts embodying these ideas about physical and sexual difference were widely available at this time. Equally significant, in terms of both their distribution and the ideas about gender they conveyed, were conduct books, a genre which has received rather less attention from historians. Conduct books form part of a long tradition of books of moral instruction, including discussions of the purpose of marriage and the proper ordering of domestic relations, which date back to before the Reformation. Such books became more common from the sixteenth century, with growing literacy and demand for printed books. As the potential market broadened, the content of some books did as well, to include, for example, cooking and medical advice. From the Restoration to the end of our period the genre really came into its own, with at least 500 separate editions published between 1693 and 1760 alone, most of which were targeted at one sex or the other rather than both. Judging by the numbers of editions published, the works were even more popular between the 1770s and the 1830s. According to Anthony Fletcher, the 'stress in this literature on inculcating behaviour according to a person's place in certain predetermined social and gender categories . . . was entirely new' in the eighteenth century. Without overemphasising the novelty of the prescriptions (comparisons with the most popular early-seventeenth-century text, William Gouge's *Of Domestical Duties* [1622] show strong continuities in ideas), Fletcher's point about the role such texts played in the *construction* of gender roles in our period is important.[12]

The popularity of this genre is evident from their publishing history: the most popular book of all, Richard Allestree's *The Whole Duty of Man*, was in print during virtually the entire period of this

11 Ludilla Jordonova, *Sexual Visions: Images of Gender in Science and Medicine between the Eighteenth and Twentieth Centuries* (1989), ch. 2.

12 Kathleen M. Davies, 'Continuity and change in literary advice on marriage', in *Marriage and Society: Studies in the Social History of Marriage*, ed. R. B. Outhwaite (1981), pp. 60–2; Fenela Childs, 'Prescriptions for manners in English courtesy literature, 1690–1760, and their social implications' (D.Phil. thesis, Oxford University, 1984), p. 32; Marjorie Morgan, *Manners, Morals and Class in England, 1774–1858* (1994), p. 13; Fletcher, *Gender, Sex and Subordination*, p. 335.

study: sixty-four editions were published between 1659 and 1842. Other publishing successes included Allestree's *The Ladies Calling* (first published 1673, it went through at least twelve editions up to 1787); an anonymous author's *New Whole Duty of Man: Containing the Faith as well as Practice of a Christian* (a competitor to Allestree's *Whole Duty of Man*; this went through thirty-seven editions between 1744 and 1853); and Sarah Stickney Ellis's *The Women of England* (ten editions between 1839 and 1850). Some books, such as the anonymously published *New Whole Duty of Woman*, were in fact largely copied from earlier books (in this case, *The Ladies Calling*), which suggests that publishers attempted to make the most of what was clearly a lucrative market.

Much of this literature was written by members of the educated elite, and it was often targeted at a middle- or upper-class audience. The full title of Allestree's *The Whole Duty of Man, Laid Down in a Plain and Familiar Way for the Use of All, But Especially the Meanest Reader*, however, demonstrates that such books were often aimed at a wider audience. (Indeed, the competing *New Whole Duty of Man* noted that Allestree's book had been 'indiscriminately put into the hands of not only the common people, but many others'.[13]) Moreover, some authors noted that their advice did not depend on the social class of the reader; in their minds, gender roles were not class-specific. While the earliest were directed at male readers, with the expansion of female literacy during the period many books were also explicitly directed at women. Given the large numbers of copies sold (the standard print run was about 1000[14]), these books must have reached a large and socially diverse audience.

Unsurprisingly, the gender roles prescribed in these texts were closely linked to the theological and medical understandings discussed above. Despite the often secular tone of their works, many of the authors had ecclesiastical connections (Allestree was a conservative Anglican divine, and Ellis was a Congregationalist involved in temperance and missionary work) and biblical justifications continued to be used to justify limitations placed on women's conduct. Medical conceptions of sexual difference were also influential. Writing about women's meekness, Allestree notes that 'nature hath befriended women with a more cool and temperate constitution, put less of fire, and consequently of choler, in their compositions'. The shift to a nerve-based understanding of physical difference in the eighteenth century is echoed in the works of James Fordyce, a non-

13 *The New Whole Duty of Man* (1853 edn), p. ii.
14 Childs, 'Prescriptions for manners', pp. 29–31.

conformist minister who advised men to pay more attention to their feelings and told women to use their greater delicacy to reform men.[15]

Based partly on perceived fundamental theological and anatomical facts, conduct-book writers assigned what they believed were characteristic virtues and faults to each sex. The female virtues mentioned most frequently by these commentators were chastity and purity; modesty, meekness, and patience; tenderness and charity; and piety and devotion. Although sexual continence was a virtue expected of both sexes, conduct manuals followed the prevailing 'double standard' in arguing that it was more important that women be chaste, because woman's infidelity had greater practical consequences (since children of doubtful paternity threatened family property) and because it was thought that, due to their weakness, once women acted immorally their passions would become uncontrollable. Indeed, since women were created subordinate to men and in order to serve their needs, sexual fidelity was the essential female virtue. Keith Thomas has argued that 'from this prime insistence on women's chastity emerged most of the other social restrictions upon her conduct'.[16] It is certainly the case that many of the other words used to describe female virtues in this period, such as shame, honour, propriety, purity, and the most common word of all, modesty, were often euphemisms for chastity. Yet modesty meant more than that; together with meekness, patience, and even silence, it was about a general pattern of reserved behaviour and self-effacement which derived from women's perceived 'softness', their lack of 'choler', and the need for obedience to their parents or husbands.

Also related to women's 'softness' were the female characteristics of affability, tenderness, compassion, and charity, virtues frequently mentioned by the conduct-book writers. Allestree argued that 'female sex . . . being of the softer mold, is more pliant and yielding to the impressions of pity[,] . . . charity . . . [and] clemency'.[17] Women were more sensitive to the needs of others, and in this sense these virtues derive from women's primary functions as mothers and wives. Due to their subjection, wives had to obtain influence over their husbands indirectly – through, in the words of Thomas Gis-

---

15 [R. Allestree], *The Ladies Calling* 6th edn (Oxford, 1693), p. 48; Barker-Benfield, *The Culture of Sensibility*, p. 346.

16 Keith Thomas, 'The double standard', *Journal of the History of Ideas* 20 (1959), p. 214.

17 [Allestree], *Ladies Calling*, p. 53.

borne, 'affection', 'example', and 'charms' rather than through boldness or strength.[18] Outside the home, women's social skills (vivacity, a sense of humour, complaisance) were perceived as a civilising influence on men.[19]

The supposed greater compassion of women also helps explain why the conduct-book writers believed that women were more pious and devout than their male counterparts. God's laws inspire fear and love, according to Allestree, and 'the female sex being eminent for the pungency of both of these, they are consequently the better prepared for the impressions of religion'.[20] In the early eighteenth century writers went further and argued that women were potentially more virtuous and moral than men, and this theme was echoed in the second half of our period by writers involved in the evangelical movement; as Sarah Stickney Ellis phrased it, 'all the noblest passions, the deepest feelings, and the highest aspirations of humanity, may be found within the brooding quiet of an English woman's heart'.[21] One author even suggested that wives could lead the household in family prayer.[22] Nonetheless, women were advised to follow their hearts rather than their minds in religious worship, and avoid 'meddl[ing] with controversy'.[23]

In sum, female virtues were primarily concerned with qualities associated with the emotions; as William Gouge noted, 'yet the man be as the head, the woman [is] as the heart'.[24] Intelligence was not generally considered a female virtue, since 'the men . . . had the larger share of reason bestowed upon them'.[25] Although female intellectual endowments were not considered of primary importance by the conduct-book writers, in the second half of our period some did point to certain types of mental abilities in which women excelled. Women's minds were commonly described as quick and imaginative, but these skills were thought primarily suitable for

18 Thomas Gisborne, *An Enquiry into the Duties of the Female Sex* (1797), p. 246.

19 Lawrence E. Klein, 'Gender, conversation and the public sphere in early eighteenth-century England', in *Textuality and Sexuality: Reading Theories and Practices*, ed. J. Still and M. Worton (Manchester, 1993), pp. 106–11.

20 [Allestree], *Ladies Calling*, p. 88. See also Gisborne, *Enquiry into the Duties of the Female Sex*, p. 248.

21 Sarah Stickney Ellis, *The Women of England, Their Social Duties and Domestic Habits* 10th edn (*c*.1850), p. 29; Amanda Vickery, 'Golden age to separate spheres? A review of the categories and chronology of English women's history', *Historical Journal* 36 (1993), pp. 407–8.

22 *The English Matron* (1846), p. 50.

23 John Gregory, *A Father's Legacy to his Daughters* (1774), pp. 13–15.

24 William Gouge, *Of Domesticall Duties* (1634), p. 273.

25 Lord Halifax [George Savile], *The Lady's New Year's Gift: or, Advice to a Daughter* (1688), p. 26.

interpersonal relations and narrowly focused problems. Gisborne thought that women excelled 'in sprightliness and vivacity, in quickness of perception, [and] in fertility of invention', but he went on to say that these powers were most suited 'to diffuse, throughout the family circle, the enlivening and endearing smile of cheerfulness'.[26] According to Ellis, while men possessed 'a more expansive range of intellect and thought' which allowed them 'to generalize', women contributed 'finer feelings' and were more sensitive to individual issues: 'The sphere of a domestic woman's observation is microscopic.'[27]

Men's intellectual powers were thus both different and superior. Gisborne had an even greater sense of the superiority of the mental powers of men, which extended to 'the abstruse researches of erudition; the inexhaustible depths of philosophy; . . . the powers of close and comprehensive reasoning, and of intense and continued application . . .'. Such powers were not necessary 'for the discharge of the customary offices of female duty'.[28] In addition to greater intelligence and physical strength, men were thought to possess other distinctive virtues such as courage, boldness, discretion, honesty, and sobriety. Given the belief that men had greater fire, choler, and strength, it is hardly surprising that they were thought to possess courage and boldness; in opposition to women's modesty and meekness, men were expected to possess ambition and determination. An anonymous publication of 1743, *The Ladies Cabinet*, described 'the true gentleman' as having 'a natural thirst of glory, and an honest pride. . . '.[29] Men, according to Ellis, value 'free agency' so highly that illness is 'trial and humiliation' to them, since it 'cuts them off from their accustomed manly avocations, and shuts them up to a kind of imprisonment . . . '.[30]

Men thus possessed an innate propensity to aggressiveness, but the writers of conduct books were keen to emphasise that the virtuous man possessed discretion, caution, prudence, and humility as well. Indeed, given the duties man assumed as a member of the superior sex, and frequently as a husband and a father, in looking out for the interests of the 'weaker vessel', he had no choice but to act responsibly. The properties of a good husband, according to an essay in 1747, included that he

26 Gisborne, *Enquiry into the Duties of the Female Sex*, p. 22.
27 Sarah Stickney Ellis, *The Wives of England* ([1843]), pp. 70–1; *idem, Women of England*, p. 33.
28 Gisborne, *Enquiry into the Duties of the Female Sex*, p. 21.
29 *The Ladies Cabinet, or a Companion for the Toilet* (1743), p. 65.
30 Ellis, *Wives of England*, p. 79.

be sober in speaking, easy in discourse, faithful where he is entrusted, discreet in giving counsel, careful of providing his house, diligent in looking after his estate, prudent in bearing the importunities of his wife, zealous of the education of his children, vigilant in what relates to his honour, and very stayed in all his behavior.[31]

Like women, men had the potential for virtuous moral behaviour, but whereas women achieved this through piety and sociability, men achieved virtue through gravity and dignity. Ellis asserted that 'it is the honest heart, the upright principle, the steady mind, and the unbiased judgement which give [man] dignity wherever he may be placed'.[32]

Just as contemporaries thought men and women had distinct sets of virtues, they assigned distinct weaknesses to each sex, failings which correspond predictably with their perceived virtues. Although both sexes were thought to be liable to pride and sexual incontinence, the sins meant different things when applied to each sex. Female pride was the opposite of the female virtues of modesty and meekness. Commentators complained about women's vanity, affectation, ambition, artifice, confidence, and stubbornness, for behaviour which might in many cases be labelled positively in men. According to the author of *The Whole Duty of a Woman*, vanity is the 'crime to which the female sex seems to be most inclined'.[33] For Allestree, who complained about the 'peevish stubbornness of many wives . . . only because they are impatient of [the] duty of subjection' to their husbands, this vanity resulted from women trying to transcend their station.[34] Yet a certain type of pride was acceptable: Lord Halifax told his daughter 'to raise yourself to a character, by which you may be distinguished, [by] an eagerness for precedence in virtue'.[35] Men, on the other hand, were guilty of exaggerating their natural superiority and being oversensitive to potential threats to that position; the synonyms to pride in this case were selfishness and haughtiness. Gisborne commented that man 'not unfrequently endeavours to aggrandise his own merits', and several authors complained about husbands who treated their wives in a haughty, tyran-

31 *The Art of Governing a Wife, with Rules for Batchelors* (1747), p. 3.
32 Ellis, *Wives of England*, pp. 84, 213.
33 *The Whole Duty of a Woman: Or, an Infallible Guide to the Fair Sex* (1737), p. 97.
34 [Richard Allestree], *The Whole Duty of Man, Laid Down in a Plain and Familiar Way for the Use of All, But Especially the Meanest Reader* (1703), p. 300.
35 Halifax, *Lady's New Year's Gift*, p. 152.

nical manner. As Richard Steele commented, such behaviour resulted from 'a false notion of the weakness of female understanding
in general, or an over-weaning opinion that we have of our own'.[36]
It is perhaps logical, therefore, that men were thought to be especially prone to jealousy, for nothing threatened a man's superior social position more than misbehaviour by his wife.

And such misbehaviour was most serious if it was sexual. Although both sexes were thought to have the potential for sexual immorality, the problem presented itself in different forms in each
sex. The extent to which contemporaries recognised male lust as a
fact of life is evident from the permissive attitude towards male
promiscuity evident in the prevailing double standard and the frequent complaints about the hypocritical, 'artful', and deceptive
methods men used to get virtuous women into bed. For men, sex
was not just a biological urge; the seduction of women was perceived in terms of conquest and submission, and thus was connected with male pride. Men even tended to brag about their
exploits: referring to adultery, Allestree complained that 'in this
age, 'tis no strange thing for men to publish their sin as Sodom, and
the offender does sometimes not only discover, but boast his
crime'.[37] Many commentators thought that women had the potential to go to either extreme on this issue; when lewd, they could be
more wicked than men. For the pseudonymous author 'Philogamus', lust was preeminently a female vice; while men were guilty of
a large number of other crimes in addition to sexual crimes,
women, who 'were principally designed for producing the species',
were more inclined than men to 'lubricity':

> Their souls seem to be of a more amorous temper; their
> constitutions are more turned to supply that passion: love, and the
> effects of it, is the darling and predominant passion of the sex ...
> What is little more than recreation in men, is the whole bent of the
> soul of a woman, if we consider her in the mere state of corrupt
> nature ...

Women, too, used deceptive means to draw the opposite sex into
bed, but in their case this was perceived as a fundamental aspect of
their nature, as illustrated by what happened in the Garden of
Eden. The power of female lust was another example of women's
greater susceptibility to be governed by the passions rather than rea-

---

36 *Tatler*, 149 (23 March, 1710).
37 [Allestree], *Ladies Calling*, p. 183.

son, but in any case it was inevitable due to their desire to become a
mother (their 'inexpressible desire of children').[38]

In addition to pride and lust, each sex was thought to have a
number of faults peculiar to itself. The most common problem
among women, as suggested by the last paragraph, was the strength
of their passions: women, according to the conduct-book writers,
were liable to be impetuous, impatient, too sincere, and to suffer
from 'violence of spirit' and 'constitutionally ardent' passions. According to *The Art of Governing a Wife*, 'the high spirit of a woman is
much more to be dreaded than the anger of a man, for a man in his
passion chides, but the woman in her fury bites . . . [you] must
never oppose a woman in her fury'.[39] Women were too weak to control their passions, and for this reason should not get involved in
areas of public life where passions were liable to run high, such as
politics and religion. Female passions, 'being naturally the more impetuous, ought to be the more strictly guarded, and kept under the
severe discipline of reason'.[40]

Women's relative weakness of mind and body led to other failings. Their physical weakness, together with their pride and mental
weakness, led them to talk too much, and say the wrong things:
women were accused of being contentious and shrewish, of engaging in impertinent tattle, scoffing, and derision. As Allestree explained, while a man has a number of different weapons with which
to offend, a woman has only the tongue, and clearly men's intolerance of female loquaciousness derived not simply from the content
of what was said but from the assertive manner in which it was delivered.[41] But the content was also objectionable: women's talk too
often was mere 'tittle-tattle', or it was irritable, peevish, capricious,
listless, or frivolous. Not only did women constantly complain, but
they could not make up their minds and nothing pleased them.
These faults derived largely from women's perceived weakness of
mind and their high-spiritedness. The eighteenth-century 'cult of
sentiment' heightened these concerns through its depiction of
women as possessing delicate nervous systems and as being easily
overcome by their emotions.

Among the weaknesses Thomas Gisborne discussed were 'fond-
ness of novelty' and 'dislike of application', and this raises a final ca-

---

38 Philogamus, *The Present State of Matrimony: Or, the Real Causes of Conjugal
Infidelity and Unhappy Marriages* (1739), pp. 11, 12, 16, 67.
39 *Art of Governing a Wife*, pp. 15–16.
40 [Allestree], *Ladies Calling*, p. 43.
41 [Allestree], *Whole Duty of Man*, p. 257.

tegory of perceived feminine faults: women were accused of being lazy and idle, and of indulging in unnecessary expenses. Women who could afford to hire servants (a growing number) were accused of 'prating and being idle'; of taking breakfast in bed and not rising until just before dinner; and of wasting their time and money on dress, fashionable amusements, visiting, and romantic novels. Instead of fulfilling their potential for virtue through charity, compassion, and tenderness, women were accused of stooping 'to be the slave of habit, of custom, and . . . of fashion'.[42] In sum, as a result of their relative weakness of mind and body, women were thought to be prone to a number of faults which, in one way or another, were all related to their tendency to be governed too much by their passions and too little by reason.

Men, on the other hand, were liable to failings characterised by the excessive use of their mental and physical powers. Using words like austerity, rigour, and sternness, commentators complained about men's tendency to adopt a serious, uncompromising, humourless attitude towards life, and especially towards their wives. Such attitudes may have been understandable, given the responsibilities of men's 'charges and employments', but men were advised to avoid any 'ungentleness, or rigour' towards their wives.[43] Even in public, men needed the civilising influence of female conversation in order to counteract their lack of social skills and common sense. Another problem was men's sublime sense of their own importance and the resulting strength of their wills. Noting 'the real and intense coarseness of the masculine character', the author of *The English Matron* stated that men tended to be obstinate, irritable, and impatient.[44] Male pride sometimes led men to be oversensitive to insults and other challenges to their authority. The dangers were first, that men were too quick to enter into disputes and quarrels, and second that, unlike women, this would lead beyond words to 'personal outrage, violence and hurt'.[45] During this period contemporaries became increasingly aware, and intolerant, of violence committed by men in all spheres of life. Men too, therefore, were liable to allow their passions to overrule their reason, but for men the consequences were different and often more serious.

Out of the perceived virtues and weaknesses of each sex, commentators drew conclusions about the proper functions of each sex

---

42 *Art of Governing a Wife*, p. 35; Ellis, *Wives of England*, p. 363.
43 [Allestree], *Ladies Calling*, p. 71; W. Fleetwood, *The Relative Duties of Parents and Children, Husbands and Wives, Masters and Servants* (1705), p. 333.
44 *English Matron*, pp. 16, 19, 28, 30.
45 Fleetwood, *Relative Duties*, p. 336.

in day-to-day life. Put simply, women were expected to stay at home while men went out into the world. Or, to paraphrase the duties as summarised by *The Art of Governing a Wife*:[46]

Men	Women
to get	to lay up and save
to go abroad and get his living	look to the house
deal with all men	talk to few
to manage all things without doors	take of all within

It is not difficult to see how this view of the different spheres of activity of men and women derived from commonly held beliefs concerning men's greater physical and natural strength and the superiority of husbands over their wives. At the same time, childcare and domestic responsibilities were believed to be more suited to the sex which was perceived to be less intelligent, but more tender and compassionate.

Nonetheless, the sexual division of labour described in the above passage was clearly schematic and should not be taken to imply that the worlds men and women were expected to inhabit were entirely separate, in which women were confined to a 'private sphere' while men acted in a 'public sphere'. While men were expected to go out into the world in order to earn a living and promote the public good, they were also expected to act in a domestic context as governors of their families, protecting and comforting their wives and leading the whole household in prayer.[47] Similarly, while women were certainly kept busy at home with their assigned duties of raising children, provisioning and ordering the house, governing maidservants, caring for sick members of the family, and acting as a companion and adviser to their husbands, women were also expected by some writers to have a positive moral influence on the wider society. Yet improving society, 'in ever so humble a way', came only after husbands and children had been cared for. Much of the charitable work which middle- and upper-class women were expected to perform was personal, in the sense that it was to be performed among friends, acquaintances and neighbours; as *The English Matron* noted, such duties 'may be performed by ladies, without stepping out of their sphere, without display, without being political economists, or politicians'. Women who adopted a public role,

---

46 *Art of Governing a Wife*, pp. 28–9.
47 See, for example, Gouge, *Domesticall Duties*, p. 262; Thomas Gisborne, *An Enquiry into the Duties of Men in the Higher and Middle Classes of Society in Great Britain* (1794), pp. 86, 620.

according to John Gregory, needed to behave circumspectly, adopting 'an easy dignity . . . but not that confident ease, that unabashed countenance' which alienates men.[48] Nonetheless, women had some public role to play, especially (as we shall see) in the second half of the period; they were clearly not expected to be confined to their homes. What differentiates prescriptions for male and female social roles is not so much that they were told to inhabit separate spheres of action defined spatially (although men were expected to have a wider range of personal contacts), but that they had separate duties and were expected to behave differently: both at home and in public, men were to be involved in governing and as the primary breadwinners, while women were expected to be responsible for caring, 'in ever so humble a way'.

Did ideals about gender characteristics and roles change significantly during this period? As outlined in the introduction, it is commonly argued that an ideology of separate spheres emerged during this period, involving an increasingly close association between women and their homes and families. In an influential article written in 1979, Catherine Hall argued that such ideas first achieved prominence through the Evangelical Revival, which dominated English religious life during the late eighteenth and early nineteenth centuries and was to have a formative influence on Victorian social attitudes. Under the leadership initially of the Clapham Sect, the movement sought to advance moral reform through the fight against the slave trade, missionary activities, and a campaign for a reformation of manners, and it expected women to play a major but distinctive role in reform. Hall argued that a new prescriptive model for women, which she labelled 'Victorian domestic ideology', was created by evangelical writers between 1780 and 1830, which introduced a new emphasis on women as domestic beings and on the home as a centre of moral virtue and women's religiosity. This involved an exaggeration of traditional feminine characteristics, in which feminine nature was seen as particularly delicate and fragile, but also as pure and especially suited to religious devotion.[49] Hall's thesis, however, has recently come under attack, notably by Amanda Vickery, who points out that 'texts extolling domestic virtue and a clear separation of the realms of men and women' had circulated

48 *English Matron*, pp. 73, 108; Gregory, *Father's Legacy*, p. 28.
49 Catherine Hall, 'The early formation of Victorian domestic ideology', in her *White, Male and Middle Class: Explorations in Feminism and History* (1992). See also Vickery, 'Golden age to separate spheres?', pp. 386–7.

since at least the seventeenth century.[50] Indeed, conduct manuals written before the Reformation stressed women's domestic duties, and this theme remained constant across the next three centuries. Allestree's *Ladies Calling* (first published in 1673) argued that 'there appear so many particulars [family duties], that if they were all duly attended, Ladies need not be much at a loss how to entertain themselves, nor run abroad . . . when they have such a variety of engagements at home', and this idea of separate spheres was repeated frequently, for example by two anonymous authors in the 1740s.[51] Further evidence of continuity comes from the fact that popular conduct books extolling these ideas such as *The Whole Duty of Man* and *The Ladies Calling*, which went through numerous editions during this period, changed little if at all from edition to edition.

This is not to suggest, however, that there was no change in ideas about gender roles during the two centuries from 1650 to 1850. It is undoubtedly the case that, under the influence of the evangelical movement, there was an increasing stress on the moral importance of women's domestic role in the second half of the period. Although the idea that women were primarily responsible for domestic duties was nothing new, in the period of social conservatism following the French Revolution one can detect in conduct books the elaboration of an image of wives providing in their homes a safe haven for their husbands away from the corruption and vexations of public life. An early example of this view comes in 1797 from Gisborne, who, in describing the three most important 'effect[s] of the female character', mentioned first, 'in contributing daily and hourly to the comfort of husbands, of parents, of brothers and sisters, and of other relations, connections and friends, in the intercourse of domestic life, under every vicissitude of sickness and health, of joy and affliction'. A somewhat more developed statement of this ideology comes from John Ovington in 1813, when he asked rhetorically, 'what can be found in the whole circle of fashionable pleasures, that can produce such exquisite feelings of delight, as the affectionate husband enjoys, when he returns home from the business and fatigues of the day, and finds his wife engaged in domestic cares . . .?'[52]

The elaboration of this domestic ideology was accompanied by subtle changes in ideas about the virtues and vices peculiar to men

50 Vickery, 'Golden age to separate spheres?', pp. 398, 411–12.

51 Davis, 'Continuity and change'; [Allestree], *Ladies Calling*, p. 230; Philogamus, *Present State of Matrimony*, p. 20; *Art of Governing a Wife*, pp. 28–9.

52 Gisborne, *Enquiry into the Duties of the Female Sex*, p. 12; John Ovington, *The Duties, Advantages, Pleasures, and Sorrows, of the Marriage State* (1813), p. 35.

and women, and the social roles ascribed to each sex. For women, the focus turned from warning them against succumbing to female weaknesses and towards emphasising their positive virtues. For example, in the second half of our period there was less concern about the dangers posed by female sexuality. In books published in the early part of the period writers followed a long tradition in depicting women's sexual behaviour as liable to go to extremes of either purity or wantonness: according to 'Philogamus', 'women are more inclined to criminal excesses of that [sexual] kind than men, when they are let without restraint . . . [yet] they are infinitely more chaste than men, if they are educated with proper care. . . .'.[53] In the second half of our period this natural inclination to virtue was given the greater weight and women were in a sense desexualised. This is evident in the writings of the evangelicals as well as in medical literature. Thomas Gisborne, for example, thought women were 'less exposed than the other sex to the temptations of open vice; they have quicker feelings of native delicacy, and a stronger sense of shame, no inconsiderable supports to virtue . . .'. As will be argued in Chapter 3, although opinion on this subject was divided, the prevailing view by the mid-nineteenth century was that the female sexual drive was far less insistent and far less likely to result in immoral conduct than the male.[54]

Concurrently, complaints that women were ruled by their passions and subject to talkativeness decreased, while more attention was paid to the nature of a woman's intellect (and there were more complaints about her pusillanimity and capriciousness which arose from her failure to develop it) and the moral influence she could exert over men. Fletcher found a growing interest in women's education, and toleration of their intellectual endeavours, in the late-eighteenth-century conduct books, as well as a more positive view of the moral influence they could exert as wives and mothers. In works by evangelical writers published in the 1790s and early 1800s this influence was extended outside the home, as middle- and upper-class women were expected to improve society through their good example, neighbourly conduct, and charity. Gisborne noted approvingly that some ladies had established 'schools of industry and of religious devotion' for the benefit of 'the wretched and the ignorant'. According to *The English Matron*, women had the potential to effect

---

53 Philogamus, *Present State of Matrimony*, p. 21.
54 Gisborne, *Enquiry into the Duties of the Female Sex*, p. 248; below, Chapter 3, pp. 63–4.

'a great moral revolution ... in society' through their efforts as good neighbours, teachers, and even writers.[55]

These changes are important, for they suggest that women's sphere of activity in this period may actually have been extended in one sense, by allowing women greater scope to act outside the home in improving society. *The New Whole Duty of Man*, first published in 1744, dismissed such activity by citing the Apostle Timothy's discussion of the duties of husbands and wives, including the phrase 'I suffer not a woman to teach (i.e., in public), nor to usurp authority over the man, but to be in silence' (1 Tim. 2: 12). In editions of this work after 1780 (of which there were several), the phrase '(i.e., in public)' was dropped. This alteration of the text in a book which was generally republished without alteration may reflect a significant change of attitude toward women's public activity, activity which was concurrently being encouraged by evangelical writers such as Gisborne and Ellis.[56] This greater willingness to see a public role for women did not imply, as we have seen, a diminution of their domestic duties: concurrently, there was increased interest in women's moral influence at home as the idea of the home as a virtuous retreat from a corrupt world gained currency. Moreover, as Judith Newton has pointed out, influence is not the same as control, and women in public were expected to work behind the scenes: 'having influence ... [and] having the ability to persuade others to do or to be something that was in *their* own interest, was made contingent upon the renunciation of such self-advancing forms of power as control or self-definition.' While women's opportunities may have expanded in some respects, they narrowed in others. As the tendency to desexualise women at this time and the growing attention paid to the supposed debilitating effects of menstruation, motherhood, and menopause suggests, contemporary notions of femininity were reshaped in this period rather than simply broadened. Women benefited from a broader range of opportunities outside the home, but they were simultaneously constricted by the higher moral standards they were expected to uphold and beliefs concerning the debilitating influence of their nerves and biological functions. Ellis's characterisation of women as concerned with 'the

---

55 Fletcher, *Gender, Sex and Subordination*, pp. 396–400; Judith L. Newton, *Women, Power, and Subversion: Social Strategies in British Fiction, 1778–1860* (Athens, Georgia, 1981), pp. 2–3; Gisborne, *Enquiry into the Duties of the Female Sex*, pp. 220–1; *English Matron*, pp. 73, 106, 185. See also Ellis, *Wives of England*, ch. 12.

56 *New Whole Duty of Man* (1763 edn), p. 221.

minute and particular observance of . . . trifles' as opposed to men's concern with 'expansive and important measures' illustrates the serious limits which conduct-book writers continued to impose on women's sphere of activity at the end of our period.[57]

The new emphasis on how women could exert a positive moral influence on men suggests, as Olwen Hufton points out, 'some re-distribution of virtue' from men to women during the early modern period. Nonetheless, the standards expected of men in conduct books also became more demanding. As Anthony Fletcher has shown, in the eighteenth century there was a new emphasis on civility and manners, or as it was often labelled, politeness, which rested 'upon an inner self discipline, and exhibit[ed] itself in a set of acceptable patterns of carriage and demeanour, affability, speech and benevolence to others'. As is reflected in the increased complaints in conduct books after 1750 about men's insolence, pride, and potential for violence, previous masculine habits such as drunkenness, boorishness, and brutality were attacked. In 1794, for example, Thomas Gisborne advised men to avoid 'the brutish spectacles of cockpits and boxing matches . . . [and] the ruinous occupations and infamous society of race-courses and gaming tables' as well as 'disputes and quarrels of every kind'. Some of the virtues men were advised to adopt came perilously close to the feminine, and for this reason men were advised to avoid womanish displays of emotion and to ensure they continued to possess manly courage and independence. Concern about male sexual misbehaviour also decreased in the conduct books published in the second half of the period, though as Fletcher explains informal toleration of promiscuity under the double standard if anything increased: under the new emphasis on deportment, what was now unacceptable was to advertise such behaviour publicly. These changes suggest that changing gender ideals simultaneously expanded and constricted men's sphere of activity just as they did women's: while there was less scrutiny of men's private behaviour, in public they were expected to lead more virtuous and civilised lives than they had done in the past.[58]

By the late eighteenth century the tradition of conduct-book literature examined here became increasingly class-specific, as evangelical writers such as Fordyce and Gisborne celebrated middle-class

57 Newton, *Women, Power, and Subversion*, p. 4; Ellis, *Women of England*, p. 38.
58 Olwen Hufton, *The Prospect Before Her: A History of Women in Western Europe, Volume 1* (1995), p. 501; Fletcher, *Gender, Sex and Subordination*, ch. 16 (quote from p. 332); Gisborne, *Enquiry into the Duties of Men*, pp. 628–30.

domestic virtues and in some cases compared them unfavourably with alleged aristocratic luxury and moral corruption, vices which sometimes were portrayed as 'feminine'. Consequently, such writings probably had little direct impact on the poor, though by the 1820s the gender differences inherent in domestic ideology were also articulated in advice books written for a lower-class audience. William Cobbett's *Cottage Economy* (1822) placed women firmly in the home, where they were expected to be virtuous and diligent in completing the household tasks. Echoing evangelical writers, Cobbett painted a picture of 'the labourer, after his return from the toils of a cold winter day, sitting with his wife and children round a cheerful fire'.[59] Nonetheless, in his expectation that the wife would manage all the details of running the household and its finances Cobbett gave lower-class women somewhat more substantial responsibilities than their middle-class counterparts. For more information on the ideas about gender which reached a lower-class audience, and indeed those parts of the middle and upper classes not allied with evangelicalism, it is necessary to broaden our focus and examine other genres of printed literature.

LITERARY REPRESENTATIONS

Conduct books are only one, though perhaps the most obvious, genre of print in which ideas about gender were communicated in this period. Other forms of fiction and non-fiction, including popular ballads, plays, poetry, novels, and political writing, much of it published in periodicals, were even more widely read and, judging by the frequent concerns expressed over the impressionability of women readers, influential in the ideological construction of gender roles. Indeed, the novel has even been called the fictional version of the conduct books. Yet the wide variety of subjects covered and approaches taken by writers meant that representations of gender in literature were more varied than those found in conduct books. This literature also includes the voices of women: whereas most conduct books were written by men (of the authors cited in the previous section, only one, Sarah Ellis, was a woman), women authored an increasing number of other types of literature during this period, much of which was specifically written for female readers. It would be impossible in a short section to examine repre-

59 Cited in Catherine Hall, 'The tale of Samuel and Jemima: gender and working-class culture in early nineteenth-century England', in her *White, Male and Middle Class*, p. 140.

sentations of gender in the entire body of printed literature in this period; attention will be focused on three of the most widely available types of publication: popular ballads, periodicals, and novels.[60]

Popular Literature

Probably the most popular form of literature in the seventeenth and eighteenth centuries was the ballad or chapbook. Inexpensively priced, these sought to entertain and instruct an audience which was both male and female (though most were probably written by men), and extended far down the social scale: those who could not read could hear them sung or see their messages depicted in woodcut prints. In contrast to the conduct books, the image of gender roles which comes across in these tales is ambiguous. Turning the world upside down, women are frequently portrayed as disorderly, sexually voracious (often cuckolding their husbands), and shrewish. Frequently they win the battle for supremacy in marriage and they are sometimes depicted as wearing the breeches. Correspondingly, husbands are depicted as weak and sexually impotent. Most such representations can be seen as products of male anxieties and as such are intended to provoke laughter and ridicule, thereby upholding patriarchal gender roles. This corresponds with the positive representations in some stories of ideal women as docile and chaste, and of men as assertive, courageous, and adventurous. Yet some depictions of women as passionate, resolute, and strong can, even if they are satirical, be seen as celebrations of female power and independence. Some ballads even positively recommended the single life for women as the only way of preserving their independence. Even here, however, it is notable that the primary weapon women were seen to possess in asserting their power was through the exercise or suppression of their sexuality.[61]

One type of ballad went even further towards subverting gender boundaries. Tales of women who disguised themselves as men and who followed their lovers off to war were particularly popular in the eighteenth century. Because such heroines successfully adopt male traits such as assertiveness and courage and are successful soldiers and sailors, these ballads, in the words of Dianne Dugaw, 'highlight

---

60 The phenomenon of female authorship is discussed in more detail in Chapter 7, pp. 283–91.

61 J. A. Sharpe, 'Plebeian marriage in Stuart England: some evidence from popular literature', *Transactions of the Royal Historical Society*, 5th series, 36 (1986), pp. 69–90; Joy Wiltenburg, *Disorderly Women and Female Power in the Street Literature of Early Modern England and Germany* (1992).

the theatricality of gender markers' at this time and therefore 'subvert . . . the very category of gender itself'. (Male characters can also
be found adopting stereotypically feminine traits such as weeping
and fainting, and they nurse their lovers.) Yet the inversion of normal gender roles, though celebrated in these ballads, is always temporary. In the end the heroine almost always reveals her disguise,
marries her lover, and both husband and wife settle back into accepted gender roles. Although in this sense such roles are ultimately affirmed, these ballads nonetheless suggest to their audience, in
an extraordinarily positive fashion, the idea that gender identity is
artificial and mutable.[62]

Although the popularity of female warrior ballads waned in the
early nineteenth century, one can still find a variety of gender roles
portrayed in popular literature in the second half of our period. In
an attempt to provide a morally sound alternative to ballads, the
evangelical Hannah More published her *Cheap Repository Tracts* in
the 1790s. These presented a type of domestic ideology for the
working class in which wives stayed at home and were subordinate
to their breadwinning husbands, but it has been argued that the impact of these tracts on popular culture was limited. In contrast, female readers in the early nineteenth century could turn to a
number of published songs with titles like 'I'll Be No Submissive
Wife', which, borrowing from the political rhetoric of the day
against slavery and tyranny, advised women to rebel against repressive husbands. Representations of gender relations in popular
literature at this time varied considerably, but the common themes
are inequality and conflict: the companionate marriage sometimes
found in earlier ballads has disappeared. While some songs celebrated wife-beating, others condemned the practice. Similarly,
while some celebrated female independence, others, including
Chartist songs, adopted a central theme of domestic ideology and
advised men to shield women from the hardships of the world.[63]
During this period readers thus could find an extraordinary variety
of possible models of gender roles in popular literature, but in its
concentration on issues of male brutality and female sexuality this
literature nonetheless tended to reinforce some fundamental sexual
stereotypes.

  62 Dianne Dugaw, *Warrior Women and Popular Balladry, 1650–1850* (Cambridge,
1989), quotes from pp. 151, 159.
  63 Susan Pedersen, 'Hannah More meets Simple Simon: tracts, chapbooks, and
popular culture in late eighteenth-century England', *Journal of British Studies* 25
(1986), pp. 84–113; Anna Clark, *The Struggle for the Breeches: Gender and the Making of
the British Working Class* (1995), pp. 67–71, 252–9.

Periodicals

In the late seventeenth and early eighteenth centuries one of the most rapidly expanding forms of publication was the periodical. Though they attracted a wealthier audience than the ballads or chapbooks, early periodicals such as the *Athenian Mercury*, the *Tatler*, and the *Spectator* also sought explictly to attract both female and male readers. However, they served through their commentaries and articles to construct ideals of masculinity and femininity which were very different from those portrayed in the ballads. Kathryn Shevelow has argued that men and women were portrayed in the early periodicals according to a model of separate spheres, as different 'in kind rather than degree', possessing ' "separate but equal" area[s] of activity and authority'. In the *Tatler* and the *Spectator* Richard Steele and Joseph Addison argued there was 'a sort of sex in souls' in which men's 'minds have different, not superior qualities' to those of women. While feminine virtues included innocence, vivacity, kindness, and prudence, and women's domains were identified as the reproductive, private, and domestic (including leisure), masculine virtues were identified as gravity, responsibility, and wisdom and their domains were the political and the productive. Yet it is important to note that the ideal male was also seen to possess a capacity for feeling and softness, and was expected to be a companionable and faithful husband and participate in domestic management. This is an early example of the attempt to civilise male behaviour that we found in the conduct books.[64]

The model of gender roles promoted in these periodicals is not new, in the sense that the basic division of male and female virtues and responsibilities can be found in earlier conduct books, nor does it involve a rigid separation of spheres: both men and women are seen to have an important domestic role, while women are not entirely excluded from discussions of political, scientific, or historical issues. Indeed, in 1709 female readers of the *Tatler* were told by a fictional female correspondent that the journal 'designs, for the use of our sex, to give the exact characters of all the chief politicians who frequent any of the coffee houses from St. James to the Change'. Around the middle of the eighteenth century, however, as separate periodicals were published for men and women, the focus in magazines intended for women became more exclusively domestic, with more attention paid to achieving marital happiness and to

64 Kathryn Shevelow, *Women and Print Culture: The Construction of Femininity in the Early Periodical* (1989), chs 1–4, esp. p. 3; *Tatler* 172 (13–16 May 1710); *Spectator* 128 (27 July 1711).

cookery, needlework, and domestic management, with fewer essays on science and history. Under the influence of the Evangelical Revival, in the first half of the nineteenth century greater attention was paid in periodicals for women to their moral and religious duties, and the influence (but not power) they could thereby exert in the wider world. Thus, the changing concept of femininity in the periodicals paralleled that of the conduct books, but comes across more clearly in this new genre.[65]

The Novel
Another widely read genre in the eighteenth and nineteenth centuries was the novel, a new form of writing which was particularly attractive to women, both as readers and as authors, as well as men. Although the content and approach of novels changed considerably over the period, the increasingly dominant tone was sentimental, depicting women as sensitive, virtuous, vulnerable, and domestic. The earliest novels written in the late seventeenth and early eighteenth centuries presented less confining images of femininity: Aphra Behn, for example, wrote about relations between the sexes in her plays and prose narratives in terms which placed less stress on difference, recognising female as well as male sexual desire and initiative (while admitting the social disadvantages it could cause) and depicting men as occasionally impotent rather than always threatening. Such open discussions of sexuality were much less acceptable by the 1730s, however, when the new paradigm of sensibility took hold. Stressing women's more delicate and sensitive nerves which rendered them weak and vulnerable but also morally superior, novels explored the conflict between female innocence and aggressive male sexuality, as pioneered in Samuel Richardson's novels *Pamela: or, Virtue Rewarded* (1740) and *Clarissa* (1747–8). (Richardson's interest in women's nerves can be attributed to the influence of his doctor, George Cheyne, who was instrumental in the development of a nerve-based understanding of physiology.) As in so many conduct books, women in sentimental novels were depicted as emotional, affective, and virtuous. Yet, due to their irrationality and weakness, their best means of exerting influence in the world was indirectly, through their family responsibilities.[66] That

65 Shevelow, *Women and Print Culture*, ch. 5; Ros Ballaster et al., *Women's Worlds: Ideology, Femininity and the Woman's Magazine* (1991), pp. 48–9, 58–9, 86–8; Newton, *Women, Power, and Subversion*, pp. 3–4.
66 Janet Todd, *The Sign of Angellica: Women, Writing and Fiction, 1660–1800* (1989), ch. 4; Barker-Benfield, *Culture of Sensibility*, ch. 1.

this portrayal of female virtues was new and controversial is suggested by the fact that *Pamela* was parodied in Henry Fielding's *Shamela*, in which Pamela's 'virtue' was depicted as hypocritical.

As suggested by the story of Pamela, who managed to reform Mr B. after he attempted to rape her, the sentimental novel produced a reformed ideal of masculinity as well as a more virtuous form of femininity. Richardson's novels, for example, criticise the selfishness and conceit of characters like Lovelace in *Clarissa* who treat women as property and as sexual objects and set in contrast the Christ-like qualities of the eponymous hero of *Sir Charles Grandison* (1753–4), a man who, though powerful and patriarchal, was sensitive, charitable, and refined. Similarly, the male characters in sentimental novels written by women are typically considerate, thoughtful, and diffident, while arrogant and aggressive behaviour is criticised.[67] In promoting the man of feeling, however, there was concern that he retain a degree of masculine fortitude, lest he become effeminate, though there was some disagreement on this point. When Henry MacKenzie's novel *The Man of Feeling* was published in 1771, it was celebrated for portraying the superiority of feeling as a guide to virtue, despite the fact the author intended 'to satirize such unrestrained sensibility in a man'.[68]

As MacKenzie's intended approach suggests, sentimental and romantic fiction came under attack in the late eighteenth century as promoting unrealistic and self-indulgent fantasy. Despite its portrayal of women in weak and passive terms, this literature could be read as promoting images of female power. There was concern, however, that such images were unrealistic, that women were encouraged to place undue reliance on their passions as well as reformed male saviours to keep them out of trouble. In gothic novels, pure heroines implausibly survive their harrowing experiences in terrifying spaces such as castles and dungeons under the protection of a male authority figure. In response to these criticisms, and to the French Revolution, the 'Jacobin' novels, written by radicals such as William Godwin, Mary Wollstonecraft, and Mary Hays, sought to harness sensibility to the cause of political reform and feminism. While attempting to join reason with sensibility, these novels were also notable for their largely sympathetic treatment of female sexuality, a point of view which had been absent for most of the century.

67 Katharine Rogers, *Feminism in Eighteenth-Century England* (Brighton, 1982), pp. 160, 162, 173.

68 Barker-Benfield, *Culture of Sensibility*, p. 144.

The inevitable conservative response to the Jacobin novels spelled out the negative consequences of female initiative in sex or any other activity and brought a renewed emphasis on the moral importance of women's domestic duties, echoing the contemporary conduct books discussed earlier. The fusion of evangelicalism with sensibility (as in the works of Hannah More) led to a moralised sensibility which was firmly identified as female. A host of 'domestic novels' were published in the early nineteenth century which examined women's emotional lives and social conduct within the home and emphasised the moral influence such women could exert; this idea was later stated most forcefully in Coventry Patmore's poem, 'The Angel in the House', written in the 1850s. Yet, in contrast perhaps to earlier depictions of sentimental women, the images of women in early-nineteenth-century novels could be empowering. In the works of Jane Austen, women's emotions and behaviour were portrayed as more complex and analysed in a more sophisticated manner. A 'feminine heroic tradition' developed which emphasised female capabilities and celebrated the feminine virtues of mercy, flexibility, perceptiveness, and openness, thereby offering 'some of the most positive images of women that [English] literature has produced'. At the very end of our period, a few works such as Charlotte Brontë's *Jane Eyre* (1847) portrayed strong-minded, passionate, and self-conscious heroines, though it is significant that, having deviated from conventional expectations, Brontë published the work under a male pseudonym. Thus by the mid- nineteenth century women were increasingly represented in fiction as a sex which had an important and distinctive public role to play in society. This is evident not only in the political novels of the period of the French Revolution or the social and factory novels of the 1840s, but also more generally in the way feminine or domestic values were projected as means of resolving tensions between the individual and society, though we should note that some female characters, such as Jane Eyre, transcended traditional feminine virtues. In the words of Susan Morgan, 'the ideology of the angel in the house . . . was transformed, and even inverted, into a call for the public role of women.'[69]

Elaborating on ideas found in the conduct books, therefore, representations of women in literature became more confining, in

69 Susan Morgan, *Sisters in Time: Imagining Gender in Nineteenth-Century British Fiction* (Oxford, 1989), pp. 10–11; Newton, *Women, Power, and Subversion*, p. 6; Elizabeth K. Helsinger et al., *The Woman Question: Society and Literature in Britain and America, 1837–1883* 3 vols (1983), 3, chs 2–3.

their rejection for the most part of women's sexuality and their focus on domestic responsibilities, but also more positive. By the nineteenth century the early-modern obsession with women as disorderly and lustful was replaced with the sense that women had a positive (if limited) role to play in society. Much more work needs to be done on representations of masculinity in literature, especially since by the end of the period 'manliness' had become a frequent topic of discussion. It is possible to identify some important, and sometimes conflicting, themes. We have seen that under the influence of sensibility men were expected to lead more disciplined lives. Patmore's poem 'The Angel in the House', for example, criticised male assertiveness, particularly sexual aggression, as well as idealising feminine passivity and asexuality. Indeed, it has been argued that men formulated this vision of the ideal woman as a result of fears and insecurities about their own lack of aggressive qualities. Yet alternative notions of masculinity developed in the nineteenth century which, while retaining a sense of moral purpose, depicted upper-class men in particular as active, strong and heroic. The novels of the Scottish writer Sir Walter Scott promoted a cult of chivalry in which gentlemen protected their wives and children. Other novelists, such as Thomas Hughes and Charles Kingsley, celebrated 'manly' moral and physical strength and athleticism tied to a Christian purpose, as is evident in Thomas Hughes's novel, *Tom Brown's Schooldays* (1856).[70]

Despite the dominant trends of sensibility and domesticity, therefore, alternative definitions of masculinity and femininity were available in printed literature in this period. Moreover, as we have seen with MacKenzie's novel *The Man of Feeling*, even individual texts could be interpreted in different ways. In the case of texts propounding a subordinate or domestic role for women, modern feminist critics have shown that deeper, more radical levels of meaning can often be detected where masculine values and control were critiqued and subverted. Terry Castle has recently pointed out, for example, that eighteenth-century novels often include masquerade scenes which 'coincide with a peculiar reversal of those conventional male–female power relations encoded elsewhere in eighteenth-century fiction . . . [as] female characters acquire unprecedented intel-

---

70 Carol Christ, 'Victorian masculinity and the angel in the house', in M. Vicinus (ed.), *A Widening Sphere: Changing Roles of Victorian Women* (1977), pp. 146–62; David Newsome, *Godliness and Good Learning: Four Studies on a Victorian Ideal* (1961), ch. 4; Norman Vance, *The Sinews of the Spirit: The Ideal of Manliness in Victorian Literature and Religious Thought* (Cambridge, 1985).

lectual and emotional influence over [men]'. While such scenes are typically the subject of moral disapproval, they in fact often play a crucial role in transforming the narrative and have positive consequences.[71] As is evident from works such as the Jacobin novels, however, more explicitly feminist arguments were also emerging at this time.

FEMINISM

The 200-year time span covered by this book constitutes a crucial period in the history of feminism. Whereas texts advocating women's rights were largely defensive at the start of our period, by 1850 the ideological justifications for modern women's movements had been largely set out. Such ideas were reflected only marginally in the conduct books which, with their attempt to reach a wide audience and their evangelical tone in the second half of the period, adopted largely conservative approaches. Even here, however, we have seen the growth of a more positive view of women's potential over the course of this period, as traditional misogynist views of women, which focused on women's potential vices, came under attack as increasing emphasis was placed on women's perceived moral qualities and the positive influence these could exert on society as a whole. These trends were more apparent within fiction. A minority of writers went further, explicitly expressing views which can be labelled as 'feminist' due to their high estimation of women's potential abilities. In this section we will consider these points of view in more detail, and expand the focus to include polemical writing as well as fiction. Feminist writings did not exert as much influence on society in the short term as the works discussed so far, but by the end of this period their ideas had broadened the terms of debate about women's nature considerably, and this had implications for conceptions of masculinity as well.

The origins of feminism in England can be traced back to the 'Querelle des femmes', a European-wide debate among intellectuals over the relative merits and status of women which, initially stimulated by the Renaissance, lasted from the fifteenth century to the French Revolution. This dialogue started with Christine de Pisan in France in the early fifteenth century who, angered by the misogynist

---

71 Ballaster et al., *Women's Worlds*, pp. 75–93; Elaine Showalter, *A Literature of Their Own: British Women Novelists from Brontë to Lessing* (rev. edn, 1982); Newton, *Women, Power and Subversion*; Terry Castle, *The Female Thermometer: Eighteenth-Century Culture and the Invention of the Uncanny* (Oxford, 1995), ch. 7, quote from p. 111.

literature of her time, wrote a number of works defending the female sex. In these she introduced the crucial idea that the prevailing character of the sexes was determined not only biologically, but also by culture. The ensuing debate over four centuries followed this pattern of attacks on and subsequent defences of the female sex. The first works in English were published in 1578 and 1589, with several more published in the seventeenth and eighteenth centuries.[72]

Although the feminist side of the debate was for a long time largely defensive and the debate, after Christine de Pisan, stimulated few new ideas, during the period of this study one can detect a growing assertiveness and confidence on the female side. As Joan Kelly points out, the language of the titles of the works shifted from words like 'bastions', 'sanctuaries', and 'protections' of women in the fifteenth and sixteenth centuries, to 'ladies' defences' and 'female advocates' in the late seventeenth and eighteenth centuries.[73] More than that, a sense of female superiority emerges in works with titles like *Haec & Hic; or, the Feminine Gender More Worthy than the Masculine* (1683) and *Beauty's Triumph, or the Superiority of the Fair Sex Invincibly Proved* (1751), in which it is suggested that, had they not been cruelly deprived of a proper education, women could actually be superior to men in some virtues (including courage) and skills (rhetoric, law, and medicine).[74]

This growing assertiveness reflects broader intellectual changes which undermined the traditional scriptural arguments on which male superiority was based. The patriarchal model of the family was seriously challenged by John Locke's theory of the development of human society, in which marriage, like political institutions, was seen as a contractual relationship rather than a divinely ordained institution. Subject to natural rather than divine law, marriage became a partnership in which the natural abilities of each sex, and an agreed contract, determined the relative power and functions of each sex. Although Locke envisioned that man's superior strength and abilities normally gave him the leading role, his theory clearly if implicitly undermined arguments for patriarchal authority and en-

72 Joan Kelly, 'Early feminist theory and the *Querelle des femmes*, 1400–1789', in her *Women, History and Theory* (1984); Moira Ferguson (ed.), *First Feminists: British Women Writers 1578–1799* (Bloomington, Ind., and New York, 1985), pp. 2–10.

73 Kelly, 'Early feminist theory', p. 78.

74 [James Norris], *Haec & Hic; or, the Feminine Gender More Worthy than the Masculine* (1683), esp. pp. 25, 29; and *Beauty's Triumph, or the Superiority of the Fair Sex Invincibly Proved* (1751), esp. pp. 44–8.

couraged a more companionate approach to relations between spouses.[75]

More fundamentally, the philosophical thought of René Descartes, Locke, and later Enlightenment thinkers prompted serious reconsideration of commonly held assumptions about what were thought to be the fundamental qualities of each sex. Perhaps because neither Descartes nor Locke spelled out the implications of their ideas for conceptions of gender, contradictory interpretations emerged. On the one hand, new ways of thinking could easily be incorporated within existing paradigms. Many interpreted the mind/body dualism in Cartesian thought as gendered, with men associated with rational thought and women associated with nature. Similarly, we have seen that the sensationalist psychology of the eighteenth century, which was strongly influenced by Locke, presumed that women's nerves were much more sensitive to external stimulation than men's. Yet the Cartesian method of sweeping away traditional preconceptions and grounding all judgements on self-conscious thought, together with Locke's argument that human mental development is a product of experienced sensations, could lead to scepticism about claims that men and women had fundamentally different natures from birth. François Poulain de la Barre published a Cartesian critique of traditional notions of women in a work first published in France in 1673 as *De L'Egalité des deux Sexes*, and loosely translated into English and published as *The Woman as Good as the Man* in 1677.[76] If, as Descartes claimed, all humans possessed the capacity for reason, why should men and women have different intellectual capacities? And if men and women are fundamentally shaped by their lived experiences as argued by Locke, then what would happen if those experiences were altered, if, for example, women received the same upbringing and education that men did?[77] Reflecting this belief in the importance of socialisation, some conduct-book writers came to the conclusion that men and women could, if properly educated, acquire equal intellectual skills.

In assessing the implications of these ideas, eighteenth-century thinkers were forced to reevaluate all the presumed sexual differen-

75 John Locke, *Second Treatise of Government* (1690), chs. 6 and 7; Lawrence Stone, *The Family, Sex and Marriage in England, 1500–1800* (1977), p. 239.

76 This text was reprinted in *Beauty's Triumph*. See Ferguson, *First Feminists*, p. 20.

77 Joan K. Kinniard, 'Mary Astell and the conservative contribution to English feminism', *Journal of British Studies* 19 (1979), pp. 61–2; Schiebinger, *Mind Has No Sex?*, pp. 171–2.

ces. Even the most fundamental female virtue, chastity, was scru-
tinised: David Hume came to the conclusion that it was an artificial
virtue, from which society 'derived that vast difference between the
education and duties of the two sexes'.[78] This was not a commonly
held view, but it illustrates that all aspects of human nature came
under scrutiny in this period, as writers sought to determine, on the
basis of observation and critical thinking rather than scripture,
which sexual differences were innate, and which were a product of
society. On that basis new conclusions could be drawn about the
proper qualities and social roles of each sex, especially women.

English feminism first appears in print from about 1650. Prior to
then, it is difficult to find writers who advocated improved conditions for women as a whole, as opposed to complaining about specific injustices.[79] The first such writing occurred in the context of
the Interregnum, when claims for religious equality (including the
participation of women in preaching) led to questioning of 'the
very foundations of the old patriarchal family'.[80] The Quaker argument that all men and women had an 'Inner Light' that gave them
the potential to express the word of God was especially important.
In 1667, the Quaker Margaret Fell Fox published a pamphlet,
Women's Speaking Justified, in which she argued for the equality of
men and women in all religious activities. Although the broader social implications of such ideas were not developed, the idea of the
equality of men's and women's souls was influential. If that was true,
did not women have the same intellectual potential as men, a
potential which could only be realised if women received a proper
education? A chorus of complaints about the poor state of female
education surfaced during the Restoration, even before Locke's
ideas on epistemology and education were published. Hannah
Woolley wrote in 1675 that 'certainly man's soul cannot boast of a
more sublime original than ours, [women] had equally their efflux
from the same eternal immensity, and [are] therefore capable of
the same improvement by good education.'[81]

These ideas were stated more forcefully by Mary Astell, who is
often regarded as the first English feminist because of her syste-

78 Quoted by Jane Rendall, *The Origins of Modern Feminism* (Basingstoke, 1985),
p. 14.
79 Hilda Smith, *Reason's Disciples: Seventeenth-Century English Feminists* (Urbana,
Ill., 1982), pp. 4–5.
80 Keith Thomas, 'Women and the Civil War sects', *Past and Present* 13 (1958),
p. 55.
81 Hannah Woolley, *The Gentlewoman's Companion* (1675), p. 2; quoted by
Kinniard, 'Mary Astell', p. 53.

matic and sustained arguments for women's equality.[82] Influenced
by Descartes, Astell believed women had the same intellectual
potential as men, and, like men, should be governed by reason
rather than their passions. She proposed, in *A Serious Proposal to the
Ladies* (1694), the establishment of a 'monastery' or 'religious retirement' for women where they could receive a proper education,
which included reading substantial works such as philosophy rather
than 'idle novels and romances'.[83] In addition to stating the case for
proper female education more forcefully than previously, Astell's
proposal is remarkable for its approval, and indeed encouragement,
of women living independently of men, where they could form virtuous friendships. (She severely criticised marriage, since men so
often abused their superior position.) Moreover, Astell justified the
education of women for their own sake, not, as was commonly argued, so that they could be helpful to men.[84] More generally, Astell
rejected biblical justifications of the subordination or inferiority of
women (except in marriage), arguing that the relevant passages
simply described common practice and were not prescriptive.[85]

Although the implications of her arguments were quite radical,
Astell was nonetheless a conservative on social issues. While she advised women against marriage (it involved acquiring a 'monarch for
life'), she believed that the Bible dictated that when married the
'husband must govern absolutely and entirely', and the wife 'has
nothing else to do but to please and obey'.[86] Moreover, she thought
that within marriage women's tasks should be confined to the domestic sphere of raising children and helping their husbands. Only
single women were expected to have any public influence, and that
was confined to intelligent and Christian discourse, and philanthropy: 'women have no business with the pulpit, the bar, or St.
Stephen's Chapel [parliament]'.[87] Fundamentally, Astell believed
that, although equal to men in terms of their souls and rational fa-
culties, women possessed different temperaments, sensibilities, and
gifts, which resulted from physical differences.[88] Thus, although in
one major respect Astell broke free from biological and scriptural

82 Ferguson, *First Feminists*, p. 180.
83 Mary Astell, *A Serious Proposal to the Ladies* (1694), pp. 60–1, 85–6; Kinniard,
'Mary Astell', pp. 59–62.
84 Rogers, *Feminism*, pp. 72, 74.
85 Mary Astell, *Reflections Upon Marriage*, 3rd edn (1706), preface.
86 Astell, *Reflections Upon Marriage*, pp. 31, 56.
87 Mary Astell, *A Serious Proposal to the Ladies, Part II* (1697), pp. 192, 211–15;
Kinniard, 'Mary Astell', p. 65.
88 Kinniard, 'Mary Astell', p. 74.

determinism, she remained wedded to the idea that men and women were naturally different and possessed distinct capabilities. Similarly, while her *An Essay in Defence of the Female Sex* (1696) went so far as to suggest that women were more capable of mental activity than men, it nonetheless stated that, due to physical differences, women were more suited to domestic duties while men should be the breadwinners.

Although her books were quite popular, few followed Astell and took up the feminist cause polemically in the early eighteenth century; the important developments which occurred at this time occurred in fiction. A number of female authors writing in the late seventeenth and early eighteenth centuries, including Aphra Behn, Lady Anne Winchilsea, Lady Mary Chudleigh, Lady Mary Wortley Montagu, and Eliza Haywood, can be considered feminist due to their defence of women's right to express themselves and publish their writings; their advocacy of female education and intellectual activity; their emphasis on the pleasures of female friendship; the presentation of strong heroines in their works; and their fictional portrayals of the suffering women encountered due to economic dependence on their husbands. Nonetheless, these works did not present any significant new interpretations of women's position. The writers were arguably limited by the lack of a suitable literary form for expressing feminist views. Neither plays, poems, nor the early novels provided authors with significant opportunities for feminine characters to develop fully.[89]

This changed with the development of the sentimental novel. Although the emphasis on the value of women's emotions and feelings in these novels often did little more than reinforce accepted stereotypes of women as weak and self-sacrificing, the novels of Richardson opened up a form of literature which could actually contribute towards changing the image of women. Like many sentimental novelists, Richardson analysed feelings and perceptions from a feminine point of view. However, he went further and gave his heroines intelligence and strength, and he explored their emotions thoroughly and gave them legitimacy. Moreover, like Mary Astell, he expressed the hope that women could live independently of men and he exposed the oppressive social and cultural conditions which prevented them from doing so. Thus, despite the fact that Richardson's heroines remained within conventional definitions of femininity which emphasised the dominant role played by

89 Rogers, *Feminism*, pp. 89–113; Smith, *Reason's Disciples*, pp. 151–91.

emotions and limited their social influence to a moral influence, Richardson's obvious empathy for women elevated their status and raised questions about their treatment by men. This approach was echoed by a number of female novelists who, by giving their female characters increased intellectual and moral capabilities, exploited this genre with increasing confidence during the remainder of the period.[90]

This respect for women's feelings was greatly increased by the Evangelical Revival. Building on seventeenth-century arguments for the spiritual equality of women and exalting the traditional feminine qualities of purity, humility, and tenderness, the evangelicals adopted a positive, if in many ways limited, view of women and expected them to play a prominent role in their campaign. As we have seen in the conduct books of Thomas Gisborne, who was closely associated with the Clapham Sect, and Sarah Ellis, women in the second half of our period were seen as potentially morally superior to men and were depicted as such in many novels. Emphasising woman's selflessness, Sarah Lewis argued in 1839 that 'the moral world is ours . . . ours by the very indication of God himself' and suggested that God intended women to act as 'his missionaries upon earth, – the disseminators of his spirit, the diffusers of his word'.[91] This increase in women's moral status, however, was sharply constrained by the fact that the evangelicals envisioned limited opportunities in which women could exert this influence. They were encouraged to participate in philanthropy and Sunday schools, but the primary method by which they were expected to change society was through the good example they set in interactions with their family and friends.[92] Yet in its heightened estimate of feminine worth and its introduction of traditionally feminine concerns into the public sphere, evangelicalism was an important development. As Jane Rendall has pointed out, many of the leading feminists of the 1840s and 1850s had been closely exposed to evangelical teaching, even if they subsequently rejected it.[93]

In fact, the most important developments in feminist thought which occurred in the late eighteenth century occurred in opposition to evangelicalism. Stimulated by the French Revolution and political radicalism in England, Mary Wollstonecraft's writings on

90 Rogers, *Feminism*, pp. 119–80; below, Chapter 7, pp. 289–90.

91 S. Lewis, *Women's Mission* (1839), pp. 128–9, quoted in Rendall, *Origins of Modern Feminism*, p. 75.

92 Rendall, *Origins of Modern Feminism*, pp. 89–90.

93 Ibid., p. 322.

women's education and women's rights gave renewed impetus to arguments for women's mental equality with men. Rather than stressing women's distinctive qualities, as the evangelicals did, Wollstonecraft, along with the radical Catherine Macaulay, condemned the idea of sexual character (the idea that each sex possessed a different combination of virtues), and criticised sentimental novels, conduct books (notably those by Gregory and Fordyce), and medicine for promoting this way of thinking. Building on the sensationalist philosophy of Locke, both writers argued that it was only poor education which prevented women from becoming fully rational beings like men.[94]

In her *Vindication of the Rights of Women* (1792), Wollstonecraft carried these ideas further, arguing that women's current weaknesses were due to institutions which prevented them from reaching their true potential. In addition to education, most fundamental among those was marriage. Wollstonecraft argued that women's subordination to their husbands was degrading and proposed that husbands and wives should be 'equally necessary and independent of each other' while each fulfills 'the respective duties of their station'.[95] (In her novel *Maria; or, The Wrongs of Women* (1798), which was unfinished at the time of her death, Wollstonecraft went further and suggested that women in unhappy marriages should be able to leave their husbands and live with another man.[96]) Freed from subservience to their husbands, women, Wollstonecraft advocated, should adopt a more public role than ever before. She suggested broader work opportunities: they could become 'physicians as well as nurses', for example, or manage farms or shops.[97] This plea was echoed by Priscilla Wakefield in her *Reflections on the Present Condition of the Female Sex* (1798). Hesitantly (she was aware that the idea would be ridiculed), Wollstonecraft also proposed that women 'of a superior cast' should have political representation in government.[98]

Wollstonecraft's hesitancy in advocating political change is not the only conservative aspect of her ideas. By seeking to combine rationality in women with a respect for their feelings she was clearly influenced by the eighteenth-century 'cult of sensibility'. She still saw the primary role of women as wives and mothers, though given

94 Mary Wollstonecraft, *Thoughts on the Education of Daughters* (1787); Catherine Macaulay, *Letters on Education* (1790).

95 Mary Wollstonecraft, *A Vindication of the Rights of Woman* (1792; Norton edn, 1967), p. 215.

96 Rogers, *Feminism*, p. 192.

97 Wollstonecraft, *Vindication*, pp. 221–3.

98 Ibid., p. 220.

her emphasis on female independence she stressed the latter rather than the former. Although Wollstonecraft was keen to emphasise women's contributions to society as full citizens, she thought the most useful way for them to make such a contribution was through motherhood. Like the evangelical writers, she conjured up a picture of domestic harmony, in which the wife 'prepare[s] herself and children . . . to receive her husband, who returning weary home in the evening found smiling babes and a clean hearth'.[99] Conservative as they seem now, Wollstonecraft's ideas on female equality and independence were nonetheless too radical for her time. Discredited both by her political radicalism and her views (and actions) with respect to female chastity, Wollstonecraft's feminism had far less social or political influence in the short term than evangelicals such as Gisborne, whose *An Enquiry into the Duties of the Female Sex* (1797) was a critical response to Wollstonecraft's *Vindication*.

Nevertheless, by 1800 claims for female equality included the assertion of spiritual, moral, and mental equality and had begun to include claims for a limited public role for women. Still unchallenged, however, despite critiques of inequalities within marriage, was the fundamental equation of married women with domestic life and motherhood. Over the first half of the nineteenth century, this basic assumption was challenged in several ways: by attacking the fundamental inequality of the institutions of marriage and the nuclear family; by questioning the role motherhood played in women's lives; by opening up the public activities of work and politics still further to women; and, finally and crucially, by challenging the notion of masculinity to which the domestic conception of femininity was set in opposition.

Wollstonecraft had already gone some way towards arguing against the fundamental inequality of husbands and wives in marriage, but early-nineteenth-century writers went further in challenging the cultural and legal rules which upheld the husband's superior position. Feminist novelists and radicals attacked the double standard of sexual morality which restricted respectable female sexual activity to marriage while allowing husbands to indulge in extramarital affairs. John Stuart Mill and his wife Harriet Taylor Mill and others argued against the legal basis of male domination: the property laws which gave husbands control of their wives' property, the definition of assault which permitted husbands to discipline their wives physically, and the laws of divorce which

---

99 Rogers, *Feminism*, p. 246; Wollstonecraft, *Vindication*, p. 215.

prevented women from escaping from unhappy marriages.[100] In 1837 Caroline Norton attacked the laws which prevented women who were separated from their husbands from having access to their own children, and in the 1850s a committee of feminists lobbied in support of a proposed married women's property bill which would have allowed married women to own their own property.[101] Owenite socialists like William Thompson and Catherine Barmby went further, however, claiming that it was necessary to abandon the traditional household unit; only with collective possession of property and the sharing of childcare and education would true equality within marriage become possible.[102]

But who would perform the childcare? The assumption that married women would become mothers and assume responsibility for their children was almost universally held during this period, among feminists and non-feminists alike. Increased discussion about birth control (a very controversial topic, and not one to be openly discussed by women), however, opened up the possibility of breaking the link between women and motherhood, and thereby, in the words of John Stuart Mill, reducing the 'disproportionate preponderance' of the 'exclusive function' of child rearing in their lives.[103] Nonetheless, birth control was not envisaged as a way of preventing women from becoming mothers. It was to be used simply to reduce the size of families, and thereby improve the health and well being of mothers.[104]

Freed from some of the burdens of childcare, women might be able to participate more fully in the public sphere. We have seen that Wollstonecraft hesitantly called for political representation for some women in 1792, and further written demands for political rights for women were made by William Thompson and Anna Wheeler in 1825. Discussion of women's suffrage was stimulated by the reform bill of 1832, which for the first time specifically *prevented*

---

100 Rendall, *Origins of Modern Feminism*, pp. 216–18, 285–6; John Stuart Mill, *On the Subjection of Women* (1869; Crofts Classics edn, 1980), ch. 2.

101 Rendall, *Origins of Modern Feminism*, p. 227; Mary Poovey, *Uneven Developments: The Ideological Work of Gender in Mid-Victorian England* (1988), ch. 3. The bill failed, although a bill which legalised divorce and provided some protection for separated women was passed in 1857; full reform of married women's property law did not occur until 1882.

102 Rendall, *Origins of Modern Feminism*, p. 218; William Thompson, *Appeal of One-Half the Human Race, Women, against the Pretensions of the Other Half, Men, to Retain them in Political, and thence in Civil and Domestic Slavery* (1825).

103 John Stuart Mill, *Principles of Political Economy* (1848), quoted by Rendall, *Origins of Modern Feminism*, p. 287.

104 Rendall, *Origins of Modern Feminism*, pp. 225–6.

women from voting. Arguments in favour of enfranchising women on the same terms as men were put forward by a number of writers in the 1840s.[105] This was followed, in the late 1840s and 1850s, by a number of writers, including Harriet Taylor and J. S. Mill, who called for expanded occupational opportunities for women.[106]

By 1850, therefore, most of the arguments which had been used to define women as separate from, and inferior to, men had been challenged. The ideas that chastity was a fundamental female virtue; that women possessed inferior mental capacities to men and were instead ruled by their passions; that women should be subordinate to their husbands in marriage; and that women should have few if any political rights and opportunities to fulfil public roles were all challenged by feminist writers during the period from 1650 to 1850. Nonetheless, an important gender difference remained: the association of women with domesticity. Only a few feminist writers were willing to challenge the division of labour within the home. The freethinker Richard Carlile and a number of radical unitarians directly challenged the ideology of separate spheres by rejecting the idea that housework was naturally women's work. One writer, Mary Leman Grimstone, even went further and argued that women could work for a living while their husbands performed the domestic chores.[107] But these were very much minority viewpoints. Even J. S. Mill, whose arguments in favour of expanded occupational and political opportunities have already been mentioned, suggested that, within marriage, 'the common arrangement, by which the man earns the income and the wife superintends the domestic expenditure, seems to me in general the most suitable division of labour between the two persons.' Mill expected wives to assume 'the whole responsibility of [the children's] care and education in the early years'; the total burden of these responsibilities meant that 'it is not, therefore, I think, a desirable custom, that the wife should contribute by her labour to the income of the family.'[108] For the most part, even feminists thought that when women had children they should still be primarily concerned with their care, though those duties did

---

105 Ibid., pp. 307–11; Barbara Taylor, *Eve and the New Jerusalem: Socialism and Feminism in the Nineteenth Century* (1983), pp. 180, 215.

106 Rendall, *Origins of Modern Feminism*, pp. 286–7, 311, 316, 317.

107 John R. Gillis, *For Better, For Worse: British Marriages 1600 to the Present* (Oxford, 1985), p. 222; Kathryn Gleadle, *The Early Feminists: Radical Unitarians and the Emergence of the Women's Rights Movement, 1831–51* (1995), pp. 96–106.

108 Mill, *Subjection of Women*, p. 47.

not necessarily mean that they should be completely excluded from public functions.[109]

Despite this limitation, a new, more sympathetic view of the characteristics and potentialities of women's nature had clearly developed during this period, one which was radically different from that propounded in the Bible. (Indeed, the most radical feminists in the 1830s and 1840s rejected Christianity or sought to reinterpret the sections of scripture which justified female inferiority.[110]) Feminist views, of course, did not predominate at the end of this period; as Rendall points out, such views were held by a small minority of English women and men, and these people were 'frequently ridiculed, treated with often brutal hostility, and even imprisoned'.[111] But the creation of this new position meant that there was a far wider range of definitions of femininity in print, including far more positive estimates of women's capabilities, at the end of this period than existed at the beginning (though even then, as the 'Querelle des femmes' suggests, there were important differences of view).

Significantly, this applies to views of masculinity as well, for all this thinking about the nature and role of women in society necessarily involved a reconsideration of the position of men. Current research suggests that definitions of masculinity were stretched far less during this period than was the case with femininity, but there were nonetheless some significant developments. As noted earlier in this chapter, conduct-book writers when discussing male faults paid decreasing attention to lust over the course of this period, and increasingly criticised male insolence, pride (something previously thought to be a problem only if it appeared in women), and violence. Similarly, in the writings of Astell and Wollstonecraft and in sentimental novels there was criticism of men's brutal and arrogant behaviour in their relations with women during courtship and marriage. This encouraged the formation of an ideal of masculinity which involved greater sensitivity and consideration for others. Significantly, in her discussion of the benefits of education for women, Mary Wollstonecraft suggested that a proper education could lead to a similar transformation in aristocratic male behaviour: instead of training boys to become 'selfish and vicious' and set themselves above others, schools could teach men affection, modesty, and delicacy of mind, as well as respect for chastity.[112]

109 Rendall, *Origins of Modern Feminism*, pp. 286–7, 290, 310.
110 Taylor, *Eve and the New Jerusalem*, pp. 144–6.
111 Rendall, *Origins of Modern Feminism*, p. 321.
112 Wollstonecraft, *Vindication*, pp. 241, 242, 246.

In sum, over the course of the eighteenth century an image of masculinity developed which to a certain extent moved closer to traditional femininity: the ideal man was modest, diffident, and caring as well as having the traditional male virtues of intelligence, strength, and courage. This line of thought could ultimately lead to the breakdown of all gender differences and the advocacy of an androgynous personality: this actually happened in the 1840s in the thought of Catherine and Goodwyn Barmby, Chartists and Owenite socialists, who sought to transcend and combine 'woman-nature' and 'man-nature'. In terms of conceptualisations of gender this was an extremely important development, but, needless to say, it was not influential, and the Barmbys later retreated somewhat from this position.[113] Nonetheless, at the very end of our period feminists were perceiving significant similarities between the sexes. Harriet Taylor Mill advocated a strict equality in the treatment of men and women and argued that individuals, regardless of sex, should be able to choose whichever calling in life they preferred.[114] As we have seen, one writer, Mary Leman Grimstone, even argued that traditional gender roles could be reversed. John Stuart Mill failed to adopt quite such a radical stand, but even so in his *The Subjection of Women*, written in 1860–1, he noted that with the progress of civilisation men had become more domestically oriented: 'The association of men with women in daily life is much closer and more complete than it ever was before. Men's life is more domestic.'[115]

CONCLUSION

Feminist thinkers during the period 1650–1850 developed visions of femininity and masculinity which were unprecedented in terms of the similarities of the characteristics possessed by each sex and in their challenges to male superiority and privilege, though few broke down gender distinctions altogether and the assumed link between women and domestic activities was rarely attacked. In contrast, we have documented from the conduct books, periodicals, and some fiction in the second half of the period the increasing prominence

---

113 Rendall, *Origins of Modern Feminism*, p. 105; Taylor, *Eve and the New Jerusalem*, pp. 178–80.

114 Harriet Taylor Mill, 'The enfranchisement of women', *Westminster Review* 55 (July 1851), 289–312; reprinted in Rossi (ed.), *Essays on Sex Equality*, p. 105.

115 Mill, *Subjection of Women*, pp. 94–5.

of domesticity as a prescriptive ideology for women, an ideology which stressed the fundamental differences between male and female natures. At the same time alternative representations stressing female independence and assertiveness could be found in popular ballads and chapbooks and in some novels. Thus, the terms of debate about the nature and social functions of women (and to a lesser extent men) broadened significantly over the course of this period. By the mid-nineteenth century the 'woman question' had become a popular subject of discussion, and there was a lot to discuss.[116] Masculinity, of course, was not a subject of such conscious debate, but even here alternative possibilities were discussed, in part because changing ideas about women, especially their relations with men in marriage, inevitably forced some reconsideration of male as well as female gender roles. In this chapter we have only been able to scratch the surface in analysing arguments about gender and representations of men and women in printed literature. Much more could be said on this topic, not only on the specific texts and genres discussed, but also on genres such as poetry and verse, and travel writings. Nonetheless it should be apparent even from this limited discussion that a variety of ideas about gender were in circulation in this period, and that the range of ideas expanded significantly.

What impact did these ideas have on gender roles as actually lived in English society? There is good reason to be sceptical about the extent to which prescriptive ideologies were followed in day-to-day life. Large numbers of people, especially women, were unable to read any of the texts discussed in this chapter. Moreover, we need to recognise that even when texts were read they were subject to multiple and potentially subversive readings. Evidence from diaries shows that conduct-book advice could be reshaped into a more palatable form. As Vivien Jones has argued, when conduct books were read alongside works of fiction in which women were active protagonists, readers could be led to fantasise about the possibilities of female independence and sexual desire, in spite of the conduct books' firm denunciations of such behaviour. It has recently been demonstrated that the conduct books of Sarah Ellis were given contradictory readings at the time they were published: while some commentators praised her for advocating an entirely domestic, supportive and subordinate role for women, others thought she encouraged women to seek power through cunningly manipulating

---

116 For a review of this debate, see Helsinger et al., *The Woman Question* (3 vols, 1983).

men. Finally, we must note that at any one time readers could find
alternative visions of gender roles on offer by reading different
texts. Ellis's writings, for example, were an intervention into a
broader debate about the proper roles of middle-class women. Even
direct emulation of what was read, therefore, involved a positive
choice on the part of the reader. Printed literature exerted a profound influence on people's lives, but clearly that influence was
often limited, indirect, and complex. We must now turn our attention to men's and women's lives as actually lived in order to assess
how close the correspondence was between gender roles in theory
and in practice.[117]

117 Fletcher, *Gender, Sex and Subordination*, pp. 409–10; Vivien Jones, 'The
seductions of conduct: pleasure and the conduct literature', in *Pleasure in the
Eighteenth Century*, ed. R. Porter and M. M. Roberts (1996), pp 108–32; Henrietta
Twycross-Martin, 'Woman supportive or woman manipulative? The "Mrs Ellis"
woman', in C. C. Orr (ed.), *Wollstonecraft's Daughters: Womanhood in England and
France, 1780–1920* (Manchester, 1996), pp. 109–20; Dror Wahrman, '"Middle-class"
domesticity goes public: gender, class, and politics from Queen Caroline to Queen
Victoria', *Journal of British Studies* 32 (1993), pp. 430–1.

CHAPTER THREE

Sexuality

It almost goes without saying (indeed it has done, since the topic was largely ignored by historians until recently) that sexual attitudes and practices are fundamental aspects of society. Reproductive activities shape demographic patterns, while attitudes towards sexual practices, in terms of what is considered 'normal' and what is 'deviant' for both men and women, help shape the construction of gender roles. At a time when all licit sexual behaviour took place within courtship and marriage, gender differences in attitudes towards sex shaped important aspects of the roles played by men and women in forming families and in conducting family life. Moreover, historians are increasingly becoming aware that such attitudes had a public significance as well, in the sense that gendered understandings of sexuality shaped social and political behaviour in a number of ways.

Recent research has suggested that some significant changes in understandings and practices occurred during the period of this study, changes which have potentially important implications for our understanding of gender roles. As we have seen, Thomas Laqueur's work on conceptions of the body has posited a shift in the eighteenth century from a 'one-sex' model which interpreted male and female bodies as fundamentally similar, to a 'two-sex' model of sexual difference, a shift which can be seen as related to arguments about the growth of separate spheres. Other historians have argued for important changes in sexual behaviour. As part of his argument for the growing importance of affection in marriage (discussed in Chapter 4), Lawrence Stone argued that there was a growing sexual permissiveness in the eighteenth century, which was, however, reversed in the nineteenth century. This section of Stone's book has been the most heavily criticised, however, and most historians now see the eighteenth century as a period of increasingly restrictive sexual attitudes rather than the reverse. An important argument, advanced by Henry Abelove and Tim Hitchcock, is that sexual practices became restricted to heterosexual, penetrative, vaginal intercourse, as mutual masturbation and fondling became less common. While this provocative argument may seem impossible to prove, a variety of supporting evidence has been advanced, notably changes in the descriptions of sexual behaviour in men's diaries; the increasing rates of illegitimacy and prenuptial pregnancy; the growth in pornography, which gave primacy to penetration, and anti-masturbation literature; and the growing popularity of sex manuals (which were primarily guides to achieving conception). This evidence will be considered carefully in this chapter. If true, this change in sexual practice has important implications for women, not least because they were much more likely to become pregnant. Parallel changes occurred in attitudes towards homosexuality, according to the work of Randolph Trumbach and others, as homosexual acts became less tolerated and were increasingly confined to a homosexual subculture. Trumbach sees these changes, which occurred at different times for men and women, as part of a process of increasing differentiation of gender roles, as anyone whose behaviour transcended the line between accepted male and female roles was increasingly marginalised.[1] Once again, this process can be seen as facilitating the development of separate spheres. The cumulative effect of these arguments thus presents a relatively coherent picture of an increasing concentration of expectations on one type of heterosexuality to the exclusion of other forms of sexual expression, leading to a narrowing of sexual opportunities and an increasing differentiation of expected behaviour between men and women.

Each of these theories, however, can be criticised for being based on insufficient evidence, for sources concerning sexual attitudes and sexual behaviour in this period are extremely scanty. We must be careful to distinguish between changing ideas and practices, for evidence about the former is much more plentiful than the latter. Analysis of the medical literature, popular sex manuals, conduct

1 Thomas Laqueur, *Making Sex: The Body and Gender from the Greeks to Freud* (Cambridge, Mass., 1990); Lawrence Stone, *The Family, Sex and Marriage in England 1500-1800* (1977); Henry Abelove, 'Some speculations on the history of "sexual intercourse" during the "long eighteenth century" in England', *Genders* 6 (1989); Tim Hitchcock, 'Redefining sex in eighteenth-century England', *History Workshop Journal* 41 (1996), pp. 73–90; Randolph Trumbach, 'London's sapphists: from three sexes to four genders in the making of modern culture', in *Body Guards: The Cultural Politics of Gender Ambiguity*, ed. J. Epstein and K. Straub (1991), pp. 112–41.

books, and pornography certainly suggests that understandings and expectations of sexuality did change considerably over this period. Nonetheless, consideration of the limited available evidence of sexual behaviour suggests that we should be careful not to overemphasise change at the expense of the evident continuities in gender roles in sexual behaviour throughout this period.

UNDERSTANDINGS OF THE BODY AND SEXUALITY

As we saw in Chapter 2, medical understandings of sex were directly connected with interpretations of the differences between male and female bodies. Under the humoral or Galenic model, which was still influential at the start of our period, the body consisted of hot and cold, wet and dry fluids, with men tending to be the former, and women the latter. Under this model the genitalia were perceived as essentially the same in both men and women, but the heat in male bodies was thought to cause their genitalia to be fully developed whereas in women they remained inverted inside them. This understanding of the body had important implications for ideas about sexuality. Because men had what women lacked, women were thought to have a fundamental desire to copulate with men and obtain their hot, dry semen. This is one of the reasons why at the start of our period women were perceived as lustful, and men were not: men did not need sex in the way that women did. (In fact, sexual activity was seen as a cure for many female diseases.[2]) Such was the perceived female need to have sex that while men's primary sexual dysfunction was thought to be a lack of sexual appetite, for women the danger was that they might be too lustful. Concerns about female lust were heightened by the prevailing ideas that women were less rational and more prone to be be governed by their passions. So much emphasis was placed on women's enjoyment of sexual activity that some thought that women could not conceive if they did not experience an orgasm. As the popular sexual advice book *Aristotle's Masterpiece* states, 'it is . . . necessary, that in their mutual embraces [husbands and wives] meet each other with equal ardour; for if the spirit flag on either part, they will fall short of what nature requires, and the woman must either miss of conception or else the

2 Hilda Smith, 'Gynecology and ideology in seventeenth-century England', in *Liberating Women's History*, ed. Bernice A. Carroll (1976), p. 101.

children prove weak in their bodies.'[3] This idea led to the assumption that women could not have been raped if sexual intercourse led to pregnancy. Fear about unleashing women's uncontrollable lust is one of the reasons, in addition to men's desire to control their wives and legal concerns about establishing the legitimacy of children, that there was a 'double standard' of sexual morality at the time, in which men's sexual pecadilloes were often tolerated and the sexual misbehaviour of women was widely condemned.

As we have seen, medical understandings of the body shifted over the course of this period to an interpretation of men's and women's bodies as fundamentally different. This 'two-sex' model of sexual difference evolved over a long period, from the late seventeenth to the early nineteenth century, and it involved new ways of characterising the sexual organs and sexual activity, ways which accentuated differences between men and women. For example, from the late seventeenth century a new language of sexual difference was developed by anatomists. From the 1670s there is evidence of the use of the term 'vagina' to label a cavity which had previously been labelled the neck of the womb and characterised as an inverted penis. Around the same time the sexual secretions of women and men were identified separately. In 1672, Regnier de Graaf published his discovery of the ovarian follicle, and argued that eggs were produced there. In the same decade, Anton van Leeuwenhoek and Niklaas Hartsoeker discovered active sperm in men's semen. By the eighteenth century the word 'testicle' was no longer used for both sexes: testicle became male, while the word ovary was used for women.[4]

By the end of the eighteenth century equally fundamental changes occurred in perceptions of women's role in sexual intercourse: it began to be questioned whether women needed to experience sexual pleasure, or orgasm, in order to conceive. In 1845, Dr Adam Raciborski discovered spontaneous ovulation in dogs, and postulated that this was true of women too. This meant that women's active participation in sexual intercourse was unnecessary in order for ovulation, and therefore conception, to take place. Reproduction, which was now seen as a biological rather than a mental issue, would henceforth be governed by a woman's ovaries,

---

3 Quoted by Roy Porter, in '"The secrets of generation display'd": *Aristotle's Master-piece* in eighteenth-century England', in *'Tis Nature's Fault: Unauthorized Sexuality during the Enlightenment*, ed. R. P. Maccubbin (Cambridge, 1987), pp. 8–9.

4 Laqueur, *Making Sex*, pp. 158–61, 171.

which were increasingly viewed as her defining biological characteristic.[5]

Needless to say, these new ways of thinking about the process of sexual reproduction had important implications for understandings of the nature of male and female sexuality. As women's conscious participation in intercourse was de-emphasised, less attention was paid to women's supposed lust and increasingly women were viewed as sexually passive, even passionless. In the seventeenth and early eighteenth centuries, although men were expected to take the initiative, men and women were both seen as lustful and intercourse was expected to lead to mutual orgasm (as reflected in the passage from *Aristotle's Masterpiece* cited earlier).[6] Even before the new medical understandings became influential, the intensity of female sexual pleasure began to be questioned in literature. It has been argued that the eighteenth-century cult of sentiment portrayed women as too delicate to be affected by coarse sexual feeling. In eighteenth-century fiction, female heroines were increasingly depicted as chaste and, according to Ruth Perry, 'maternity came to be imagined as a counter to sexual feeling'. Perry argues that motherhood became women's essential function, as there was increasing pressure on them to breast feed their babies even though it delayed the resumption of sex after childbirth (intercourse was thought to spoil the milk). The emphasis on the sensibility and imagination of heroines in literature has been interpreted by other modern scholars as a recognition of female sexuality, since contemporaries were worried that the images of overwhelming passion in sentimental novels encouraged women to act irresponsibly.[7] Yet after 1750 conduct-book writers ceased to discuss female lust. In 1850 *The Westminster Review* went so far as to argue that, with the exception of 'fallen women', nature had made sexual desire in women dormant 'till excited by undue familiarities; almost always till excited by actual intercourse'.[8]

---

5 Ibid., pp. 162–3, 184–9; Thomas Laqueur, 'Orgasm, generation, and the politics of reproductive sexuality', in *The Making of the Modern Body: Sexuality and Society in the Nineteenth Century*, ed. C. Gallagher and T. Laqueur (Berkeley, 1987), pp. 3, 27.

6 Anthony Fletcher, *Gender, Sex and Subordination in England 1500–1800* (1995), pp. 55, 58–9, 114.

7 Ruth Perry, 'Colonizing the breast: sexuality and maternity in eighteenth-century England', *Journal of the History of Sexuality* 2 (1991), pp. 209–11; G. J. Barker-Benfield, *The Culture of Sensibility: Sex and Society in Eighteenth-Century Britain* (1992), p. 328; P. M. Spacks, "Ev'ry woman is at heart a rake"', *Eighteenth-Century Studies* 8 (1974), p. 38.

8 Quoted by Keith Thomas, 'The double standard', *Journal of the History of Ideas* 20 (1959), p. 215.

By the early nineteenth century many doctors also denied that women had a sexual drive. Yet the notion that the Victorian ideal woman was so innocent she was not even conscious of sexual desire has recently been questioned. Michael Mason has argued that professional opinion on this question was 'far from unanimous' and has shown that there was widespread recognition (and approbation) of female sexual appetite and passion, as is evident, for example, in the continuing belief (despite the discovery of spontaneous ovulation) that women needed to experience an orgasm in order to conceive. Indeed, it was suggested that suppression of sexual desire was far more likely to lead to ill health in women than in men. Confronted with such contradictory advice, some writers on sex and marriage, according to Peter Gay, adopted an intermediate position, which recognised erotic feelings in women but characterised male sexuality as more insistent and dominant. To the extent that one can identify a common position among commentators at the end of our period, this view probably comes closest. The situation among the working class, however, was different. Middle-class concerns about the lasciviousness of female workers in the mines and in agriculture suggest that such women were thought to have strong sexual feelings. These views were echoed in Victorian popular ballads, where it was assumed that the male and female libido were both powerful.[9]

Nonetheless men, whose sperm had been identified as the primary component in the reproduction process in the late seventeenth century, were increasingly seen by the medical profession as the most active participant in intercourse, with the male orgasm given the central role. Whereas in the early part of our period it was women's sexual aggressiveness that was the subject of most concern, by the early Victorian period it was men's. One aspect of male sexual indiscipline was adultery. In the debate on the 1857 divorce bill, William Gladstone argued that the causes of adultery were different for women and men: 'I believe that a very limited portion of the offences committed by women are due to the mere influence of sensual passion. On the other side, I believe that a very large proportion of the offences committed by men are due to that influence.'[10] An-

9 Michael Mason, *The Making of Victorian Sexuality* (Oxford, 1994), pp. 177, 195–205; Peter Gay, *The Bourgeois Experience: Victoria to Freud. Volume 1: Education of the Senses* (Oxford, 1984), pp. 155–6; J. S. Bratton, *The Victorian Popular Ballad* (1975), pp. 159–61, 184–6, 195–6 (I am indebted to Professor John Tosh for this reference). For concerns about female sexuality at work, see below, Chapter 5, p. 203.

10 Quoted in Thomas, 'Double standard', p. 207.

other example of indiscipline was masturbation. From the early eighteenth century to the end of our period there developed a growing concern about the ill effects of this practice. Although both female and male masturbation were condemned, the focus was primarily on men and on the dangerous consequences of the waste or excessive expenditure of semen. As Mason has argued for the nineteenth century, although it was thought that 'masturbation could damage a woman's internal genitalia', 'in general female masturbation was not singled out for condemnation in this period in the elaborate and persistent fashion that male masturbation was'. Even with men, however, Victorian medical opinion was not unanimous: a well respected doctor like James Paget did not view the practice as harmful.[11]

Another manifestation of the increasing concentration on sexual behaviour from a male point of view in this period is the growth in pornographic literature. Stimulated by the growth of obscene publications on the continent (especially France) from the mid-seventeenth century and the development of a philosophy of libertine pleasure, and encouraged by the growth in press freedom stemming from the expiration of the Licensing Act in 1695, this was the first period in English history in which there was a significant and burgeoning market in published erotic and pornographic literature. Although explicit images of sexual activity in a variety of forms (art, novels, poetry, drama, satire, street-ballads, and para-medical works) violated the bounds of the permissible, they reflected and helped shape sexual norms.

Most obscene literature was written by and for men, and it encouraged them to have penetrative sex with women. The central theme in most fiction depicts men actively seducing women, though particularly at the start of our period the women are often depicted as more than willing participants. As Rachel Weil has noted, the Restoration poem 'Sardanapalus' includes images of 'huge and magnificent penises, [with] the women literally dying to be penetrated'.[12] Restoration poems and libertine literature also include

---

11 Tim Hitchcock, *English Sexualities, 1700–1800* (1997), ch. 4; Robert H. MacDonald, 'The frightful consequences of onanism: notes on the history of a delusion', *Journal of the History of Ideas* 28 (1967), pp. 423–31; Mason, *Making of Victorian Sexuality*, p. 204; M. J. Peterson, 'Dr. Acton's enemy: medicine, sex, and society in Victorian England', *Victorian Studies* 30 (1986), pp. 580–1.

12 Rachel Weil, 'Sometimes a scepter is only a scepter: pornography and politics in Restoration England', in *The Invention of Pornography: Obscenity and the Origins of Modernity, 1500–1800*, ed. Lynn Hunt (New York, 1993), p. 131.

depictions of women sexually overwhelming men. Indeed, the men depicted in Restoration erotica were often impotent and unable to satisfy their female partners.[13]

In contrast, reflecting the growing focus on male rather than female lust over the course of this period, most eighteenth- and nineteenth-century pornography celebrated male erotic desire and depicted the female body as its object. Reflecting eighteenth-century interests in topography, geography, and botany, erotica depicted the female body as a '"terra incognita" . . . to be discovered and explored.' As the origins of the term implies, much pornographic work was about prostitution, with some including biographies and lists of prostitutes, such as *Harris' Lists of Covent Garden Ladies* (published between 1760 and the early 1790s), which included prices and anatomical descriptions. Stephen Marcus describes the central focus of mid-nineteenth-century pornography as an 'immense, supine, female form', while men are depicted as 'an enormous erect penis . . . [which is] creator and destroyer, the source of all and the end of all being'.[14] The images of men and women in erotic prints and drawings reflect these preoccupations, with men typically fully clothed, with the exception of their trousers dropped to their ankles to reveal an erect penis, while women's bodies are much more exposed.[15]

The image of the man as active and virile and women as receptors was not all-pervasive, however. Some pornography did go beyond the conventional. Eighteenth-century pornographic novels which were influenced by materialist philosophy depicted women, who were often the narrators, as 'activated [and] energised . . . participants'.[16] The most famous eighteenth-century pornographic work, *Memoirs of a Woman of Pleasure* by John Cleland, is narrated by a woman, Fanny Hill, who not only engages in masturbation and lesbian acts, but also seduces young men. Like Restoration erotica, other works depict men as unable to satisfy or control their wives, and satirise men as impotent or as cuckolds.

13 Roger Thompson, *Unfit for Modest Ears: A Study of Pornographic, Obscene and Bawdy Works Written or Published in England in the Second Half of the Seventeenth Century* (1979), p. 212.

14 P.-G. Boucé, 'Chthonic and pelagic metaphorization in eighteenth-century English erotica', in *'Tis Nature's Fault*, ed. Maccubin, p. 204; Stone, *Family, Sex and Marriage*, p. 539; Steven Marcus, *The Other Victorians: A Study of Sexuality and Pornography in Mid-Nineteenth-Century England* (1967), p. 275.

15 See the images in Peter Wagner, *Eros Revived: Erotica of the Enlightenment in England and America* (1988).

16 Margaret C. Jacob, 'The materialist world of pornography', in *The Invention of Pornography*, ed. Hunt, pp. 157–202, esp. p. 164.

It is often assumed that the readers of pornographic works were male, and indeed this must have often been the case. Yet women were not excluded. Promoters of pornography certainly tried to encourage women as well as men to buy the products: Francis Place reported that the owner of a stationery shop in the 1780s 'used to open a portfolio [containing obscene prints] to any boy or to any maidservant' who came into the shop.[17] That women actually read and enjoyed pornographic literature is suggested by a number of prints from the second half of our period which depicted women masturbating while reading such books, though of course these can be interpreted as male fantasies.[18]

Since much pornography was stimulated by libertine philosophy it is hardly surprising that it depicted a range of sexual acts which were unconventional. Nonetheless, there were limits to what could be depicted, even in pornography: female masturbation was acceptable but male masturbation was not. The former was seen as far less dangerous, but also far less satisfying: invariably in pornographic literature it was only a prelude to 'more serious food' (heterosexual sex). Similarly, lesbianism was acceptable, if equally unsatisfying, but male homosexuality was not, as was very rarely portrayed. (Although a homosexual act between young men is described in detail in *Memoirs of a Woman of Pleasure*, it is almost immediately condemned.) Thus even pornography tended to encourage heterosexual penetrative, vaginal sex (anal intercourse was also condemned). It has been argued that even in *Memoirs of a Woman of Pleasure* female sexuality was portrayed as unrealistic and passive.[19] Even libertines could not escape prevailing gender roles. Indeed, although pornography transgressed conventional sexual norms, it largely conformed (and contributed) to shifting cultural conceptions about appropriate sexual behaviour.

LICIT SEXUALITY

In sum, there is considerable evidence that over the course of this period interpretations of the extent and nature of men's and women's sexual desire changed significantly. The adoption of a two-

17 Cited by Stone, *Family, Sex and Marriage*, p. 621.

18 For example, see P. A. Baudouin, 'Midi' (undated) and Issac Cruickshank, 'Luxury' (1801), both reproduced in Wagner, *Eros Revived*, plates 53 and 59.

19 Randolph Trumbach, 'Erotic fantasy and male libertinism in enlightenment England', in *The Invention of Pornography*, ed. Hunt, p. 266.

sex model of the body emphasising the primary role played by men in intercourse and conception, the shift from worries about excessive female lust to concern about male lust, and the growing emphasis on penetrative sex can all be seen as part of the same phenomenon, which emphasised the male role in sex and focused on women's maternal responsibilities rather than their sexuality (though at the end of our period women were by no means seen as entirely asexual). It is far more difficult to determine whether similar changes occurred in sexual practice, for, to cite a modern country western song, 'no one knows what goes on behind closed doors'. Nonetheless, some sources, such as diaries and letters, are available, and it is important to examine them for what they can tell us about gendered patterns of sexual behaviour.

The vast majority of sexual activity in this period took place within the context of marriage or an impending marriage (as we shall see, sex played an important role in courtship rituals). While the major purpose of sex was thought to be procreation, the pleasurable aspects of sex were recognised for both partners. It is nonetheless possible that men took a more proactive approach to sex than women. Women rarely mentioned sex in their diaries (though their discussions of love and romance can be interpreted in erotic terms), while the subject is discussed in great detail in a number of male diaries. Since women were socialised not to talk about sex, it is difficult to draw conclusions on this point. Even so, the language men used to discuss sex is significant, and suggests control and dominance: they write of 'the use of her body', of having their 'will and pleasure' of a woman, or of satisfying an 'itch'. Edmund Harrold, a wig-maker of Manchester, recorded in his diary in June 1712 'on the 9th I did wife two times couch and bed in an hour an[d] half time.'[20] Evidence from descriptions of sex in defamation cases in the early seventeenth century (which, however, concern extramarital sexual relations) suggests that 'while men were consistently described as looking for sexual satisfaction, women's agency seems to lie entirely in consent'.[21] Some men publicly bragged about their sexual exploits, such as John Daniel, who in 1670 told Mary, the wife of Henry Jones, that she was a 'common whore . . . and that he

---

20 Ralph Houlbrooke, *English Family Life, 1576–1716: An Anthology from Diaries* (Oxford, 1988), p. 95.

21 Angus McLaren, *Reproductive Rituals: The Perception of Fertility in England from the Sixteenth Century to the Nineteenth Century* (1984), pp. 45, 81; Stone, *Family, Sex and Marriage*, pp. 493–4; Laura Gowing, *Domestic Dangers: Women, Words and Sex in Early Modern London* (Oxford, 1986), p. 78.

had often times layne with her and could when he pleased'. In contrast, women who discussed sex publicly were more likely to *condemn* other women for sexual misbehaviour, insulting such women by calling them whore, bitch, bawd, and bastard-bearer.[22]

It is of course virtually impossible to find out what actually happened during intercourse. Contemporary sex manuals advised men to lie on top of their partner and enter from the front (what would later be called the 'missionary position'), though pornographic works and medical treatises suggested other possible positions. If the missionary position was adopted, it could support the view that men were the dominant actors in sexual activity; certainly the position was associated with male dominance at the time. This is not to say that women did not fully participate in intercourse, or experienced less pleasure. There is plenty of evidence that both women and men pursued sexual pleasure throughout the period. Margaret Spufford has shown that seventeenth-century chapbooks depict women as 'after the first shynesses of virginity, taking positive pleasure in lovemaking'. Similarly, there is evidence of female sexual assertiveness in the testimony of eighteenth-century divorce cases, and Peter Gay's analysis of the surviving letters and diaries of nineteenth-century middle-class women has shown that such women experienced 'joint pleasure in the physical aspects of eroticism', though due to decorum there were few ways of expressing such feelings in writing.[23] Women could also use sex instrumentally for other purposes. All the women who had full intercourse with Samuel Pepys, for example, used their relationships with him to further their husbands' careers, and it is likely that women act equally purposefully within their own marriages.[24] In courtship, as we shall see, some women were expert at allowing just the right amount of sexual encouragement to their suitors to allow the courtship to proceed, without losing control. Indeed, while men took the initiative, women, as typically the more cautious partners, often controlled the pace in sexual intercourse.

We have seen that historians have made a number of arguments

22 Greater London Record Office, MJ/SR/1392, R. 142 (August 1670); Tim Meldrum, 'A women's court in London: defamation at the Bishop of London's Consistory Court, 1700–1745', *London Journal* 19 (1994), pp. 8–10.

23 Stone, *Family, Sex and Marriage*, pp. 643–5; Margaret Spufford, *Small Books and Pleasant Histories: Popular Fiction and its Readership in Seventeenth-Century England* (Cambridge, 1981), p. 63; Lawrence Stone, *Broken Lives: Separation and Divorce in England 1660–1857* (Oxford, 1993); Gay, *Bourgeois Experience, Vol. 1: Education of the Senses*, pp. 126, 133.

24 Stone, *Family, Sex and Marriage*, p. 555.

about changes in sexual practices between the seventeenth and nineteenth centuries. Stone argued that while in the seventeenth century sexual activity in the propertied classes was restricted to marriage and enjoyed by both partners, the eighteenth century was a period of permissiveness, especially for men, and the nineteenth century issued in a period of prudishness, especially for women, who were increasingly uninterested in sex. Recent research has cast doubt on these assertions, particularly (as we have seen) the last. Although sexual activity in general may have been been more open and tolerated in the eighteenth century than before, in terms of the range of acceptable sexual practices the climate appears to have become more rather than less restrictive.

The Hitchcock and Abelove argument that sexual activity between men and women during the eighteenth century became increasingly centred around penetrative vaginal sex, with less time spent fondling and in mutual masturbation, is supported by some significant evidence. A comparison of the diaries of three sexually active men (Samuel Pepys, a secretary in the Navy Office in the 1660s; John Cannon, a farm labourer and then excise officer in the early eighteenth century; and James Boswell, a largely unemployed Scottish gentleman whose papers cover the period from 1758 to 1795) reveals a significant change: while in the late seventeenth and early eighteenth centuries Pepys and Cannon appear to have engaged in a considerable amount of petting, fondling, and mutual masturbation with their mistresses, Boswell, in the words of Stone, had an appetite which was 'stronger and grosser. His main need was frequent and violent intercourse without preliminary foreplay or even conversation.'[25] The earlier pattern of sexuality is evident in the practice of 'bundling', by which courting couples (in all but the highest social classes) spent the night together with their clothes on, kissing and petting, without vaginal intercourse taking place.[26] It is argued that the increases in illegitimacy and prenuptial pregnancy which took place over the course of this period were the result of the decline of this practice, as couples increasingly engaged in full penetrative sex in courtship but were not always able to marry. If this change towards exclusively penetrative sex took place, it has important implications for gender roles. While it would be wrong to assume that one type of sex necessarily involves greater in-

---

25 For Cannon, see Hitchcock, *English Sexualities*, ch. 3. For Pepys and Boswell, see Stone, *Family, Sex and Marriage*, ch. 11, esp. p. 598.

26 Lawrence Stone, *Uncertain Unions: Marriage in England 1660–1753* (Oxford, 1992), pp. 9–11.

itiative by, or pleasure for, men or women, this change did put greater emphasis on the role of the phallus in sex. Moreover, in an era where birth-control methods were largely ineffective, penetrative sex led to more pregnancies for women, and therefore women more frequently became mothers, both inside and outside marriage (though some women resorted to abortion or infanticide).

Nonetheless, there are a number of objections to this argument. There is plenty of evidence of the primacy of penetrative sex in the early part of our period. Fletcher cites the example of a young man, Theophilus, Earl of Huntingdon, who in 1672 was unable to penetrate his new bride. In correspondence, his uncle assured him, according to Anthony Fletcher, 'that his niece would enjoy sex once the physical problem of lack of elasticity in her vagina was solved'. The language men used to describe sex is very suggestive of penetration: men wrote of 'tak[ing] her by storm' or described their penis as a 'plough'. Similarly, women described sex in terms of men 'occupying' or having the 'pleasure and use' of their partners.[27] Moreover, the increases in illegitimacy and prenuptial pregnancy rates which occurred in this period can be explained without reference to changing sexual practices. New economic opportunities encouraged the young to enter courtship and sexual activity earlier. Together with the disruption to normal courtship and marriage practices caused by the insecurity of many employments and growing geographical mobility, this meant that couples who engaged in penetrative sex were often unable to marry or chose to marry only when the woman became pregnant. If penetrative sex did become more common, one would expect higher levels of fertility *within* marriage as well as prior to marriage, but this was not the case. In sum, the evidence suggests that penetration was the dominant sexual practice throughout this period, though not to the exclusion of other forms of sexual intimacy.

Given the sources available, it is at this point impossible to determine whether any significant changes occurred in gender roles in heterosexual relations within marriage in this period. Further research, especially on women's sexual attitudes, is clearly necessary. In the interim, we should note that, though women discussed sex much less openly than men, there is continuing evidence of female initiative and pleasure in sex through to the end of our period, which suggests that the growing ideological importance placed on

---

27 Fletcher, *Gender, Sex and Subordination*, pp. 59, 93, 343; Meldrum, 'A woman's court', p. 8; Gowing, *Domestic Dangers*, p. 73.

the male role did not diminish women's active involvement in intercourse. We can, however, learn more about these issues through an
examination of sexual attitudes and practices outside marriage,
where, due to greater efforts of policing, there is much more evidence available.

SEXUAL DEVIANCE

The gendered nature of sexual practice is more apparent when we
examine sexual activity outside its legitimate context in marriage,
whether as extramarital sex, prostitution, or homosexuality. An
examination of these activities will demonstrate that even where society's rules were broken, sexual conduct was highly gendered, and
that over the course of this period those differences changed in
some significant ways.

While sexual behaviour outside marriage by both men and
women was condemned by the church, a double standard was built
into the law, whereby men's promiscuity was deemed far less harmful than that of women, and was far less likely to be punished.[28] To
a great extent the double standard is also evident in social attitudes.
Conduct books treated adultery involving married women as a
crime far worse than theft, while women whose husbands cheated
on them were told not to complain, but to reform their husbands by
setting a virtuous example.[29] Defamation cases reveal that women
were frequently publicly insulted for engaging in sexual misbehaviour, while virtually nothing was said about male fornication, unless the activity involved complicating factors such as sodomy,
brothel keeping, or a bastard child, and even then such public accusations against men disappeared over the course of this period.
Similarly, rough music, the traditional neighbourhood shaming
demonstrations, were frequently directed at men whose wives had
cheated on them, but not the reverse.[30] This is not to say that men's
pecadilloes went unchallenged: men could come under significant
pressure to exercise self control, particularly among the middle
classes and at times of intense religiosity (such as early-seventeenth-
century puritanism and late-eighteenth-century and early-nine-

28 Thomas, 'Double standard'; Carol Smart, 'Disruptive bodies and unruly sex:
the regulation of reproduction and sexuality in the nineteenth century', in
Regulating Motherhood: Historical Essays on Marriage, Motherhood and Sexuality (1992),
pp. 7–32.

29 For example, see *The Whole Duty of Woman: Or, an Infallible Guide to the Fair Sex*
(1737), p. 122.

30 E. P. Thompson, *Customs in Common* (1991), ch. 8.

teenth-century evangelicalism). And diary entries demonstrate that when they did stray from their wives men could feel intense guilt. Nonetheless, men were never subject to the public scrutiny and condemnations that women experienced.

Of course, both men and women engaged in sex outside marriage, though the available evidence suggests that such activity was typically initiated by men, and, while it involved men of all social classes, a narrower range of women participated. While the vast majority of women appear to have kept their virginity until they were on the verge of marriage, if not actually married, men's sexual activity started long before, commencing with masturbation (occasionally in groups) from early adolescence, and often involving pre-marital sex with prostitutes or servants. Although the tradition of aristocratic libertinism was in decline by 1850, for most of our period aristocratic fathers accepted that their sons would experiment with prostitutes. Moreover, respectable men often kept mistresses with whom they appeared in public, and they often recognised their bastard children. Politicians such as John Wilkes and Charles James Fox actually profited in terms of public acclaim from their sexual exploits.[31]

With the exception of prostitution, the illicit sexual activities of women are rarely documented, but in contrast to men descriptions of female mutual masturbation before marriage are rare, though it is possible that such activity occurred in the context of the romantic friendships between women discussed below. On the whole, women engaged in fondling with men only as a part of courtship, and they kept their virginity intact until marriage had been promised or taken place. Those who had children outside marriage typically had engaged in intercourse with the promise of marriage, but for a variety of reasons the intended marriage never took place. But this was not always the case: certain groups of women were prone to, or vulnerable to, sexual activity outside courtship and marriage. There is some evidence of adultery committed by elite women, especially where the liaisons were discreet and sustained. Somewhat lower down the social scale a minority of unmarried women, including actresses, slept with men like Boswell, but in doing so they chose a lifestyle which to a certain extent marginalised them from respectable society. Among lower-class women there is evidence of casual sex

---

31 Randolph Trumbach, *The Rise of the Egalitarian Family: Aristocratic Kinship and Domestic Relations in Eighteenth-Century England* (1978), p. 282; Roy Porter and Lesley Hall, *The Facts of Life: The Creation of Sexual Knowledge in Britain, 1650–1950* (1995), pp. 23–6.

among 'vagrant women, former parish apprentices, young women ill-equipped to deal with the death of parents on whom they were financially dependent, and those women of the town who consorted with soldiers and sailors'; it will be apparent that such women (of whom there were many) were frequently forced into sex by their precarious economic circumstances, though they often did not consider themselves prostitutes. In any case, such women had little incentive to conform to the norms of respectable society. One group of women was particularly vulnerable to sexual exploitation: servants. Samuel Pepys, for example, frequently groped and fondled the maids working in his house. Although he never engaged in penetrative sex with them, other masters used their superior position and physical strength to force servants to engage in full intercourse, and if they got pregnant they were often immediately dismissed.[32] A conduct book for servants told them that, whereas it was 'exceedingly shocking and unnatural' that male servants would be pursued by their mistresses, it was very likely that maids would be attacked by their masters or fellow servants.[33]

Despite the strictures of the double standard, a number of married women did engage in extramarital sexual activity, though often under duress. Stone's conclusion from his examination of Pepys's diary that 'most women [of all social classes] were quite willing to be kissed and to allow their breasts to be seen and handled' is contradicted by evidence from the diary that, in the words of Margaret Hunt, 'many of the women *did* mind, found the experience humiliating, and tried to resist'. As we have seen, however, Pepys did have full intercourse with some women, all of whom were his social inferiors. James Boswell, who was both more aggressive and less willing to be deterred by the possibility of pregnancy or venereal disease, propositioned a large number of married women of his own class, and was successful with some, including two wives of close friends and two women who had separated from their husbands. Although in both Pepys's and Boswell's diaries it is usually the men who seem to take the initiative, at least three women 'simply threw themselves into [Boswell's] arms'. Nonetheless, Boswell's record suggests that willing women were in short supply, and such activity was not widely tolerated. Boswell himself felt particularly guilty about his affairs

---

32 Nicholas Rogers, 'Carnal knowledge: illegitimacy in eighteenth-century Westminster', *Journal of Social History* 23 (1989), p. 363; Stone, *Family, Sex and Marriage*, pp. 552–61.

33 Trumbach, *Rise of the Egalitarian Family*, p. 148.

with married women, and his wife, though she always ultimately forgave him, was clearly disturbed by his transgressions.[34]

For these reasons, men were most successful with women over whom they could exert some power, through the use of force or because they could offer them social or economic benefits in return for sex, or penalties if they refused. The male beliefs that they had a right to molest women in the streets, that 'unchaste' women were available to all men, and that violence and conquest were a normal part of sex led to a significant, but unknown, number of women being raped.[35] In many other cases, women were enticed or compelled into sex by the man's superior social position. The mistresses of Pepys, Cannon, and Boswell were mostly below them in social status: Cannon, an excise officer, consorted with servants; Pepys, a gentleman civil servant, pursued his wife's maids, tavern girls, and especially the wives of the men he supervised; and Boswell, a gentleman, slept with actresses, a wet nurse, and servants. There were simply too many legal, social, and practical reasons which discouraged women from their own social class from engaging in extramarital sexual activity. More than the dangers of pregnancy and disease, there was the social stigma of being liable to be called a 'whore'. Even among the more dissolute aristocracy, female sexual promiscuity could be problematic: women who obtained divorces in order to marry their lovers were shunned by respectable society.[36] When women did have affairs, therefore, it may well have often been for ulterior motives, such as social or economic advancement.

Such activity is of course closely related to prostitution, perhaps the clearest example of the gendered nature of sexual behaviour at this time. In a variety of different contexts, women engaged in intercourse with men in exchange for money or goods throughout this period, but there is no evidence of male prostitution, except for a limited amount in a homosexual context. This is because extramarital sexual activity had a completely different meaning for women than for men. When they sought it, diary evidence suggests that they apparently had no problem finding willing men. But due to the costs of such activity, in pregnancy, disease, and social disapproval, women were much less likely to seek such activity for pleasure.

34 Stone, *Family, Sex and Marriage*, pp. 552–61, 572–99; Margaret Hunt, *The Middling Sort: Commerce, Gender and Family in England, 1680–1780* (1996), pp. 354–5. See, for example, the description in Pepys's diary of his encounter with Betty Michell on 23 December 1666.

35 Anna Clark, *Women's Silence, Men's Violence: Sexual Assault in England, 1770–1845* (1987).

36 Trumbach, *Rise of the Egalitarian Family*, p. 159.

For men, of course, there were far fewer disadvantages, though venereal disease was a constant threat and they also had to contend with some social and moral disapproval and their own religious conscience. But because it was hard to find willing women, men frequently had to pay. Similarly, the even greater social opprobrium associated with homosexual sex (discussed below) explains why men seeking sex with men occasionally paid for male prostitutes.

Many, probably most, women entered prostitution because they were poor. The nineteenth-century social investigator Henry Mayhew thought that the 'greatest' cause of prostitution was 'the low rate of wages that the female classes of this great city [London] receive, in return for the most arduous and wearisome labour'. Compared to most work opportunities for women, prostitution, despite the obvious disadvantages, offered better pay and shorter hours. Even then it was mostly young women with nowhere else to turn for help, because one or both parents had died and/or they had left home, who turned to prostitution. In contrast to arguments of the time that prostitutes were usually women who had been 'seduced' and then abandoned by gentlemen, it appears that most women turned to prostitution because they had no other means of supporting themselves, not because they had lost their honour. For some women, however, it may have been a way of rebelling against their upbringing and achieving some independence. As one nineteenth-century brothel keeper remarked, adolescent women had few other opportunities if they wished to rebel and assert their independence: while boys could run away to sea, women who sought such independence had few opportunities for supporting themselves beyond selling their bodies. Although the dangers of such a course of action were considerable, prostitution offered the possibility of participating in a distinctive female subculture, where women lived together and 'adopted an outward appearance and a more affluent style of life that distinguished themselves from other working class women'.[37] Most women, however, must have turned to prostitution less because it fulfilled social aspirations than because it was simply the least unattractive way available of supporting themselves.

Social attitudes towards prostitution were ambiguous. On the one hand, it was condemned, especially by religious figures, along with all other forms of non-procreative, extramarital sex. On the other hand, many legal and social commentators viewed prostitu-

37 Henry Mayhew, *London Labour and the London Poor* (4 vols, 1861–62; repr. edn New York, 1968), 4, p. 213; Judith R. Walkowitz, *Prostitution and Victorian Society: Women, Class and the State* (Cambridge, 1980), pp. 21, 26.

tion as a necessary evil, in that it served a useful function in satisfying men's lust while keeping respectable women pure. Taking this attitude to its logical conclusion, in the early eighteenth century Bernard Mandeville proposed the creation of state-run brothels, which would allow men to satiate their lust while eliminating the ill effects of unregulated prostitution, including venereal disease.[38] Attitudes towards prostitution were thus very much part of the double standard, and the double standard is evident in how it was treated. When attempts were made to curb prostitution, for public order or public health reasons, it was the women who were harassed, not their male clients. Prostitution was not itself illegal, except to the extent that it caused a public nuisance. Under this rubric, both brothels and street walkers were liable to be prosecuted, with the latter often sent to houses of correction for whipping and a stint of hard labour. Their male clients were very rarely prosecuted, and almost the only time they appear in the records is when they were forced to act as prosecutors, implausibly blaming such 'loose, idle and disorderly women' for corrupting them. Thus the calendars of the Middlesex House of Correction for 1721 include the name of Thomas Brass, who, as an alleged victim, was responsible for the commitment of a woman for 'picking him up in the streets and carrying him into a tavern and agreeing to let him lie with her for 4s 6d'.[39]

Concern about the social problems caused by prostitution, such as the spread of venereal disease, also focused on women, as is evident in Mandeville's proposal for state-run brothels. Beyond disease, prostitution was seen as the embodiment of a wide range of social and economic ills, and therefore it was thought that suppressing it could contribute to the wealth of the nation at home and success at war abroad. The founding of the Magdalen Hospital in London in 1758, with its unprecedented strategy of attempting to reform 'penitent' prostitutes, can thus be ascribed not simply to the religious and philanthropic good will of the benefactors, but also to concern over the need to contribute to Britain's efforts in the Seven Years War and in colonial expansion. The reform of female sexuality was thus linked with the future of the nation.[40] In sum, re

38 Bernard Mandeville, *A Modest Defence of Public Stews* (1724); Thomas, 'Double standard', p. 197.

39 Greater London Record Office, MJ/SR/2374, House of Correction Calendar, October 1721.

40 Donna Andrews, *Philanthropy and Police: London Charity in the Eighteenth Century* (Princeton, 1989), pp. 119–27.

sponses to prostitution indicate that, despite the fact that men provided the demand, it was deemed a female problem.

Although it is impossible to know how frequently prostitution occurred, the everpresent gendered construction of sexual honour meant that it was widespread. According to an observer in 1859, 'there are few men who, in some period of their lives, have not dealt in mercenary sex'.[41] It was most visibly an urban phenomenon, but the evidence suggests that prostitutes could also be found in rural areas. In his study of early-seventeenth-century rural Somerset, G. R. Quaife found a wide variety of casual, semi-amateur prostitution not only among spinsters, but also among wives and widows. Some were vagrants, others were the 'private whores' of particular men, while others occasionally offered sexual favours in exchange for cash, goods, or help on the farm. The phenomenon of the small minority of bastard bearers who were 'repeaters' has been adduced as further evidence of village prostitution.[42] A wider variety of both casual and professional prostitution could of course be found in cities, ranging from long-term relationships to casual encounters in the street. Examples of the former can be found at both ends of the social spectrum, including both mistresses of aristocrats or gentry kept in lavish apartments in the west end of London and 'sailor's whores' in the east end who lived with sailors when they were in port. The fact that such relationships were often described as tantamount to marriage illustrates the point that, given women's fundamental economic dependence on men at this time, it is often very difficult to draw a line between mercenary sex and other types of sexual relationships.

It is generally assumed that prostitution increased considerably during this period. It is certainly possible that it was encouraged by the declining range of work opportunities for women in the nineteenth century. Since the most visible prostitution could be found in cities, and the country experienced considerable urban growth during this period, it is likely the amount of *visible* prostitution did increase. It has been estimated that in the 1830s there were over 900 brothels and 850 houses of 'ill fame' in London; in 1858 the Metropolitan Police counted 7261 prostitutes. Nonetheless, there is

41 John Wade, *Women, Past and Present* (1859), cited by Mason, *Making of Victorian Sexuality*, pp. 119–127.

42 G. R. Quaife, *Wanton Wenches and Wayward Wives: Peasants and Illicit Sex in Early Seventeenth Century England* (New Brunswick, NJ, 1979), pp. 146–52; Peter Laslett, *Family Life and Illicit Love in Earlier Generations* (Cambridge, 1977), p. 149.

considerable evidence of prostitution in both the towns and villages of England in the early part of our period. Prostitution in the nineteenth century was not a qualitatively different phenomenon from preceding centuries, and indeed a recent survey suggests that the amount of prostitution declined over the course of the nineteenth century.[43] There is some evidence of more tolerant attitudes in the eighteenth century, as attempts were made to reform prostitutes, rather than punish them, as in the Magdalen hospital. Yet although these were important developments, they did not herald a long-term trend of toleration: in the nineteenth century prostitution came to be seen as 'the social evil', a threatening vice which epitomised the dangers of the new marketplace economy and whose perversity 'was thought to be visited on the bodies of prostitutes' through venereal disease and their supposed infertility.[44] Attitudes towards prostitution appear to move cyclically, with waves of intolerance occasionally disrupting the fundamental social acceptance of it as a necessary consequence of the double standard.

While the double standard continued to sanction certain forms of illicit heterosexual sex throughout our period, attitudes towards homosexuality changed, stimulated in part by the new ideological emphasis on heterosexual penetrative sex. In theory homosexual activity of any type, by both men and women, was disapproved of throughout this period, given that sexual activity was thought to be primarily for the purpose of procreation and any violation of this God-given function was seen as 'part of an anarchy that threatened to engulf the established order'. Thus, legally, sodomy was described as the 'detestable and abominable sin, amongst Christians not to be named'. Yet in practice at the start of our period attitudes were relatively tolerant, in part due to the nature of homosexual behaviour at the time and in part as a consequence of the one-sex model of the body, in which homosexuality could be interpreted as part of a continuum of varieties of sexual behaviour involving men and women. The fact that men and women were thought to inhabit the same bodies, except for the degree of heat and dryness present, meant that each could be more or less like the opposite sex depending on the amount of heat and moisture they possessed. The line

---

43 Stone, *Family, Sex and Marriage*, p. 619; Mayhew, *London Labour and the London Poor*, 4, p. 215; Mason, *Making of Victorian Sexuality*, pp. 72–103.

44 Thomas Laqueur, 'Sex and desire in the industrial revolution', in *The Industrial Revolution and British Society*, eds P. O'Brien and R. Quinault (1993), pp. 120–1.

between being a man and woman, and between male and female sexual behaviour, could thus be easily crossed. For example, women who engaged in excessive sexual activity, such as libertines and those who masturbated excessively, were thought to have an excess of heat in their bodies and were expected to have a small 'penis'.[45] With the adoption of the two-sex model of gender difference by the end of our period, however, homosexual behaviour was more explicitly differentiated from heterosexual sex and was more likely to be condemned.

Because, according to the one-sex model, the male body was thought to be more fully developed, it was expected that women would naturally seek male rather than female partners for sex. Consequently, homosexuality among men was considered far more likely to occur, and it was treated much more seriously than sexual activity between women. Sodomy, whether between man and man, or man and woman, or man and beast, was a capital offence, but, unlike in some other European countries, the offence was not interpreted to include sexual acts between women. Although some men were executed for this crime, there was nonetheless a degree of tolerance of sodomy, especially at the start of our period and in certain contexts, especially if it was committed in such a way as not to undermine gender roles. There was some tendency to overlook sexually aggressive men who had sex with other men, as long as their partners were young (and thus not fully developed as men), the older man assumed the active role of penetrator, and that man also slept with women. Among the elite, it was understood, if not totally acceptable, for a libertine to have 'his mistress on one arm and his "catamite" on the other'. Such men established their masculinity through the use of their penis and by having intercourse with women as well as young men. If they adopted women's clothing or other feminine ways they were condemned for undermining gender roles. This libertine behaviour, however, took place largely among the elite. It is difficult to determine how common male homosexual behaviour was further down the social scale, though there is evidence of it among the navy and army. It has recently been argued that the male homosexual subculture which developed in the eighteenth century was primarily composed of lower-middle-class shopkeepers and tradesmen, and the working class. This possible shift in

---

45 Trumbach, 'London's sapphists', pp. 118–19; Alan Bray, *Homosexuality in Renaissance England* (1982), pp. 61–2; Emma Donoghue, *Passions Between Women: British Lesbian Culture 1668–1801* (1993), pp. 26–7.

social composition may reflect changing attitudes towards homosexuality in the eighteenth century, which will be discussed below.[46]

Because women were thought to have sexual desires only for men, and because definitions of sex were so phallocentric, female homosexuality was arguably inconceivable in this period. Indeed, there was no clear feminine equivalent of the term 'sodomy' to describe sexual acts between women. In a libel case involving allegations of such activity in 1811 in Scotland, a judge ruled that 'the crime here alleged has no existence'. Consequently, sex between women, which clearly existed, is relatively rarely explicitly described, and attitudes towards it were confused. Nonetheless, Emma Donoghue has shown that sexual passion between women was documented in some songs, pornographic pictures, and medical and literary books of the time. To the extent that contemporaries were aware that female homosexual acts took place, they explained them by suggesting that one of the partners was not truly female, but had acquired the equivalent of a male penis: such women were often labelled 'tribades' or 'hermaphrodites'. These women were thought to have either an enlarged clitoris or a prolapsed vagina which could be used as the equivalent of a penis to engage in penetrative sex; in this way, female homosexual activity could be construed as not contradicting normal gender relations.[47]

Given women's presumed sexual desire for men, however, female homosexual acts were generally not thought of as satisfying, likely, or significant, which means that although there was not much of a language with which to discuss it, a wide range of homosexual behaviour between women was unwittingly tolerated because the relationships were thought to be innocuous. Close female friendships could develop without public disapproval; indeed, with the development of the concept of romantic friendship in the second half of the eighteenth century such relationships were idealised. The im-

46 Randolph Trumbach, 'The birth of the queen: sodomy and the emergence of gender equality in modern culture, 1660–1750', in *Hidden from History: Reclaiming the Gay and Lesbian Past*, ed. M. B. Duberman, M. Vicinus, and G. Chauncey, Jr. (New York, 1989), pp. 129–40; *idem*, 'London's sodomites: homosexual behavior and western culture in the eighteenth century', *Journal of Social History* 11 (1977), pp. 1–33; *idem*, 'Sex, gender and sexual identity in modern culture: male sodomy and female prostitution in Enlightenment London', *Journal of the History of Sexuality* 2 (1991), pp. 186–203; Bray, *Homosexuality in Renaissance England*, p. 34; Rictor Norton, *Mother Clap's Molly House: The Gay Subculture in England 1700–1830* (1992).

47 For two opposing interpretations of the nature and extent of lesbianism in the eighteenth century, see Donoghue, *Passions Between Women* and Lillian Faderman, *Surpassing the Love of Men: Romantic Friendship and Love Between Women from the Renaissance to the Present* (1981) (citation from p. 149).

possibility of determining how often such relationships had a sexual dimension has led historians to draw contradictory conclusions about the nature and scale of lesbianism in the period. The truth is, we simply do not, and probably will not ever, know which type of female friendship was more common in our period: the apparently asexual (though some suspected otherwise) but deeply passionate and committed relationship between two women, such as Sarah Ponsonby and Eleanor Butler (the 'Ladies of Llangollen'), who lived together in Wales for over fifty years in the late eighteenth and early nineteenth century; or the eroticism of an Anne Lister, who had numerous middle- and upper-class lovers in Yorkshire and Paris in the early nineteenth century (both cases are unusually well documented in diaries and correspondence). Given the lack of public recognition of sexual attraction between women as well as the commonplace sharing of beds by women at this time, both kinds of relationship were equally possible. In all likelihood, there was a continuum of female homosocial and homosexual activity between these two types, and it is impossible to identify any one type of behaviour as typical.[48]

Female same-sex interest may account for some of the large number of women who cross-dressed as men during this period. On stage, women dressed as men in about a quarter of the plays performed in the eighteenth century, and female cross-dressers were also depicted in plays and literature. While directors of such plays may have intended to titillate male audiences, it has been suggested that some women saw these actresses as objects of desire.[49] In real life, some women cross-dressed for most of their adult lives and even married other women. Once again, it is impossible to determine the sexual content of such relationships. While it has been argued that cross-dressing allowed women an acceptable context in which they could love other women, the widespread tolerance of cross-dressing combined with the paucity of evidence of explicit sexual activity makes such an argument difficult to prove. Although such women in disguise could be punished when found out, this was primarily because they were thought to have behaved fraudu-

---

48 Helena Whitbread (ed), *I Know My Own Heart: The Diaries of Anne Lister* (1988); Elizabeth Mavor, *The Ladies of Llangollen: A Study in Romantic Friendship* (1973). See Hitchcock, *English Sexualities*, ch. 6, for a survey of this historiography.

49 Donoghue, *Passions Between Women*, pp. 87–108; Kristina Straub, 'The guilty pleasures of female theatrical cross-dressing and the autobiography of Charlotte Charke', in *Body Guards*, ed. Epstein and Straub, pp. 144, 161.

lently for financial gain, rather than because it was suspected that such women sought homosexual sex.[50]

This largely tolerant approach to both male and female homosexual sex disappeared during this period, and the new intolerance can be seen as a response to a number of factors, including changing patterns of homosexual activity and broader changes in ideas about sexuality and gender roles. As Alan Bray and Randolph Trumbach have argued, the eighteenth century witnessed the creation for the first time of a male homosexual subculture in London, with its own network of meeting houses and distinctive gestures, language, dress, and pick-up signals. This was not yet a full-fledged homosexual identity, in that few of the men organised their whole lives around their sexuality, and it was present only in London and possibly other cities.[51] Yet unlike previous homosexual activity, this subculture subverted the gender hierarchy because at least some of those involved chose to have sex only with men, and effeminate behaviour was widespread. These men were called 'mollies', and were described by the Grub Street writer Ned Ward as 'fancy[ing] themselves women . . . affecting to speak, walk, tattle, curtsy, cry, scold and mimick all manner of effeminacy'.[52] By the late eighteenth century, homosexual couples often included a partner who adopted feminine traits and such couples engaged in mock marriage ceremonies and even pregnancy rituals. Because this new approach inverted normal definitions of masculinity, homosexuality was condemned as subversive and subjected to unprecedented levels of prosecution. For the first time in English history groups of homosexuals, as opposed to isolated individuals, were charged with sodomy in the courts. Waves of prosecutions started in 1699, and continued periodically throughout the eighteenth century, with the number of prosecutions (and executions) increasing still further in the early nineteenth century. As a result, Trumbach suggests, men in the dominant heterosexual culture had to stop having sex with other men, or else risk the threat of being labelled as a 'molly', an effeminate homosexual. This persecution further encouraged the confinement of homosexual activity to a deviant subculture and it

50 Trumbach, 'London's sapphists', pp. 121–5; Donoghue, *Passions Between Women*, pp. 59–62, 107.

51 Bray, *Homosexuality in Renaissance England*, ch. 4; Trumbach, 'London's sodomites'; Jeffery Weeks, *Sex, Politics and Society: The Regulation of Sexuality since 1800* (1981), p. 110.

52 Quoted in Trumbach, 'London's sodomites', pp. 12–13, from Edward Ward, *The History of the London Clubs* (1709).

led to a decline in public physical intimacy between heterosexual men.[53]

A similar, but far less dramatic, change occurred with female homosexuality. Trumbach has argued that towards the end of the eighteenth century the female equivalent of the 'sodomite' developed, as women who were sexually attracted to other women came to be separately labelled as 'sapphists' or 'tommies' (a word, first used for this purpose in 1751, which clearly suggests concerns that such women were transgressing gender roles). Combined with the increased importance of romantic friendship, this suggests that new lesbian roles for women were emerging, which, unlike earlier forms of lesbianism, apparently excluded masculine sexual references (such as the dildo) entirely. Further research is clearly necessary, but it appears that unlike male homosexuality this did not involve the development of a subculture with its own distinctive practices; it did not lead to persecution (indeed, we have seen evidence of judicial scepticism that such activity ever took place); nor did a dominant culture of femininity develop which was based on the avoidance of sex with other women. Even so, the increasing use of these terms, which were terms of abuse, suggests that there was growing public intolerance of female homosexual activity. Thus, fears about homosexuality led to a decline in the number of female actors who dressed as men at the end of the century.[54]

The growing intolerance of sexual activity which was thought to undermine gender roles suggests that those roles may have been solidifying at this time. Indeed, Trumbach has argued that changing attitudes towards homosexuality occurred in response to the anxieties caused by a growing equality in relations between the sexes, which created a need to reinforce gender differences by eliminating behaviour which crossed gender boundaries.[55] This argument is based on a premise (the development of the companionate marriage) which, as we shall see, is questionable. It is possible, as Alan Bray and Tim Hitchcock have argued, that the development of a male homosexual subculture occurred in response to broader intellectual and social changes which encouraged individualism and

53 Hitchcock, *English Sexualities*, ch. 5; A. D. Harvey, 'Prosecutions for sodomy in England at the beginning of the nineteenth century', *Historical Journal* 21 (1978), pp. 939–48; Alan Bray, 'Introduction' to article by Valerie Traub, *History Workshop Journal* 41 (1996), pp. 21–2.
54 Trumbach, 'London's sapphists'; Straub, 'The guilty pleasures of female theatrical cross-dressing'; Hitchcock, *English Sexualities*, ch. 6. See also Donaghue, *Passions Between Women*, pp. 10–11.
55 Trumbach, 'Sex, gender, and sexual identity'.

the development of a pluralist society.[56] Yet it is also likely that changes in attitudes to homosexual behaviour *were* related to broader changes in gender roles. The increasing value placed on the distinct sexual roles of men and women can be seen as related to other changes discussed so far, including the development of the two-sexed body and the growing ideological emphasis on penetrative vaginal sex, both of which prescribed different roles for each sex and sought to confine sexuality to heterosexual intercourse. It remains unclear, however, how much homosexual practice, as opposed to attitudes towards it, changed during this period. Although the available evidence does suggest that activity was increasingly confined to distinct subcultures, we still know far too little on this point to draw definite conclusions.

CONCLUSION

In sum, the body and sexuality were significant areas for the construction of gender differences in this period, and we have seen that such differences were reflected in textual and pictorial representations of sex and, as far as can be determined with the limited available evidence, in actual sexual practices. In approaches to heterosexual intercourse in courtship and marriage, in extramarital sexuality and homosexuality, and in pornography, men and women were expected to behave differently, and usually did. And because such differences were culturally and socially constructed, they could change over the course of this period, as conceptions of the body itself shifted to a two-sex model. Taken together, the ideological changes we have examined accentuated the already existing differences between male and female sexuality. The active, initiating role taken by men was given greater prominence, and any activity (such as homosexual intercourse) in which they could be seen as acting passively was further marginalised. Correspondingly, women were less likely to be seen as sexually aggressive, but their presence, whether as wives or prostitutes, was increasingly deemed a necessary part of all sexual activity. These changes could be seen as encouraging the development of separate spheres, with women increasingly defined in terms of their maternal functions and men rejecting any sexual behaviour which might be deemed feminine.

We should not, however, exaggerate the extent of change in sexual attitudes, given the strong continuities which persisted

56 Bray, *Homosexuality in Renaissance England*, pp. 105ff.; Hitchcock, *English Sexualities*, ch. 5.

throughout the period. Profound gender differences already
existed in the seventeenth century, when men's bodies were viewed
as hotter and more fully formed than women's and the double
standard already tolerated male but not female promiscuity. Despite
the wealth of the evidence concerning deviant sex, we should not
forget that the normative form of behaviour, heterosexual sex within courtship and marriage, remained constant. Moreover, we have
seen that opinions were often divided, notably on the possibilities of
lesbianism and on the nature of female lust.

Finally, and most importantly, the evidence for changes in sexual
practices is still very limited: it does not appear that there was a
close correspondence between changing ideas about sex and actual
behaviour. Representations of sexuality may have increasingly concentrated on penetrative sex, but this was already the dominant
(but not exclusive) sexual practice in the seventeenth century, and
there is little evidence to suggest that this pattern changed. Moreover, despite the denial of female lust by many writers in the second
half of the period there is clear evidence of continuing female initiative and pleasure in sex. The best case for changing sexual practices is probably found with male homosexuality, but even here the
evidence is limited, and the changes can be interpreted as resulting
from broader social forces (such as the emergence of a pluralist society) as opposed to changing ideas about sex and gender. Whether
there actually was an increasing separation of male and female roles
during this period is best considered through an examination of
somewhat less intimate activities, where the evidence is richer. We
now turn our attention to how men and women conducted their
lives in courtship and family life, as husbands and wives, and as
fathers and mothers.

CHAPTER FOUR

Family and Household Life

The family and household were units of central importance in English society at this time, a point which undermines any attempt to
draw a firm distinction between the nature of public and private
life. Demographically, the family was important as the key unit of reproduction: the vast majority of births took place within it (though
as we shall see, conceptions often occurred prior to marriage).
Economically, through inheritance practices, the family controlled
the passage of wealth from one generation to the next. The somewhat larger unit of the household was also of fundamental importance: it was the most common unit of economic production at the
time, since the factory did not replace household-based manufacture as the primary unit of production until after the end of this
period. Socially and culturally, the household was the key environment in which children, as well as apprentices and domestic servants, were socialised, and it was an important site for social
interaction both between and within generations. The household
was also of fundamental political importance. At the start of our
period hierarchies within the household were seen to mirror, and
to be a guarantee of, the obedience of subjects to the state (all
members of the household were subject to the authority of the
household head). Although this link between the subjection of
families to fathers and subjects to kings in political thought was
broken by John Locke, in the eighteenth century middle-class political discourse sought to maintain the connection between family life
and public life by basing claims for political authority on the virtue
and order allegedly found in middle-class, but not aristocratic,
families.[1] Throughout this period, the household was thought of as

---

1 Susan Amussen, *An Ordered Society: Gender and Class in Early Modern England*
(Oxford, 1988), pp. 64–5; Margaret Hunt, *The Middling Sort: Commerce, Gender and
the Family in England, 1680–1780* (1996), ch. 8.

the basic building-block of society, and men and women of both sexes who were not members of a household were viewed suspiciously.

The family and household were not only basic units of economic, social, and political life, they also had an important role to play in the construction of gender roles. At the centre of the family was the most common meeting ground of the two sexes: marriage. Relations between husbands and wives, in terms of the division of paid labour, housework and childcare, and the distribution of power in family decision-making, were fundamentally shaped by, and shapers of, gender roles. Even more important perhaps were children's experiences of growing up within a family, as they learned about gender roles from watching their parents and formed their own masculine or feminine identities in the process. By examining these and other aspects of family and household life, this chapter will provide a number of insights into how gender roles were lived and constructed at this time.

If family life provides an important window on gender relations, then changes in the nature of family life would have important implications for our understanding of gender roles. As with other aspects of English society at this time, historians have seen the years between 1650 and 1850 as an important period of change in the history of the family. Most basically, there was an important shift in definition. In the early modern period the family and household were seen to be relatively synonymous and were all-encompassing terms, including, in addition to the nuclear family of the mother, father, and their children, co-resident servants, apprentices, kin, and lodgers.[2] However, in the late eighteenth and early nineteenth centuries definitions of the family began to be restricted to the nuclear family. This shift can be related to a number of other postulated changes in household life, including its economic functions, and in the nature of affective relations within the family.

Historians have argued that economic changes during the period, such as the decline of the household-based economy and proletarianisation, had a significant impact on gender relations within the family. Bridget Hill has argued that, because these changes severely restricted women's economic opportunities, women became 'more

2 Naomi Tadmor 'The concept of the household-family in eighteeth-century England', *Past and Present* 151 (1996), pp. 111–40. In this study the term 'family' will be used in its modern sense of a group of people related by marriage or blood – what is often referred to as the 'nuclear family' – while 'household' will be used to refer to the entire group of people living in the same residence.

dependent on their husbands', and lost power within their marriages, enduring 'greater servitude and conditions where they had no defence against the arbitrary wielding of patriarchal power'.[3] As we shall see, however, the decline in women's work and in the family as a unit of production in this period has been exaggerated. In fact it has been argued that the growth of industrial employments in the household gave some women greater power within the home, since they were now earning their own wages. Given the limited surviving evidence concerning the dynamics of power relations within marriages, such arguments need to be treated sceptically. Both because economic change was a long-term process, and because such changes can have contradictory effects on gender roles, arguments about the gender implications of changing economic circumstances have thus far proved problematic.

A second, and more pervasive, argument about changes in the English family in this period focuses on 'sentiments'. In particular, Lawrence Stone and Randolph Trumbach have argued that over the course of the eighteenth century emotional relations within the family became warmer and more affective. (For Stone, these changes occurred first among the urban bourgeoisie and gentry, spread a little later to the aristocracy, and did not influence the lower classes until the nineteenth or early twentieth centuries; for Trumbach, they occurred first among the aristocracy.) The allegedly more egalitarian relations between spouses in the 'affective' family would have important implications for our understanding of gender roles. Whereas, according to Stone, in the seventeenth century under the influence of puritanism and the state patriarchal authority and wifely obedience were the norm, in the eighteenth century 'the authority of husbands over wives and of parents over children declined as greater autonomy was granted to, or assumed by, all members of the family unit . . . [and women] were granted greater status and decision-making power within the family . . .'. At the same time, greater individualism and the growing emotional attachment to children encouraged the development of separate spheres of activity for each sex: as women withdrew from economic activities, they 'were occupying themselves with the supervision of the servants, child care, and a round of status-enhancing leisure activities'. Thus women became more equal, but also more separate, from men. Although neither Stone nor Trumbach carried their

---

3 Bridget Hill, *Women, Work and Sexual Politics in Eighteenth-Century England* (Oxford, 1989), p. 263.

research into the next century, Stone suggests that patriarchal authority returned after 1800.[4]

The 'sentiments' approach to the history of the family in general and Lawrence Stone's theories in particular have come in for a number of criticisms. From the point of view of gender, what is most problematic are the arguments for the strength of patriarchal power in the seventeenth century and for the diminution of that power in the eighteenth century. Citing considerable evidence of deep love and affection in seventeenth-century marriages, early modern historians have argued that Stone was wrong in suggesting that the affective family was new in the eighteenth century, while feminists have questioned whether in any case such a family necessarily involved more equal relations between spouses. Stone's 'companionate marriage' has been described as a 'gentle tyranny', in which male dominance was maintained, even if it became more subtle.[5] One of the ways male dominance was maintained, according to Susan Moller Okin, was through the very idea of separate spheres. The potentially liberating effect of individualism, Okin argues, was undermined by political theorists who defined women's tasks as primarily domestic, and who characterised women as 'creatures of sentiment and love rather than rationality . . .'.[6] The 'sentiments' approach has thus come under attack both for overstating the extent of change and for misinterpreting its impact on gender roles. Recent research on the family has shied away from grand theories of change and has emphasised the basic continuities in the history of the family, while stressing how at any one time experiences of family life varied depending on region, social class, and individual personality. Historians have also been warned not to mistake prescriptive evidence (such as conduct books or sermons) for actual behaviour, which often differed. As with other aspects of this topic,

---

4 Lawrence Stone, *The Family, Sex and Marriage in England, 1500–1800* (1977), pp. 656–7.

5 Lois Schwoerer, 'Seventeenth-century English women engraved in Stone?', *Albion* 16 (1984), pp. 389-403; Randolph Trumbach, 'Europe and its families: a review essay of Lawrence Stone, *The Family, Sex and Marriage in England, 1500–1800*', *Journal of Social History* 13 (1979), pp. 136–43; E. P. Thompson, 'Happy families', *New Society* 41 (779) (8 Sept. 1977), pp 499–501; Martin Ingram, 'The reform of popular culture? Sex and marriage in early modern England', in *Popular Culture in Seventeenth-Century England*, ed. B. Reay, (1985), pp. 133–4; Ruth Perry, 'Radical doubt and the liberation of women', *Eighteenth-Century Studies* 18 (1985), p. 475.

6 Susan Moller Okin, 'Women and the making of the sentimental family', *Philosophy and Public Affairs* 11 (1981), p. 74.

historians need to be alert to both the continuities and the complexities in writing the history of gender roles within the family.[7]

This chapter is organised according to the lifecycle of the family. Our discussion will commence with the moment when the family is formed, courtship and marriage, and then discuss relations between spouses, the division of tasks between spouses, and parenthood. After discussing how mothers and fathers related to their offspring, we will shift the focus to an examination of how the process of growing up in a family and household helped shape the gender identities of children and adolescents. Finally, we will look at those people in English society who, either temporarily or permanently, were without families: widows and widowers; and those who never married.

COURTSHIP

Marriage was an important event, not only in the lives of the bride and groom, but also for the entire community. Not only did marriages form the units in which reproduction was intended to take place, they also cemented important economic, religious, and class alliances. But marriage meant something different for men and women. Not only did men acquire authority over their wives (including control over most of their property and the right to chastise them, physically if necessary), but it also gave them the status of householders, which made them liable to taxation and gave them a political voice in the community. Although wives, too, possessed more status in the community than unmarried women, in an important way marriage reduced the status of women, by turning them into dependants who were expected to obey their husbands (though this change may have been of less significance for those who had previously been living under the authority of their fathers). For this reason, some women, especially middle-class women whose opportunities for work within marriage were limited (and who had less independence than their upper-class counterparts), 'seem to have regarded the serious step of marriage as a not unmixed blessing'.[8] Yet marriage was a social and financial necessity for most women. Women were expected to marry and breed, and as

7 See for example, Ralph Houlbrooke (ed.), *English Family Life, 1576–1716: An Anthology from Diaries* (Oxford, 1988), p. 253; Mary Abbott, *Family Ties: English Families 1540–1920* (1993); Rosemary O'Day, *The Family and Family Relationships, 1500–1900: England, France and the United States of America* (1994).

8 Leonore Davidoff and Catherine Hall, *Family Fortunes: Men and Women of the English Middle Class, 1780–1850* (1987), p. 325.

we shall see those who didn't faced disapproval. More importantly, it was very difficult for an independent woman to support herself financially; a women's financial security depended to a large extent on her choice of a husband. For these reasons, choosing a spouse was the most important decision a woman made in her life, far more important than it was for a man.

The choice of a spouse was not solely left up to the suitors. Parents and even the wider community had an interest in securing suitable matches, between men and women of similar status, wealth, and age, and they exerted pressure accordingly. Except perhaps among the upper classes, such pressure was never overwhelming: even at the start of our period the ideal was that both parents and children consented to any proposed match. One of the most important findings of the 'sentiments' school of the history of the family was that parental interference decreased in the eighteenth century, leaving young men and especially young women with greater control over their choice of a partner than they had had previously. Of course, men and women did not approach this choice on equal terms. Men were expected to take the initiative in courtship, and women could only reject unwanted advances. Nonetheless, the woman's role was important. In particular, the role that sex played in courtship negotiations among the lower classes gave women an important means of influencing the pace and results of courtship.

The first point to make about the gendered nature of courtship is that men and women married at different ages. In general, English people in the early modern period married relatively late, due to the expectation that couples should have sufficient resources to be able to set up an independent household upon marriage. On average, at first marriage men were one to two years older than their brides, with men marrying in the late seventeenth century at an average age of 27.7 and women at 26.6. Over the course of the period the marriage ages of both sexes declined, with women's decreasing slightly faster so that the gap between men and women increased to 1.8 years.[9] Of course these are only statistical averages, and there were many cases where the bride was older than the groom, as well as cases where the groom was much older than the bride. In general, the gap in marriage ages increased higher up the social scale. There was a five-year gap among the London middle class in

9 E. A. Wrigley, 'Marriage, fertility and population growth in eighteenth-century England', *Marriage and Society: Studies in the Social History of Marriage*, ed. R. B. Outhwaite (New York, 1981), p. 147.

the early eighteenth century, which extended to as much as ten among the wealthiest groups, such as merchants, the gentry, and the aristocracy.[10]

These age gaps reflect both gender differences in the process of courtship and the important role played by parents and property considerations in middle- and upper-class marriage arrangements. The extent of parental control of marriages depended very much on the status of the family and the amount of property involved. Among the upper classes, arranged marriages were still common, with the father of the suitor or the suitor himself approaching the parents of the prospective bride and often conducting long negotiations over the marriage settlement before the daughter was even informed. When Nicholas Blundell sought to arrange a marriage with Frances, daughter of Lord Langdale, he conducted negotiations with her father and grandmother for three weeks before he had his first contact with Frances.[11] Because the property came from their fathers in such marriages and daughters played such a minor role in negotiations, it is not surprising that upper-class brides were younger, both absolutely and in relation to the age of the groom, than in marriages where less property was at stake. Where the woman herself was expected to contribute savings and/or earning power to the marriage, the age difference between bride and groom was much smaller.

Parental control was thus less evident in middle- and lower-class marriages, but it was still expected that the consent of the parents, especially parents of daughters, was necessary. If the parents were wealthy enough to be able to contribute financially to the marriage settlement, they wanted to have a voice in the choice of the man who would benefit from it. But even where little or no property was at stake, parents of daughters (much more than parents of sons) seem to have wanted to be consulted, especially when the daughter was still living at home, in part because they thought young women were ignorant and wilful and could not be trusted to find a man with a good character and sufficient economic prospects.[12] In the early nineteenth century the radical weaver Samuel Bamford's attempt to woo one woman was vetoed by her mother, who thought

10 Peter Earle, *The Making of the English Middle Class: Business, Society and Family Life in London 1660–1730* (1989), p.182; Stone, *Family, Sex and Marriage*, p. 48.
11 See the extract from Blundell's diary in Houlbrooke (ed.), *English Family Life*, pp. 40–1, and, for a similar example, the account of Samuel Jeake's marriage, pp. 35–8.
12 Earle, *Making of the English Middle Class*, p. 186.

Bamford was not wealthy enough: according to her, 'no one should marry her daughter who could not fetch her away on his own horse.'[13]

While parents, if still alive (the high mortality rates of the time ensured this was often not the case), outside the upper classes were frequently consulted, they rarely initiated courtship; that role, as should be evident from the examples already given, was primarily undertaken by the man, regardless of social class. Men were expected to make the first move, and women could either encourage or discourage men's advances. On Monday, 11 September 1791, William Jones, a weaver, woke up with 'a desire to have an help meet and companion' and went to the home of the woman he chose and proposed (she turned him down).[14] Among the lower classes, popular courtship customs accentuated the role of men. Hiring fairs, for example, often involved courting in addition to the business of hiring servants for the coming year. Once the hiring was completed, 'the girls began to file off, and gently pace the streets, with a view of gaining admirers; while the young men ... follow after, and having eyed the lasses, pick up each a sweetheart, whom they conduct to a dancing room, and treat with punch and cake.'[15] Even where marriages were arranged, the groom was expected to take the first steps in getting to know the bride. Once the marriage between Jemima, daughter of the first Earl of Sandwich and Philip, the eldest son of Sir George Carteret, was negotiated in 1665 with the help of Samuel Pepys, Pepys took Philip aside and explained to him what to do when the two were finally introduced to each other: 'take the Lady away by the hand to lead her; and ... make these and these compliments ...'.[16]

While men were expected to initiate courtship, popular courting customs normally accorded women an opportunity to reject unwanted attentions. Night visiting, for example, involved male suitors coming to a woman's home for all-night courting. The suitor tapped on the window to gain entrance, but the woman or a servant girl could refuse entry to someone she objected to.[17] Women could

13 Cited by David Vincent, *Bread, Knowledge and Freedom: A Study of Nineteenth-Century Working-Class Autobiography* (1981), p. 51.

14 Cited by Hill, *Women, Work and Sexual Politics*, p. 176.

15 Cited by Robert Malcolmson, *Popular Recreations in English Society 1700–1850* (Cambridge, 1973), p. 54. Popular courting customs are described in John Gillis, *For Better, For Worse: British Marriages, 1600 to the Present* (Oxford, 1985), pp. 25–37.

16 R. Latham and W. Matthews (eds), *The Diary of Samuel Pepys* (11 vols, 1970–83), 6, p. 159 (16 July 1665).

17 Gillis, *For Better, For Worse*, p. 31.

also encourage suitors indirectly, for example by using brothers, sisters, or friends to act as go-betweens to encourage a young man to act. Moreover, during popular festivals such as on Easter Monday and Tuesday or at wakes, women were given opportunities to express their preferences openly.[18]

In choosing their potential spouses, men and women looked for somewhat different combinations of qualities. Money was a key issue for both sexes. The future solicitor-general Dudley Ryder was persuaded by his father not to marry Sally Marshall because she would not bring him sufficient economic benefits: 'her fortune could not be anything considerable . . . her family was nothing, could bring me no acquaintance nor friends that could serve me in my business.' This was despite the fact her fortune amounted to as much as £1500.[19] Middle-class men were equally concerned about money, for they depended on their wife's portion to help set themselves up in business.[20] Lower down the social scale, women brought fewer funds to marriage, and attention turned to the skills which they could bring to the family business or which increased their earning potential outside the home. Bridget Hill cites a popular chapbook of 1783 in which a man discusses the necessity of marriage: 'For a man of my trade must have both journeymen and apprentices, therefore I cannot well be without a wife.'[21] Yet in the nineteenth century the growing influence of the ideal of the male breadwinner led some men to expect to be the sole provider in a marriage, and such men refused to marry until they were in a position to do so. Gillis argues that nineteenth-century artisans 'refused to contemplate any [marriage] arrangement that would violate the traditional artisan notion of husbandhood, the ideal of the protector or provider'. This ideal, which given the wages of most artisans was probably very difficult to achieve in practice, is also reflected in the comment of a needlewoman to Henry Mayhew about her unrealised marriage: 'it's not in his power to marry me, his work won't allow it; and he's not able to support me in the manner he wishes and keep himself.'[22]

If anything, women were even more conscious of the economic

---

18 Davidoff and Hall, *Family Fortunes*, p. 326; Gillis, *For Better, For Worse*, pp. 25, 28.

19 Houlbrooke (ed.), *English Family Life*, p. 50.

20 Earle, *Making of the English Middle Class*, p. 190.

21 Hill, *Women, Work and Sexual Politics*, p. 192.

22 Gillis, *For Better, For Worse*, pp. 181, 184; E. P. Thompson and Eileen Yeo (eds), *The Unknown Mayhew: Selections from the Morning Chronicle 1849–50* (1971), p. 171.

aspects of their choice of a partner for life. This was a particular concern of women in the middle and upper classes, who were less likely to work and therefore knew that their marriage alone would primarily determine their future economic and social position in society. Thomas Wright, who was to become a farmer, noted in his autobiography that the women he courted rejected him 'as I had made but little show in trade' and had 'but little spare money'.[23] Yet working-class women were also concerned about the earning potential of their future spouses: one woman in the mid-nineteenth century refused to marry her suitor until he 'got a permanent situation, either on the railway or in the post office'.[24] These concerns were especially acute when women were in a position (as in the rural southeast) where they had few opportunities to work themselves, and they help explain why men tended to get married somewhat later than women.

Monetary considerations were of course by no means the only factors influencing the choice of a marriage partner. Although in recent years historians have stressed the important and possibly increasing role played by affect and love, practical considerations may have been more important, with loving relationships often resulting from marriage rather than leading to it. It was the sex with the more secure economic position which could most afford to look for other qualities in a spouse. In particular, men wanted someone who would run a household for them. We have already seen the example of William Jones, who was looking for 'an help meet and companion'; other men, in the words of Dr Johnson, sought 'domestic comforts'. In anticipating marriage, an Essex solicitor not so much looked forward to 'the intenseness of pleasures' as 'the pursuits of comfort'.[25] The apparent selfishness of these comments is spelled out in Dudley Ryder's thoughts in anticipation of marriage: 'it ravishes me to think of a pretty creature concerned in me, being my most intimate friend, constant companion and always ready to soothe me, take care of me, and caress me.'[26] Other virtues looked for in a wife were, according to Thomas Turner, the Sussex shopkeeper, industriousness, sobriety, and prudence. As Theodore Koditschek has pointed out, middle-class men looked for women

23 Cited by Hill, *Women, Work and Sexual Politics*, p. 179.
24 Cited by Vincent, *Bread, Knowledge and Freedom*, p. 51.
25 Alan MacFarlane, *Marriage and Love in England: Modes of Reproduction 1300–1840* (Oxford, 1986), p. 150; Davidoff and Hall, *Family Fortunes*, p. 323.
26 Cited by Earle, *Making of the English Middle Class*, p. 189.

'who possessed feminized versions of the same qualities of character and industriousness that they valued in themselves'.[27]

In contrast, it is difficult to find evidence of other qualities, beyond personal compatibility and wealth or earning potential, which women looked for in men, though the relative paucity of women's diaries from this period makes it difficult to draw conclusions on this point. Since women did not normally initiate courtship, but could only reject advances, it would appear that they needed to be more flexible than men in their choice of a spouse, and some felt the pressure to accept the first plausible offer for fear that another suitable man might not come along; this may help explain the lower age of marriage for women. As a result, as the conduct-book writer John Gregory commented, 'without an unusual share of natural sensibility, and very peculiar good fortune, a woman in this country has very little probability of marrying for love.' When a woman found an attractive suitor and he turned out to be unacceptable to her parents she was devastated: the seventeenth-century case books of Dr Richard Napier include a number of cases of such women who suffered mental instability; women were three times more likely than men to appear before Napier with this complaint.[28]

Important changes took place in the nature of courtship over the course of this period, changes which gave women more opportunities to take the initiative, but which made the process more dangerous for some. Among the upper and middle classes, arranged marriages became less common and parents increasingly let young men and women choose their own spouses. Although throughout this period middle- and upper-class wives were expected to remain chaste until formally married, among the lower classes pre-marital sex began to play a more important role in courtship. Even in the early part of our period, the practice of betrothal among the lower classes allowed men and women who had promised to marry each other to have full intercourse, since marriage was expected to follow whether or not the woman got pregnant. Although not universal, the practice was sufficiently widespread in the late seventeenth century for around 15 per cent of brides to be pregnant when they got married.[29] It has been suggested that the custom of betrothal was

27 Hill, *Women, Work and Sexual Politics*, pp. 192–3; Theodore Koditschek, *Class Formation and Urban-Industrial Society* (Cambridge, 1990), p. 213.

28 John Gregory, *A Father's Legacy to his Daughters* (1774), p. 80; Michael MacDonald, *Mystical Bedlam: Madness, Anxiety and Healing in Seventeenth-Century England* (1981), p. 94.

29 Wrigley, 'Marriage, fertility and population growth', p. 156.

advantageous for women since they were virtually guaranteed marriage if they got pregnant, but they were not yet legally subservient to their husbands (as they would be in marriage) and they were able to break their marriage plans if they decided that their potential husband was unsuitable.[30] Moreover, it allowed them to take the initiative in sexual relations. In his analysis of the pre-marital courtships of John Cannon, Tim Hitchcock has shown how some of the women Cannon interacted with used 'the offer and reality of sex as an integral part of their behaviour towards men'. For example, a young widow named Hester flirted with John Cannon and on a subsequent visit informed Cannon 'by her motions she would yield to anything' if Cannon agreed to marry her.[31]

In the eighteenth and nineteenth centuries however, sex began to play a more important role in negotiations leading to marriage. Lord Hardwicke's Marriage Act of 1753 ended legal protection for the betrothed, which had forced men to marry women whom they had promised to marry if they became pregnant. In any case, by that time young people had apparently started engaging in sex *before* there was any formal agreement to marry, although pregnancy was still expected to lead to marriage. This situation further allowed women to use sex, hoping to get pregnant, as a means of taking the initiative in courtship. Nicholas Rogers has suggested that poor female servants or ex-servants in London 'use[d] their sexuality to secure marriage partners . . . [because they saw] early marriage as a safeguard against unemployment or economic marginality'.[32] For such strategies to work, marriage was expected to follow when the woman became pregnant. And, whether because the father was fully in agreement with this approach to marriage or because of his sense of responsibility, it often did: prenuptial pregnancy rates doubled over the course of our period, so that by the early nineteenth century about a third of brides were pregnant at the time of their marriage.[33] It was reported that in the arable counties in the early nineteenth century 'there has been no increase in chargeable bastards [to the poor law], but a great increase of marriages to prevent it.'[34]

30   Gillis, *For Better, For Worse*, p. 183.
31   Tim Hitchcock, *English Sexualities, 1700–1800* (1997), pp. 30–1.
32   Nicholas Rogers, 'Carnal knowledge: illegitimacy in eighteenth-century Westminster', *Journal of Social History* 23 (1989), p. 366.
33   Wrigley, 'Marriage, fertility and population growth', p. 157.
34   *Report of His Majesty's Commission to Inquire into the Poor Laws*, 1834, cited by Gillis, *For Better, For Worse*, p. 115.

Needless to say, this was a very dangerous game for women to play. For a variety of reasons marriages often did not follow pregnancy, and there was a concurrent increase in illegitimacy during the period, from about 1.5 per cent of all births to 5 per cent. (The period of this study forms a distinctive period in the history of bastardy, in which illegitimacy was constantly increasing; ratios had declined in the early seventeenth century and would decline again in the late nineteenth century).[35] If we focus only on first births (only a very small proportion of subsequent births took place outside marriage), illegitimacy ratios were even higher: it has been calculated that about 16% of first births in mid-eighteenth-century London were illegitimate. As we shall see, some illegitimate births took place within stable informal ('common law') marriages, but in the vast majority of cases these births resulted from relationships which had broken down. In this sense the increase in illegitimacy was bad news for women, often the result of a calculated gamble which they lost, and many such births must have been unwanted, and the children very difficult to provide for. Some women had the opportunity to leave their babies at the London Foundling Hospital (the first admissions took place in 1741), and it is astonishing how many did so: during the period of 'general reception', when the hospital adopted its most liberal admissions policies (1756–60), almost half of all first births in London were delivered there.[36]

There are a number of reasons why pregnancy so often failed to lead to marriage, especially in the second half of our period, the most common of which was poor economic conditions which prevented the couple from setting up a household. It has been shown that the number of illegitimate children in London, and foundlings at the Foundling Hospital, increased during times of hardship.[37] In such cases the couple may have mutually decided not to marry, or the decision may have been taken unilaterally, almost always by the man (many men absconded when faced with imprisonment for debt). In many, perhaps most, cases, men simply wished to evade their responsibilities, but in other cases the situation was more complicated. Where the man was unable to support the family, his departure made it more likely that the mother and

35 Peter Laslett et al., (eds), *Bastardy and its Comparative History* (1980), table 1.1(a).

36 Adrian Wilson, 'Illegitimacy and its implications in mid-eighteenth-century London: the evidence of the Foundling Hospital', *Continuity and Change* 4 (1989), p. 136.

37 Ibid., p. 134.

child could receive poor relief, and could thus be seen as being in the family's interest. In other cases, it was the woman who wanted to avoid marriage, in order to preserve her independence. It has been suggested that where plenty of work was available for women (such as in framework knitting in Leicestershire or handloom weaving in Lancashire), unmarried mothers might prefer to collect maintenance payments from the father and remain independent, especially in cases where they could remain in their parents' home.[38] Moreover, Gillis argues that there were an increasing number of 'common law' marriages in the nineteenth century where couples cohabited and had children without legal sanction. These arrangements were more equitable than traditional marriages because they allowed for the possibility of separation if the relationship did not work out.[39] For most women, however, illegitimacy was not a matter of choice; it was a social and economic catastrophe for them.

In sum, in a number of ways courtship and marriage became less governed by ritual and more flexible over the course of our period. Among the upper and middle classes, it was young men who benefited most from the decline in arranged marriages, since it was they who initiated most courtships, even if women helped shape their outcome. Lower down the social scale, where young men had always played a significant role in selecting their marriage partner, women acquired a greater role, since they became able, in the words of John Gillis, to use 'their sexuality, savings, and labour power' aggressively in courtship, with sexual activity and often stable relationships occurring outside the formal institution of marriage.[40] Despite the frequent depiction of women as sexually passive in the second half of the period, lower-class women were able to use their sexuality for their own ends. However, these changes in courtship practices also enabled some men to exploit women, and many ended up as single mothers with only the poor law or charity to support them. As Bridget Hill has argued, 'customary alternatives to lawful marriage . . . all too often seem to have . . . favoured men at the expense of women.'[41] With the very real possibility that their male partners might desert them and leave them literally holding

---

38 Gillis, *For Better, For Worse*, p. 129; Bridget Hill, 'The marriage age of women and the demographers', *History Workshop* 28 (Autumn 1989), p. 133, citing G. N. Gandy, 'Illegitimacy in a handloom weaving community: fertility patterns in Culcheth, Lancashire 1781–1860', unpublished PhD thesis, Oxford University, 1978.

39 Gillis, *For Better, For Worse*, ch. 7.

40 Gillis, *For Better, For Worse*, pp. 181–2.

41 Hill, *Women, Work and Sexual Politics*, p. 220.

the baby, the breakdown of traditional courtship practices often spelled disaster for women.

RELATIONS BETWEEN SPOUSES

Once married, men and women had to sort out the distribution of authority and responsibilities in their relationship. They had a lot of advice, from the church, the law, conduct manuals, and their own family and neighbours, advice which emphasised the husband's authority over his wife and a sexual division of labour. Nonetheless, in theory, and even more in practice, a number of different approaches to the marital relationship were available.

The Bible made it clear that the primary duty of wives was to obey their husbands, while the first duty of husbands was to love their wives. At common law, as Lawrence Stone has noted,

> a married woman was the nearest approximation in a free society to a slave. Her person, her property, both real and personal, her earnings, and her children all passed on marriage into the absolute control of her husband. The latter could use her sexually as he wished, and beat her (within reason) or confine her for disobedience to any orders. The children were entirely at the disposal of the father.[42]

We have seen that the superior position of men was echoed in conduct books and in popular customs such as rough music, which punished husbands who failed to control their wives (as indicated by the fact that their wives beat them or committed adultery). Similarly, although popular ballads often depicted marital relations as a 'struggle for the breeches', they usually demonstrated the disastrous consequences that would follow if the husband's authority was undermined.

Although the religious and legal basis of patriarchal authority in marriage did not change in this period, we have seen that the historians Lawrence Stone and Randolph Trumbach have argued that the eighteenth century witnessed a significant change from this patriarchal approach to marriage to a more companionate, affectionate model, especially among the middle and upper classes (though Stone argues that there was a reassertion of patriarchal authority in the early nineteenth century). Since spouses increasingly chose each other on the basis of affection, it is argued, they had more rea-

---

42 Lawrence Stone, *Road to Divorce: England 1530–1987* (Oxford, 1990), p. 13.

son to treat each other as equals.[43] As we have seen, Stone's arguments have been heavily criticised as being overly schematic and failing to recognise the variety of marital practices in existence at any one time. In fact, evidence from a variety of sources reveals that patriarchal authority and love were not inconsistent with one another and were both common aspects of marriage throughout this period; it is difficult to trace a clear pattern of chronological change.

In conduct books, for example, the extent of expected husbandly authority was often qualified as authors attempted to reconcile the possible contradiction between the necessity for wives to submit to their husbands' authority and the expectation that spouses form a relationship based on love and friendship. In 1705, for example, William Fleetwood advised wives to obey their husbands, but noted that wives should not be treated as slaves or menial servants, but as 'friends and companions in all their fortunes'. St Paul, he notes, left it 'as much a duty on the husbands to love their wives, as on the wives to submit themselves to their own husbands', and he goes on to advise husbands not 'to use, neither in word or deed, any ungentleness, or rigour towards' their wives, who were 'equal [in] dignity' to them.[44] A century later, John Ovington's tract on *The Duties, Advantages, and Sorrows, of the Marriage State* includes both instructions for wives to 'submit yourselves unto your own husbands as unto the Lord' and the comment that 'the husband and wife must be like the primitive Christians, of one heart, and of one soul: and each must endeavour in all things to please the other, that they may live in love and peace'.[45] And the anonymous author of *The English Matron* wrote in 1846 that although the household should be governed as a 'limited monarchy', 'marriage was never intended to be a state of subserviency for women . . . the very word "union" implies a degree of equality.'[46]

In sum, many authors qualified the husband's patriarchal authority by emphasising aspects of equality, mutual obligations, and affection in the marital relationship. Some authors, of course, thought patriarchal authority was absolute: the anonymous author of the appropriately titled *The Art of Governing a Wife* wrote in 1747

43 Stone, *Family, Sex and Marriage*; Randolph Trumbach, *The Rise of the Egalitarian Family: Aristocratic Kinship and Domestic Relations in Eighteenth-Century England* (1978).

44 W. Fleetwood, *The Relative Duties of Parents and Children, Husbands and Wives, Masters and Servants* (1705), pp. 170, 297, 333, 336.

45 John Ovington, *The Duties, Advantages, Pleasures and Sorrows, of the Marriage State* (1813), pp. 8–9.

46 *The English Matron* (1846), pp. 17, 22.

that the husband 'must govern with absolute power', while the duty of wives was 'not . . . to understand, but to obey'.[47] For others, the only power women could exercise was indirect. In his published letter to his daughter, Lord Halifax explained that the best way women could influence their husbands was through deceit and the use of their tears. 'You have it in your power not only to free yourselves, but to subdue your masters', he wrote, 'and without violence throw both their natural and regal authority at your feet.' A century and a half later the conduct books written by Sarah Ellis could be interpreted as encouraging women to counteract their husbands' unreasonable behaviour by surreptitiously 'managing' them.[48] Nonetheless, by confirming female subordination and the stereotype of female irrationality such behaviour could ultimately reinforce patriarchal authority. Conduct books thus contain a spectrum of ideas about the distribution of power within marriage, ranging from the the strongly patriarchal to the patriarchal mitigated by companionship or deceit, and there is no clear pattern of chronological change in terms of which model of prescribed marital relations was dominant.

An even greater diversity can be found in marital practice, though the evidence of how husbands and wives actually related to one another is extremely limited (and comes largely from a male point of view, in their letters and diaries). Strong evidence of patriarchal marriages can be found in a number of places. Sara Mendelson has shown that pious women in the seventeenth century internalised contemporary religious teachings concerning wifely obedience: writing in their diaries, they 'felt obliged to confess and repudiate all manifestations of marital insubordination'. Stone's suggestion that patriarchal marriages were most common among the lower classes is supported by some evidence. Michael MacDonald's analysis of the complaints of the lower- and middle-class clients of the early-seventeenth-century astrological physician Richard Napier shows that women were far more likely to complain about unhappy marriages than men, citing husbands who were cruel, unfaithful, profligate, or drunkards. Anna Clark has suggested that the adoption by the working class of a separate-spheres model of marriage in the early nineteenth century enhanced the

47 *The Art of Governing a Wife, with Rules for Batchelors* (1747), pp. 44, 55.
48 Lord Halifax [George Savile], *The Lady's New Year's Gift: or, Advice to a Daughter* (1688), p. 27; Henrietta Twycross-Martin, 'Woman supportive or woman manipulative? The "Mrs Ellis" woman', in C. C. Orr (ed.), *Wollstonecraft's Daughters: Womanhood in England and France, 1780–1920* (Manchester, 1996), pp. 109–20; A. James Hammerton, *Cruelty and Companionship: Conflict in Nineteenth-Century Married Life* (1992), p. 77.

patriarchal character of marriages in that class. John Burnett's analysis of nineteenth-century working-class autobiographies supports this: the father was often portrayed as 'frequently a drunkard, often thoughtless and uncaring of his wife and children' even if he was 'occasionally over-generous and sentimental'.[49] There is similar evidence, however, of patriarchal marriages higher up the social scale. Thomas Jolly, the son of a clothier, wrote of his fourth wife that 'she was a most loving wife and tender nurse to me; if she at any time offended me, she could not be quiet until she had acknowledged her offence and was reconciled.'[50] Among the upper-middle class, patriarchal relationships were no doubt facilitated by the large gap in ages between husbands and wives. Stone quotes the example of Hester Thrale, who married Henry, a wealthy brewer twelve years older than her, and who wrote in her diary 'I never offer to cross my Master's fancy ... unless on some truly serious occasion where virtue, life or fortune are concerned. I have never opposed his inclination three times in the fifteen years I have been married.'[51]

Further evidence of the patriarchal character of marriage can be found in the practice of wife beating, the double standard of sexual morality, and the laws and practice of marital breakdown. Yet in each case, the evidence suggests that husbands were not all-powerful. In this hierarchical society violence was an accepted method of disciplining social inferiors who misbehaved, whether they were servants, children, or wives. Husbands thus had the legal right to use 'moderate correction' to chastise their wives physically for misbehaviour: it was suggested that if a stick was used it should not be thicker than a man's thumb. While such limited violence against wives was legal, attacks by wives on their husbands were seen as a very serious offence which undermined the social order: wives who killed their husbands were guilty not simply of murder, but of petty treason, which was punishable by burning at the stake.

It is impossible to measure how much wife beating took place, and to gauge accurately popular attitudes towards it. For a number of reasons victims often chose to ignore or suppress the evidence. Even where the beating was far from moderate, some victims were ashamed of the fact and blamed themselves for provoking their hus-

---

49 Sara Heller Mendelson, 'Stuart women's diaries and occasional memoirs', in *Women in English Society 1500–1800*, ed. Mary Prior (1985), p. 194; MacDonald, *Mystical Bedlam*, pp. 99–100; Anna Clark, *The Struggle for the Breeches: Gender and the Making of the British Working Class* (1995), ch. 14; John Burnett, *Destiny Obscure: Autobiographies of Childhood, Education and Family from the 1820s to the 1920s* (1982), p. 233.

50 Cited by Houlbrooke (ed.), *English Family Life*, p. 88.

51 Cited by Stone, *Family, Sex and Marriage*, p. 369.

bands. Others who strove to maintain their respectability were worried about the damage such a complaint might inflict on their reputation, while others recognised that making a complaint, whether to the neighbours or the courts, could very well be counterproductive in the sense that it could stimulate further abuse, or cause their husbands to desert them or be imprisoned, leaving them without any means of support. Given this reluctance to complain, we will never know the extent of wife beating which occurred during this period, though we can identify some of the contexts in which it took place. Matrimonial disputes in the late-seventeenth-century Court of Arches include cases in which men beat their wives for failing to prepare their dinner on time, putting too much butter in the pudding, and not dressing appropriately. Similarly, in eighteenth-century London husbands beat their wives over a wide range of perceived misbehaviour, including 'what they saw as women's extravagance, over labour contributions to their husbands' businesses, over the provision of sexual or emotional services, and over subtleties such as whether or not their behaviour or appearance reflected the rank to which husbands aspired.' Among the middle class, husbands beat wives who refused to allow them access to the property in their 'separate estate', or who failed to secure them financial support from their families.

The underlying current in most of these cases is clearly the husband's frustration at not being able to control his wife. Although the abuse could be quite violent, it is surprising that there is not more evidence of cases where it proved fatal. Margaret Hunt concludes that 'most English men in the eighteenth century probably assumed that they had a right to beat their wives ... and the bulk of the population ... supported them in this belief.' Indeed, men often arranged for relatives to witness the beating, and when accused, they rarely denied the fact, and instead simply justified their actions by their wives' supposed disobedience. Community members were reluctant to intervene, unless they thought the situation was getting out of hand. Amussen quotes a case from 1696 in which a neighbour told a man that 'he was very ill man to beat his wife *at that rate*' (emphasis added). Elizabeth Foyster has argued that excessive violence towards wives was regarded as 'unmanly', shameful, and dishonourable in the late seventeenth century.[52]

52 Elizabeth Foyster, 'Male honour, social control and wife beating in late Stuart England', *Transactions of the Royal Historical Society* 6th series, 6 (1996), pp. 215–24; Margaret Hunt, 'Wife beating, domesticity, and women's independence in eighteenth-century London', *Gender and History* 4 (1992), pp. 16, 18, 23; Hunt, *The Middling Sort*, pp. 154, 160; Amussen, *An Ordered Society*, p. 129.

There is, however, evidence of more general hostility towards wife beating throughout this period, and this hostility increased, as all types of violence in English society, whether exercised by individuals or the state, became less acceptable. Wife beating was condemned in print in a pamphlet printed in 1609 and reprinted in 1682, and was criticised in the early eighteenth century by proponents of a new 'polite' code of elite behaviour, such as that advanced by Joseph Addison and Richard Steele in the *Tatler* and the *Spectator*.[53] In 1765, Blackstone noted that, although the legality of 'correcting' wives had been in doubt for a century, the practice was still common 'among the lower rank of people'. Although Blackstone did not rule out physical chastisement altogether, in 1853 it was prohibited by the Aggravated Assaults Act, the result of a 'moral panic' about the offence and the difficulties of punishing it.[54] Evidence of popular attitudes towards the practice can be found in the history of rough music, the communal shaming ritual which punished antisocial practices. In the seventeenth and early eighteenth century these demonstrations were often targeted at husbands who allowed their wives to beat them, but in the second half of our period they increasingly punished husbands who beat their wives.[55] Despite this change, recent research has emphasised that wife beating continued to be common in the nineteenth century, and not only among the working class. Although owing to public condemnation it was now more likely to be conducted in private, even neighbours continued to tolerate it, within limits. Arguably, wife beating may have even increased in the early nineteenth century as a result of tensions arising from the growing articulation of the ideal of companionate marriage despite the continued patriarchal expectations of husbands. Thus, Anna Clark has argued that domestic violence was particularly common among artisans who found themselves torn between the demands of their wives and the attractions of the 'homosocial world of workshop and pub'.[56]

As the evidence of rough music suggests, on occasion wives did

53 Hunt, 'Wife beating', pp. 10, 25; W. Heale, *The Great Advocate and Orator for Women* (1682).

54 William Blackstone, *Commentaries on the Laws of England* (4 vols, Oxford, 1765–9), 1, pp. 432–3; Anna Clark, 'Humanity or justice? Wifebeating and the law in the eighteenth and nineteenth centuries', in *Regulating Motherhood: Historical Essays on Marriage, Motherhood and Sexuality* (1992), pp. 189–92, 200.

55 E. P. Thompson, *Customs in Common* (1991), pp. 505–13.

56 Nancy Tomes, 'A "torrent of abuse": crimes of violence between working-class men and women in London, 1840–1875' *Journal of Social History* 11 (1978), pp. 331, 335–6; Hammerton, *Cruelty and Companionship*, chs 2 and 4; Clark, *Struggle for the Breeches*, pp. 71–82.

physically attack their husbands. There is, however, very little other evidence of this practice, though a reading of the satirical literature on marital strife 'suggests that many women could be expected, so far as they had the courage and the physical strength, to give as good as they got in marital quarrels'. Of course, unlike wife beating there was no question of this activity ever being tolerated, legally or socially. Moreover, women must have been inhibited by the prevalent cultural ideal of the subordination of wives to their husbands, as well as in many cases by relative physical weakness. Instead, women were forced to resort to insulting words (hence the stereotypical image of the scold), together with the occasional act of violence. In response to physical abuse from their husbands, women could also fight back by bringing their husbands before justices of the peace and charging them with assault. Nonetheless, such women could only get sympathy by portraying themselves as passive and dutiful wives and emphasising that the beatings they had endured were exceptionally severe, or 'inhuman.'[57] Even when fighting back, it was difficult to escape the patriarchal framework of marriage.

Further evidence of women's unequal position in marriage comes from attitudes towards adultery. As we have seen, although all sexual activity outside marriage was frowned upon, a double standard applied in which male adultery was much more likely to be tolerated. This is especially evident in the development of the legal action of 'criminal conversation' during this period, whereby husbands could sue their wives' lovers for damages (to the husband's honour) caused by adultery, often as a prelude to a divorce by parliamentary act.[58] The reverse was of course not possible, since a wife could not sue on her own and in any case a husband's infidelities were not thought to damage *her* honour. We have seen that social practice reflected this double standard, in the sense that married men were more likely to initiate and engage in extramarital sex. Nonetheless, women did commit adultery; indeed, their affairs provided men with the pretexts they needed to justify separation and divorce.

When, owing to cruelty, adultery, or personal incompatibility, marriages broke down, spouses faced a difficult situation, since divorce, except by statute, was illegal in England until 1857. Although there were a number of ways of achieving formal or *de facto* separ-

57 Anthony Fletcher, *Gender, Sex and Subordination in England 1500–1800* (1995), p. 198; Clark, *Struggle for the Breeches*, pp. 192, 194; Hunt, 'Wife beating', p. 24.
58 Stone, *Road to Divorce*, ch. 9.

ation and even remarriage, the tactics involved differed by social class and were far less available to women than to men. The surest but most expensive approach was to obtain a formal divorce by act of parliament, but this required considerable financial and political resources and was rare even among the rich. Even then it was designed largely for men, as is evident from an examination of what were considered acceptable grounds for such an act. While a wife's adultery was considered by itself sufficient cause (because, as we have seen, it endangered the transmission of property), wives could not seek a divorce unless the husband's adultery was compounded by other serious misbehaviour such as bigamy, rape, incest, or sodomy. Consequently, only four divorce acts in the entire period were passed at the instigation of the wife.[59]

Another option, for those who could afford the cost of approximately £20, was to pursue a legal separation, either in the church courts or by private agreement. Stone has shown that most separation suits in the church courts were brought by husbands, who, as in parliamentary divorce cases, justified the case on the basis of the wife's adultery. In principle, private agreements were more favourable to wives since they did not depend on an accusation of misbehaviour, they included maintenance, they gave them full economic freedom, and they often included clauses preventing the husband from disturbing his (ex-) wife, but due to the uncertain legal status of such agreements these clauses did not always hold up in court. Stone suggests that private agreements were also used more by men than by women, in this case as a means of allowing men to live with their new lovers.[60]

For the bulk of the population who did not possess the financial resources to pursue any legal form of separation or divorce, there were a number of other options. The first was simple desertion, when one spouse (most often the husband) simply left home, often leaving his wife and children with no means of support except the poor law. Recent research has demonstrated that this practice became increasingly common in the late eighteenth century, apparently for economic reasons. In Colyton, Devon about 10% of all marriages which took place between 1725 and 1765 resulted in separation. Men seem to have been most prone to desert their wives when they were unemployed, when the family was impoverished by the presence of a large number of young children, and when new job possibilities in other places opened up, such as with the militia

59 Hill, *Women, Work and Sexual Politics*, pp. 210–11.
60 Stone, *Road to Divorce*, chs 7 and 8.

or the navy. In other cases, men abandoned their wives in order to live with another woman. Whatever the reason, it was typically the man who left, because a women who deserted her husband was still considered to be legally married and therefore had no right to any property, nor to the custody of her children. Of thirty-nine marital separations in Colyton between 1741 and 1769 where the evidence is complete, thirty-three were initiated by the husband and only six by the wife.[61]

Where a still legally married man or woman wanted to live with another partner, it was necessary to cancel the husband's responsibility to provide for his legal wife. It was widely believed that this could be achieved through a number of popular rituals which formalised separations, involving such activities as returning the wedding ring or jumping backwards over a broom. John Gillis has argued that the popular rules governing these practices were 'relatively egalitarian' and demanded the consent of both parties.[62] Although such common-law divorces and remarriages were widespread, they had no legal standing, and with the passage of Hardwicke's Marriage Act of 1753 remarriage became more difficult because it became easier to detect bigamy. Consequently, a new, more formal (but still extra-legal) form of divorce, the 'wife sale', became popular in the century after 1750.

In a wife sale a husband placed a halter around his wife's neck and led her to the market, where she was sold by auction to the highest bidder. The social meaning of this extraordinary ritual is difficult to determine. On the one hand, women were clearly treated as forms of property. The obvious parallels to the sale of livestock (the use of the halter; the fact that tolls were paid to market officials) suggest that such women were treated like animals; another comparison, to the annual hiring fairs for servants, suggests they were being treated as servants. Men, of course, could not be treated this way: sales of husbands were very rare. But it has been pointed out that these rituals did not occur without the wife's consent, that in many cases the purchaser was in fact the wife's lover, and that the 'purchase' had often been agreed between the three parties in advance. This does little to diminish the demeaning quality of the rit-

61 Pamela Sharpe, 'Marital separation in the eighteenth and early nineteenth centuries', *Local Population Studies* 45 (Autumn 1990), pp. 66–70; David A. Kent, ' "Gone for a soldier": family breakdown and the demography of desertion in a London parish, 1750–91', *Local Population Studies* 45 (Autumn 1990), pp. 27–42; Keith Snell, *Annals of the Labouring Poor: Social Change and Agrarian England 1660–1900* (1985), pp. 359–64.

62 Gillis, *For Better, For Worse*, pp. 199, 209–10.

ual, but it does suggest that this form of divorce often worked to the woman's advantage (though the husband also benefited, in the sense that he was discharged of his financial responsibility for his wife). But some sales occurred due to the sudden impulse of the husband, and the purchaser had not always been arranged in advance. Perhaps it was cases like these which led crowds of women to disrupt wife sales in the 1820s and 1830s.[63]

In many ways, then, the wife sale epitomises the patriarchal nature of marriage in this period. The demeaning nature of the ritual, as well as the possibility that a woman might be involuntarily 'sold' to enter into a common-law marriage with a man who was totally unknown to her, highlight women's legal and social inferiority in marriage in this period. Yet the fact that in the vast majority of the cases such 'sales' freed women from an unhappy marriage and allowed them to move in with their lovers suggests that in practice women, especially in the lower classes, were able to achieve a degree of control over their marital circumstances.

Indeed, there is a considerable amount of evidence throughout this period that the marriage relationship was not always completely hierarchical, that instead decisions were reached jointly and there was a great deal of mutual affection and respect (though this was not necessarily incompatible with a hierarchical relationship). The fact that women frequently assumed significant responsibilities within the household (as discussed in the next section) meant that wives were likely to want to participate in decision-making, and that husbands sought their participation. In the seventeenth century, according to Wrightson, 'decision making . . . was frequently based on prior discussion between husband and wife' and 'marital bickering was not usually cut short promptly by assertions of the husband's patriarchal authority.'[64] J. A. Sharpe concluded from an analysis of popular ballads that, although male superiority was acknowledged, it was generally thought that 'marriage could and ought to be loving, companionate, and affective . . . [with] decisions about marital matters being reached jointly, after a frank and loving discussion between what were conceived of, for most normal purposes, as more or less equal partners.'[65] Similarly, MacDonald concluded

---

63 S. P. Menefee, *Wives for Sale: An Ethnographic Study of British Popular Divorce* (Oxford, 1981); Thompson, *Customs in Common*, ch. 7.

64 Keith Wrightson, *English Society 1580–1680* (1982), pp. 92–104, esp. 94–5; Fletcher, *Gender, Sex and Subordination*, pp. 173–9.

65 J. A. Sharpe, 'Plebeian marriage in Stuart England: some evidence from popular literature', *Transactions of the Royal Historical Society* 5th series, 36 (1986), p. 84.

from his analysis of the marital cases heard by Napier that women had strong expectations that 'the tie between their husbands and them [should] be a bond of love and not merely of obligation'. It has been suggested that such marriages were most common among the lower class, where spouses were most likely to be the same age, and women's joint participation in breadwinning placed them in a partnership with their husbands,[66] but there is also strong evidence of mutual affection from higher social classes. Love and companionship could characterise middle-class marriages, especially where husband and wife shared firmly held religious or mercantile values. Fletcher argues that 'affection and loving familiarity between spouses shines through many of the collections of the gentry's correspondence'.[67]

In some cases the balance of power in a marriage was even in favour of the wife. Strong women could persuade or intimidate husbands into surrendering some power, and this was not necessarily seen as a problem: it has been argued that the proverbs 'better to marry a shrew than a sheep' and its opposite were both in use in this period. Earle argues, on the basis of divorce records pertaining to the London middle class, that in marital conflicts 'wives . . . often gave as good as they got, or better. They were independent individuals who would strike and abuse a husband they did not like or who treated them badly. They would say that they would do as they please and then proceed to do as they pleased.'[68] Adam Eyre, a Yorkshire yeoman who kept a diary in the late 1640s, was frequently in conflict with his wife over money matters and his drinking. She refused his request to sign over her property to him, and he only made peace with her by persuasion and making promises, as he notes in his diary entry for 1 January, 1648:

> This morn I used some words of persuasion to my wife to forbear to tell me of what is past, and promised her to become a good husband to her for the time to come, and she promised me likewise she would do what I wished her in anything, save in setting her hand to papers [to turn over her property]; and I promised her never to wish her thereunto.[69]

66 MacDonald, *Mystical Bedlam*, p. 103; Amussen, *An Ordered Society*, p. 119; Gillis, *For Better, For Worse*, pp. 117, 159.

67 Hunt, *The Middling Sort*, pp. 166–70; John Tosh, 'From Keighly to St. Denis: separation and intimacy in Victorian bourgeois marriage', *History Workshop Journal* 40 (1995), pp. 193–206; Fletcher, *Gender, Sex and Subordination*, p. 174.

68 Martin Ingram, 'Ridings, rough music and the "reform of popular culture" in early modern England', *Past and Present* 105 (1984), p. 98; Earle, *Making of the English Middle Class*, p. 204.

69 Cited in Houlbrooke (ed.), *English Family Life*, p. 68.

Similarly, the diary of Edmund Harrold reveals a man who often gave way in conflicts with his wife. One Sunday in 1712 he wanted to take the sacrament in church, but his wife told him not to, accusing him of being 'presumptuous' in taking communion so often. Edmund gave in 'for fear of giving offence to my weak wife . . . so I sinned for peace . . .' His strategy for marital peace was made explicit in another entry, when he wrote, 'I observe that it's best to keep good decorum and to please wife; it makes everything pleasant and easy . . .'.[70]

As Sharpe has noted, the image of the shrewish wife and scold was a common one in popular fiction, which suggests that there was a certain degree of popular concern (at least among men) about the potential for female insubordination. In such literature the ambiguities and contradictions between patriarchal ideas and the ideal of a companionate marriage, as well as the concerns raised by the inevitable practical difficulties men had in actually maintaining authority in their marriages, could be aired and addressed in a humorous fashion, in a manner which, Sharpe suggests, ultimately reinforced male dominance.[71] Yet women with strong personalities could find role models of assertive women in such literature, and other evidence suggests that they did achieve *de facto* power in marriages, despite the widely repeated injunctions to them to obey their husbands. In doing so, they transgressed normal gender roles, but their actions probably did little in the long run to alter those roles.

In sum, arguments for the development of companionate marriages in this period are undermined by evidence that such marriages can be found throughout the period. At the same time, the overall patriarchal character of marriage is also a constant: whether one considers the property laws, wife beating, the double standard, or divorce and separation practices, men clearly retained the upper hand. What Martin Ingram has written of the seventeenth century applies to this whole period: 'in practice, the balance of authority between husbands and wives in marriage varied considerably',[72] depending no doubt on individual personalities and the internal dynamic of each relationship (which was often shaped by age differences). Although marital experiences in many ways differed by social class, the evidence presented here suggests that both patriarchal and companionate marriages could be found at all social levels. Only in the case of attitudes towards wife beating is there significant

---

70 Cited in ibid., p. 95.
71 Sharpe, 'Plebeian marriage', pp. 81–9.
72 Ingram, 'Ridings, rough music and the "reform of popular culture" ', p. 97.

evidence of change in the character of marital relations in this period, but even here there is considerable evidence of continuity in actual practice.

THE DIVISION OF LABOUR BETWEEN SPOUSES

Not only was the balance of power in marriage typically (if not universally) weighted firmly towards men, but there were significant differences in the responsibilities and tasks performed by husbands and wives. Just as they faced a chorus of ideological advice that wives should be subservient to their husbands, husbands and wives faced clear instructions throughout this period regarding the duties each partner should take up: the husband should be the primary bread-winner, while the wife should run the household and take care of the children. Although such ideas were articulated with increasing frequency and intensity in the late eighteenth and early nineteenth centuries as an ideology of domesticity for women and the ideal of the breadwinning husband developed, we have seen in Chapter 2 that this separation of duties was frequently articulated throughout our period. But did married couples actually follow these precepts? Is there any indication in marital practices of an increased differen-tiation of tasks into separate male and female spheres in the second half of our period? We need to consider how married couples divided up the tasks of marriage: earning income, housework, and (in the next section) childcare.

Unless they were able to live off their investments (or, at the other social extreme, could not find work), all men worked for in-come during this period, but as we shall see in the next chapter, they were joined by vast numbers of married women, especially from the lower class, working full- or part-time. Most married women engaged in a number of different paid employments, many of which took place in the home. When working at home, women could, alongside the housework, contribute to the family business, engage in protoindustrial manufacture, or carry out a considerable amount of work which combined household responsibilities with earning extra income, such as taking in washing, cultivating fruit or vegetables, or raising poultry.

Middle-class wives, on the other hand, were less likely to work for income. When the family could afford it, many wives ceased paid working. A number of historians have argued that the phenomenon of the 'idle' middle-class wife increased dramatically over the course of this period, ascribing the cause of this change to the rise of capi-

talism or the influence of domestic ideology, but what is more impressive is the fact that evidence of this practice can be found
throughout the period. In 1678, an anonymous author complained
that London women did not have the skills needed to be able to
contribute to their husbands' businesses. In 1726, Daniel Defoe
devoted an entire chapter of his *Complete English Tradesman* to a dia-
tribe against tradesmen's wives, who 'generally speaking . . . scorn to
be seen in the counting house, much less behind the counter' and
instead 'sit above in the parlour, and receive visits, and drink tea,
and entertain her neighbours, or take a coach and go abroad . . .'.[73]
Historians of the London middle class disagree over how common
this practice was. Peter Earle concluded from his study of the period
between 1660 and 1730 that 'the majority of middle-class wives
played little or no part in the running of their husbands' businesses,
especially if their husbands were reasonably well off.' In another
study of a cross section of Londoners of all social classes, Earle
found that, when asked how they were maintained or got their living, 42% of the wives mentioned no paid employments. Instead,
most indicated that they were maintained by their husbands (94%
of wives with no paid employment) or other relatives and friends, or
lived off income from property and/or investments.[74] Yet Margaret
Hunt has shown that many aspects of middle-class women's work
are obscured by these statistics. Status-conscious wives did not always
fully report their income-earning activities, such as the fact that they
helped with retail sales in the family shop. And even when they did
not participate directly in their husband's business, wives, and their
natal families, frequently contributed capital and provided business
contacts which were vital to the success of the family enterprise.
Wives also sometimes failed to report jobs they held independently
of their husbands: insurance records suggest that some ran their
own shops. Finally, as we shall see, many aspects of housework
generated income. Thus few middle- (or lower-) class women did
not contribute to the family income in some way.[75]

It is impossible to tell whether the proportion of wives who were
not engaged in paid employments increased during this period. It
may be that any increase in the number of women not working is

73 *Advice to the Women and Maidens of London* (1678); Daniel Defoe, *The Complete
English Tradesman* ([1726] 1987), pp. 201, 205.
74 Earle, *Making of the English Middle Class,* p. 166; Peter Earle, *A City Full of
People: Men and Women of London, 1650–1750* (1994), pp. 114, 152.
75 Hunt, *The Middling Sort,* pp. 128–9, 132–3, 151–61; Davidoff and Hall, *Family
Fortunes,* pp. 279–89.

best explained by the vast increase in the size of the middle class which occurred over the course of this period, rather than a growing tendency for middle-class wives not to work. Nonetheless, there is also some evidence of the latter: Davidoff and Hall cite the case of a man in the early nineteenth century who noted that whereas his mother had participated in the family auctioneering business, women had withdrawn from business life during his lifetime. Although few working-class families could afford this division of labour, the growing influence of middle-class values and of the ideal of the breadwinning wage (the idea that working men should be paid a wage sufficient to support a whole family), led some wives of artisans also to stop working for income. Henry Mayhew reported in 1849 that 'the more respectable portion of the carpenters and joiners "will not allow" their wives to do any other work than attend to their domestic and family duties.' The difficulty of maintaining such a position, however, is clear from Mayhew's subsequent qualification of this point, where he admits that 'some few of the wives of the better class of workmen take in washing or keep small "general shops".'[76]

It is important to note that middle-class husbands, too, avoided paid work when they could afford it. A foreign observer noted in the 1690s that 'no sooner do [English merchants] acquire wealth, but they quit traffick, and turn country gentlemen.'[77] Earle's study of the London middle class between 1660 and 1730 found this comment to be true, except that they invested their money in the city as well as in country estates. Professional tradesmen quite often retired early and invested their assets in housing, stocks, shares, and personal loans. Thomas Harris made enough money in trade with India to retire when he was thirty-four. Although this was unusually early, it was 'not uncommon', according to Earle, for businessmen to retire in their forties. Early retirement continued to be the case a hundred years later, when successful businessmen and professional men gradually transferred their wealth to less active forms of investment in order to spend more time with their families, their religious devotions, and voluntary activities. Men who had ceased working made up 11% of Davidoff and Hall's sample of middle-class male heads of households from the 1851 census; their average age was 59.4. In the end, Earle's comment for the period 1650–1750 that 'few people worked if they could afford to be idle' applies to both

---

76 Davidoff and Hall, *Family Fortunes*, pp. 272, 312–13; Thompson and Yeo (eds), *The Unknown Mayhew*, p. 338.
77 Cited by Earle, *Making of the English Middle Class*, p. 152.

sexes (and for the whole period); the only significant difference between men and women was that if a married couple could afford to have only one person not working, it was the woman who first gave up paid employment.[78]

Whether or not they worked for income, wives, or the servants they supervised, did the vast majority of the housework, including virtually all of the cleaning, shopping, and cooking. Such work was far more onerous during this period than at present, for although lower standards of cleanliness, smaller houses, and fewer possessions made for less cleaning, the lack of running water, electricity, and gas meant that what are today fairly simple chores such as doing the laundry were immensely laborious and time-consuming. Moreover, housework in this period was generally considered to include a number of tasks which are no longer done at home, such as brewing, dairy work, growing fruits and vegetables, caring for lodgers, keeping pigs and poultry, spinning, and providing medical care. Many such tasks produced goods for the market as well as the home, which further emphasises the point that it is difficult to draw the line between housework and work for income. It also underlines the fact that even when they do not appear in the records to be working, most wives contributed directly to the family income.

Seventeenth-century women's diaries reveal that middle- and upper-class wives spent much of their time on housework, either doing it themselves or closely supervising servants (most of whom, as we shall see, were also female).[79] A foreign observer noted in 1748 that 'English women generally have the character of keeping floors, steps, and such things very clean'.[80] Nonetheless, men performed some tasks around the home, including outdoor work such as carrying water, fetching fuel, and working in the garden; processing food such as grinding corn, storing grains and root vegetables, preserving fruit, and salting meat; brewing; and decorating rooms (in many of these tasks husbands and wives must have worked together). Nicholas Blundell, a gentleman from Lancashire who lived in the early eighteenth century, for example, managed and disciplined the servants, kept the household accounts, fed the pigs, preserved food, cut bread, brewed beer and ale, and helped arrange the house when guests were expected. Important as the tasks per-

78 Earle, *Making of the English Middle Class* pp. 152–7; Davidoff and Hall, *Family Fortunes*, pp. 225–7; Earle, *City Full of People*, pp. 99–100.

79 Mendelson, 'Stuart women's diaries', pp. 189–90. For the sexual composition of servants, see below, Chapter 5, pp. 175–8.

80 Cited by Hill, *Women, Work and Sexual Politics*, p. 117.

formed by men are, however, they do not include any cleaning or
day-to-day cooking. Blundell 'never did any routine cleaning' and
his greatest contribution to the household, according to Caroline
Davidson, was that he was a 'great handyman: he was always fixing
things'. The husbands of women who were in full-time employment
occasionally performed some extra household tasks, such as cleaning walls and windows or blacking stoves, but these tasks were clearly peripheral. Only in extraordinary circumstances, such as when
only the wife was able to find paid employment, as in Manchester
between 1839 and 1842, did men do a significant amount of cooking, cleaning, or nursing.[81] Normally, however, the wife did the bulk
of the household work even when both spouses worked for income:
among powerloom weavers, where men and women worked for
similar wages, the responsibility for housework and childcare remained with wives. Such practices left women to work longer hours
than their husbands, seven days a week. The popular custom of
'Saint Monday', a day of leisure at the start of the working week, was
observed by men, but not women, who spent their day off washing,
shopping, and doing other household tasks.[82]

In sum, the division of labour in marriage was significantly gendered throughout this period. Nonetheless, men and women did
not fully live up to the expectations (found in conduct books) that
men should spent all their time outside the house earning a living,
while only women should 'look to the house'. Whether in terms of
the physical location of their activities or the tasks performed, there
was a degree of overlap. Wives often went outside to garden or work
in the farmyard, or left home entirely to work in workshops or
shops or attend markets. Husbands, on the other hand, frequently
worked at home, and did some types of housework. But the tasks
performed by men and women were still for the most part divided.
As we have seen, the domestic tasks men performed were in many
ways peripheral, just as, as will become evident in the next chapter,
women's opportunities for wage labour were significantly limited.

A number of changes affected the nature of housework over the
course of this period which may have served to accentuate its

---

81 Caroline Davidson, *A Woman's Work is Never Done: A History of Housework in the British Isles 1650–1950* (1982), pp. 185–7; Davidoff and Hall, *Family Fortunes*, p. 387; Hill, *Women, Work and Sexual Politics*, ch. 7; Clark, *Struggle for the Breeches*, p. 256.

82 Sonya Rose, *Limited Livelihoods: Gender and Class in Nineteenth-Century England* (Berkeley, 1992), pp. 164–5; Catherine Hall, 'The history of the housewife', in *idem, White, Male and Middle Class: Explorations in Feminism and History* (Cambridge, 1992), p. 67.

already gendered character. The adoption of a more prosperous and genteel lifestyle by the middle classes led to an increase in the number of household tasks, especially cleaning. Substituting wood floors for bare earth or stone created more work washing and polishing, while the adoption of coal fireplaces, often in many rooms, created a considerable amount of work cleaning and polishing grates and removing soot.[83] Such tasks were performed by women, whether as wives or female servants. Similarly, the growing social value placed on the possession of consumer goods during this period meant that women's traditional responsibility for marketing became both more important and more burdensome. Analysis of the diary of Elizabeth Shackleton, a Lancashire gentlewoman from the second half of the eighteenth century, has shown that although her husband purchased certain types of luxury goods, like snuff, wine, and barrels of oysters, as well as one-off purchases like expensive furniture, Elizabeth performed most of the shopping for the household. At the same time, men lost some household tasks, since some activities in which they had often participated (or which had been performed by both men and women), such as brewing, were no longer performed in the home, as commercial products and services became available.[84]

Another reason why housework may have become more exclusively feminine during this period is that there was a growing ideological distinction, and physical separation, between housework, which was seen to be female, and (real) work, which was seen to be male. Evangelically inspired 'domestic ideology', with its emphasis on the moral value of women's domestic moral and social duties and their distinction from men's public responsibilities, was increasingly influential in the early nineteenth century, especially among the middle class, though as we have seen the association of women with household tasks was hardly a new idea. Nancy Folbre has analysed the categories used in census returns to argue that the concept of the 'unproductive housewife' developed in the nineteenth century among political economists, as housewives came to be seen as 'dependants' or as 'unoccupied' in contrast to men, who worked for the market. The strongest evidence for such a change, however, comes from the second half of the century. In 1851 the census returns still included categories for women in both non-market house-

---

83 Hill, *Women, Work and Sexual Politics*, pp. 107, 116.
84 Amanda Vickery, 'Golden age to separate spheres? A review of the categories and chronology of English women's history', *Historical Journal* 36 (1993), pp. 280–1; Hall, 'History of housewife', pp. 51–2.

hold work and paid occupations, and the commentary noted that household duties in Britain were performed by both 'the husband' and 'the housewife'.[85]

Nonetheless, it is possible that the increasing physical separation of home and the workplace during industrialisation helped reduce the already limited amount of household work performed by men. As middle-class men increasingly left home to go to work, women were left at home to do the housework, with fewer opportunities to participate in their husband's occupation. Although many middle-class families still lived close to their workplaces, living spaces within the home began to be divided, with areas of men's work, whether the shop or the study, separated from the kitchen and other domestic areas.[86] By the mid-nineteenth century some men appear to have had very little interest in domestic duties: it has been noted that even the feminist John Stuart Mill performed only one domestic chore: he made tea when he returned home in the evening. Similarly, there is some evidence that working-class husbands who helped with the housework were regarded as 'unmanly'.[87]

It may be that the vast increase in the use of female domestic servants during this period, especially among the middle class, helped push men away from domestic duties. When the wife had no one else to turn to, husbands helped out with the less gendered household tasks, but when there were servants to do the work, there was no perceived need for male participation. Although servants performed the most tedious and laborious of household tasks, wives were not totally relieved of domestic activities. Even though she had a waiting woman and three maids, Elizabeth Pepys was kept busy planning purchases, shopping, cooking, doing needlework and 'participat[ing] when required in the household wash'.[88] Two hundred years later, according to Davidoff and Hall, middle-class wives were still involved in some aspects of housework including sewing, cooking, overseeing the buying of provisions, and childcare (discussed in the next section). Although 'genteel women in the wealthiest households' had much less to do (if they had a housekeeper

85 Cited by Hill, *Women, Work and Sexual Politics*, p. 122; Nancy Folbre, 'The unproductive housewife: her evolution in nineteenth-century economic thought', *Signs* 16 (1991), pp. 463–84, esp. pp. 470–1.

86 Davidoff and Hall, *Family Fortunes*, p. 359.

87 Cited by John Tosh, 'Domesticity and manliness in the Victorian middle class: the family of Edward White Benson', *Manful Assertions: Masculinities in Britain since 1800*, ed. Michael Roper and John Tosh (1991), p. 49; Clark, *Struggle for the Breeches*, p. 256.

88 *Diary of Samuel Pepys, Volume 10: Companion*, p. 196.

they did not even have to supervise the servants), they still arranged
flowers, did fancy embroidery, and possibly distilled flower essences
and baked special confections.[89] The more servants there were, the
less housework there was for wives, but they still had to manage the
household and they continued to take an interest in cooking and
the overall appearance of the house.

With the exception of purchasing certain luxury items, and assisting wives in the purchase of furniture and carpets,[90] middle-class
men did none of this, but in theory they did retain control of the
running of the household, including the hiring and firing of servants and overall control of the finances. This could be difficult,
given the contradiction between men's expected patriarchal control
of the household and their lack of involvement in its day-to- day
running. Conduct books were somewhat ambiguous on this point,
but in general they told wives to manage domestic affairs, subject to
their husband's instructions or veto. Thus *The English Matron* advised wives in 1846 that a wife should have 'the daily command of
her household, subject to a reference from her husband'.[91] Actual
arrangements no doubt depended on the personality and skills of
the individuals involved, but they often echo this advice. Elizabeth
Pepys supervised the Pepys household and appointed and dismissed
most of the female servants. Yet as head of the household Samuel
took considerable interest in the conduct of his servants and once
ordered his wife to beat a disobedient maid.[92] Davidoff and Hall
found evidence among the middle class of wives supervising the servants, but noted that the husbands 'retained ultimate authority,
and, except in female headed households, the mistress acted only as
deputy'.[93] It is less clear who controlled the family finances. As the
primary shoppers and supervisors of the servants, wives clearly
played an important role. Among the lower class such basic expenses were likely to consume virtually the total family income; this
may explain the practice among some nineteenth-century working husbands of giving their wives total control over expenditures.
David Vincent found from his analysis of working-class autobiographies that 'the wife was in charge of the household budget.' In
wealthier households women's responsibilities often included not
only the management of the accounts but also on occasion the run-

---

89 Davidoff and Hall, *Family Fortunes*, pp. 380–8, quote at 388.
90 Ibid., p. 387.
91 *The English Matron* (1846), p. 23.
92 *Diary of Samuel Pepys*, 6, p. 39 (19 February 1665).
93 Davidoff and Hall, *Family Fortunes*, pp. 384, 391.

ning of estates. This applied particularly if their husbands spent long periods of time away from home, and to the property wives had brought to the marriage, which they could expect to inherit if they were widowed. Nonetheless, husbands retained the ultimate legal control over all the property in a marriage, except where their options were limited by legal devices such as separate estates.[94]

The husband's authority as head of the household also extended to moral and religious issues, though here too there was a potential conflict between female action and male control. Conduct books throughout the period told husbands to lead the family prayers and assume responsibility for the moral and religious welfare of their wives and the rest of the household. In 1659, husbands were told to provide instruction to their wives 'in the things that concern her eternal welfare'; two centuries later, the husband was told to 'consider himself the divinely appointed priest of his own household'.[95] Yet women were expected to lead the family prayers if their husbands were absent. Wives were also expected to contribute to the moral and spiritual welfare of their spouses, but only indirectly, through example and persuasion, so as not to undermine their husband's authority. To convince a husband not to drink too much, for example, the wife was told to make 'herself and her house agreeable in a degree superior to which those scenes [drunkenness] pretend'.[96]

With the growing importance, stimulated by evangelicalism, given to the positive moral influence women could exert in the home, conduct books from the late eighteenth century advised women to take a more active role in improving their husbands, who in their daily lives were exposed to the corruption of the public world. Wives were encouraged to 'endeavour to correct any deviation from the path of Christian rectitude' (1797), to 'mildly correct' husbands who were behaving uncharitably (1813), and 'gently to combat all that is faulty and weak in her husband's character' (1846).[97] Although conduct-book writers stressed that women

---

94 Snell, *Annals of the Labouring Poor*, p. 357; Vincent, *Bread, Knowledge and Freedom*, p. 53; Fletcher, *Gender, Sex and Subordination*, pp. 174–9; Amy Louise Erickson, *Women and Property in Early Modern England* (1993), pp. 225–7.

95 [Richard Allestree], *The Whole Duty of Man* (1659; 1703 edn), p. 304; W. B. MacKenzie, *Married Life, Its Duties, Trials, Joys* (1850, 2nd edn 1852), p. 120.

96 Juliana-Susannah Seymour [pseudonym for John Hill], *The Conduct of a Married Life* (1753), p. 16.

97 Thomas Gisborne, *An Enquiry into the Duties of the Female Sex* (1797), pp. 246–7; John Ovington, *The Duties, Advantages, Pleasures and Sorrows, of the Marriage State* (1813), pp. 66–74; *English Matron*, p. 184.

should not forget their subservient position, those who attempted to reform their husbands in this manner clearly threatened the balance of power in a marriage. How common such behaviour was and what its consequences were for marital relations are impossible to determine, though there is some evidence of women taking over from men in encouraging family religiosity in the second half of our period, even to the extent of leading family prayers.[98] The idea that wives could reform men is also present among working-class men in the nineteenth century, who appear to have seen marriage as a means of becoming, in the words of a self-improving compositor, 'the most respectable, and the most intellectual and humanised (I cannot think of a better word) of their class'.[99]

In sum, the sexual division of labour at home, which was already distinctly gendered in the seventeenth century, appears to have been further accentuated over the course of our period as a result of economic and ideological changes which undermined men's participation in domestic life and, as we shall see, removed work opportunities for some wives. Although there was some overlap in the distribution of domestic tasks between husbands and wives, household work was almost as gendered as the conduct books prescribed. Such differences in the allocation of tasks necessary to keep the household going were echoed in childcare, as we shall see in the next section. The separation of male and female activities gave women autonomy in some marriages, but in general the patriarchal character of marriage continued, since most men sought to retain the ultimate decision-making powers: the conflicts which this situation gave rise to are evident in the wife-beating cases which persist throughout this period.

MOTHERHOOD AND FATHERHOOD

Like housework, the day-to-day care of babies and children was clearly the wife's responsibility throughout this period, though fathers played an important peripheral role. And like housework, it is is possible that the activity of child-rearing became even more gendered over the course of the period as a result of the growing influence of the ideology of separate spheres. An increasing emphasis placed on motherhood may have also been encouraged by the

98 Trumbach, *The Rise of the Egalitarian Family*, p. 145; Davidoff and Hall, *Family Fortunes*, p. 384.
99 Quoted by Vincent, *Bread, Knowledge and Freedom*, p. 55.

changing attitudes towards female sexuality in the second half of our period discussed in Chapter 3.

Maternal care for children was seen as natural. In a book published in 1673 and reprinted several times over the next 114 years, Richard Allestree wrote that 'a mother is a title of so much tenderness . . . that nature seems to have secured the love of mothers to their children.'[100] Yet women did not have a monopoly on child raising. The mother's responsibility was greatest with babies and young children and decreased to some extent after the age of seven, especially for boys. (By this point many mothers will have had younger children consuming their attention.) Childbirth was a primarily female domain, as midwives and nurses were joined by female kin and neighbours. No men were present, with the possible exception of the father and, in the second half of our period among better-off families, a male midwife.[101] The lying-in extended this period in which women resided in a largely female domain, which arguably gave them a degree of power; there followed the religious ceremony of 'churching'. Although originally a possibly humiliating ritual which 'purified' new mothers from the sinful taint of sex and childbirth, by our period churching was popular among women because it 'legitimated the wider ceremony of childbirth' which they controlled.[102] Mothers dominated the care of babies and young children. As the Marquis of Halifax wrote in his manual of advice to his daughter in 1688, 'the first part of our life is a good deal subjected to you in the nursery, where you reign without competition.' Although women were often aided by wet nurses (in elite families, especially at the start of our period), and female servants, many mothers devoted 'a good deal of their time' to their children; Linda Pollock has noted that mothers who wrote diaries in the eighteenth century (there are few before then) claimed to devote 'every waking moment to the care of their offspring'.[103]

Fathers also took considerable interest in their children's upbringing, especially as they got older, though theirs was a very different role. According to Anthony Fletcher, 'there is much evidence in diaries and letters of the intense involvement husbands often

100 [Richard Allestree], *The Ladies Calling* (1673), p. 201.
101 For the increasing use of male midwives, see below, Chapter 5, pp. 182–3.
102 Fletcher, *Gender, Sex and Subordination*, p. 187; Adrian Wilson, 'The ceremony of childbirth and its interpretation', in *Women as Mothers in Pre-Industrial England*, ed. V. Fildes (1990), pp. 78–9, 88–93.
103 Halifax, *Lady's New Year's Gift*, p. 28; Stone, *Family, Sex and Marriage*, p. 449; Linda Pollock, *Forgotten Children: Parent–Child Relations from 1500 to 1900* (Cambridge, 1983), p. 120.

showed in their wives' pregnancies, in childbirth and in concern about infants, even if the day-to-day management of babies was seen as effeminate and not men's business.' Fathers performed few of the daily tasks of raising children, though some participated in selected activities as a matter of personal choice. James Boswell was delighted to learn that the Duke of Gloucester 'put his little daughter to bed every night', as he did; but it is significant that he found this worth noting.[104] More often fathers devoted time to playing with their children, reading with them, and going on walks and other outings. But often these recreational and instructional activities were quite limited. The Reverend Philip Frances reported in a letter to his absent wife that 'the two children and I played together this morning about half an hour on the carpet', which suggests this was not a common activity for him.[105]

Fathers saw their primary role as providing economic support, authority, and discipline, and in preparing their children for a career. Fathers were expected, and expected themselves, to provide economic support for the family, and viewed themselves as personal failures when they were unable to provide it.[106] In addition, they controlled all-important decisions affecting their children's future – from the choice of whether the child should be wet-nursed or breast-fed by its mother (it was reported in 1695 that 'very oft the father is unwilling that his wife should undertake this office') to questions of schooling, apprenticeship, careers, and choice of marriage partners, though in some marriages, such as that of Ralph Josselin, wives had considerable influence.[107] Fathers also enforced discipline, though there are a number of examples where mothers, who were the front-line troops in the battle against childhood misbehaviour, carried out punishments themselves.[108] Depending on their temperament, fathers used a variety of disciplinary strategies, ranging from the permissive to the authoritarian, but they always retained ultimate authority over their children.

One of the most important paternal functions, and one which mothers could fulfill only to a small extent and then primarily with

104 Cited by Stone, *Family, Sex and Marriage*, p. 456; Fletcher, *Gender, Sex and Subordination*, p. 184.

105 Cited by Stone, *Family, Sex and Marriage*, p. 455.

106 Davidoff and Hall, *Family Fortunes*, p. 334; Pollock, *Forgotten Children*, p. 118.

107 Valerie Fildes, *Wet Nursing: A History from Antiquity to the Present* (Oxford, 1988), pp. 83–4; Davidoff and Hall, *Family Fortunes*, p. 332; Alan MacFarlane, *The Family Life of Ralph Josselin* (Cambridge, 1970), p. 109.

108 Stone, *Family, Sex and Marriage*, pp. 461, 467, 473; Davidoff and Hall, *Family Fortunes*, p. 331.

their daughters, was helping their children, especially their sons, get started in a career. From an early age sons were acquainted with their father's work or business, and as they got older fathers often provided training and put them to work. If a father did not or could not take his son into his own business or occupation, he sought suitable apprenticeships and/or job prospects elsewhere. The non-conformist minister Henry Newcome secured an apprenticeship for his son Daniel in 1668, and when this didn't work out he arranged for him to go on a trading voyage two years later. When Daniel returned home his father tried once again to find him a job.[109] While such actions could provide a son with a crucial leg-up in life, one author complained that upper-middle-class fathers took too much control of this process out a concern for social advancement and ignored the views and qualifications of their sons: 'the genius, the natural talents, nor so much as the constitution of youth are seldom or never consulted.'[110] Lower down the social scale fathers worked equally hard training and finding jobs for their sons, but in the nineteenth century their efforts were sometimes undermined by the factory system.[111]

The one significant area of overlapping responsibilities between mothers and fathers was in moral and religious instruction and general schooling, but even here there was a division of labour. Mothers appear to have provided (or supervised) most instruction of younger children, which included reading, writing, and spelling. After middle-class boys reached the age of about six they went to school, but mothers typically continued to look after the instruction of their daughters. As children got older fathers began to play a greater role in the training of all their children, providing some religious education and teaching skills in such subjects as handling money and outdoor activities, as well as helping them prepare lessons for school.[112] Henry Newcome recorded in his diary that he 'catechized and instructed' his children, prayed with them, 'helped the boy with his Latin', and sat in on one of his son's tutorials.[113] Recalling her role as mother, Lady Sarah Lennox reported around 1820 that as her children 'rose out of infancy, I left them to their father's management, and studied to become their friend, not the

109 Wrightson, *English Society 1580–1680*, p. 110.

110 Quoted by Stone, *Family, Sex and Marriage*, p. 447; R. Campbell, *The London Tradesman* ([1747] 1969), p. 2.

111 Vincent, *Bread, Knowledge and Freedom*, pp. 66, 85.

112 Davidoff and Hall, *Family Fortunes*, pp. 331, 339–40; Stone, *Family, Sex and Marriage*, pp. 453–4.

113 Quoted in Houlbrooke, *English Family Life*, pp. 158–9.

tutoress of my sons'.[114] The distribution of the responsibility of instruction thus depended very much on the child's age and sex.

As part of the argument that this period witnessed a shift of the weight of domestic responsibilities more firmly on to women's shoulders as a consequence of evangelically inspired domestic ideology, many historians have argued that mothers took on a greater share of the child-raising responsibilities in the eighteenth and nineteenth centuries, not only among the middle class, but also within sections of the working class. In the words of Davidoff and Hall, there was a 'progession to a model of full-time motherhood'; similarly, Lawrence Stone wrote that 'the mother became the dominant figure in children's lives' over the period 1640–1800. And John Tosh suggests that in the early and mid-Victorian period motherhood acquired a greater moral importance 'than [it had] at any other time', as 'all questions relating to the upbringing of children were increasingly resolved by the mother.'[115]

Some compelling evidence can be marshalled in support of this argument. A study of child-rearing manuals from the seventeenth through the nineteenth centuries using content-analysis methodology revealed that, while such manuals were aimed at both mothers and fathers in the seventeenth century, in the next century they were targetted at mothers only, 'with some anxiety expressed about this', and in the nineteenth century they were aimed at mothers without such anxiety.[116] Ruth Perry uses two different types of evidence in support of her claim that maternity became 'a serious duty and responsibility' for women in the eighteenth century: literature, and the practice of wet nursing. In literature, 'newer "feminine" sentiments were being elicited and demonstrated by the novels of the age – sentiments connected with maternity, such as pity, tenderness, and benevolence.' This was reinforced by the parallel decline in wet nursing in the eighteenth century, as middle- and upper-class mothers adopted the new fashion of maternal breast-feeding. Thus, Perry argues, women came to be defined more in terms of their maternal functions than their sexuality. In the nineteenth century, according to John Tosh, the evangelical stress on

114 Quoted by Stone, *Family, Sex and Marriage*, p. 456.

115 Clark, *Struggle for the Breeches*, part 3; Davidoff and Hall, *Family Fortunes*, p. 338; Stone, *Family, Sex and Marriage*, p. 448; John Tosh, 'Authority and nurture in middle-class fatherhood: the case of early and mid-Victorian England', *Gender and History* 8 (1996), pp. 53, 59.

116 Abigail J. Stewart, David G. Winter, and A. David Jones, 'Coding categories for the study of child-rearing from historical sources', *Journal of Interdisciplinary History* 5 (1975), p. 701.

the mother's responsibilities for the moral upbringing of her children even 'extended to the manliness of her son'.[117]

Parallel arguments have been made about the withdrawal of men from child raising. With the separation of work from home, it is often thought that men spent less time with their children and correspondingly had less interest in their upbringing. According to Barbara Fass Leavy, 'a study of *The British Mothers' Magazine* from its inception in 1845 till it ceased publication in 1864 suggests that the mother acquired increased importance at the expense of father, whose role became increasingly passive, his patriarchal authority paradoxically exercised in response to what was becoming his intensifying helplessness and dependency in family matters.' Tosh argues that by the mid-nineteenth century a number of factors had altered the relationship between middle-class fathers and their children: the increasing use of nurseries in middle-class homes; economic changes which made it more difficult for fathers to secure jobs for their sons; the increasing ideological importance placed on the mother's moral qualifications for child rearing; and a growing concern that fathers needed to be hard-hearted in order to prepare their sons for the harshness of the public world. Although Tosh stresses that a number of different approaches to fatherhood can be found in the nineteenth century, he argues that the most common was the emotionally distant father, who cared deeply about his children but withheld those feelings from them. Thus, it has been argued that the boys who became successful middle-class businessmen in nineteenth-century Bradford experienced far closer and more intense relationships with their mothers than with their fathers during their upbringing.[118]

It would seem, then, that increasing ideological emphasis was given to maternity during this period, which, together with economic and other changes, undermined the role of fathers. But we should note that much of the evidence for this argument is prescriptive, that evidence of changing practices is so far somewhat limited and derives mostly from the middle class, and that this

---

117 Ruth Perry, 'Colonizing the breast: sexuality and maternity in eighteenth-century England', *Journal of the History of Sexuality* 2 (1991), pp. 204–34, esp. p. 215. For the decline of wet nursing, see also Fildes, *Wet Nursing,* chs 8 and 12; John Tosh, *Men at Home: Domesticity and the Victorian Middle Class* (forthcoming), ch. 5. I am grateful to Professor Tosh for allowing me to read and cite from his manuscript in advance of publication.

118 Barbara Fass Leavy, 'Fathering and *The British Mother's Magazine,* 1845–1864', *Victorian Periodicals Review* 13, (1980), pp. 10–17; Tosh, 'Authority and nurture', pp. 54–9; Tosh, *Men at Home,* ch. 4; Koditschek, *Class Formation and Urban-Industrial Society,* p. 188.

evidence must be placed alongside considerable evidence of continuities in the gendering of childcare. Most mothers had always
taken the primary responsibility for childraising. The majority of
women had always breast-fed their children, for example, since
lower-class women could not afford wet nurses and even in the
seventeenth century many middle- and upper-class women (43%,
according to diary evidence) chose to breast-feed their own children.[119] Men, on the other hand, had always played only a limited, if
significant, role in raising their children. Even in 1748, William Cad-
ogan, a physician who specialised in children, complained that, although men clearly made the decision about whether or not their
child was to be breast-fed, they had no interest in the process. Instead, they 'suffer it to be made one of the mysteries of the *Bona
Dea*, from which men are to be excluded'.[120] As we have seen with
respect to housework, the significance of the growing separation of
home and work for men's domestic responsibilities has been exaggerated, partly because a large proportion of men still worked in or
near their home at the end of our period, and partly because
middle-class men had always restricted their role in child raising to
decision-making and relatively peripheral activities such as playing
with them, going on Sunday walks, and finding employment opportunities. We have little evidence of the role played by working-class
husbands, who may well have been forced to play a greater role in
childcare due to the lack of servants. Among the middle class, even
at the end of our period there is strong evidence that fathers continued to participate in domestic decision-making and family intimacy.
While paternal emotions may have been more hidden, Tosh points
out that early Victorian fathers continued to assume 'an acute sense
of personal responsibility' for their children's future.[121] In sum,
there is no evidence that nineteenth-century fathers spent considerably less time with their children than in earlier periods. On the
basis of the present available evidence it is best to conclude that, although the gendered division of childcare responsibilities may have
been somewhat accentuated, it is the continuities in parental roles
over this long period rather than the changes which are most striking.

119 Pollock, *Forgotten Children*, p. 215.
120 Cited by Fildes, *Wet Nursing*, p. 114.
121 Tosh, 'Domesticity and manliness', pp. 60–1; *idem*, 'Authority and nuture',
p. 54.

THE EXPERIENCE OF CHILDHOOD

While growing up, children not only witnessed the contrasting gender roles adopted by their mothers and fathers, but were themselves treated very differently according to their sex. By the time they reached adulthood, boys and girls had very different skills, characteristics, and expectations. As Sarah Stickney Ellis complained in 1843, from their very infancy boys were 'accustomed to a mode of treatment as much calculated to make them determined, frank and bold, as that of girls to induce the opposite extremes of weakness, artifice, and timid helplessness'.[122] Although child-rearing manuals (including those written by Ellis) noted and encouraged gender differentiation most strongly in the nineteenth century, in practice parents treated boys and girls very differently throughout the period.

Even at birth, in some cases sons were welcomed more than daughters, especially among the upper classes where it was important to ensure the continuity of the family name and estate through a male heir. When his daughter gave birth to a girl in 1671, Thomas Chichely assured her that 'although it be a girle that God hath sent', 'in time' she would have a boy as well.[123] Unlike in some cultures, this did not extend to deliberate infanticide of girls, but such preferential attitudes may nonetheless have affected their life chances. There is some evidence of differential mortality rates between girls and boys, especially among younger daughters in larger families, which suggests that some female children may have been relatively neglected by their parents. But there is no actual evidence of such neglect, and in fact a recent study of seventeenth-century probate accounts concluded that virtually identical amounts of money were spent on maintaining sons and daughters.[124] Likewise, there is no evidence that decisions about maternal breastfeeding and the age of weaning depended on the sex of the child. More research is needed, both to document and to explain differential childhood mortality rates.

During childhood boys and girls learned about gender from observing the actions of adult men and women. From a psychoanalytic

122 Sarah Ellis, *The Wives of England* [1843], p. 85.
123 Cited by Patricia Crawford, 'The construction and experience of maternity in seventeenth-century England', in *Women as Mothers in Pre-Industrial England*, ed. V. Fildes (1990), pp. 19–20.
124 Richard Wall, 'Inferring differential neglect of females from mortality data', *Annales de Demographie Historique* (1981), pp. 119–40; Erickson, *Women and Property in Early Modern England*, p. 50.

perspective, Nancy Chodorow has suggested that the kind of gender differentation in parenting discussed in the previous section could, through its impact on the unconcious in infants and children, have a significant impact on the development of female and male personalities. Both boys and girls spent far more time with their mothers than their fathers, she argues, but girls were expected to emulate their mothers and boys their fathers. Because mothers were present girls could form close personal relationships with them; boys, on the other hand, were forced to distance themselves from their mothers' feminine influence, and were unable to form such close relationships with their fathers. As a consequence, as adults women were more adept at interpersonal relations, while men were more independent, but also more insecure. Although arguments concerning the development of the unconscious are difficult to prove, this theory may be particularly relevant to understanding nineteenth-century gender roles. Because the role of mothers in upbringing was even greater in the mid-nineteenth century than at other times, Tosh argues, middle-class men found it difficult to achieve a secure sense of masculine identity, and this insecurity arguably helps explain the persistence of domestic violence (despite increasing public revulsion) and the phenomenon of the Victorian 'tyrannical father' in this period.[125]

Chodorow's theory is not inconsistent with what we know about the impact of the process of socialisation on the development of gender identity in this period. From at least the age of five there is strong evidence that boys and girls were socialised differently. Davidoff and Hall note that 'very small children were dressed and treated more alike but by the age of 5 or 6, boys were taken out of petticoats in the ritual of breeching, the first step towards manhood', while girls continued to wear petticoats. The awareness of gender difference thus encouraged was reinforced by the different toys and games they played with. According to Davidoff and Hall, middle-class boys played with 'hoops, balls, and other toys associated with physical activities' while girls played with 'dolls, doll houses, needlebooks, and miniature work baskets'. Children also learned about gender from their observations of the different tasks performed by their mothers and fathers (and by male and female servants in the household) as well as the considerably greater authority exercised by their fathers both at home and in the wider

---

125 Nancy Chodorow, 'Family structure and feminine personality', in *Women, Culture, and Society*, ed. M. Z. Rosaldo and L. Lamphere (Stanford, 1974), pp. 43–66; Tosh, 'Authority and nurture', pp. 59–60.

world. Moreover, parents actively encouraged the development of different personality traits in boys and girls. While boys were encouraged to be aggressive and physically tough, girls were expected to be more polite and sensitive and have higher standards of cleanliness.[126] Concern was expressed when girls were rude, or boys cried: Sir Ralph Verney questioned in private a boy of twelve he was looking after 'about crying when he is chid[ed], and he tells me t'was only after his last sickness, and that he hath left it.'[127] As middle-class boys grew older, they were taught skills in time management and accounting and encouraged to become diligent and independent. In contrast, their sisters learned about duty, self-sacrifice, and submission to authority. Yet it is important to note that, among the propertied classes at any rate, girls were allowed to be spirited and wilful, as long as they also knew when to be modest, humble, and obedient. Because such girls would grow up to preside over estates which they would often need to manage during their husbands' absences, their upbringing was designed, Linda Pollock argues, 'to induce selective deference and subordination rather than produce incompetent, spineless women'.[128]

Schooling reinforced gender differences. Boys were much more likely to leave home to go to school (from the age of six or seven), while girls were usually trained at home, often by their mothers. Wealthy families often provided male tutors for their sons or sent them to all-male boarding schools, where they were virtually deprived of female company. The growing number of schools for girls during this period led to a significant improvement in female education, but it did not alter the fact that, as we shall see, the sexes were educated quite differently. While, depending on their class, boys learned Greek and Latin, accounting, vocational skills, or simply reading and writing, girls learned domestic and finishing skills, or just reading and/or sewing. Not only did boys and girls learn different skills, but schooling exacerbated personality differences. While boys' grammar schools and public schools encouraged self-control, endurance, striving, and athletic prowess, girls were taught subservience and to combat vanity and pride.[129]

126 Davidoff and Hall, *Family Fortunes*, p. 344.
127 Miriam Slater, *Family Life in the Seventeenth Century: The Verneys of Claydon House* (1984), p. 130.
128 Hunt, *The Middling Sort*, chs 2 and 3; Linda Pollock, ' "Teach her to live under obedience": the making of women in the upper ranks of early modern England', *Continuity and Change* 4 (1989), p. 246.
129 Fletcher, *Gender, Sex and Subordination*, chs 15 and 18; David Newsome, *Godliness and Good Learning: Four Studies on a Victorian Ideal* (1961); below, Chapter 5, pp. 193–4.

Schooling, especially for girls, was often interrupted by the need to contribute to the family economy. Among poorer families children were expected to help out from a very early age. Ben-Amos found that 'the division of tasks between boys and girls, especially among the very poor, was anything but clear-cut', with both performing tasks such as 'fetching water and milk, gathering sticks, picking and spreading dung, and doing errands'. But gender divisions were not slow to develop, even among childhood chores, as children grew older, especially in wealthier families. When growing up, William Stout and his brothers helped with husbandry, while his sister Elin worked with their mother in childcare, cooking, and sewing.[130]

Such differences were accentuated by the fact that children, especially sons (who would carry on the family name), were being prepared for their future careers. As we have seen, fathers undertook the responsibility of laying the groundwork for their sons' future careers, by providing suitable training and helping them find jobs. At an early age, boys often assisted their fathers at work. In Kent, Surrey, and Sussex in 1843, it was 'very common for the flail and the sickle to hang in labourers' cottages, where they are seen by the young [boys], and looked at as implements of manly labour . . . they are sometimes carried, partly as a toy and partly as a tool, by the young husbandman to the scene of labour, which he soon fills seriously and for life.'[131] The responsibilities given to sons accrued with age: the fourteen-year-old Thomas Isham accompanied his father into the fields 'to decide where new ditches should be dug and hedges set'.[132] David Vincent's analysis of nineteenth-century male working-class autobiographies demonstrates that working-class boys were strongly influenced by their father's occupational identity, and depended on their fathers 'for a major contribution in the arrangement of [their] own occupational future'.[133] Although the lack of equivalent female writings unfortunately makes it difficult to compare the experiences of boys and girls, it is likely that girls fell more under the influence of their mothers and were less influenced than their brothers by their father's occupational identity. According to one middle-class father, 'daughters neither require nor admit of the same tuition' as sons.[134] Davidoff and Hall report that the associ-

---

130 Ilana Ben-Amos, *Adolescence and Youth in Early Modern England* (1994), p. 42.
131 *Parliamentary Papers: Report on the Employment of Women and Children in Agriculture* (1843), p. 133.
132 Cited by Houlbrooke, *English Family Life*, p. 165.
133 Vincent, *Bread, Knowledge and Freedom*, pp. 8–9, 64–74, esp. p. 66.
134 Quoted in Davidoff and Hall, *Family Fortunes*, p. 332.

ation of men with manufacture started with childhood play, where boys played with drawings, tools, and pieces of machinery; girls who showed talents in this direction were not encouraged. While boys developed career skills, girls, as Margaret Hunt has argued, were taught to subordinate 'their individual needs and aspirations to the labour needs of the family group'. Since what the family needed most from girls was housework and (depending on economic position) extra income from piece work, sewing was the key skill which most girls were taught.[135]

As a consequence of these sex-specific child-rearing practices, closer, if sometimes more contentious, relationships formed between fathers and sons, and mothers and daughters, than between parents and children of the opposite sex. We have seen that fathers supervised their sons' education and acquisition of career skills, while appearing to be less interested in their daughters' fate (except when it came to marriage). The father/son relationship was not always happy or close, but it had an intensity not found in father/daughter relations: Francis Place wrote that his father beat and terrorised his sons, but never touched his daughters.[136] It has been suggested that the economic partnerships formed between fathers and sons in commerce helped sustain male domination by teaching sons 'to sustain their position through the subordination and objectification of desirably "dependent" women'.[137] Since daughters, unlike sons, often did not leave home until marriage, mothers and daughters spent more time together than the male half of the family and formed closer and more complicated personal relationships, and therefore mothers may have had even more influence over their daughters. According to Harriet Blodgett, in their diaries women indicate 'a conscious willingness to take their mothers . . . as models and mentors, not to mention what they take in without conscious will'.[138]

Historians are coming to realise that the transition to adulthood (from the mid-teens to the mid-twenties) formed a significant stage of development in this period in which a limited degree of independence was achieved, but this experience was very different for boys and girls. Although some sons remained at home because they

---

135 Ibid., pp. 311–12; Hunt, *The Middling Sort*, pp. 81–3.

136 Stone, *Family, Sex and Marriage*, p. 469.

137 Shawn Lisa Maurer, ' "As sacred as friendship, as pleasurable as love": father–son relations in the *Tatler* and *Spectator*', *History, Gender and Eighteenth-Century Literature*, ed. Beth Fowkes Tobin (Athens, Georgia, 1994), pp. 14–38.

138 Harriet Blodgett, *Centuries of Female Days: Englishwomen's Private Diaries* (New Brunswick, NJ, 1988), p. 230.

expected to inherit the family business, teenage boys (who may have already attended school from around the age of six) were more likely than their sisters to leave home to take up an apprenticeship or a job. In the exaggerated prose of Robert Campbell, 'a youth may be set afloat in the world as soon as he has got a trade in his head ... but a girl is such a tender, ticklish plant to rear, that there is no permitting her out of leading-strings till she is bound to a husband.' Leaving home so early could be traumatic, but it was seen, in the words of Davidoff and Hall, 'as part of the hardening process of becoming a man'. Because boys needed to learn how to become independent, they needed to sever their dependence on their mothers. Often this led them to join a youth culture which, for those not brought up in a godly environment, was characterised by drinking, fighting, and sexual promiscuity.[139]

In contrast, where possible daughters stayed at home until marriage, but due to the death of parents or economic need many daughters left home in their mid-teens in order to work, often as domestic servants. (If their fathers had died, however, daughters often stayed with their mothers.) Like boys of all social classes, working-class young women in their late teens and early twenties experienced a degree of relative independence and responsibility which was denied to women of the same age who were their social superiors. Nonetheless, while men in their twenties often lived independently, young women in service typically lived in their master's household before marriage, except when, as was often the case, they were unemployed.[140]

This section has outlined the socialisation processes which shaped the gender roles of men and women from the early childhood years to adulthood. Although the impact on children of the increasing value placed on motherhood in the period is difficult to measure, the upbringing process does not appear to have changed much over the course of this period. We can see clearly from this evidence how gender roles were perpetuated from generation to generation, as children learned both from how they were treated by adults and from watching their parents and servants the different patterns of behaviour expected from each sex. Such differences

139 Campbell, *London Tradesman*, p. 228; Davidoff and Hall, *Family Fortunes*, p. 345; Fletcher, *Gender, Sex and Subordination*, p. 92. Gender differences in experiences of apprenticeship are discussed below, in Chapter 5, pp. 194–5.

140 Ben-Amos, *Adolescence and Youth in Early Modern England*, pp. 229–32; Patricia Seleski, 'Women, work and cultural change in eighteenth and early nineteenth-century London', in *Popular Culture in England, c. 1500–1800*, ed. Tim Harris (1995), p. 149.

were probably greatest among the middle and upper classes, where families could afford to educate boys and girls separately, enforce standards of cleanliness among girls, and keep daughters at home until marriage. In contrast, the demands of work shaped lower-class children's experiences from an early age, and especially among young children the sexual division of labour was minimal. Nonetheless, as children grew older, both the household chores and paid employments they performed were increasingly gendered.

MEN AND WOMEN OUTSIDE MARRIAGE

Up to this point this chapter has assumed that all adult men and women were married, but this was clearly not the case. Not only did men and women often not get married until they were in their late twenties, but high mortality led to a marital breakdown rate of a similar magnitude to that created by the large number of divorces today. Moreover, a significant number of women and men never married at all. Yet the existence of significant numbers of unmarried, previously married, and never married men and women did not threaten the family, or the gender roles shaped by family and household life, in part because such people were frequently members of a household as servants, kin, or lodgers. We have already seen that in the years prior to marriage young women often remained at home, and when they did leave home they frequently lived and worked as domestic servants in other households. Men were more likely to live independently in the period between leaving home and marriage, though when they did so they occasionally created their own households by hiring female servants to do their household chores. Although male apprentices and servants often lived in the homes of their masters or employers, this practice declined over the course of this period.

On the other hand, when a spouse died it was men who were more likely to move quickly to reestablish a family unit. While widowers typically remarried after a short period, widows were much less likely to do so. Together with the fact that women married earlier than men and typically lived longer, this explains why there were far more widows than widowers in the population. This is a difficult point to establish statistically, because men are very rarely identified in records by their marital status (while women are often *only* identified this way), but in a sample of 4118 male and female householders who were liable to the poll tax in late-seventeenth-century

London, D. V. Glass found only 48 widowers and 142 widows. It is probable that the ratio of widows to widowers was even larger, since many widows were too poor to pay the poll tax or resided with other family members and thus were not identified as householders.[141] In the late seventeenth century, Gregory King estimated that there were 89,500 widowers and 273,800 widows in England. Remarriage rates for both sexes fell over the subsequent 150 years, and the ratio of widows to widowers appears to have declined: according to the 1851 census there were only twice as many widows as widowers.[142]

Much less is known about widowers than about widows, but it is likely that they remarried more frequently for the simple reasons that they were richer, and they wanted help with the household chores, especially if young children were present, as well as in some cases assistance with their work. A late-eighteenth-century Essex farmer explained his reasons for remarrying: 'man was not born to live alone. Having experienced much comfort in the married state, and my children requiring some careful female to manage and bring them up, I soon determined to look out again.'[143] As Amy Erickson put it, such men were more likely to remarry than hire help since 'it was more economical for a man to marry his house-keeper than to pay her.' Although young women who had never married were preferred (they did not have children from a previous marriage to provide for), among the working class in the second half of the period widows with children were sought after by miners, fishermen, and weavers, all of whom needed the additional cheap labour the children could provide. As Erickson concludes, the fact that men were far less likely to live alone than women shows that 'men were actually more dependent on women's labour than the reverse.'[144]

In contrast, only between 16 and 24% of the women in one parish in the late seventeenth century who lost their husbands married again.[145] There are a number of explanations for the low remarriage rate among widows. People were frequently suspicious or hos-

141 D. V. Glass, 'Socio-economic status and occupations in the City of London at the end of the seventeenth-century', in *Studies in London History Presented to P. E. Jones*, eds, A. E. Hollaender and W. Kellaway (1969), table 5.

142 Joan Thirsk and J. P. Cooper (eds), *Seventeenth-Century Economic Documents* (Oxford, 1972), p. 773; *Parliamentary Papers: Census of Great Britain, 1851, Part II* (1854), 1, p. cci.

143 Quoted in Davidoff and Hall, *Family Fortunes*, p. 325.

144 Erickson, *Women and Property in Early Modern England*, p. 195; Gillis, *For Better, For Worse*, p. 123.

145 Barbara Todd, 'The remarrying widow: a stereotype reconsidered', *Women in English Society 1500–1800*, ed. Mary Prior (1985), p. 60.

tile towards widows in this period, no doubt because they were seen to have no social role, they were not subject to any male authority, and they were seen as a potential financial burden on the parish. In an earlier period, of course, they had often been suspected of witchcraft. Yet, there was also social and religious criticism of widows remarrying, which is reflected in negative stereotypes. Because widows were expected to remain loyal to their deceased husbands, remarriages were thought to result from base motives. Having been introduced to sexual activity by their late husbands, widows were thought to be sexually voracious. According to a contemporary proverb:

> He that woos a maid, must fain lie and flatter
> But he that woos a widow, must down with his breeches and at her.[146]

While widows were thought to marry for lust, it was thought that men chose widows for brides primarily for their money. Although this was sometimes prevented by legal constraints placed around widows' inheritances, this popular belief provides further evidence of the prevailing hostile attitude towards remarrying widows. Husbands were of course especially unhappy about the possibility that after their deaths other men might replace them in their beds.

Many widows, however, had their own reasons not to remarry. Some declined offers out of continuing feelings for their former husbands. Others sought to enjoy their new freedom and status as head of a household, a status which gave them for the first time control over their lives and property. Sara Mendelson noted that some female diarists responded to their husbands' deaths with 'barely disguised relief'. Barbara Todd cites the diary of Katherine Austen, a London widow who lived in the late seventeenth century, who chose not to remarry primarily because she wanted to preserve her legal rights in order to protect the interests of her children. The idea that widows chose to remain unmarried in order to enjoy their new-found freedom and rights is also evident in some published writings, though Todd notes that it 'appears only in obscure works, not widely circulated'.[147] Among aristocratic women, the increasing value placed on 'rational friendship' in the late seventeenth and eighteenth centuries led to the formation of extramarital platonic relationships with both sexes which legitimised delay or refusal of

---

146 Cited in Sharpe, 'Plebeian marriage', p. 74.
147 Mendelson, 'Stuart women's diaries', pp. 198–9; Todd, 'The remarrying widow', pp. 55, 77, 82.

offers of remarriage or even of a first marriage.[148] For some women, there were also financial advantages to remaining single. Out of a concern to protect the interests of the children, husbands occasionally included in their wills penalties on their widows which would deprive them of their home and/or their land if they remarried. Between 7 and 10% of husbands in the late seventeenth century imposed such limitations.[149]

Whether a widow could actually maintain her standard of living without the presence of a husband depended on a number of factors, including her status and wealth, the occupation of her deceased husband and whether she was familiar with her husband's occupation. The socio-economic position of widows varied considerably. Generally, those most likely to stay single were the rich and the poor; the former because they could afford to, and the latter because their poverty rendered them undesirable candidates for remarriage. Through marriage settlements which preserved their 'separate estate', elite and middle-class women were often well provided for. Aristocratic widows had the opportunity to pursue masculine activities such as managing their estates and engaging in lawsuits without interference.[150] Gentry and middle-class widows often invested their money in loans or property and lived off the proceeds; recent research suggests that widows 'owned a sizeable proportion of the London housing stock' and 'played a vital role in the provision of loan capital through the bond and mortgage markets'.[151] Other middle-class widows with sufficient capital could carry on the family business. (Those with less capital, but who had some resources, could only maintain their living standards by remarrying, which, because of their wealth, they were often able to do.) It was legally and socially acceptable for widows to carry on their husbands' businesses and some did so, running farms or working in male-dominated trades such as metalwork or woodworking, and prospering. Erickson notes that in the seventeenth century widows often died with the same or even greater wealth than they had received on their husband's death.[152]

148 Irene Q. Brown, 'Domesticity, feminism, and friendship: female aristocratic culture and marriage in England, 1660–1760', *Journal of Family History* 7 (1982), pp. 406–24.

149 Erickson, *Women and Property in Early Modern England*, pp. 166–7; Todd, 'The remarrying widow', pp. 72–3.

150 See, for example, Katharine Hodgkin, 'The diary of Lady Anne Clifford: a study of class and gender in the seventeenth century', *History Workshop Journal* 19 (1985), pp. 148–61.

151 Earle, *Making of the English Middle Class*, pp. 172–3.

152 Erickson, *Women and Property in Early Modern England*, p. 193.

Yet widows who tried to carry on their husbands' businesses faced a number of obstacles. First, they were often in a weak financial position. By common law they were entitled to only a third of their husband's estate (though they often received more), and the increasing use of jointures (as part of a marriage settlement) instead of dower was not always to their advantage. Moreover, the terms of many bequests prevented widows from selling property to raise capital. At the same time, the husband's death was a time of reckoning for his debts, which reduced or even eliminated the estate: in the seventeenth century, a quarter of all husbands left their widows in debt.[153] Second, widows often did not have the necessary skills to carry on their husband's business, particularly if his work had taken place outside the home and she had not had the opportunity to become acquainted with the business (as was the case with mercantile trades, seafaring occupations, and the building trades). As we have seen, however, even when they did have the opportunity, many middle-class women who sought to maintain a genteel lifestyle unsullied by trade chose not to take advantage of it.[154]

Consequently, relatively few widows carried on with their husbands' businesses, especially in predominantly male trades: Earle found that of the 295 employed widows in his sample of London church deponents, only 7% worked in occupations outside the usual female employments. Clearly, few were working in their husbands' trade. Indeed, when widows did carry on with their husband's business, they sometimes felt the need to advertise the fact publicly. Many others, faced with the difficulty of carrying on by themselves in an all-male trade, either remarried or sold up and took up a more suitable trade. Those doing the latter frequently ended up making or repairing clothing, running a food, drink, or lodging house, or teaching. The widows of wage earners or poor cottagers had even fewer opportunities: they were forced to try and piece together a living from such low-paid activities as spinning, knitting, laundry work, keeping a cow, and/or gathering shrubs, fuel, and berries from common land. With the loss of common rights through enclosure, many of these opportunities disappeared.[155]

153 Ibid., pp. 186, 200; Susan Staves, *Married Women's Separate Property in England, 1660–1833* (1990), ch. 4.

154 Ben-Amos, *Adolescence and Youth in Early Modern England*, pp. 147–8; see above, pp. 113–15.

155 Earle, *City Full of People*, p. 123; Alice Clark, *Working Life of Women in the Seventeenth Century* ([1919] 1982), pp. 169–89; Hill, *Women, Work and Sexual Politics*, p. 247; Jane Humphries, 'Enclosures, common rights, and women: the proletarianization of families in the late eighteenth and early nineteenth centuries', *Journal of Economic History* 50 (1990), pp. 17–42.

For many women widowhood was a time of poverty, the combined result of inheriting little or nothing from their husbands, the
difficulties of carrying on with their husbands' businesses, and the
low wages women received when working in traditionally female
trades. Such difficulties were compounded if they had children to
support, as was often the case. According to the London poll-tax
records from the late seventeenth century, widowers were far wealthier than their female counterparts. Whereas two-thirds of the widowers who paid tax had estates worth £300 or more, this was true of
only 19% of the widows.[156] In fact, rather than paying taxes, widows,
especially those with young children, frequently dominate poor-relief lists, despite their reluctance to ask for help (after all, with their
husbands they had usually been able to support themselves up until
widowhood). In the parish of St Peter in Derby in the late eighteenth century, almost half of the adult recipients of parish pensions
were widows.[157] Women with so little money were not, needless to
say, attractive marriage partners.

Those Who Never Married

If widows often found themselves destitute and distrusted, women
who never married were even more marginal social figures. Owing
to overseas military service, greater male than female emigration,
and lower mortality rates for women, there were more women than
men in the English population, and although some men never married, more women remained permanently single (and at far greater
cost). In 1851 there were 20% more unmarried women than men
over the age of 40 in England and Wales.[158] Certain types of women
were particularly likely never to marry. In a society where men were
expected to take the initiative in courtship, some women were probably never asked, especially if they were poor and could not contribute financially to a match. On the other hand, wealthier women
sometimes rejected all their suitors as unacceptable, often because
they were thought to be socially inferior. This was particularly common among the younger daughters of the aristocracy, who had
small portions and consequently only attracted suitors of a lower social class. Because upon marriage women took on the status of their

---

156 Glass, 'Socio-economic status and occupations', table 5.
157 Calculated from the table in Bridget Hill, *Eighteenth-Century Women: An
Anthology* (1984), pp. 166–7; Tim Wales, 'Poverty, poor relief and the life-cycle:
some evidence from seventeenth-century Norfolk', in *Land, Kinship and Life-Cycle*,
ed. Richard Smith (1984), pp. 351–404.
158 *Parliamentary Papers: Census of Great Britain, 1851, Part II* (1854), 1, p. clxv.

husbands, aristocratic women were much more reluctant than aristocratic men to marry beneath them.[159] Other women were unwilling to surrender their independence: Davidoff and Hall cite the case of an Essex woman who dreaded 'the selfishness, the littleness, the increase in worldly cares which accompanie[s] marriage'.[160]

But the most common explanations for permanent spinsterhood were probably locally imbalanced sex ratios in the population, and the responsibilities which some unmarried women took on for other members of their families. In rural protoindustrial parishes like Colyton, greater employment opportunities for women than men led to a surplus of women in the parish, many of whom never married.[161] There was a similar surplus of women in towns during this period due to the large number of women employed as servants. Some young women, having been brought up to make sacrifices for the good of the family, found themselves adopting the role of a pseudo-wife or mother and looking after a widowed or sick father or mother, or an unmarried or widowed brother, and by the time they were freed from such obligations they may have been considered too old for marriage (especially since men preferred to court younger women). According to Davidoff and Hall, younger daughters whose mother had died often did not marry until after their father's death. But even then other family members could require their services. After the father of Elin Stout (the sister of William Stout) died, Elin helped her mother with the housework, assisted her brother William in his shop and with housekeeping, looked after her mother in old age, and, in her early sixties, took care of two children of another brother. She died unmarried at the age of sixty-four. Unmarried or widowed brothers seem to have expected as a matter of course that, if requested, unmarried sisters would run their households and take care of their children. Of course, if the brother married, the sister found her presence no longer necessary. At this point, she may have been considered too old for marriage.[162]

Despite the important social functions they often filled, unmar-

---

159 Hill, *Women, Work and Sexual Politics*, pp. 222–3; Olwen Hufton, 'Women without men: widows and spinsters in Britain and France in the eighteenth century', *Journal of Family History* 9 (1984), p. 359.

160 Davidoff and Hall, *Family Fortunes*, p. 325.

161 Pamela Sharpe, 'Literally spinsters: a new interpretation of local economy and demography in Colyton in the seventeenth and eighteenth centuries', *Economic History Review* 44 (1991), pp. 46–65.

162 Davidoff and Hall, *Family Fortunes*, pp. 346–50; Hill, *Women, Work and Sexual Politics*, pp. 226–9.

ried women faced considerable prejudice. In a world in which bearing and raising children within marriage was seen as a woman's
natural role, those who didn't even marry were marginalised. During this period the word 'spinster' came to be used to designate the
unmarried state, rather than the occupation (though as we shall
see, many spinsters continued to spin), and it was largely used pejor-
atively, as was the term 'old maid', which came into use in the eighteenth century. Such women were thought to be sour and morose;
any woman who lived 'without answering the end of her creation',
according to William Hayley, must be 'utterly devoid of tenderness
and of every amiable sensation'.[163] Since the family was a fundamental social unit, men who remained single could also be
viewed suspiciously, but there were fewer of them and they faced
much less prejudice. Moreover, if such men hired a servant they
could still head a household. Because women were generally expected to submit to the authority of a man, whether as father, master, or husband, single women threatened to undermine the social
order in a way that single men did not; this is one of the reasons
why single women walking unaccompanied on London's streets
were so often arrested on suspicion of prostitution or 'loose idle
and disorderly' conduct and committed to a house of correction.[164]

Not only were never-marrying women viewed suspiciously, but
those who were not supported by their families faced severely
limited opportunities for supporting themselves. Usually lacking
any capital for investment, they had no entrée into male occupations and were confined to the narrow range of what was considered women's work. Among the gentry and middle class, these
problems were compounded by attitudes that women of those
classes should not perform any labour that was not genteel. Such
women were thus limited to choosing professions such as teaching,
nursing, acting as companions to the elderly, and writing (or, somewhat lower down the social scale, running a small shop or keeping
lodgers). Even then, they could be despised for having to work for a
living. It is not surprising that the lack of suitable employments for
educated but impoverished middle- and upper-class women was an
early concern of feminists.[165]

Lower-class women of all marital states were expected to work,
but those who never married faced the most limited opportunities

---

163 Hill, *Eighteenth-Century Women: An Anthology*, pp. 128–9.
164 See below, Chapter 7, pp. 271–3.
165 Hill, *Women, Work and Sexual Politics*, p. 231; Hill, *Eighteenth-Century Women: An Anthology*, pp. 130–2.

due to their lack of access to the world of men's work. Their most common occupations were probably domestic service (though as they got older there were fewer opportunities); laundry work; spinning, lacemaking, and other textile work; hawking and peddling; and nursing. Often poor women were forced to try to sustain themselves through an 'economy of makeshifts', performing a collection of odd jobs and activities, including keeping chickens and cows, and/or cultivating a small plot. Frequently parish officers paid them to take in lodgers, help in childbirth, care for the sick, or lay out the dead. Historians have noted that such women, as well as widows, often lived together, and this may have been in order to share costs (though some may have had lesbian relationships).[166] Like all women's work, these jobs were low-paid, and such women frequently ended up dependent on poor relief, as those who worked for the parish in a sense already were. According to the 1851 census, from the age of forty single women were less likely to be employed and as they got older they became increasingly unable to support themselves: by the age of sixty-five, a third of both widows and spinsters were dependent on the state or charity, and many ended up in workhouses or other institutions. However, unattached women without children often received very low levels of relief from parish officials, who hoped to force them out of the parish or into some form of employment.[167]

In sum, life outside marriage was far more difficult for women than for men, for the simple reasons that women on their own had fewer economic resources and women's social roles were to a much greater extent defined in terms of their family responsibilities. Women who were not married were distrusted because they were not under the authority of a male household head. The low wages and limited work opportunities available to all women were in a sense predicated on their being wives who benefited from a family economy in which they received financial support in return for housework and assistance in the family business; outside marriage this essential pillar of support was removed. Consequently, it was primarily when single women or widows were able to remain within a family context, as an unpaid carer for family members or as a

166 Sharpe, 'Literally spinsters', pp. 55–62; Hill, *Women, Work and Sexual Politics*, p. 233; Hufton, 'Women without men', pp. 361, 363–4. For lesbianism, see above, Chapter 3, pp. 81–4.

167 Michael Anderson, 'The social position of spinsters in Victorian Britain', *Journal of Family History* 9 (1984), p. 380 (table 2), and 390–1; Ivy Pinchbeck, *Women Workers and the Industrial Revolution* (1930; 1969), pp. 80–1.

hired servant in another household, that they enjoyed the best living conditions; only the wealthiest women were able to prosper on their own.

Paradoxically, although single men encountered less prejudice and fewer economic difficulties, there were fewer of them outside marriage, except for the years between leaving home and first marriage when they were establishing their careers. Because men depended on the unpaid or low-paid labour of women in the home and often at work, they quickly sought to remarry when widowed, and such men were able to find willing partners, largely because their superior wealth and earning power made marriage an attractive prospect for most women.

CONCLUSION

This chapter has shown that experiences of family and household life, from infancy to old age, were fundamentally gendered, and it has demonstrated the important role family life played in shaping and perpetuating gender roles. We have also seen that, despite significant changes in the intellectual and economic environment, the gendered aspects of family life changed less during this period than is usually argued. Even changing ideas and conduct in the realm of courtship and child rearing failed to have much impact on the balance of power in marriage, the division of labour between husbands and wives, and the roles of mothers and fathers. While the evidence on many, if not most, of these issues is still very limited, it seems clear that there was a limited separation of spheres between men and women throughout this period, with overlap in areas such as working for income and some aspects of housework and parenting. In some respects, there was an accentuation of differences as men withdrew from some household tasks, motherhood became more highly valued (with more women electing to breast-feed their babies), and middle-class fathers became more emotionally distant, but it is the continuities in spousal and parental roles over this long period which are most impressive. Finally, we have seen (especially in this last section) how the different work opportunities open to men and women fundamentally shaped their lives, both inside and outside the family. It is to this topic that we now turn.

CHAPTER FIVE

Work

In the field of women's history, one of the subjects which has received the greatest attention is the history of women's work. Much less, of course, has been written about the sexual division of labour from the point of view of men. Yet as we shall see, it is impossible to understand fully the distinctive features of either women's or men's work without an awareness of what the other sex was doing, as well as a broader understanding of gender roles and the forces which shaped them.

We have seen in the previous chapter that in marriages husbands tended to perform more of the income-producing labour, while women spent more time on the equally labour-intensive, but not always directly income-producing, housework. The very definition of work adopted in this chapter (and in the historiography more generally), as that which earns monetary income (thereby excluding any housework which did not generate products or services for the market), can be seen as one of the ways in which women's labour has been ideologically undervalued by historians. Yet this distinction was drawn by contemporaries, who viewed housework as an important, but fundamentally different kind of activity than paid labour: it was a duty, rather than an occupation. And even if women were expected to devote their efforts first and foremost to the unpaid labour of caring for their families, it is important to note that the vast majority of women also engaged in income-producing work during this period, and if we are to understand the extent to which such work was or became marginalised for women it is important to analyse precisely how it was distributed between the sexes in this period and how this changed.

The historiography of women's work has tended to rely on long-term linear models of historical change, in which it is argued that opportunities for women have constricted over time. In the words of Amanda Vickery, historians have tended to see women's work as moving from a 'golden age' in which the overlap between the types of work women and men did was significant, to 'separate spheres', where that overlap was much reduced. As noted in the introduction, the early work of Alice Clark and Ivy Pinchbeck which embodies this approach remains influential. According to Clark, men and women typically worked together in family businesses up to the seventeenth century, but with the separation of home and work due to the growth of 'capitalism' in that century women were no longer able to participate in their husbands' employments. According to Pinchbeck, the crucial period of change occurred later, between about 1790 and 1840 as a consequence of industrialisation, but it had the same result of reducing employment opportunities for women. Similar arguments about the progressive marginalisation of women's work during this period have been made more recently, by Bridget Hill in her survey of women's work in the eighteenth century and Deborah Valenze in her study of the consequences for women of the economic and ideological aspects of industrialisation.[1]

As other historians are now arguing, however, these models assume that in earlier periods women's opportunities were greater than was actually the case. Judith Bennett, a medieval historian, has argued that as far back as 1200 women's work was 'low-skilled, low-status, and low-paying', and this has continued to be the case up to the present day. Thus there was no 'golden age'. Bennett argues that the history of women's work is characterised largely by continuity; while the specific tasks performed change, the basic fact that women's opportunities were more limited and lower in status than men's has remained a constant despite the advent of capitalism and industrialisation.[2] While this is undoubtedly the case, it would nonetheless be wrong to conclude that the relationship between women's work and men's work, both in terms of status differences and degrees of overlap, has remained completely unchanged over the centuries.

1 Amanda Vickery, 'Golden age to separate spheres? A review of the categories and chronology of English women's history', *Historical Journal* 36 (1993), pp. 383–414; Alice Clark, *Working Life of Women in the Seventeenth Century* (1919); Ivy Pinchbeck, *Women Workers and the Industrial Revolution* (1930); Bridget Hill, *Women, Work and Sexual Politics in Eighteenth-Century England* (1989); Deborah Valenze, *The First Industrial Woman* (Oxford, 1995).

2 Judith Bennett, 'History that stands still: women's work in the European past', *Feminist Studies* 14 (2) (1988), pp. 269–83. Her arguments are more fully developed in 'Medieval women, modern women: across the great divide', in David Aers, ed., *Culture and History, 1350–1600* (1992), pp. 147–75.

Another approach to the problem is to argue that historical changes in women's work are circular rather than linear, in that women's opportunities have increased at some points in history, but only temporarily. One such period, according to Maxine Berg, was the industrial revolution. A similar model, advocated by Katrina Honeyman and Jordan Goodman, posits that the history of gender at work involves long periods of stability interrupted by occasional periods of 'gender conflict', when improvements in women's position upset the equilibrium and men reassert their control of the workplace. Honeyman and Goodman identify two periods of gender conflict, from the late fifteenth to the late sixteenth centuries, and in the early to mid-nineteenth century, in response to industrialisation. Thus, the periodisation used in a gendered history of work may need to be somewhat different from that normally used by historians, in that the periods of study need to be longer and have different starting and ending points, and we need to recognise that the direction of change is not always the same. Moreover, we need to recognise the diversity of women's experiences. In her study of women's work in eighteenth- and early-nineteenth-century Essex, Pamela Sharpe found that the growth of capitalism had contradictory effects on women's work opportunities and wages, depending on where they lived and the type of employment involved.[3]

Whatever model of change is adopted, it is important to recognise the advantages of studying women's work from the perspective of gender. What is important in the history of both women's and men's work is to determine which occupations pursued by that sex are conducted solely by members of that sex, and thus can be defined at particular moments in time as masculine or feminine, and which occupations are pursued by both men and women. This can only be done by analysing the work experiences of both sexes. Bennett's argument that women's work is 'low-skilled, low-status, and low-paying' defines women's work in relation to that of men, and it is therefore necessary to examine changes in the types of work performed by men as well in order to determine the significance of any changes in the tasks performed by women. And in explaining why sex-specific patterns of work occurred, it is necessary to examine occupational characteristics as an integral part of the construction of gender roles. As recent research has demonstrated,

3 Maxine Berg, 'What difference did women's work make to the industrial revolution?', *History Workshop Journal* 35 (1993), pp. 22–44; K. Honeyman and J. Goodman, 'Women's work, gender conflict and labour markets in Europe 1500–1900' *Economic History Review* 44 (1991), pp. 608–28; Pamela Sharpe, *Adapting to Capitalism: Working Women in the English Economy, 1700–1850* (1996).

changes in the nature of women's work have often come about as
the result of efforts by men, using sexual stereotypes, to define femininity and work in ways which restrict women's employment opportunities.[4]

Problems of Evidence

Despite the rich historiography, the study of women's work presents
serious difficulties for the historian, for, reflecting its low status,
women's employments are often poorly recorded in the sources.
Since their work was generally regarded as much less important
than their marital status, women are typically identified in the sources (such as tax records or judicial records) as spinsters, wives, and
widows, while men are always identified by their occupation or social status (i.e., gentleman). But it is also the nature of much of the
work performed by women which made it less likely to be recorded.
Part-time, seasonal, and casual work was rarely recorded, for informal arrangements were not regulated by institutions such as the
guilds. This was especially true if the work took place at home (such
as laundry work or spinning), involved geographical mobility (such
as migrant harvest work or hawking and peddling), or occurred as
part of a family team (in which case any records of wages or payments made only identify the male household head). An additional
factor is that in a desperate attempt to make ends meet many
women worked in a number of different occupations. The employments of Mary Risebrook, a young widow from the east end of London, for example, were described as follows: she 'has sold . . . butter
and eggs and has wound silk for throwsters and has washed linen
and nursed a child. She has left off one employment and taken up
another in hopes to get a better livelihood.'[5] There is no simple
answer to the question of what Risebrook's occupation was.

The opposite distortion affects the records of men's work. Because masculine identity was largely defined in terms of their work,
men were frequently identified by an occupational label. Quite
often such labels give a spurious impression of stability, when in fact
men's work could be almost as variable as women's. Men, too, suffered from under- and un-employment, and often combined employments, but they were still likely to identify themselves in terms
of only one (no doubt their most prestigious) occupation. As John

4 Valenze, *First Industrial Woman*; Honeyman and Goodman, 'Women's work,
gender conflict and labour markets'.

5 Peter Earle, *A City Full of People: Men and Women of London 1650–1750* (1994),
p. 146.

Patten has argued, despite the 'apparently growing occupational sophistication' among men in early modern towns, they actually engaged in a 'quite unsophisticated diversity of part-time and unspecialised activities'. If women's work is underreported, Maxine Berg has suggested, men's work has often been 'double counted'.[6]

A good example of the problems of evidence facing the historian of the sexual division of labour are the nineteenth-century census returns. Even after the census started identifying, in 1851, the 'rank, profession, or occupation' of all members of the household, and not just the household head, serious distortions remained. In the words of Edward Higgs, the census returns 'were constructed by men . . . who had certain assumptions about the position of women in society. In broad terms, women tended to be defined as dependants, whatever their productive functions, whilst men were classified according to the nature of their labour.'[7] One of the most serious problems for historians results from the fact the census requested information about the occupations of only those people who were 'regularly employed'. There were no instructions about how to record part-time, casual, seasonal, or multiple employments, which of course were more frequently engaged in by women.

In the face of this uncertainty, the enumerators adopted a number of different strategies in recording women's work, which unfortunately vary considerably from district to district. In many areas they simply left the space for occupation blank, and as a result more than half of the adult women in London were listed with no occupation, which is implausible. Another tactic employed was to give the occupation of wives in terms of their husband: for example 81,037 'shoemaker's wives' and 5860 'shopkeeper's wives' were listed in 1851. It is unclear in such cases whether the wife actually worked in her husband's occupation, or worked in some other occupation (or no occupation) and was simply identified in terms of her husband's work. As a result of these practices, a number of known women's occupations, such as laundry work, street trading, market work, and prostitution, are underrecorded in the census or not recorded at all. Census data about women's occupations must therefore be viewed sceptically, though Higgs's heroic attempt to remedy some of these deficiencies, which makes it possible to form some more reliable estimates of the numbers of women working in different sec-

6 John Patten, 'Urban occupations in pre-industrial England', *Transactions of the Institute of British Geographers* n.s. 2 (1977), pp. 301–3; Berg, 'What difference', p. 29.

7 Edward Higgs, 'Women, occupations and work in the nineteenth century censuses', *History Workshop Journal* 23 (1987), p. 60.

tors of the economy, will be discussed later. Although the recording
of men's work in the census returns is less problematic, underem-
ployment and multiple employments remain hidden.[8]

In sum, in analysing the sexual division of labour, the historian
has to be extremely careful to distinguish between differences in
the ways in which men's and women's work was recorded and differences in the actual nature of the work performed by each sex.

As we have seen, over the course of this period there were two contradictory movements in ideologies of gender: on the one hand a
growing emphasis on women's sex-specific domestic virtues and
moral duties, and on the other hand the articulation of feminist
ideas concerning the similarity of the potential characteristics possessed by each sex. This debate inevitably called into question ideas
about what constituted 'men's work' and 'women's work'. Thus when
fundamental economic transformations, especially in the agricultural and industrial sectors, altered levels of demand for many occupations in this period, there were many non-economic as well as
economic forces encouraging changes in the sexual division of labour. This chapter will examine the impact of these ideological, social, and economic forces on patterns of men's and women's work
during this period.

AGRICULTURE

At the start of our period the majority of the English people worked
in the agricultural sector, so it is appropriate to commence our discussion with an analysis of the sexual division of labour on farms.
Due to the enormous regional variations in soil types and crops
planted, the story is complicated, and it becomes more complex
over the course of this period as changing techniques (sometimes
termed the 'agricultural revolution') resulted not only in significant
improvements to productivity, but also increasing regional specialisation, especially the contrast between the grain-growing areas in
the south and east of the country and the pasture-dominated farms
of the north and west. Before considering how between 1650 and

---

8 Higgs, 'Women, occupations and work'; Hill, *Women, Work and Sexual Politics*,
pp. 148–56; Sally Alexander, 'Women's work in nineteenth-century London: a study
of the years 1820–50', in J. Mitchell and A. Oakley, *The Rights and Wrongs of Women*
(1976), p. 64; *Parliamentary Papers: Census of Great Britain, 1851. Population Tables II,
Vol. I* 88 (1852–3), p. ccxxvi. Although the census did include space for additional
employments (of men only), in the compilation of the data only one occupation
was counted: Hill, *Women, Work and Sexual Politics*, pp. 151–2.

1850 the gendered pattern of work in agriculture was affected by these changes in farming practices we need to survey the situation at the start of our period.

Both men and women worked on farms, and there was some significant overlap in the tasks they performed. Nonetheless, labour patterns were gendered. The primary tasks of men were ploughing and harrowing (breaking up clods of dirt and covering seeds), reaping and mowing, and caring for and working with draught animals. They were also responsible for hedging, ditching, and threshing. Women were involved in a much wider range of tasks. They relatively rarely ploughed, but they planted seeds, hoed weeds, spread muck, and removed stones from the fields. They did less reaping than men and never used the scythe, but at harvest time they followed the reapers or mowers and raked and gathered the grain or hay. But not all women's work involved helping men. Women had virtually complete control over the dairy, where not only did maidservants milk the cows but farmers' wives controlled the production of cheese and butter, both for home consumption and the market. Farmers' wives also played a major role in managing the farm, including training and looking after the servants (both domestic and farm), taking care of the finances, and marketing. Wives of agricultural labourers often grew vegetables in small cottage gardens, allotments, or plots on the common land, and kept cows, chickens, and pigs. They also took advantage of the customary rights of gleaning (gathering grain left behind by harvesters) and of gathering fuel and fruits from the common land. Finally, female labourers played a major role in the market gardens around London, and in the hop gardens of the southern counties, weeding, gathering crops, and carrying produce to market. Agricultural work for women was thus more varied than for men. According to Bridget Hill, women's work 'filled the gaps ... [it] was of necessity flexible, ranging over a great variety of skills and in consequence ill defined.' Hill has analysed the diary of a farmer's wife, Mary Hardy of Norfolk (1733–1808). Hardy's tasks were multifarious: she sowed barley, helped with the harvest, ground malt for brewing, kept pigs and poultry, made cheese, looked after a vegetable garden, and supervised servants.[9]

There was, however, considerable overlap in the jobs performed by men and women. Servants in husbandry (unmarried youths who

9 Hill, *Women, Work and Sexual Politics*, pp. 45 and 28–9, citing B. Cozens-Hardy (ed.), *Mary Hardy's Diary*, Norfolk Record Society vol. 37 (1968).

were hired for a fixed period of typically a year to work both on the farm and in the household) were both male and female, and the women were expected 'to do most of the tasks involved on the farm, even the heaviest'.[10] When jobs needed to be done in a hurry, it mattered less whether one was a man or a woman than how strong one was. At harvest time, in particular, the whole community was involved in bringing in the crops before they were damaged by the weather. In this situation strong women were involved in reaping and carting. On a farm in Yorkshire in 1641 women and men reaped in equal numbers and there was 'always one man, or else one of the ablest of the women, to abide on the mow . . . whose office is to help to team' [to unload the cart].[11] And Hill notes that 'the smaller the farm or landholding, the less any sexual division of labour appears'; women could even be involved in ploughing. Other jobs, such as shearing sheep, seem to have been performed by both men and women. This fluidity in the sexual division of labour is further reinforced by evidence of considerable local and regional variation in the distribution of agricultural tasks, with chores like reaping, weeding, and threshing performed by either sex, depending on local customary practices.[12]

Despite these areas of overlap, there was still a strong element of gender segregation in agricultural work at the beginning of our period. While men did most of the core task of ploughing and played a more important role in harvesting, women performed a wider range of tasks which, while important in that many provided essential extra income or food for the household, were often tedious, peripheral, or required women to act as accessories to men. Men's work varied too, according to the seasons and the nature of the soil, but it was largely restricted to a number of principal tasks. The relatively marginal status of women's work was reflected in remuneration. Depending on the job and the age of the worker, women received wages that were between one-third and three-quarters of those paid to men for the same job. Female reapers, for example, received between 50% and 71% of the wages received by male reapers, while female servants in husbandry were paid be-

10 Hill, *Women, Work and Sexual Politics*, p. 70.

11 Michael Roberts, 'Women's work and men's work at harvest time', *History Workshop Journal* 7 (1979), p. 10, citing C. B. Robinson (ed.), *Rural Economy in Yorkshire in 1641* (Surtees Society) (1857).

12 Hill, *Women, Work and Sexual Politics*, p. 35; I. Pinchbeck, *Women Workers*, p. 17; Sharpe, *Adapting to Capitalism*, pp. 74, 81.

tween 37% and 60% of the wages received by their male counterparts.[13] Sheep shearers in seventeenth-century Norfolk were paid 6d
per day (with meat and drink) if they were female, and between 7d
and 14d if they were male.[14]

A number of economic and social changes occurred in the eighteenth and early nineteenth centuries, some as a consequence of the
'agricultural revolution' and some which were part of broader social
trends, which could have potentially altered this division of labour.
The most relevant changes, which were largely stimulated by the
growing demand for food due to population growth, are growing
regional specialisation, the increased use of the scythe, the acceleration of enclosure, and the commercialisation of the dairy industry.[15]

The growing specialisation in corn growing, in rotation with fod-
der crops like turnips, in the south and east of the country led to
fewer types of jobs being available to women: dairy work in particular declined. Using a quantitative analysis of settlement examinations to determine the seasonality of male and female
unemployment, Keith Snell has argued that in the second half of
the eighteenth century women's work in this part of the country became concentrated on spring-time tasks such as hoeing, weeding,
planting, and spreading manure (tasks which increased with the
new emphasis on the cultivation of root crops), while their autumn
work declined as men virtually monopolised the harvest work (with
the exception of gleaning).[16] Snell's use of settlement examinations
to make this argument has been questioned on a number of
grounds, however, including the fact that it overemphasises both
women's earlier opportunities and the extent of the change which
took place.[17] Indeed it is clear that women continued to play a significant role in the harvest, though possibly in reduced numbers and
in less important tasks. Women may have spent less time reaping,
due to the increased use of the scythe (discussed below). (In contrast, in the north they did most of the reaping after 1750, probably

13 Roberts, 'Women's work and men's work', p. 19.

14 Alice Clark, *Working Life of Women in the Seventeenth Century* (1919; 1982), p.
60; Ann Kussmaul, *Servants in Husbandry in Early Modern England* (1981), pp. 37,
143.

15 For a survey of major agricultural changes which occurred in this period, see
R. Floud and D. McCloskey (eds), *The Economic History of Britain since 1700,
Volume 1: 1700–1860* (1981), chs. 4 and 10.

16 K. D. M. Snell, *Annals of the Labouring Poor: Social Change and Agrarian England
1660–1900* (1985), ch. 1.

17 Norma Landau, 'Going local: the social history of Stuart and Hanoverian
England', *Journal of British Studies* 24 (2) (1985), pp. 278–80; Sharpe, *Adapting to
Capitalism*, ch. 4.

due to a shortage of available men.) But women continued to do the lighter work of raking, gathering, and gleaning. Although evidence from parliamentary commissions in the early nineteenth century reveals that women continued to participate in harvests in the southern counties,[18] it is possible that the decline of some types of women's work did result in lower importance being placed on those employments still dominated by women, as suggested by their declining wages. This may have led many women to seek employment elsewhere, particularly in domestic service and industrial by-employments, as Snell has argued.

The growing use of the scythe, especially after 1790, certainly contributed to the marginalisation of women's work in the southeast. A longer and heavier instrument than the sickle, the scythe has historically only been used by men, and only the strongest men at that. Irish immigrant men, for example, who were shorter and weaker than their English counterparts, were often unable to wield the scythe.[19] Its increased use, which occurred unevenly (both geographically and chronologically) during this period, appears to have been stimulated by economic pressures (although mowers were paid more than reapers, the greater efficiency of the scythe meant that farmers could save money by introducing it), changes in crops, and, in some cases, labour shortages. The consequence for women was to change the nature of their contribution to the harvest, but not reduce their participation in it. Where the scythe was used women lost the opportunity to act as reapers, but the demand for followers and rakers, less-skilled female jobs which were lower paid increased.[20] As Arthur Young noted in his tour of the north of England published in 1770, 'a woman follows every mower, to gather the corn and lay it in order for binding.'[21] Thus, the growing importance of the scythe served to sharpen the sexual division of labour in agriculture.

The acceleration of the pace of enclosure from about 1760 to 1820 also had negative effects for women. Enclosure led to a decrease in the number of small landholdings and loss of common land. Consequently, women frequently lost the opportunity to cultivate garden plots, to raise livestock on the common land, and to gather fruits, berries, nuts, and fuel from forests; it also restricted

18 Pinchbeck, *Women Workers*, pp. 56, 72.
19 J. A. Perkins, 'Harvest technology and labour supply in Lincolnshire and the East Riding of Yorkshire, 1750–1850', *Tools and Tillage* vol. 3, pp. 54, 128.
20 Roberts, 'Women's work and men's work', pp. 17–18.
21 Quoted by Hill, *Women, Work and Sexual Politics*, p. 57.

their opportunity to glean. Many of these activities were increasingly viewed as unjustifiable intrusions on property rights and were now defined as theft. Enclosure thus destroyed the common-right economy, and women had exercised those rights more than men. All these activities had been ideally suited to women who had small children to look after while they worked, and they had provided vital contributions to the family income.[22]

Another important change in agricultural practice was the decline in the number of servants in husbandry employed. In the early part of our period the number of such servants increased, but a decline set in in the 1750s in the southern and eastern counties which accelerated after 1790, with the western counties following a similar pattern but with a twenty-year lag. (The decline was not total: 'farm-servants' still comprised 15–38% of the agricultural labour force in the south in 1831.) There were a number of causes of the decline, including specialisation in grain growing, with its sharper seasonal fluctuations in demand for labour (servants in husbandry were hired on annual contracts); population growth, which made wage labour cheaper than servants in husbandry; the rising costs of feeding living-in servants due to the increase in grain prices; and a desire to avoid giving labourers a settlement in the parish (which would make them eligible to receive poor relief).[23]

Although both men and women were affected by this decline, the consequences differed. While men often continued to work on the farm as labourers on shorter contracts, women were often pushed out of agricultural work altogether, often into domestic service (an occupation which, for women, had always overlapped with service in husbandry), at least until after marriage. Concurrently, the practice of putting young female parish apprentices to work on farms decreased. By 1843, the assistant poor law commissioners reported that most of the women who worked in the fields were married or widows.[24] Consequently, boys were introduced to agricultural work far earlier than girls, and while men continued to view such work as a career, women increasingly viewed it as a tem-

---

22 J. M. Neeson, *Commoners: Common Right, Enclosure, and Social Change in England, 1700–1820* (1993); Jane Humphries, 'Enclosures, common rights, and women: proletarianization of families in the late eighteenth and early nineteenth centuries', *Journal of Economic History* 50 (1) (1990), pp. 16–42; Valenze, *First Industrial Woman*, ch. 2.

23 Kussmaul, *Servants in Husbandry*, part 3; Snell, *Annals of the Labouring Poor*, ch. 2.

24 *Parliamentary Papers: Report on the Employment of Women and Children in Agriculture* (1843), pp. 6, 13, 293.

porary way of supplementing the family income. It was reported in 1843 that thirty years ago 'it appears to have been a common practice ... to send the girls into the fields with boys to work, no difference being made in their occupations; but this is no longer the case; and when female apprentices now work out of doors (by no means a common practice), it is only occasionally in the hay or corn harvest.'[25]

Farmers' wives also lost an important responsibility, running the dairy, during this period. As we have seen, the dairy was an aspect of agricultural work which was dominated in the first half of our period by women, who milked the cows and carried out the production of cheese and butter. As Deborah Valenze has argued, the early-eighteenth-century dairy turned normal gender roles on their head: 'women combined decision-making with industry, and showed ceaseless commitment to a never-ending workday, while men appeared on the scene only sporadically in order to contribute unskilled labour' such as helping to carry milk in from the pasture, churn the butter, or turn heavy rounds of cheese.[26] This anomalous situation was reversed, however, in the second half of the eighteenth century by the combined force of growing commercial pressures and the efforts of 'scientific' investigators to place dairy production on a more 'rational' footing.

As a result of an increase in demand for dairy products, cheese factors (who were essentially middlemen) interfered with the activities of dairy women by seeking to secure dependable supplies of products of consistent quality, thereby undermining the dairy women's independence. Yet economic pressures alone did not necessarily exclude women, since many adapted to the new demands of the market. What fundamentally weakened their position was the introduction of scientific discourse into the world of dairying, in which male authors and practitioners evaluated production techniques according to 'rational' standards and depicted female working practices as irrational and tradition-bound. Women, it was argued, could not be trusted to produce a reliable product of consistent quality; male managers were needed to introduce proper scientific methods, including the use of careful measurements of times and quantities. The consequence of this change is not that women ceased to work in the dairy, for dairy maids continued to be used for milking and other routine tasks. But increasingly the

---

25 Ibid., p. 28.
26 D. Valenze, 'The art of women and the business of men: women's work and the dairy industry, c. 1740–1840', *Past and Present* 130 (1991), p. 160.

farmer's wife's role of supervising the production of butter and cheese was supplanted by male managers. This was a gradual process: even in the 1840s the 'controlling mistress [of the dairy] was still in evidence', but by the mid-nineteenth century male factors and managers largely controlled the industry.[27] The fact that women were perceived to be less capable of scientific practices made them less likely to participate in other farming innovations as well, including new methods of stock breeding and the use of machinery and chemical fertilisers.[28]

Thus, in a number of aspects of agricultural practice the role of women was marginalised in this period. These changes, together with the increasing influence of domestic ideology, led to the withdrawal of some women, especially middle-class women, from agricultural labour altogether. One woman in Gloucestershire complained in the early 1800s that 'a woman undertaking to farm is generally a subject of ridicule.'[29] The commercialisation of dairying and the decline of servants in husbandry (and thus the need to supervise them) had largely eliminated two major tasks for farmer's wives. Yet we should not exaggerate this change: even in 1850 middle-class women still performed some agricultural tasks. Most of the evidence that they withdrew from such work comes from the south and east of the country, while in the west farmers' wives or dairy women continued to be responsible for 'the entire management of the dairy . . . [as well as] the actual labour attending the dairy, more particularly that of attending to and cleaning the cheeses'.[30] Though many middle-class women did spend less time outdoors, they continued to work hard indoors 'smoking, pickling, and preserving food as well as cooking and baking'. While their husbands also engaged in less manual work, they continued to be actively involved in managerial and supervisorial tasks on the farm.[31]

To determine the extent to which women lower down the social scale withdrew from outdoor agricultural labour at the end of our period it is helpful to consider the findings of the poor law commissioners who investigated the employment of women in 1832–4 and 1843. When compared with what is known about women's work in

27 Valenze, 'Art of women'; Pinchbeck, *Women Workers*, p. 41.
28 L. Davidoff and C. Hall, *Family Fortunes: Men and Women of the English Middle Class, 1780–1850* (1987), pp. 274–5, 309.
29 Pinchbeck, *Women Workers*, p. 30.
30 *Report on the Employment of Women and Children in Agriculture*, p. 5.
31 Davidoff and Hall, *Family Fortunes*, pp. 255–6, 283–4.

the first half of our period, the report provides evidence of considerable continuity. In all parts of the country women continued to be involved in haymaking, hoeing, weeding, picking stones, pulling and dressing turnips or potatoes, and similar tasks, much as they had done in the seventeenth century. Indeed, Pinchbeck argued that there was an increase in the early nineteenth century in the amount of work performed by women (often with their husbands), as day labourers, in agricultural gangs (in the eastern counties) and in the bondage system (in the north), as farmers came to realise the benefits of hiring women. Not only could they be paid less than men, but new farming techniques increasingly demanded the kinds of work women typically performed, such as hoeing and weeding. Advocates of new methods such as Arthur Young actually promoted the greater use of female labour on the grounds of cost.[32] At this time women's work was common in many parts of the country. In the west and southwest, women continued to work on the hay harvest. In the south, there are reports of full employment of men and women at harvest time. Women reaped corn in Devon and Northumberland (but apparently not in Yorkshire).[33] And despite the progress of enclosure, gleaning continued to be an important activity in many counties.

But in some counties female reapers and dairy workers *were* harder to find in the first half of the nineteenth century. In many parts of the south and east, commissioners found that women were relatively rarely involved in field labour, including the harvest, with the exception of some haymaking, weeding, and gleaning.[34] In some cases, women even ceased to be involved in milking.[35] There is some evidence that in the mid-nineteenth century women began to shun field work in favour of domestic service. Mary Puddicombe, a forty-one-year-old wife of an Exeter labourer, told an assistant poor law commissioner in 1843 that when she had been an apprentice in the 1810s she had been required (among other tasks) to drive bullocks to and from the field and lead horses or bullocks to plough, but 'maidens would not like that work now.'[36] In the 1860s women

---

32 Pinchbeck, *Women Workers*, pp. 53–66, 86–8, 91, 100–1.

33 *Report on the Employment of Women and Children in Agriculture*, pp. 27, 300; Pinchbeck, *Women Workers*, p. 72. For evidence of women reapers in the north from the 1790s onwards see: Hill, *Women, Work and Sexual Politics*, p. 57; E. Hostettler, 'Gourlay Steell and the sexual division of labour', *History Workshop Journal* 4 (1977), pp. 95–6.

34 Snell, *Annals of the Labouring Poor*, pp. 54–5.

35 Pinchbeck, *Women Workers*, p.110.

36 *Report on the Employment of Women and Children in Agriculture*, p. 109.

in Somerset were reported to be 'above working out now, it makes their hands dirty'; it has been argued that this reluctance to work in the fields caused a labour shortage which encouraged increased use of the scythe.[37] In many parts of the country it was noted that the number of girls and young women who did agricultural work was declining. Perhaps because such dirty, outside labour was increasingly seen to be inappropriate for women, young women went into domestic service, and only picked up some field work after marriage or when they became widows. Middle-class observers shared this sense that women's agricultural work was not only less common, but also less important than it had been previously. The commissioner for the counties of Kent, Surrey, and Sussex in 1843 described the work of women and children as 'the lightest known to agriculture' and as involving primarily 'acts of neatness and economy, which might be dispensed with altogether'. Similarly, the commissioner for Wiltshire, Dorset, Devon, and Somerset argued that women's agricultural work was less important than and different in kind from what men performed.[38]

Important as these discontinuities are, they do not represent any fundamental structural transformation in the sexual division of labour in agriculture. Rather, this period witnessed some accentuation of differences which had existed already in the seventeenth century. Even then, as we have seen, women's work was in many ways less central than that performed by men, and over the course of this period women continued to perform such tedious but vital tasks as weeding, hoeing, and haymaking, though in some parts of the country they lost the more prestigious tasks of managing the dairy and reaping. Meanwhile, men monopolised the increasingly common (and vitally important) task of mowing with a scythe. As women were increasingly defined as less suitable for skilled tasks, their wages, in relation to those of men, decreased in the second half of the eighteenth century in those parts of the country where they lost their main tasks.[39] Yet women remained an important part of the agricultural labour force. While the amount of work they performed may have have decreased in the second half of the eighteenth century, we have seen that there is evidence it increased from the early nineteenth century. Change in the history of women's work is often cyclical rather than linear.

37 E. J. T. Collins, 'Harvest technology and labour supply in Britain', *Economic History Review* 2nd series, 22 (3) (1969), p. 470.

38 *Report on the Employment of Women and Children in Agriculture*, pp. 27, 28, 130–1, 217, 293, 299.

39 Snell, *Annals of the Labouring Poor*, pp. 23–39, 65.

MANUFACTURE AND INDUSTRIALISATION

Even at the start of this period manufacturing was an important component of the English economy. Because much of this activity took place in the countryside, with many households involved in both agricultural and industrial work, it is impossible to draw a sharp distinction between the two. Indeed, the agricultural changes of the period contributed to the growth of rural manufacture, since the residents of areas specialising in pastoral farming frequently had time on their hands which could usefully be spent on other types of work. As David Hey has shown, the economy of the Sheffield region, one of the most rapidly growing industrial areas in the country, depended on workers who combined metal work with farming small plots of land, or who at the very least dropped their tools at harvest time in order to gather in the crops. Similarly, in the textile areas of Lancashire and the West Riding, the combination of spinning and weaving with small agricultural holdings was common. The mixture of occupations found in such areas and the fact that much work was based in the home greatly enhanced work opportunities for women. Nonetheless, there was a definite division of labour by gender within each family: in Lancashire and the West Riding, women and children did the spinning and dairy work while men did the weaving and field work on the farm.[40]

The rapid industrial expansion which occurred during this period encompassed not only the 'classic' period of the industrial revolution from around 1760 to 1850 but also the significant expansion of 'protoindustrial' activity in the period up to 1760. Industrialisation involved not only changes in manufacturing techniques, but also changes in the organisation of labour, including the decline of the guild system of regulating craft production, the expansion of the putting-out system, and the introduction of factories. We have seen that changes in farming techniques and the organisation of agricultural labour altered somewhat the sexual division of labour, with women increasingly performing more marginal tasks; can the same be said about the changes involved in industrial expansion?

In order to assess the impact of these changes it is best to start with an examination of the period before the acceleration of industrial growth in the late eighteenth century. A very wide variety of products were manufactured in preindustrial England, both in rural and urban areas. The period 1650–1760 witnessed a dramatic ex-

40 David Hey, *The Rural Metalworkers of the Sheffield Region* (Leicester, 1972); Hill, *Women, Work and Sexual Politics*, pp. 40–3.

pansion of handicraft production, a process which is often termed 'protoindustrialisation', which was stimulated by the development of the world market for consumer goods. Protoindustrialisation had a number of key characteristics: much of the production was rural, it was often organised by merchants who used the 'putting-out system' to take advantage of cheap underemployed rural labour, and the primary producers were women and children. This first stage of industrialisation thus involved an expansion in the amount of women's work: did this lead to greater overlap in the types of work performed by men and women?

By far the most common type of manufacture in preindustrial England was in textiles. Unsurprisingly, given the fact that maintaining and making clothing was an important household task, women predominated. Whether one looks at the trades of female apprentices, labourers, wives, or widows, the most common occupation (outside domestic service) is invariably some form of spinning, weaving, or needlework. In early-eighteenth-century London, for example, 92% of the female apprentices were in trades involving 'the making, maintenance, or selling of clothes', and the 'needle trades' were the largest category of occupation mentioned by female witnesses who testified in the church courts.[41] In southern rural areas in the eighteenth century, female apprentices were more likely to be placed in the clothing trades than in any other occupational group, with the exception of 'housewifery'.[42] Men, however, also worked in the textile trades, and they tended to monopolise some of the most important tasks. While women, together with children and the elderly of both sexes, primarily worked at the preparatory tasks of washing, carding, and spinning, did some weaving, and picked over the completed cloth, men were engaged in the preliminary sorting of the wool, in weaving, and in dyeing the finished product.

Spinning was the most widespread female activity, both for the household and the market, and it was only done by women, for low pay. As suggested by the use of one of the tools used, the distaff, as a symbol of femininity in popular culture, spinning was the quintessential female employment. A commentator in 1788 explained that it was the perfect employment for the female poor, since women could be 'employed in it consistently with the necessary cares of their families; for the business being carried out in their houses,

41 Earle, *City Full of People*, pp. 116, 118.
42 Snell, *Annals of the Labouring Poor*, pp. 279–82.

they can at any time leave it when the care of their families requires their attendance, and can reassume the work when family duty permits it . . . .'[43] Before mechanisation, several spinners were needed for each weaver, and this goes a long way towards explaining why so many more women than men worked in the textile industries in the first half of our period. Although weaving was primarily a male activity, some weaving, depending on the type of cloth, the extent of guild regulation, and the nature of the machinery used, was done by women. Maxine Berg has argued that weaving 'was widely practiced by women, particularly in the silk industry, but also to a considerable extent in wool, linen and cotton'. In the Essex worsted wool industry the introduction of the one-handed loom, which required less strength to operate, together with the decline of apprenticeship regulation, allowed women to take over the weaving. In the silk industry of Staffordshire and Warwickshire, three-quarters of the hand weavers were women, but in Spitalfields in London the introduction of broad silk weaving in the 1680s led to a division of labour in which men did most of the weaving (women had dominated narrow silk weaving) and women and children did the winding, quilling, and warping. It was reported in 1691 that while the linen industry employed few men, in the woollen industry large numbers of men were employed weaving, combing, dressing, shearing, and dyeing. Hand and framework knitting was divided into gender-specific tasks. Hand knitting was primarily a female activity, but framework knitting was carried out by men, with assistance from women (usually wives) in winding the yarn, filling shuttles, and finishing the article. Over the course of the century, however, as apprenticeship regulations began to be ignored, women and children increasingly worked the frames.[44]

In textiles, every sector of the industry has its own story, but the general pattern is of an expansion of work opportunities for women, as can be seen most clearly in the development of the ready-made clothing industry in the late seventeenth and early eighteenth centuries. Previously, clothes making was a male preserve, carried out by tailors and others, whose activities were regulated by the guilds. With the development of a new type of women's clothing in 1676, the mantua, the situation changed. Mantuas were

43 Quoted in Bridget Hill, *Eighteenth-Century Women: An Anthology* (1987), p. 204.

44 Maxine Berg, 'Women's work, mechanisation, and the early phases of industrialisation in England', in P. Joyce (ed.), *Historical Meanings of Work* (1987), pp. 71, 74, 80; Sharpe, *Adapting to Capitalism*, p. 33; M. D. George, *London Life in the Eighteenth Century*, pp.183–4; Clark, *Working Life*, pp. 127–9.

loose-fitting and hence did not require individual tailoring. Women who set themselves up as mantuamakers, milliners, and dressmakers evaded the controls of guilds (there were none in these trades), and in the eighteenth century they came to dominate the making of women's clothing, including accessories such as headwear, gloves, petticoats, and bodices, as well as children's coats. Although tailors continued to make men's suits, women made a number of men's accessories, including shirts and cravats.[45] The only part of women's clothing which was still made by men were stays, an undergarment made out of tabby (coarse silk), canvas, and whale bone which determined the shape of women's clothes. It was claimed that working with whale bone 'requires more strength than [women] are capable of, to raise walls of defence about a Lady's shape, which is liable to be spoiled by so many accidents'. Women assisted in the manufacture of stays, however, by stitching together the tabby and canvas parts. With the exception of those women who ran millinery businesses, where profits could be quite high, women in these trades were poorly paid: Campbell noted in 1747 that while milliners 'have vast profits on every article they deal in; yet [they] give but poor, mean wages to every person they employ under them'. He reported that the profits of mantuamakers 'are but inconsiderable, and the wages they give their journeywomen small in proportion'. Similarly, women who stitched stays earned 'poor bread'.[46] Taking over work previously performed by men did not lead to higher wages for women.

In sum, women dominated the textile industry in the period before industrialisation, although a few important tasks such as weaving and tailoring were primarily or exclusively carried out by men. In some cases both men and women can be found doing the same jobs, notably some types of weavers, the makers of sail cloth, and 'fine-drawers', who repaired imperfections in fabric. Further research, however often reveals a sexual division of labour within specific trades. Thus, while both men and women worked in the related trade of shoemaking, their work was divided such that men measured the customers' feet and cut out the leather, while women (and children) stitched the pieces together. The men's work occurred in the workshop, while women did theirs at home.[47]

45 Earle, *City Full of People*, p. 140; M. Prior, 'Women and the urban economy, Oxford 1500–1800', in M. Prior (ed.), *Women in English Society 1500–1800* (1985), pp. 110–11.

46 R. Campbell, *The London Tradesman* ([1747]; 1969), pp. 208, 224–5, 227.

47 George, *London Life*, pp. 167, 196–8; Campbell, *London Tradesman*, p. 199; L. Schwarz, *London in the Age of Industrialisation* (1992), p. 194.

Metal work, in contrast, was dominated by men. First, although a smattering of women can be found in a wide range of metal-working businesses, including as cutlers, blacksmiths, wiredrawers, plumbers, and braziers, women worked primarily in a small number of low-skilled occupations.[48] In Sheffield, women other than widows continuing a family business were not allowed by the Cutlers' Company to practice as cutlers, though they did work on bone handles and on inferior cast cutlery.[49] In those trades which were not controlled by guilds, due to their location or their recent origins, women often played a more important role, though a sexual division of labour remained.

In Birmingham, where there were no guilds, women were involved in the manufacture of nails, screws, pins, chains, buttons, jewellery, watches, and toys, though they did not participate in every aspect of these trades. Although some work was quite skilled, much of it was not, as it involved stamping and punching out small metal pieces, drilling, and polishing. The making of buttons and screws was done primarily by women, but nailmaking was probably their most common trade.[50] William Hutton's famous observation (in 1781) of female nailmakers ('in some of these shops I observed one, or more females, stript of their upper garment, not overcharged with their lower, wielding the hammer with all the grace of her sex') does not indicate any sexual division of labour in the industry (though there may well have been),[51] but in other trades the division is clear. In pinmaking, women spun the heads of the pin with a wheel, 'much like a spinning wheel', while men separated the pins from one another 'with another little machine like a pair of shears'. In many trades women were responsible for the finishing tasks, such as lacquering and japanning (varnishing in imitation of Japanese work), and other types of delicate hand painting. Although there is insufficient evidence to detect any division of labour in the toymaking industries, the markedly lower wages received by women suggests that they performed less skilled tasks. Even in trades historically controlled by guilds, the breakdown of guild control and the increasing subdivision of tasks opened up opportunities for

---

48 Snell, *Annals of the Labouring Poor*, pp. 279–82; Ilana Ben-Amos, 'Women apprentices and the trades and crafts of early-modern Bristol', *Continuity and Change* 6 (1991), pp. 238–9; Berg, 'Women's work', pp. 86–7.
49 D. Hey, *The Fiery Blades of Hallamshire: Sheffield and its Neighbourhood, 1660–1740* (1991), p. 140; Pinchbeck, *Women Workers*, p. 276.
50 Pinchbeck, *Women Workers*, pp. 273–7.
51 William Hutton, *An History of Birmingham* (2nd edn, 1783), p. 84*.

women: in the goldsmiths' trade, women were involved in polishing and finishing tasks and in the sale of goods.[52]

The same principles even apply in the heaviest industries of the period, including iron smelting and various types of mining. Although women's role in iron forges has been described as primarily 'casual labour', the work could be quite hard, involving as it did breaking limestone and ore, wheeling ore to furnaces, making coke, operating bellows, and removing cinders from furnaces.[53] In the first half of our period women commonly worked underground in coal mines, primarily as part of family teams. While men worked the coal face, women carried or dragged the coal in sledges or tubs through the tunnels to the lifts, or on occasion even up to the surface. In larger tunnels girls and women drove horses carrying baskets full of coal. Above the surface, they engaged in shovelling, sorting, and screening. At lime kilns, women were employed carrying baskets of coal and chalk, while men broke the chalk loose, screened it, lifted the baskets onto the women's heads, and threw the chalk into the kiln. Both sexes helped hack the coal and chalk into small pieces and fill the baskets. Although women's tasks were often accessory to the primary work which was carried out by men, the work in these industries exemplifies the wide range of occupations in which women worked in the first half of this period, and it puts paid to the idea that women were not strong enough to perform heavy manual labour. Women were employed in the loading of slate onto boats in Devon (after it was quarried by men), where the work was described as 'immoderately hard', yet women 'accomplish as much in a given time as the men do'.[54]

The Impact of the Industrial Revolution

How was the sexual division of labour affected by the accelerated growth in manufactures in the century after 1750, the period of economic change usually termed the 'industrial revolution'? The dramatic increase in output which occurred over the years 1780–1830 in particular was achieved by a number of changes in the organisation of labour and the technology of production. The

52 Arthur Young, *The Farmer's Tour through the East of England* (1771), cited in Hill, *Eighteenth Century Women*, p. 216; Berg, 'Women's work', pp. 86–7; A. Laurence, *Women in England 1500–1760* (1994), p. 127.

53 Pinchbeck, *Women's work*, pp. 270–1.

54 Hill, *Eighteenth Century Women*, pp. 212–14, 218, 221, in the last case quoting Richard Ayton, *A Voyage round Great Britain* (1814), vol. 1, p. 28.

extensive use of water- or steam-powered machines and the desire to reduce costs and increase control over quality led to the concentration of workers in some industries into factories. At the same time, however, there was a further expansion in the amount of work which took place in the home under the putting-out system. Both these changes had a significant impact on patterns of men's and women's work.

The first area where machines made a significant impact was in the largest sector of female employment, spinning, and the gendered aspects of this story are complicated. The first inventions, Arkwright's water frame and Hargreaves's spinning jenny, which took place in the 1760s, dramatically reduced the amount of labour required. While this led to widespread female loss of employment in agricultural areas (where alternative by-employments were not available), it is important to note that women operated these new machines, which were still located in households and small workshops. Other displaced spinners took up handloom weaving, which had previously been a largely male occupation. With the development of the still more efficient spinning mule, however, men took over. The spinning mule required substantial physical strength and technical skill. Nonetheless, women did work on smaller mules into the 1830s, despite attempts by unions to exclude them. It was only with the introduction of longer mules and the doubling up of smaller mules, which required still greater strength, that women were excluded from this work. Although the subsequent introduction of the mechanised 'self-acting' mule (which required far less strength) in the 1840s could have led to the reintroduction of female labour, the process of transmission of spinning skills to the next generation had been broken, and few women worked on the new mules. According to Mary Freifeld, it was the loss of craft knowledge rather than technological change and union obstruction which finally led to the exclusion of women from what for centuries had been a female-dominated occupation.[55]

As we have seen, weaving was predominantly (but by no means exclusively) a male occupation prior to mechanisation, and here the introduction of machine looms facilitated greater female participation. Initially, the new technologies such as the Jacquard loom and the Dutch loom, which were regarded as high skilled, were worked by men. In the Coventry ribbon-weaving industry, for

---

55 Berg, 'Women's work', pp. 78–80; M. Freifeld, 'Technological change and the "self-acting" mule: a study of skill and the sexual division of labour', *Social History* 11 (1986), pp. 332–9.

example, men operated the Dutch engine looms while women continued to use single handlooms. But employers sought to use
women to lower their costs and by the early nineteenth century, in
Coventry, Yorkshire, the West Country and elsewhere, in silk, wool,
and cotton, women were working on the new machines alongside
men, receiving the same piece rates. As one weaver from Bolton
testified in 1808, 'women's talent is equal to men's when the work is
not too heavy; we have some women whose talent is equal to any
man's in the middle kind of work.' For some types of work, such as
silk throwing, women were preferred. As a factory commissioner reported in 1844, 'a vast majority of the persons employed at night
and for long hours during the day are females. Their labour is
cheaper, and they are more easily induced to undergo severe bodily
fatigue than men.' As another commisioner put it, girls and women
were more 'docile'. Yet even in these types of work men could end
up earning more money, because they worked on different grades
of cloth, they secured better jobs (as supervisors or mechanics), or
because women were forced to work shorter hours due to their domestic responsibilities.[56]

The continuing, or in some cases increasing, role played by
women in these mechanised industries masks an important change
in the types of women employed. Whereas women of all ages
worked at home, young single women predominated in the factories, where they often worked under the supervision of their
fathers. Of the women employed in the mills of the West Riding
woollen industry, over half were under twenty-one. In the factories
of the cotton industry in 1833, women outnumbered men by 65,000
to 60,000, but only one-sixth of the women were married. Although
there is some evidence that the proportion of married women in
the factory workforce increased after 1850, it is unsurprising that
where possible married women, especially those with children,
preferred to work at home, or in jobs with more flexible hours.[57] In
many areas this continued to be possible through an expansion in
home-based industry.

The expansion of work performed by hand, often at home and
using relatively simple techniques, is a feature of the industrial rev-

56 Berg, 'Women's work', pp. 81–2; Anna Clark, *The Struggle for the Breeches:
Gender and the Making of the British Working Class* (1995), pp. 126–7; Sharpe, *Adapting
to Capitalism*, p. 47; Valenze, *First Industrial Woman*, p. 96.
57 P. Hudson, 'Proto-industrialization: the case of the West Riding', *History
Workshop Journal* 12 (1981), p. 61; E. Richards, 'Women in the English economy
since 1700: an interpretation', *History* 59 (1974) p. 346; J. Rendall, *Women in an
Industrializing Society: England 1750–1880* (1990), p. 59.

olution which has only recently been properly recognised, perhaps because it was women who carried out much of this labour. Mass production of goods during the industrial revolution was achieved as much by multiplying small units of production through the protoindustrial 'putting-out' system organised by capitalist entrepreneurs as by the concentration of production in factories. While women benefited from mechanisation in some, but not all, industries, they benefited much more, in terms of the amount of work available if not the pay, from the increase in home-based work. For many tasks home-based labour was cheaper for employers because overheads were lower, guild controls could be more easily evaded, and, most important of all, cheap labour by women and children could be utilised. With the decline of work in spinning and agriculture, many women were desperately seeking employment. Many of these 'cottage' industries which employed considerable numbers of women were traditional domestic industries which avoided mechanisation until well into the nineteenth century, such as lacemaking, stocking knitting, glovemaking (where there was a division of labour between the men who tanned, dyed, and cut the leather and the women who stitched) and handloom weaving. The number of female handloom weavers increased rapidly in the late eighteenth and early nineteenth centuries due to the expansion of the trade, the failure to enforce apprenticeship regulations, the effects of war (which removed many male workers), and the greater use of machine-spun yarn (which was easier to work with). Even before the introduction of machine looms, therefore, women had begun to take over many types of weaving.[58]

In some cases, tasks which had previously been controlled by the male-dominated guilds were farmed out to cheaper, largely female labour. Initially stimulated by government contracts for cheap clothing for the army and navy during the Napoleonic wars, a ready-made men's clothing industry developed as a putting-out system beyond the control of the tailors. Manufacturing processes were subdivided into separate, relatively unskilled stages and middlemen employed primarily women to work on the garments in their own homes or workshops, work which came to be labelled 'slop work'.[59] Similarly, new technical developments in calico printing allowed employers to bypass skilled craftsmen. Processes were broken down

58 Pinchbeck, *Women workers*, pp. 157–78; Valenze, *First Industrial Woman*, pp. 113–18.

59 Rendall, *Women in an Industrializing Society*, pp. 29, 68; Schwarz, *London in the Age of Industrialisation*, pp. 186–94.

into a number of tedious but delicate operations which could be performed by girls and women in workshops. Significantly, other innovations such as copper-plate printing could have eliminated the need for such labour-intensive work, but because they required the employment of highly paid craftsmen they were not adopted.[60]

In many sectors of the economy an expansion of outwork occurred alongside mechanisation and the growth of factory work, and often this involved a division of labour with men working in the factories and women at home or in workshops. Thus nailmaking became a predominantly female activity, with men providing the raw materials through their work in the puddling and rolling mills. Similarly, chainmaking was divided into the larger and heavier chains, which were made in factories by men, and the lighter and smaller chains, mainly made by women at home or in small workshops.[61]

The price of this expansion in women's work was that much of it was 'sweated'. As production processes were broken down into their component parts, the skill level needed to perform each task was reduced. This led to an oversupply of available labour, which drove down wages and forced workers to work long hours to earn a subsistence wage. Although 'sweating' was particularly common with women, it often led to reductions in the wages of men as well, despite the efforts of male unions to prevent it. As a journeyman tailor reported to Henry Mayhew, 'since the increase of the . . . sweating system, masters and sweaters have sought everywhere for such hands as would do the work below the regular ones. Hence the wife has been made to compete with the husband . . . if the man will not reduce the price of his labour to that of the female, why he must remain unemployed.'[62] Faced with such a choice, many men must have sought other employment.

In contrast to most of the other industries under discussion, changes in the mining industry led to a reduction in the number of women working at a time when the industry was undergoing a period of marked expansion. Organisational changes led to the abolition of the system of subcontracting family labour, in which male hewers hired their own help (typically their wives and children). Moreover, the introduction of horses pulling carts along rails in the late eighteenth century greatly reduced the demand for the type of labour women performed underground. The job of leading the

60 Berg, 'Women's work', pp. 82–3.
61 Rendall, *Women in an Industrializing Society*, p. 68.
62 Henry Mayhew, *London Labour and the London Poor* 4 vols (1861–2), 2, p. 314.

horses was given to boys, perhaps because it was seen as part of their training to become hewers. In addition, from the early nineteenth century, there was increasing middle-class moral revulsion at the idea of women working underground. This was greatly increased by the report of the Children's Employment Commission of 1840, which exceeded its brief in highlighting the alleged physical and moral problems caused by the employment of female miners. This led to the passage of the 1842 Mines Act which forbade women and children to work underground. Although there was initially a considerable amount of evasion of this law, female underground work, which was already in decline, did largely disappear. In the second half of the nineteenth century, however, women increasingly performed surface work at mines.[63]

In sum, industrialisation, whether in the form of mechanisation and factory work or the expansion of the putting-out system, failed to alter radically the sexual division of labour. Despite the expansion in the number of female workers and the fact that women were often paid the same piece rates as men and on occasion performed the same tasks, work remained for the most part gendered. As Hudson argued with respect to the expansion of work for women under protoindustrialisation, 'there was a sexual hierarchy of labour within most protoindustrial trades, processes and households, which may have endorsed female subordination rather than emancipation.'[64] Similarly, the technological and organisational developments which occurred during the later phases of industrialisation caused numerous changes in the actual tasks performed by men and women, but the more skilled tasks invariably continued to be allocated to men, and the new jobs women performed often resulted from the breakdown of complex tasks into simpler, lower-paid processes. It is also important to note that most of the work opportunities for women which opened up in industry were largely in textiles, a traditional area of women's work, while women were excluded from some more male-dominated expanding areas of activity such as mining.

Nevertheless, the industrial revolution did involve a very important discontinuity, in the sense that the number of women employed in manufacturing work increased dramatically. As Maxine Berg and

63 Angela John, *By the Sweat of Their Brow: Women Workers at Victorian Coal Mines* (1980), pp. 21–5, 55–7, 78; Jane Mark-Lawson and Anne Witz, 'From "family labour" to "family wage"? The case of women's labour in nineteenth-century coal-mining', *Social History* 13 (1988), p. 167.

64 Pat Hudson, *The Industrial Revolution* (1992), p. 227.

Pat Hudson have demonstrated, the productivity gains which led to unprecedented economic growth occurred most markedly in industries which achieved higher productivity less by technical innovations than by the increased employment of low-wage women and children in putting-out work, especially in the textile (except cotton) and small metalware trades. In this sense what was revolutionary about industrialisation was the increasing number of women working: 'in terms of their proportionate contribution to the manufacturing labour force, women workers played a greater part over the whole course of the eighteenth century than they had done previously and were to do in the later stages of industrialisation.'[65] As this last comment suggests, that increase was temporary. Starting in some industries as early as 1815, and continuing until the end of the nineteenth century, women's participation in manufacturing decreased, for a number of reasons (discussed below, pp. 199–207). One important factor is that women played very minor roles in the new nineteenth-century industries such as the railroads, engineering, and gas and electricity, and in reorganised industries such as deep coal mining and iron and steel production. Few women, for example, worked for the railroads, which began to employ large numbers of men from the 1830s: only fifty-five women were recorded in the 1851 census.[66] Thus the expansion of female labour during the early stages of the industrial revolution was a temporary phenomenon, and in the long run it did not fundamentally destabilise the traditional sexual division of labour.

TRADE, SERVICES, AND THE PROFESSIONS

Each of these other key sectors of the economy had a distinctive sexual division of labour, depending on the nature of the tasks involved, the levels of skill and capital demanded, and the extent to which occupations were regulated by guilds, professional organisations, or the state.

Trade

The products manufactured in the early stages of industrialisation were primarily consumer goods, and thus this period also witnessed dramatic growth in the retail sector, with increases in the numbers

---

65 Berg, 'What difference', p. 40; Hudson, *The Industrial Revolution*, pp. 161–2.
66 E. Jordan, 'The exclusion of women from industry in nineteenth-century Britain', *Comparative Studies in Society and History* 31 (1989), pp. 276, 287, 295.

of itinerant hawkers and peddlers, market sellers, and, somewhat later, shopkeepers. Much of this activity was unregulated by guilds and apprenticeship regulations, so women were able to play a greater role than in some other areas of the economy. Nonetheless, in commerce, as in agriculture and industry, men dominated the most profitable occupations.

Hawking and peddling goods on the streets of towns and cities as well as throughout rural England was an activity with a long history, but the practice greatly increased with the expansion of protoindustrial manufacture. In rural areas travelling hawkers and peddlers sold a variety of goods that were otherwise unobtainable outside towns, such as hosiery, haberdashery, china, and glasses, as well as chapbooks, newspapers, and other printed literature. A similar activity involved the buying up of farm products such as eggs, milk, butter, and cheese for subsequent sale. Alice Clark suggested that, despite the fact that hawking involved carrying heavy packs over long distances, it was almost monopolised by women in some districts. Margaret Spufford's work, however, suggests that about 90% of the licensed itinerant sellers at the end of the seventeenth century were men, with only a small number of women operating independently or in husband-and-wife teams. Women may have worked more intermittently, however, and it is likely that many female peddlers were unlicensed. A study of the retail providers to a gentry household in late-seventeenth-century Lancashire suggests that the sexual division of labour in this line of work was complicated: while both men and women supplied the house with dry goods, meat, hay and manure, women were the primary providers of bread and dairy products and men provided the peat, coal and livestock.[67]

In urban areas a much wider range of goods was sold on the streets, including cooked foods, and women seem to have played a greater role. In the first half of our period women, especially the wives and widows of the poor, seem to have dominated the selling of fish, fruit, vegetables, flowers, milk, meat pies, apple dumplings, sausages, flowers, and a wide variety of non-food goods (especially newspapers) on the streets of London. In particular, they had a 'virtual monopoly' over the sale of the first five items in this list.[68] By

67 Hill, *Women, Work and Sexual Politics*, pp. 170–2; Clark, *Working Life*, p. 206; M. Spufford, *The Great Reclothing of Rural England* (1984), *passim*; Carole Shammas, 'The world women knew: women workers in the North of England during the late seventeenth century', in *The World of William Penn*, ed. R. S. Dunn and M. M. Dunn (Philadelphia, 1986), pp. 106–8.

68 Hill, *Women, Work and Sexual Politics*, pp. 168–9; Earle, *City Full of People*, pp. 144–45.

the early nineteenth century, however, men appear to have played a much greater role in street trading in London, and a division of labour had developed with women still dominating the sale of fish, fruit, and vegetables, as well as a wide range of small wares such as firescreens, ornaments, laces, pin cushions, and 'anything cheap and small' while, according to Henry Mayhew,

> what may be called the 'heavier' trades, those necessitating the carrying of heavy weights, or the pushing of heavily laden barrows are in the hands of men; and so are, even more exclusively, what may be classed as the more skilled trades of the streets, viz. the sale of stationery, of books, of the most popular eatables and drinkables (the coffee stalls excepted), and in every branch dependent on the use of patter.

Nonetheless, there continued to be considerable overlap in the activities of each sex. Mayhew stated that 'I do not know of any street trade carried on *exclusively* by women', and he noted that women frequently worked in the same trades as their husbands.[69]

Although street selling was frequently an activity of the very poor, and was in some ways almost akin to begging, many hawkers and peddlers were petty capitalists who cooked or manufactured or processed the goods they sold. Milk women, for example, often owned their suppliers, the cows. Clearly these trades required substantial business acumen, for the wrong decisions on prices of purchases or sales would cause serious hardship. Yet women as well as men were able to enter them because they required no formal training, involved relatively low levels of capital (sometimes this was raised by pawning possessions), and were often very low paid and low in status (Mayhew's evidence suggests that both men and women turned to street selling as a last resort when all other sources of income dried up).

On the other hand, women were largely excluded from markets, where, especially in the first half of our period, a large proportion of food products and livestock were sold. Because most market traders needed to be licensed and the activity required a considerable amount of capital, women were rarely involved, except on a relatively small scale or as the wives or widows of other traders. In Billericay, Essex, around the turn of the eighteenth century men paid most of the tolls for established stalls at the weekly market, but women paid tolls for movable carts. In her study of markets in Ox-

---

69 Alexander, 'Women's work', p. 101; Mayhew, *London Labour and the London Poor*, 1, pp. 457–8.

fordshire in the eighteenth century Wendy Thwaites found few women involved in the sale of horses, livestock, and grain; only with the sale of home-grown vegetables and fruit were women active in significant numbers. A number of changes further narrowed women's opportunities over the course of the century, including the declining position of small agricultural producers, the advent of large capitalist businesses acting as middlemen, new business practices such as selling by sample in local inns, and the increasing prevalence of the view that such work was not respectable for middle-class women. In 1800 a commentator complained that the farmer's wife would now 'faint at the idea of attending at market, like her mother or grandmother, with a basket of butter, pork, roasting pigs, or poultry, on her arm'.[70]

Over the course of the period shops increasingly supplemented hawkers and markets as providers of goods. Although in some towns guilds restricted entry to some trades, most shop work required no formal training and was equally open to both sexes. In any case, the few girls who were apprenticed were far more likely to be apprenticed to shopkeepers than to manufacturers. Both men and women ran shops, and there is considerable overlap in the types of shops they operated. According to the 1851 census, chandlers in London were more or less equally divided between men and women, and substantial numbers of both sexes can also be found as butchers, drapers, and milliners, often as husband-and-wife teams. Similarly, eating, drinking, and lodging establishments were run more or less equally by men and women (with help from girls and boys), with married couples often jointly running victualling houses and inns. (Given the limitations of the census records with regard to women's employments, the number of women working in these occupations was probably much higher, but there was still a substantial masculine presence.) Other types of shops frequently operated by women (though men also participated in these trades) include greengrocers, pawnbrokers and moneylenders. Eighteenth-century insurance records document that women also ran a number of shops selling new consumer goods such as tea, china, glass, earthenware, and above all women's clothing. The trade of millinery, which sold a range of clothes and accessories for women, was a genteel occupation for the proprietresses, though the journeywomen they em-

---

70 Pinchbeck, *Women Workers*, p. 34; Sharpe, *Adapting to Capitalism*, p. 17; W. Thwaites, 'Women in the marketplace: Oxfordshire c.1690–1800', *Midland History* 9 (1984), pp. 23–42.

ployed were poorly paid.[71] In addition, the wives of artisans often sold goods from the family workshop, though this became less common with the separation of shopkeeping from manufacturing over the course of the period, and the wives of journeymen and farmers often ran small village shops or alehouses.

Few women, on the other hand, were bakers, millers, vintners, and brewers, unless they were wives assisting their husbands or widows taking over their husbands' trades. Despite the links with women's traditional domestic skills, the small number of women in these trades can be explained by the fact that they were closely regulated by guilds and/or civic and national authorities, and women were less likely to possess or obtain the requisite licence, capital, and long-term commitment. In the case of brewing, women were largely excluded from commercial production at the end of the seventeenth century as a result of government regulation of the trade which led to its concentration among a small number of (mostly male) brewers. On the whole, industries and shops which required high levels of capital investment, including booksellers, jewellers, and chemists, were run by men. And, at the highest levels of commerce, women rarely acted as merchants. By the late eighteenth century a number of factors discouraged women from setting up shops of any type. Those women with little capital (most women) were put off by the increasing amount of capital required for premises and stocks; those with more capital, possibly deterred by the growing belief among upper-middle-class women that shopkeeping was vulgar and unrefined, took advantage of the growth of alternative types of investments, such as stocks, annuities, and rents on property.[72]

Service

Service occupations, of which the most common were domestic service and laundry work, were generally very low in status, required little or no training or capital, and involved tasks associated with housework; hence they were frequently performed by women. With an improving standard of living, among the middle class if not those below them, demand for such services increased significantly during

---

71 Schwarz, *London in the Age of Industrialisation*, p. 21; Earle, *City Full of People*, p. 91; Davidoff and Hall, *Family Fortunes*, pp. 240–1, 283, 299–302; Margaret Hunt, *The Middling Sort: Commerce, Gender and the Family in England, 1680–1780* (Berkeley, 1996), pp. 132–3; R. Campbell, *The London Tradesman* ([1747]; 1969), ch. 39.

72 Clark, *Working Life*, pp. 211–29; Davidoff and Hall, *Family Fortunes*, pp. 241, 303–4; Peter Earle, *The Making of the English Middle Class* (1989), pp. 166, 173; Hunt, *The Middling Sort*, pp. 145–6.

the period. Although these occupations were equally open to men and women, they were increasingly female dominated, especially domestic service. Whereas at the start of our period male servants were common, particularly in noble and gentry households, they were increasingly outnumbered by women. According to Gregory King's estimates, 54% of the servants in the country were women in 1688. With the loss of some other employments women flocked to domestic service in the eighteenth century, while the number of male servants was reduced by the tax introduced on them in 1777 to help pay for the costs of the American War. By 1851, according to the most recent recalculation of the census returns, 76% of domestic servants were female.[73]

The rise in the demand for servants, and the increasing predominance of women, are both related to the growing number of middle-class households employing servants (though some employers of servants were lower class), for whom servants were an important status symbol. At the same time, the middle class adopted new standards of comfort and cleanliness which greatly increased the kinds of household tasks which were given to housemaids, maids of all work, and kitchen or scullery maids rather than male servants. A manual for housekeepers published in 1796 described how much work there was for housemaids: 'keep the whole house in a state of cleanliness, by carefully washing the rooms, stair cases etc., cleaning the fire grates, irons and hearths, dusting carpets, and rubbing the furniture, as well as the locks, knockers, glasses, chimney ornaments, picture frames, etc.'[74] The overwhelming majority of households employing servants employed only one or two, and these were almost always women, who were expected to be 'maids of all work'. And 'all work' should be taken literally: in artisanal and shopkeeping households, it frequently involved helping in the workshop or at the counter. Only wealthier households had higher-status (and better-paid) positions such as housekeeper, lady's maid, and cook, as well as a number of positions for men.

Male servants were primarily employed in the wealthiest households (where there were large numbers of servants) and they were a sign of considerable status. For the most part they performed different tasks from women, such as outdoor work (as gardeners, coachmen, and grooms), and providing personal services to men

---

73 Bridget Hill, *Servants: English Domestics in the Eighteenth Century* (Oxford, 1996), p. 42; Hill, *Women, Work and Sexual Politics*, pp. 125–7. See also the table below, p. 188.

74 *Every Woman her Own House-keeper* (1796), cited in Hill, *Eighteenth Century Women*, p. 243.

(manservants, valets). In other cases, the work they did was often also performed by women, but to have a man was a status symbol, as was the case with cooks and butlers. Otherwise, it is only with the lowest ranks of male servants that men did similar tasks to women, but most such servants, such as footmen and kitchen-boys, were under the age of twenty in the early nineteenth century.[75] And even where similar (or lower) levels of skill were involved, male servants were far better paid. Priscilla Wakefield complained in 1798 that

> a footman, especially of the higher kind, whose most laborious task is to wait at table, gains, including clothes, vails, and other perquisites, at least £50 per annum; whilst a cook-maid, who is mistress of her profession, does not obtain £20, though her office is laborious, unwholesome, and requires a much greater degree of skill than that of a valet. A similar disproportion is observable among the inferior members of the establishment.[76]

The greater cost of male servants, combined with the growing number of middle-class households employing only one or two servants and the increased demand for the types of tasks normally performed by women, helps explain why by the end of our period women servants outnumbered men by a considerable margin.

Historians are divided about whether the experience of service was positive for women. D. A. Kent has argued that, compared to other female jobs, service had considerable advantages: relative job security (servants were frequently given year-long contracts), good-quality diet and lodging, and relative independence, in that they were economically self-sufficient and not under the control of parents or a husband. Kent even suggests that the female servant was 'sexually more independent and less marriage oriented than other working women and more likely to pursue an illicit relationship rather than forfeit her position by marrying'. Against this must be placed Peter Earle's point that 'it was difficult to achieve this freedom . . . when master and mistress expected a continuous appearance of obedience, humility, piety, respect and gratitude' and the suggestion, reflected in the attitudes of Daniel Defoe's fictional character Moll Flanders, that women were reluctant to enter service. Although there is some evidence that female servants contested their mistresses' authority, the possibilities of obtaining a degree of independence within the hierarchical environment of the

---

75 Earle, *City Full of People*, p. 83; Pamela Horn, *The Rise and Fall of the Victorian Servant* (1975), ch. 5.

76 Priscilla Wakefield, *Reflections on the Present Condition of the Female Sex* (1798), cited in Hill, *Eighteenth Century Women*, p. 244.

household were limited.[77] Moreover, given the restricted range of
other jobs available, many women must have felt forced to enter service as opposed to choosing it for its perceived (at least from a twen-
tieth-century vantage point) advantages. The Londoner John
Fielding commented in 1758 that 'women have but few trades, and
fewer manufactures to employ them. Hence it is, that the general
resource of young women is to go into service.'[78] We have seen that
diminishing employment opportunities in agriculture in the southeast had a similar effect on young rural women. While subordination for women was part of their prescribed gender role, for men of
course it was not, and some historians have suggested that another
reason for the relative decline in male servants in this period is that
young men increasingly rejected servitude as an activity which was
incompatible with their masculine sense of superiority.[79]

Although some men and women did remain in service during
adulthood, for most it was a lifecycle stage, which was typically abandoned upon marriage in their mid-twenties. Their experience of
service, however, often determined the nature of their future employment. Male servants went on to join the army (where habits of
obedience were put to good use), or became hackney coachmen,
stable keepers, or barbers. A common occupation for married
couples of former servants was running a food and drink establishment.[80] Probably the most common occupations for female ex-
servants were laundry work, nursing, or needlework, doing similar
sorts of tasks as domestic servants but living out. This career pattern
is evident from the age structure of these occupations. While domestic service was the most common occupation of women under
twenty-four in early eighteenth-century London, from age thirty-five
women were much more likely to be found working in the needle
trades, nursing, catering, shopkeeping, charring, and laundry work.
A similar pattern is evident in the 1851 census returns.[81]

A wide range of domestic services were provided by women who
were not (or were no longer) domestic servants, both on a part-time

77 D. A. Kent, 'Ubiquitous but invisible: female domestic servants in mid-
eighteenth century London', *History Workshop Journal* 28 (Aug. 1989), p. 118; Earle,
City Full of People, p. 128; M. Roberts, 'Images of work and gender in early-modern
England', in L. Charles and L. Duffin (eds), *Women and Work in Pre-industrial
England* (1985), pp. 122–4, 160; Patricia Seleski, 'Women, work and cultural change
in eighteenth and early nineteenth-century London', in *Popular Culture in England,
c. 1500–1800*, ed. Tim Harris (1995), pp. 161–7.

78 Cited by Hill, *Women, Work and Sexual Politics*, p. 128.

79 Hill, *Servants*, pp. 38–9.

80 Earle, *City Full of People*, p. 85.

81 Ibid., p. 85 and table 4.4, p. 119; Alexander, 'Women's work', p. 98.

and casual basis and as full-time jobs. These included all aspects of laundry work, sewing and mending clothes, and childcare. Frequently such work was performed by married women who were unable to assist their husbands in their trades. Over half of the wives of men who took out insurance policies (which suggests a certain level of wealth) in late-eighteenth-century London, where occupations of the wives were stated, were laundresses. Wives of London journeymen who worked in trades that were not open to female participation, such as hackeycoachmen and porters, were similarly employed. According to the 1851 census laundry work was an entirely female trade.[82] Women also performed a wide range of other low-waged services such as polishing shoes, singing ballads, telling fortunes, sweeping streets, and running errands for just about anyone, including prisoners. Indeed, as Dorothy George concluded from her study of eighteenth-century London, 'it can almost be said that there is no work too heavy or disagreeable to be done by women, provided it is also ill-paid.'[83] Men, too, probably performed some of these tasks, though mostly only as boys; due to the low wages for such employments women almost certainly outnumbered men. As we have seen, prostitution was another low-paid and casual 'service' occupation which was open to women, but not, for most of the period, to men.[84] Men were only involved in service occupations when they were young or poverty-stricken, or the jobs involved some status.

The Professions

Because the professions often required high levels of training, the sexual composition of the workforce was completely different.[85] Included within this category are posts in the church, law, army and navy (commissioned officers), medicine, and education, as well as clerical work. We would now call most of these occupations 'professions', and many were in fact in the process of becoming professionalised, according to the modern definition of the term, during this period. From the point of view of gender, there are three aspects of professionalism which tend to make such occupations male dominated: the requirement that entrants have significant levels of edu-

82 Schwarz, *London in the Age of Industrialisation*, p. 22; Hill, *Women, Work and Sexual Politics*, pp. 155–6.
83 George, *London Life*, p. 172; Earle, *City Full of People*, pp. 117–18.
84 See above, Chapter 3, pp. 75–9.
85 See P. J. Corfield, *Power and the Professions in Britain, 1700–1850* (1995), pp. 32 and 34 for tables indicating the number of men and women engaged in professional employments according to the 1851 census.

cation or training; formal regulation of entry to the profession by the state or guilds; and the expectation that these were life-long vocations which could not be performed part-time. The extent to which women were actually excluded from these types of work depended on two further factors: whether or not it was traditionally seen to be 'women's work' and the number of low-skilled tasks available.

Three of these professional groups had always been composed only of men, and would remain so far beyond the end of the period of this study: the church; the law (though women were often knowledgeable about the law and sometimes gave private advice); and the army and navy. Women were excluded from ministering the word of God, but because, as we shall see, they were perceived as particularly predisposed towards religious piety women did occasionally play a leading role in activities not regulated by the established church. Both the ecclesiastical and legal professions required their practitioners to possess an education in the classics, which, of course, disqualifed all but a few privileged women. The activities of the army and the navy were so totally outside the bounds of accepted female gender roles that women had no formal role to play at any rank, but a small number of women disguised themselves as men and served, and many other women accompanied armies, and sailed in naval vessels, as soldiers' wives or providers of services such as laundry or prostitution. In battle, women on ships could be found carrying gunpowder. With the reorganisation and centralisation of military life in the nineteenth century, however, such opportunities tended to disappear.[86]

The medical and teaching professions present more complicated stories, since both included very diverse groups of practitioners and involved tasks which were expected of women. As wives and mothers, women were expected to provide medical care for their families. Girls learned 'physick' from their mothers, and women augmented their skills from manuals of housewifery. As Gervase Markham, the author of one of the earliest such books, explained, 'one of the principal virtues which do[es] belong to our English Housewife . . . [is] the preservation and care of the family touching their health and soundness of body.' Although 'the depths and secrets of this most excellent art of physick, are far beyond the capacity of the most skillful woman, as lodging only in the breast of learned professors', he wrote, 'our housewife may from them receive some ordi-

---

86 Ibid., pp. 74, 188; below, Chapter 6, pp. 209–27. Dianne Dugaw, *Warrior Women and Popular Balladry 1650–1850* (Cambridge, 1989), pp. 127–8, 140.

nary rules and medicines,' including herbal remedies, the treatment of burns, broken bones, and dislocations, and certain surgical procedures (he advised 'if it be fit to be stitched, stitch it up').[87] Some women also provided unpaid medical care for their neighbours. While their husbands looked after the spiritual needs of the village, clergymen's wives provided comprehensive medical services, especially for the poor, acquiring their skills by experience, reading books and corresponding with doctors. Similarly, one aspect of the aristocratic traditions of paternalism and hospitality was that ladies provided, or arranged for, the care for the local poor. The housekeepers of 'persons of quality', according to a pamphlet in 1700, were expected 'to have a competent knowledge in Physick and Chyrurgery, that they may be able to help their maimed, sick and indigent neighbours'.[88]

While women dominated unwaged medical care, men virtually monopolised the occupations at the top end of the medical profession: physicians, surgeons, and apothecaries. As formally defined, these occupations demanded substantial training (at a university, in the case of physicians) and were regulated by the church (originally in order to prevent witchcraft) and guilds. Physicians and surgeons who were not educated in Oxford or Cambridge had to be licensed by a bishop or, in the case of surgeons, by the Company of Barber-Surgeons (which divided in 1745). The College of Physicans excluded women entirely, and the surgeons' and apothecaries' assocations only admitted practitioners who had licences or who had served an apprenticeship. Few women obtained licenses, and most of the ones who did were probably widows taking over their husband's practices. Faced with such obstacles, few women entered these ranks of the medical profession, and, according to the census returns, at the end of this period there were no female physicians and surgeons, and only 504 female druggists (compared to 15,332 men).[89]

Nonetheless, many women did perform medical care for money, as unlicensed doctors, midwives, wet nurses, nurses, and dispensers

87 [Gervase Markham], *The English Housewife, Containing the Inward and Outward Vertues Which Ought to be in a Compleat Woman* (1664), p. 4. Last passage cited by A. L. Wyman, 'The surgeoness: the female practitioner of surgery 1400–1800', *Medical History* 28 (1984), pp. 35–6.

88 *Compleat Servant-maid, or the Young Maiden's Tutor* (1700), cited by Clark, *Working Life*, p. 255. See also Wyman, 'The surgeoness', pp. 23, 32–3; Anthony Fletcher, *Gender, Sex and Subordination in England 1500–1800* (1995), pp. 233–4.

89 Wyman, 'The surgeoness', pp. 27–9, 39; *Parliamentary Papers: Census of Great Britain, 1851, Part II* (1854), 1, table 25.

of medication. Given the informal medical skills women possessed, it would be surprising if they failed to use them for profit. An examination of each of these occupations over the course of this period, however, reveals that, with the exception of nurses, they came under attack by a medicial profession bent on discrediting 'superstitious' and 'unscientific' practices. This attitude can already be seen at the start of our period in 1651 when a physician, James Primrose, wrote a book on *Popular Errours or the Errours of the People in Physick*, with a frontispiece showing a female practitioner being held back by an angel in order to allow a robed male physician to attend to a patient.[90]

The first casualties of this new attitude were midwives. We now have a more precise understanding of the chronology and causes of the growth of man-midwifery due to the recent work of Adrian Wilson. At the start of our period childbirths were entirely conducted by women, with the exception that in cases of difficult births male surgeons were often summoned, typically only in time to save the life of the mother but not the baby. In the first half of the eighteenth century surgeons developed new techniques, including the use of forceps, which allowed them to deliver live births in difficult cases. At this point surgeons, now called man-midwives, were still only summoned in difficult cases and worked alongside midwives. Starting in 1748, however, there is evidence that man-midwives were summoned in place of women in normal births, and by the 1780s the aristocracy had almost entirely abandoned midwives. Women's gradual exclusion from this profession thus took place in three stages. First, the growing role played by men in difficult cases is explained by the fact that women could not adopt the new techniques and instruments that surgeons developed for difficult births because they were denied formal training and access to this new information and in any case were prevented by custom from using instruments. Second, elite women began to choose male midwives on a regular basis, despite the substantial cost, as a form of conspicuous consumption to assert their superiority over their social inferiors; thus, Wilson argues, 'the making of man-midwifery was the work of women.' Finally, and in contrast to the last point, man-midwifery was further popularised by the actions of men, who attempted to place the practice on a rational footing by attacking midwives as ignorant, incompetent, and superstitious, and as endangering the health of both mothers and babies. Moreover, with the

90 Cited by Wyman, 'The surgeoness', pp. 34–5.

introduction of forceps men had argued that childbirth was a 'manual mechanical operation' better suited to men. Women also suffered from the fact that men increasingly used the practice of midwifery as an entrée into the practice of surgery. As men entered the practice, it gained status. Although the medical establishment initially viewed midwifery with disdain, there was a gradual recognition in the early nineteenth century that it was an important part of (male) medical practice.[91]

By 1850, female midwives had lost all respectability, and were used only by the poor. Only 2024 were identified in the 1851 census in all of England and Wales, though since most midwives operated on a part-time basis this significantly underestimates their number. Indeed, it has been argued that at that time the majority of births in the country were still attended by women, though these would have primarily been among the lower classes. Even at upper-class births women were still present, but now only as 'monthly nurses' who assisted the mother during the lying-in period. These nurses supervised women in labour and called the male midwife when the birth was imminent. Needless to say, this change represented a significant transfer of responsibility and compensation to men.[92]

A similar diminution of women's medical role came with the marginalisation of 'quacks', men and women who practised medicine without licences on the fringes of the law, but who played an important role in the provision of health care in the seventeenth and eighteenth centuries. Encouraged by the so-called 'quacks charter', a statute which allowed persons other than physicians to treat patients with herbs, roots, and waters, women as well as men (often working together as husband-and-wife teams) frequently sold cures and remedies as a part-time or full-time occupation. Some 'cunning' women claimed their curative powers were enhanced by magic, a claim which had some plausibility since it was thought that women's irrational nature led them to be in touch with supernatural powers. Early in our period two women testified to earning their living in London by 'cur[ing] cancers' and 'treat[ing] people for the pox'. A 'gentlewoman' in Hay Market sold an 'excellent paste for the shaking and trembling of the hands after hard drinking', while other women sold remedies for 'female complaints'. Poor-relief officers frequently hired such women to care for the

---

91 Adrian Wilson, *The Making of Man-Midwifery: Childbirth in England 1660–1770* (1995); J. Donnison, *Midwives and Medical Men: A History of the Struggle for the Control of Childbirth* (1988), chs 2 and 3.

92 Donnison, *Midwives and Medical Men*, pp. 62, 69.

poor, such as a woman in Torrington in 1691 who was paid £2 by
the parish for treating a man and wife for scalds and another who
received 3s. in 1694 for curing a woman's leg.[93] Quack medicine,
however, came under increasing attack from the end of the eighteenth century by the medical profession, which criticised the supposed ignorance and superstition of practitioners, and the
unscientific methods they adopted.[94] Although both male and female healers suffered from the loss of respectability of quack medicine, for women it represented the loss of one of the only ways
they were able to practise medicine independently.

The only remaining opportunity for women in medicine was in
nursing, another activity which was clearly an extension of their
domestic duties. Women were paid to act as wet nurses, to mind
children, and to care for the sick, both in private homes and in the
many hospitals which opened in this period. They were hired by
parishes to care for the poor by lodging and feeding them, cleans-
ing them of vermin, sitting up with the dying, and laying out the
dead. They were also hired to look after persons stricken with small-
pox or the plague and to search corpses for evidence of the plague.
Owing to medical and moral criticism, and the increased ideological importance accorded to maternity, the practice of wet-nursing
probably decreased somewhat after 1750, but in other respects nursing was an increasingly common occupation of women during the
period due to the growing number of infirmaries and hospitals. As
other parts of the medical profession became more male dominated, the only role left for women was as the proletariat of the
medical profession, looking after the routine physical care of patients. Indeed, before the promotional efforts of Florence Nightin-
gale, nursing was a generally untrained and low-status occupation. It
is hardly surprising that it was monopolised by women. In contrast,
the least prestigious tasks men performed in hospitals at this time
involved administering treatments as apothecaries, dressers, residents, and clinical clerks.[95]

The other profession which was increasingly open to women at
this time was teaching. This was possibly the largest professional

93 Earle, *City Full of People*, pp. 132–3; Roy Porter, *Health for Sale: Quackery in
England 1660–1850* (1989), pp. 82–4; Wyman, 'The surgeoness', p. 30; Fletcher,
Gender, Sex and Subordination, pp. 232–3, 235–6.
94 Porter, *Health for Sale*, ch. 8; M. Fissell, *Patients, Power, and the Poor in
Eighteenth-Century Bristol* (1991), ch. 9.
95 Earle, *City Full of People*, p. 135; Clark, *Working Life*, pp. 249–51; Fissell,
Patients, Power, and the Poor, p. 67; Donnison, *Midwives and Medical Men*, p. 76;
Robert Dingwall et al., *An Introduction to the Social History of Nursing* (1988), p. 7.

grouping of the time, but, since it was not yet regarded as a profession, it was the least regulated. At the start of our period teaching was primarily carried out by the clergy, which means it was performed by men. This continued to be the case in many areas, as the clergy supplemented their incomes with some private freelance teaching. Men also controlled the secondary schools, where teachers were expected to have had a grammar-school or higher education. Women (frequently the wives of schoolmasters) contributed to the running of such schools, however, by looking after the boarders and performing other domestic tasks. Women were also active in the expanding realm of primary education, which is all most students ever received. Since teaching was an extension of the child-rearing duties normally expected of mothers, it was commonly accepted that women could teach girls and boys up to the age of seven. Indeed, such teaching was seen as an occupation 'peculiarly suited to the gentle energies of women'.[96] In 'dames' schools', women earned small amounts of money teaching lower-class children to read.

The vast expansion in primary education for the poor during this period (especially from the early eighteenth century with the advent of charity schools) led to a dramatic increase in the number of female teachers. It has been estimated that in 1730 2,000 of the 12,000–17,000 teachers in the country were female, though this may be an underestimate.[97] In contrast, according to the 1851 census, 71% of the teachers in England and Wales were female. From the second half of the eighteenth century there is increasing evidence of women establishing and running schools on their own.[98] Women were able to enter this profession in such numbers due to the lack of any organisation effectively controlling entry (much teaching was freelance), the view that girls ought to be taught by women, and the fact that most female teachers worked in primary schools, where little in the way of training was required of the practitioners. The only real regulation was the requirement that licences be acquired from a bishop, but, as with licences to practice medicine, this was frequently evaded. Towards the end of this period the occupation of the governess became popular, as middle- and upper-class families frequently hired a woman to oversee (but not necessarily

96 *The English Matron* (1846), p. 106.

97 G. S. Holmes, *Augustan England: Professions, State and Society, 1680–1730* (1982), pp. 52, 71.

98 For examples, see Hunt, *The Middling Sort*, pp. 168–9; Corfield, *Power and the Professions*, p. 187.

conduct) the education of their children. This was a poorly paid occupation which was in some ways little more than an extension of domestic service, but it was one that was thought suitable for unmarried or widowed middle-class women who needed to work. In sum, the vast expansion in educational provision during this period led to the employment of more women than men, but women had the lowest paid jobs, teaching the youngest and poorest pupils and performing domestic tasks.[99]

Finally, we come to what are today called the 'white-collar' professions: clerks, scriveners, bookkeepers, accountants, notaries-public, estate stewards, and similar occupations. The number of people employed in this area increased dramatically during this period as a result of the increase in clerical and administrative posts in government (both national and local), business, and voluntary organisations. Such work demanded little capital but it required a basic education and occasionally long periods of training, and it was career work – not suitable on a casual or part-time basis. Consequently, very few women were employed in these occupations throughout this period. The few exceptions were typically in such posts as the matron of a hospital, where the responsibilities were largely domestic: in addition to supervising and praying with the female patients, a matron was required to keep accounts of provisions and ensure that the wards remained clean and orderly.[100] The lack of a domestic component in most of the other white-collar jobs is another factor which explains the small number of women employed. As we have seen, the only professions where women were a common feature were medicine and teaching, both of which can be seen as extensions of a mother's responsibilities for her children. Moreover, the occupations women pursued in these fields were largely unregulated and involved little training.

In sum, the nature and extent of the sexual division of labour in trade, services, and the professions differed according to several factors: the levels of training and capital required; the degree of formal regulation of entry into the trade (the greatest degree of overlap occurred in the trades which were the least regulated); and whether the tasks involved can be construed as domestic or maternal in content. As these factors changed over the course of this period, so did

99 Clark, *Working Life*, p. 287; Rosemary O'Day, *Education and Society 1500–1800* (1982), p. 27; Holmes, *Augustan England*, ch. 3; Davidoff and Hall, *Family Fortunes*, pp. 265–6, 293–6.

100 Earle, *City Full of People*, pp. 86–7; Holmes, *Augustan England*, ch. 8; Davidoff and Hall, *Family Fortunes*, pp. 262–7, 305–6.

the sexual composition of the workforce, with women increasingly excluded from some occupations but finding enhanced opportunities in others.

EXPLAINING THE GENDERED DIVISION OF LABOUR

A good way to summarise the situation at the end of this period is to look at the results of the 1851 census, the first to identify (in principle) the 'rank, profession, or occupation' of every individual in the population. As discussed earlier, the census evidence is distorted by the fact that the statistics collated a single occupation for each person when many people, both men and women, worked in more than one occupation, and, more importantly from the point of view of gender, household heads and enumerators tended to view women's work inconsistently, often giving misleading or incomplete information. In an attempt to rectify some of these problems, Edward Higgs has recalculated summary figures for women's occupations, with adjustments for some of the most egregious inconsistencies in earlier tabulations. These involve compensating for the fact that the census failed to include women who worked in their husbands' occupations and those who worked on the harvest, and falsely identified many relatives of household heads as domestic servants.[101] The resulting figures are only approximations based on a number of possibly questionable assumptions, but they are probably the most accurate figures we currently possess. The results of his calculations for women are presented in Table 1, together with the earlier calculations of W. A. Armstrong and Charles Booth for men.

It is evident from the table that men virtually monopolised five sectors of the economy: mining, building, transport, commerce and clerks, and general labourers. Women dominate only two sectors: domestic service, where they account for 76% of the workers, and the 'unoccupied' (those without paid employment) sector, where they account for 68% of the non-workers. (The unoccupied sector includes children, which is the main reason why there are also so many males in it.) In four other sectors, women account for around a third of all workers: agriculture and fishing, manufacture, dealing, and public service and the professions. In terms of absolute numbers, women were most commonly employed in manufacture, agriculture (but not, from more detailed census evidence, in fishing),

101 Higgs, 'Women, occupations and work'.

TABLE 1   *Occupations of men and women in England and Wales, 1851*

| | Men | | Women | | Total |
	N (in 000s)	%	N (in 000s)	%	(N=100%)
Agriculture and fishing	1,607.2	69	714.4	31	2,321.6
Mining	326.6	97	8.6	3	335.2
Building	459.8	99.8	0.9	0.2	460.7
Manufacture	1,728.6	65	1,026.2	37	2,754.8
Transport	333.9	97	11.4	3	345.3
Dealing	438.3	62	268.7	38	707
Commerce/ clerks	44.7	99.8	0.1	0.2	44.8
General labourers	324.6	98	7.2	2	331.8
Public service/ professions	200.9	67	98.8	33	299.7
Domestic service	149.7	24	466.3	76	616
Unoccupied	3,066.9	32	6,543.8	68	9,610.7
Total*	8,781.2	49	9,146.4	51	17,927.6

Sources: For men: W.A. Armstrong, 'The use of information about occupation', *Nineteenth-Century Society: Essays in the Use of Quantitative Methods for the Study of Social Data,* ed. E. A. Wrigley (Cambridge, 1972), pp. 255–81. For women: Edward Higgs, 'Women, occupations and work in the nineteenth-century censuses', *History Workshop Journal* 23 (1987), p. 75. The figure for the unoccupied sector for women was calculated by taking Armstrong's total number of women and deducting the total number of employed women provided by Higgs.

*These are the totals given in Armstrong. For unknown reasons, the figure for men is 100(000) greater than the total of the sums provided in the individual categories.

domestic service, and dealing. In sum, although there are five major occupational groupings in which women had virtually no role, women did play a significant role in the two largest sectors of the economy, manufacture and agriculture.

While these figures are broadly in line with expectations, they of course obscure vast differences in the work actually performed within each sector. Although there were areas of overlap, we have seen that in agriculture men dominated the ploughing, mowing, reaping, and care of draught animals, while women did the planting, weeding, raking (at harvest time) and dairy work (in the first half of our period). In manufacture, men dominated many aspects of metal work, though women did a great deal of small piece work, while in textiles women did the spinning, and increasing amounts of weaving and making ready-made clothing. While both sexes worked in shops ('dealing', in census terms), they tended to work in shops selling (or making) different types of goods. Similarly, while both men and women were domestic servants, they tended to engage in very different tasks. Finally, while men dominated the professions, women were significantly involved in the lower ranks of the medical and teaching professions.

There were, nonetheless, some important areas of overlap in the work performed by men and women, particularly as youths. In agriculture, we have seen that servants in husbandry of both sexes performed a wide range of tasks, and at harvest time the enormous demand for labour often led to the abandonment of normal gender roles. Other examples of work performed by both sexes include the weaving of silk, wool, and cotton, hawking and peddling, running certain types of shops (such as chandlers and butchers), and keeping victualling houses and alehouses. It may well be the case that further investigation will identify a sexual division of labour which is hidden behind these occupational labels; certainly this was often encouraged by employers and male workers. Yet in some local labour markets the existence of a single dominant industry (like powerloom weaving) could promote job integration.[102] Such areas of overlap (especially at the bottom end of the labour market) suggest that the line between men's work and women's work was sufficiently fluid that changes in the sexual division of labour could occur.

If this was the picture at the end of our period, how had it changed since 1650? The 1851 census was the first to provide even partly reliable information about individual occupations, and there is no comparable source earlier in our period, so it is impossible to answer this question with any certainty. Nonetheless, some broad trends can be identified. In three sectors of the economy the proportion of women employed probably decreased over the period. In agriculture, we have seen that several types of work performed by women became less common in the eighteenth century, especially

---

102 Sonya Rose, *Limited Livelihoods: Gender and Class in Nineteenth-Century England* (Berkeley, 1992), pp. 186–7.

in the southeast, so that in the late eighteenth century levels of female employment were lower than a century earlier. From the end
of the Napoleonic Wars in 1815, however, female employment increased in some parts of the country. In mining of course the decrease in women's work, which began in the late eighteenth
century, was much more pronounced: while in the 1650s far fewer
men and women were employed in mining, the sexual division of
labour was much more equal. Finally, the proportion of women in
dealing probably decreased over the course of this period due to
the growth in middle-class shopkeepers, whose wives often did not
work in their husbands' shops. These decreases help explain a probable increase in the number and proportion of women not working.

While work in agriculture, mining, and dealing became more
dominated by men, in three other sectors of the economy the
proportion of women increased. The impact of the expansion of
protoindustry followed by industrialisation provided increasing opportunities for low-waged female employment, leading to increasingly
high proportions of women in manufacture, though by the very end
of our period the trend had been reversed. There was a similar
large increase in the number of women in domestic service (and a
somewhat slower, but nonetheless significant increase in the proportion of servants who were women). A gradual increase probably
occurred in the professions, due to the increased number of women
in teaching and nursing, despite the concurrent decrease in the
number of female midwives and unlicensed doctors.

Overall, there appears to have been a sharpening of the sexual
division of labour over the course of the period, with women increasingly concentrated in tasks associated with household work
and motherhood, such as domestic service, teaching, and nursing,
or not working at all. Concurrently, fewer women were involved in
the distinctly less domestic tasks of mining, agricultural work, and
dealing. Only in manufacture did large numbers of women participate in work which did not have domestic connotations, though of
course much of the work for the textile trades involved traditional
female needlework skills and continued to be performed at home.

In many cases, women's work became less skilled during the period. We have seen how the introduction of the male-operated scythe
reduced the demand for female reapers, while increasing the number of women hired at lower pay as followers and rakers. Similarly,
the increase in the number of women employed in textile manufacture was largely brought about by breaking down skilled work into
simpler processes which could be performed by lower-paid, less

skilled workers: the development of the ready-made clothing industry, which replaced some of the work previously performed by male
tailors, is a good example of this phenomenon. In medicine, the increase in the number of female nurses occurred concurrently with
the declining respectability of female midwives, wet nurses, and
'quack' doctors. In all these cases, the number of women working in
that sector of the economy did not decrease, but the skill level required in their work, and levels of remuneration, declined significantly. While in some cases opportunities for skilled work decreased
for men as well, the picture is more mixed, since in some occupations, such as operating a scythe and in medicine, men acquired a
monopoly on skilled work. In a few cases, one can identify new
skilled occupations for women which emerged in this period, such
as running a milliner's shop, teaching, or writing novels, but, with
the exception of teaching, these clearly employed relatively small
numbers.[103]

Too much emphasis, however, should not be placed on what
changed during the period. Many sectors of the economy and occupational groups remained exclusively or predominantly male
throughout the period, including not only five of the categories in
the table, but also all members of the legal profession, the church,
and the army and navy. Moreover, the most common employments
of women throughout this period remained in domestic service, the
textile trades, nursing, retailing, the food and drink trades, and
agriculture. Not only do these account for over 90% of a sample of
1004 women who testified before the church courts in London in
the late seventeenth and early eighteenth centuries (agricultural
work aside), but they were the occupations of the vast majority of
the women listed as working in the 1851 census.[104] The overall patterns of men's and women's work did not change markedly between
1650 and 1850.

Why did this division of labour by gender exist, persist, and in
some ways become sharper over the course of this period? A number of possible explanations need to be considered, starting with
those which were constant factors over the whole period, and con-
cluding with those which explain the changes described above. The
most obvious possible explanations, frequently made by contemporaries, are biological: that women were weaker and less rational
than men, but more adept with their hands. Yet women often

---

103 Authorship is discussed below, in Chapter 7, pp. 283–88.
104 Earle, *City Full of People*, p. 116.

performed extremely arduous tasks in this period. With the exception of operating the scythe, they performed agricultural tasks which required as much strength and hard labour as men, such as reaping, spreading manure, carrying sacks of grain, and lifting cheeses (which could weigh over 100 pounds) in the dairy. And in the case of the scythe, it may be the design of the tool rather than the strength of the labourer per se that limited its use; only men with large frames could use it, excluding not only women, but also smaller men. We have also seen that women performed work involving strength in other sectors of the economy, including hauling coal underground in mines (until at least the end of the eighteenth century) and laundry work, which involved long hours and heavy lifting. Clearly men's generally superior upper-body strength cannot explain the sexual division of labour (although the argument that it should was used increasingly), especially since the technological changes introduced in industrialisation, which reduced the strength required in many jobs, failed to alter significantly the fact that 'the more prestigious and better-paid work' was reserved for men.[105]

Despite their alleged weakness, contemporaries thought that women's smaller and what were perceived to be more dexterous hands made them more suited to certain types of work. According to assistant poor law commissioner Henry Vaughan, 'the labour commonly assigned to [women] is suited to her character as having more discretion [and] greater strength and pliancy of hand.'[106] While the belief that women were more adept with their hands might explain why women were more involved in planting and working with hops in agriculture, spinning and lace-making in textile work, and painting pottery, it fails to explain why men dominated the tailoring, jewelling, and watchmaking industries, despite the similar types of careful handwork involved.

As we have seen from Chapter 2, women were also considered less rational than men, and the prevalence of this idea helps explain why women were excluded from the upper echelons of the professions. As this suggests, contemporary justifications of the sexual division of labour could be influential. Nonetheless, jobs weren't allocated solely according to the perceived levels of intelligence of each sex any more than they were allocated according to strength and dexterity. Women were frequently active in medicine (in the first half of the period), and street selling and market trading, for

105 Hudson, *The Industrial Revolution*, p. 228–9.
106 *Report on the Employment of Women and Children in Agriculture*, p. 134.

example, where business acumen was essential. The problem of explaining the sexual division of labour is better approached by examining the processes by which men and women acquired differential levels and types of skills in this period, and the institutional obstacles which prevented women from doing some types of work.

The people of England acquired the skills they used in employment during this period in numerous ways, the most common of which, in increasing order of importance, were probably university, schools, apprenticeship, learning from parent(s), and learning on the job. Each of these types of training, in different degrees, allowed men to acquire more skilled jobs than women. Throughout this period the universities and most grammar schools excluded women, thereby preventing them from acquiring the qualifications necessary to become physicians and lawyers. Some girls were able to attend the growing number of boarding and day schools founded in this period, but their education was entirely different from education for boys. Not only were women thought to have inferior intellectual abilities, but it was thought that girls went to school for different reasons. While men were expected to develop their intellectual and vocational skills, women were educated in order to acquire domestic skills, to become more attractive to potential husbands, and to acquire the appropriate emblems for their rank in society. (Both sexes were expected to receive religious training.)

In grammar schools and academies boys learned writing, foreign languages (those who learned Latin and Greek were able to go on to study law and medicine), casting accounts, and, increasingly over the course of this period, commercial and vocational skills such as accounting, navigation, and design. As one man testified, the skills he acquired in school 'fit him for any kind of business'. In addition, young men benefited from the increasing numbers of clubs, institutes, and societies founded during the period which taught them reading, writing, and arithmetic, as well as technical subjects (these were mostly closed to women). In contrast, in their schools elite girls learned domestic and 'finishing' skills in addition to the basic fare of reading, writing, and elementary arithmetic. In 1785, Mrs Courtney's boarding school for young ladies taught English, French, music, dancing, writing and accounts. This was a largely non-vocational education, and it remained that way throughout this period despite increasing possibilities in the nineteenth century for women to study more intellectual subjects, including the classics. As Davidoff and Hall concluded, middle-class women's education between 1780 and 1850 'reinforced the disinterest in business affairs being put forward in the prescriptive literature'.[107] Although the education available to the poor was of course much more limited, the differences between the sexes remained. While boys were taught sufficient reading, writing, and basic arithmetic to be 'fit for an employment', girls were less likely to be taught to write and cast accounts and more likely to learn 'housewifery', especially needlework. An Irish girl in London in 1750 explained that she had 'had no education but the needle'.[108] Girls at all social levels were also less likely to go to school at all; although they were often tutored at home, their education was often undermined by demands that they should care for other members of their families or engage in paid labour.

Even for boys, however, the skills taught in schools were in only a limited sense vocational. At around the age of fourteen most boys (and a few girls) entered an apprenticeship, a far more useful preparation for employment. Male apprentices typically spent seven years learning a craft or trade with a master or mistress, though much of their time, especially in the early years, was spent on menial tasks. Not only was apprenticeship a useful way of acquiring skills, but, according to the Statute of Artificers (1563; repealed in 1814) completion of an apprenticeship was necessary in order to practise most trades, and in trades regulated by guilds it was the primary method of gaining entry. Apprenticeship is often thought to have been restricted to men, but recent research has demonstrated that a significant minority of apprentices were female: between 0.6% and 10% of apprenticeships arranged by parents, and between a quarter and a third of those arranged by the parish (for orphans and the children of paupers). Moreover, female apprentices can be found in a wide range of 'male' trades such as carpentry, blacksmithing, ironmongery, and bricklaying.[109]

For most girls, however, apprenticeship meant something different than it did for boys. For one thing it was shorter: female apprenticeships usually lasted for only four years. Moreover, by far the most common type of female apprenticeship, especially for parish apprentices, was in 'housewifery'. While this meant more than housework as defined today (it included knitting and spinning, for

---

107 Earle, *City Full of People*, pp. 21–38, esp. p. 33; O'Day, *Education and Society*, pp. 179–95, 201–12; Davidoff and Hall, *Family Fortunes*, pp. 234–40, 289–93, esp. p. 293; Fletcher, *Gender, Sex and Subordination*, chs. 15 and 18, esp. p. 373.

108 Earle, *City Full of People*, p. 35.

109 Hill, *Women, Work and Sexual Politics*, ch. 6; Snell, *Annals of the Labouring Poor*, ch. 6.

example) and often included some training in the occupation practised by the master and/or mistress, its purpose appears largely to
have been to prepare such women for menial labour and domestic
duties in marriage. And even when women were apprenticed to
learn a specific trade, there is some evidence that 'the skill content
and the training component' of their apprenticeship was 'modest',
compared to the level of training received by boys. Girls were also
less likely to be given tools at the end of their apprenticeships.[110] In
light of this evidence, and the fact that women always accounted for
only a minority of apprenticeships, too much should not be made
of the fact that the number of female apprentices appears to have
decreased over the eighteenth century, and the range of occupations to which they were apprenticed became more restricted to 'female' trades.[111] Apprenticeship had never been a significant
method of occupational training for girls. In any case, after 1800
the institution of apprenticeship, for both boys and girls, was in serious decline in many parts of the country.

The paucity of formal training received by women was to some
extent remedied by the fact that they often received informal training in the households in which they were daughters, servants, or
wives. Ilana Ben-Amos has demonstrated how daughters and even
maidservants might learn aspects of the household craft or trade
through working in the shop, just as wives often did. She argues that
'women's informal learning did not greatly differ from many types
of male formal apprenticeships, based as they were on observation
and practical experience.'[112] Since such training went unrecorded,
it is of course impossible to say how extensive it was, and how far it
compensated for women's lack of formal training. Given prevailing
notions of gender roles, however, it would be surprising if in household workshops boys and girls were not introduced to different
skills. This certainly seems true of the socialisation process within
the family. While boys were introduced into their fathers' working
environment at an early age, girls were primarily exposed to household tasks and any other occupations their mothers pursued.[113]
Both formal and informal training worked to channel men and
women into what were perceived to be suitable employments for
each sex.

There were two further institutional obstacles which limited work

110 Berg, 'Women's work', p. 75; Roberts, 'Images of work and gender', p. 142.
111 Snell, *Annals of the Labouring Poor*, pp. 276–98.
112 Ben-Amos, 'Women apprentices', p. 248.
113 See above, Chapter 4, pp 132–3.

opportunities for women: the property laws, which made it difficult to run businesses, and the guilds. All women (and of course many men) were disadvantaged by the principle of primogeniture, which limited their access to landed property by giving the eldest son the right to inherit his father's land. Married women faced additional restrictions. Under the common-law principle of 'coverture', the legal identity of married women was completely subsumed into that of their husbands; married women could not own property, make contracts, or sue or be sued. Thus on the face of it it was impossible for married women, and difficult for most other women, to act as independent economic agents. There were, however, a number of ways of circumventing both primogeniture and coverture, and recent research suggests that women, both married and single, did have some control over property. In practice, parents tended to dispose of their property in relatively equal shares to their children of both sexes: though the first-born son inherited the land, the other children received movable goods. Moreover, in some boroughs, including the City of London, married women had the status of 'feme sole' trader, which allowed them to run businesses separate from their husbands. By the nineteenth century, however, this privilege had disappeared from everywhere but London, and in any case this status did not prevent women's businesses from being plundered by their husbands or subjected to unrealistic demands from their creditors. More commonly, pre-marital property settlements allowed married wives to retain property during marriage, though we should note that since the primary purpose of such settlements was to facilitate the transmission of property between men across generations, women's ability to dispose of that property was often circumscribed. Finally, despite their lack of a legal identity at common law, married women were able to protect their property through litigation in the ecclesiastical courts. In sum, in some cases married women as well as spinsters and widows could control and exploit property for their own benefit. Maxine Berg has discovered that in metal-working communities 'women owned and bequeathed real property in significant quantities.'[114]

While the property laws worked against women more in theory than in practice, the opposite was true of the guilds. Most guilds did

---

114 Earle, *Making of the English Middle Class*, pp. 158–60; Amy Erickson, *Women and Property in Early Modern England* (1993); Hunt, *The Middling Sort*, pp. 138–40; Susan Staves, *Married Women's Separate Property in England, 1660–1833* (1990), p. 67; Maxine Berg, 'Women's property and the industrial revolution', *Journal of Interdisciplinary History* 24 (1993), p. 243.

not formally exclude women, and examples of women entering guilds and practising trades can be found throughout this period. But the vast majority of women who had not served an apprenticeship could only acquire the right to practise a trade through a male relative. A few women gained the freedom of the company through patrimony, but more common was the practice of wives possessing the right to work in a trade through their husbands' membership. Such women could take apprentices, sometimes in different trades from their husbands.[115] Upon their husbands' death widows were entitled to become members of guilds on their own. Yet there is evidence that widows were discriminated against in various ways and many abandoned their husband's trade. They lost their privileges if they remarried to a man who was not a member of the guild. They could not participate in the running of the guild. And if the trade was not one commonly practised by women, they might not have learned much of the trade from their husband prior to his death, and might be forced to hire men to perform some of the tasks. Given these constraints, it is not surprising that relatively few widows carried on with their businesses.[116]

Thus, owing to various forms of discrimination women rarely participated in trades regulated by the guilds. This had the effect of pushing women into trades which were unregulated, either because of their recent origins (such as many types of retail work) or because of their location in towns without a guild structure (such as the metal trades in Birmingham). In many cases an oversupply of women competing for such work had the effect of driving down wages. The breakdown of the apprenticeship and guild systems during the eighteenth and early nineteenth centuries therefore had a potentially positive effect for women, since they were now able to enter trades such as framework knitting and aspects of the goldsmiths and tailoring trades which had previously been closed to them.

Important as the disadvantages women experienced in the realms of education, the guild system, and the law were, probably the most important factor which disadvantaged them in the labour market was their subordination within marriage, and the expectation that they would devote their time and capital primarily to the greater good of the family. Historians have probably exaggerated the influence of women's maternal duties on their work oppor-

---

115 Snell, *Annals of the Labouring Poor*, pp. 299–301; Clark, *Working Life*, ch. 5.
116 See above, Chapter 4, pp. 138–9.

tunities, not least because a significant proportion of women did
not have children, and mothers appear to have continued to work
while their children were young. Yet work opportunities and wages
for mothers clearly were affected by the number and age of their
children. As assistant poor law commissioner Alfred Austin reported
in 1843 in the context of agricultural work, 'a woman situated, with
regard to her family, so as to be always at liberty to go out to work
when wanted by the farmer, and upon whose services he can always
depend, gets higher wages than one who can only now and then
manage to get out to work, on account of young children, or other
circumstances.' The fact that married women had to fit their paid
employment around the demands of childcare and housework was
integral to the idea that women's work was supplemental to that of
their husbands, and therefore less important and lower in status.
Higher up the social scale, this meant that married women's business activities frequently suffered from the assumption that their
profits should be used for family expenses, and their capital could
be diverted into their husband's business if it ran into trouble (the
reverse, of course, did not apply). As Margaret Hunt has argued, the
idea of ' "the family economy" fostered men's disproportionate access to [the] resources' needed for business, and this prioritising of
the needs of the family and its head goes a long way towards explaining the sexual division of labour.[117]

Change
In sum, although women were formally discriminated against in a
number of ways, it was customary practices which probably contributed most to shaping gender roles at work. The property laws
discriminated against married women, and females were excluded
or discouraged from joining universities, schools, and guilds (and
later, as we shall see, trade unions). Yet married women were able to
control property and litigate. Moreover, only a small number of
men went to universities, the schools taught few vocational skills to
either boys or girls, and women were not formally excluded from
taking up apprenticeships. For most men and women, the most important determinants of the type of work they entered into were
probably cultural beliefs about appropriate behaviour for each sex,
the socialisation and informal training experienced during their
youth, family responsibilities, and local customs. The fact that these
determinants were largely informal and subject to local variation

117 *Report on the Employment of Women and Children in Agriculture*, p. 6; Hunt, *The
Middling Sort*, pp. 136–46.

suggests that they could change, and indeed, within a basic framework of continuity, we have identified in Chapter 2 some important changes in ideas about appropriate gender roles during this period. In this chapter we have documented some significant alterations in the sexual division of labour, and we now need to consider the ideological and other forces which caused such changes to occur.

One possible explanation points to changes in the economy, especially changes in the demand for labour. In a world in which men, more than women, were defined by their work, the position of women in the labour market was, more than men, dependent on the relationship between the overall demand for labour and its supply: in times of labour shortages, women were encouraged to work, but in times of labour surplus, women's work was discouraged. Thus during the Napoleonic wars, when large numbers of men were removed from the labour market due to military service, women worked in greater numbers than they had done previously and in a greater variety of tasks, but 'they made way for men immediately at the peace.'[118] Snell argues that the decline in the demand for female workers in agriculture in the southeast in the second half of the eighteenth century resulted from efforts to prioritise employment for men, due to the reduced demand for labour in grain-growing areas.[119] In contrast, women continued to play a more prominent role in agriculture in the north of England, and, as a result of the greater demand for labour due to the presence of industry, to receive higher wages. The problem with the argument that women's labour was regulated by the laws of supply and demand, however, is that the theory is better at accounting for changes in overall levels of female participation in the workforce than in explaining changes in the types of work performed. In industry in the second half of our period, for example, what was needed was not only more labour but different types of labour: a workforce which was more malleable and flexible than the existing largely male workforce. Manufacturers sought to introduce new working practices which bypassed traditional artisan customs, and the best way to do this was to hire women and children, who were less likely to resist such changes. Significantly, many machines and processes, such as calico printing and spinning, were invented with this new workforce in mind. The spinning jenny, intended for use by young girls, was built with its wheel positioned in such a way as to make it

118 *Report on the Employment of Women and Children in Agriculture*, p. 27.
119 Snell, *Annals of the Labouring Poor*, pp. 54, 61.

uncomfortable for adults to use.[120] Industrialisation led to an increased demand for women's labour, not only because women represented a source of available low-wage workers but also because it was thought that women's socialisation made them more docile and less assertive, and therefore more adaptable (and exploitable) than men.

Another common economic explanation for changes in the work performed by men and women identifies transformations in the whole structure of economic life, such as changes in the nature of capitalism. While capitalism was centuries old by this time, it is frequently argued that it underwent fundamental structural changes in this period: as economic activity became increasingly centred around large-scale businesses and factories, the family economy declined. Given their childcare and other domestic responsibilities, it is argued, women worked best when their work could be performed in the home as part of the family unit. With the decline in small agricultural holdings and family-based workshops, and the consequent growing reliance on individual wages, Alice Clark and Bridget Hill have argued, women were forced out of the home and into the labour market, where they were unable to compete due to the exclusionary tactics of men, their lack of training, and their childcare responsibilities.

It is undoubtedly the case that in some occupations there was an increasing separation of the home and the workplace, and this could work against women. The decline of small farms reduced the number of farmers' wives who tended vegetable gardens and raised poultry. In textiles, a considerable amount of work, including the core tasks of spinning and some types of weaving, that had previously been performed in the home was transferred to factories, where the inflexibility of the hours and working practices made it difficult for mothers to bring their children to work. Yet one should not overstate the magnitude of this shift away from home work, nor its significance for women. As we have seen, much of the industrial expansion during this period occurred by the multiplication of small, primarily home-based, units of production, not by gathering workers together in factories. And even where such changes restricted the types of work women were able to perform, that is not the same as saying that women were not able to work at all: due to the lower wages they received, women could still compete in the labour market, as can be seen from the fact that there continued to be a number of tasks which women could perform at home.

120 Berg, 'What difference', pp. 34–5.

Economic forces can provide only an incomplete explanation of changes in the numbers of women working and the tasks they performed. It is also necessary to consider changes in attitudes about the types of work which were suitable for men and women, such as the greater value placed on (male) rationality as a qualification for jobs; the growing ideological importance placed on women's domestic responsibilities; and the development of the concept of the 'breadwinner wage' for men.

The increasing importance placed on rational and scientific methods, for example, and a tendency to label women's ways of working as irrational and tradition-bound, pushed women out of positions of responsibility in a number of occupations. As we have seen in the dairy industry, for example, the increasing weight placed on 'scientific' dairying in the second half of the eighteenth century tended to marginalise farmers' wives, whose actions in managing the dairy were portrayed by self-proclaimed (male) experts as irrational and governed by custom. For similar reasons, women were excluded from horse breeding and other new farming methods, and from practising medicine as midwives and unlicensed doctors.

A related justification for pushing women out of some types of work was the increasing articulation of an ideology of domesticity for women. As noted in Chapter 2, this ideology, which was initially the product of evangelical writers, came to be widely accepted in the early nineteenth century, especially among the middle class. In 1834, Thomas Wakley, the founder of the medical weekly the *Lancet*, wrote that he thanked God that in England it was 'disreputable' for a wife to be required to work.[121] Although we have seen that the idea that women's primary responsibilities were in the home was a constant theme throughout this period, the greater moral value placed on domesticity in the early nineteenth century did discourage some women from engaging in paid employment. In particular, the ideological constraints on upper-middle-class women who sought to become 'genteel' appear to have tightened, as not working became an essential ingredient of respectability. In the words of Sarah Ellis in 1839, while gentlemen could engage 'in almost any degrading occupation . . . [and] may be gentlemen still; . . . if a lady but touch any article, no matter how delicate, in the way of trade, she loses caste, and ceases to be a lady.'[122]

121 The *Lancet*, 12, pp. 205–6, cited by Donnison, *Midwives and Medical Men*, p. 58.
122 Sarah Ellis, *The Women of England* (1839), p. 463; see above, Chapter 2, pp 31–2.

Although such ideas were most powerful among the middle class, attempts were made to disseminate them among the lower classes. No attempt was made to prevent such women from working, but certain occupations were seen by upper- and middle-class observers as interfering with working class women's domestic tasks, either by preventing them from spending time at home or by giving them coarse manners and habits of insubordination which were unsuitable for home life. It was argued in 1808 that allowing women to do farm work diverted them from 'the household and more domestic duties that they ought early to be made acquainted with', and thirty-five years later an assistant poor law commissioner reported that 'agricultural work, if habitual, accustoms the whole frame to action upon too broad a scale for domestic life; the eye becomes regardless of precision and cleanliness, the habits undomestic and unfavourable to personal subordination. It seems agreed on all hands that much field-work in early life is a bad exercise for a woman's future duties.' Similarly, an investigator of the coal industry argued that 'a large portion of the evils that prevail in the class of colliers' was caused by women working away from their homes.[123]

Related concerns were voiced from the late eighteenth century about the impact of heavy labour and adverse weather conditions on the physical well being of female workers. These ideas are part of the more general increase in medical attention paid to women's alleged biological inferiority in the early nineteenth century.[124] Female farm workers had always performed heavy work, but from the 1780s observers of the agricultural scene complained when women performed strenuous tasks: making cheese was deemed 'too great a labour for any woman' in 1789, and in 1794 driving ploughs and harrows by servant maids was seen as 'rough employment' which accorded ill with their 'elegant features, and delicate, nicely-proportioned limbs'.[125] Observers were also concerned about the impact of working outdoors in cold and damp conditions on female, but not male labourers. The assistant poor law commissioners in 1843 found little evidence that agricultural work was bad for a woman's health, but the significant point is that the commissioners had been asked to examine this issue.[126] As we have seen, similar concerns

123 Charles Vancouver, *General View of the Agriculture of the County of Devon*, 1808, quoted in Hill, *Eighteenth Century Women*, p. 187; *Report on the Employment of Women and Children in Agriculture*, p. 150; John, *By the Sweat of Their Brow*, p. 43.

124 See above, Chapter 2, pp. 20.

125 Quoted in Hill, *Women, Work and Sexual Politics*, p. 31 and Hill, *Eighteenth-Century Women*, p. 186.

126 *Report on the Employment of Women and Children in Agriculture*, pp. 10–12.

about the deleterious effects of women working underground were expressed in the early nineteenth century.

Moreover, it was argued that women were morally corrupted by heavy labour and working alongside men. According to one alarmed observer, women working underground in mines 'become a set of coarse, licentious wretches, scorning all kinds of restraint, and yielding themselves up, with shameless audacity to the most detestable sensuality'.[127] Similarly, observers of factory work complained of 'the savage debauchery of men – the loss of every semblance of feminine modesty in the women . . . the irreclaimable depravity of it all'.[128] Even field work in agriculture was thought to promote immorality, since women were 'thrown so much into coarse male society'.[129] Once again, the assistant poor law commissioners looked at this problem in 1843 and found little evidence in support of this charge. Nonetheless, concern that public working environments could be morally corrupting for women was widespread. Intense manual labour which took place in homes or small workshops (such as 'sweated' needlework) did not, however, raise similar concerns.

In sum, in the second half of our period an increasing volume of social criticism was directed at women's work, demanding that women work in more suitable occupations or not at all. But did women listen to this advice? As we have seen, there is strong evidence that a significant proportion of middle-class wives did not work *throughout* this period, and the increasing attention paid to this phenomenon may have been due to the growing size and prosperity of the middle class. Nonetheless, there is some evidence that an increasing proportion of women in this class shunned certain types of work, especially commerce and all forms of manual labour (outside the home). Davidoff and Hall cite evidence from occupational directories showing that the range of occupations in which middle-class women worked 'noticeably narrowed' between the 1790s and 1850s.[130]

Domestic ideology had less impact, however, on the lives of working-class women before 1850. It has been argued that such women actively rejected its beliefs, despite the efforts of middle-class missionaries.[131] Women were excluded from underground work in

---

127 Cited by John, *By the Sweat of Their Brow*, p. 31.
128 Quoted in Hill, *Eighteenth-Century Women*, p. 207.
129 *Report on the Employment of Women and Children in Agriculture*, p. 217.
130 Davidoff and Hall, *Family Fortunes*, pp. 312–13; above, Chapter 4, pp. 113–15.
131 J. Lown, *Women and Industrialization: Gender at Work in Nineteenth-Century England* (1990), pp. 162–5.

mines, but they continued to work above ground, as well as in agricultural gangs and in the metal industries. Due to financial exigen-
cies, such women had no choice but to work. There is nonetheless
some evidence that working-class men subscribed to ideas of domesticity for their wives. Some of the men on the Short Time committees in 1841 demanded 'the gradual withdrawal of all females from
the factories', contending that 'the home, its cares and its employments is the woman's true sphere' and complaining that women
factory workers could not 'make a shirt, darn a stocking, cook a dinner, or clean a house'.[132] Such ideas may have led some wives to
take up jobs involving domestic skills, and may thus have contributed to the increasing numbers of women in domestic service,
nursing, and teaching, all occupations which were seen as being
more suitable for women due their affinities with housework and
motherhood.

While women were increasingly identified with domesticity, men
came to be identified more strongly with their occupation. Although men's occupational identity had always been far stronger
than women's, in the early part of our period the Puritan idea of
the worth of all vocations or 'callings' extended to both men and
women, and it was not expected that either would necessarily confine their work to a single employment. Over the course of our period men's, but not women's, occupational identities acquired
greater fixity and importance. In the first half of the nineteenth
century the middle-class 'masculine self', according to Davidoff and
Hall, came to be 'more deeply implicated in what they did rather
than in who they were in terms of kinship or religious loyalties'. Instead of pursuing a number of different lines of work, employment
came to be seen increasingly in terms of a single career, and occupational titles became more precise and sophisticated.[133]

In the working class, the idea of the breadwinner wage developed
in the early nineteenth century. The male counterpart of domesticity was the argument that the male head of the household should
be solely responsible for supporting his family and should be compensated accordingly. Men of course had always played a leading
role in the family economy, but in the preindustrial period their
masculinity was defined in terms of their position as head of the
household business. When this was undermined by the increasing
role of wage labour (open to all members of the family as individuals

132 Quoted by Pinchbeck, *Women Workers*, p. 200.
133 Roberts, 'Images of work and gender', pp. 130–44; Davidoff and Hall, *Family Fortunes*, p. 230.

and subject to the authority of an external employer) and the threat posed by cheaper female labour, men defended their role with the new argument that they should be the *sole* economic providers. Although not fully accepted among the working classes before 1850, the idea was gaining ground, especially among the unions, although it was seen by some as a long-term ambition which was not yet practical. Evidence of its acceptance by their social superiors is the fact that it is embodied in the provisions of the New Poor Law of 1834.[134] Earlier, the employment of wives was more widely accepted: artisans, for example, expected their wives to assist them in their work, and/or bring in their own income from by-employments. In 1743 female servants were advised that they would be expected to work after marriage, for 'none but a fool will take a wife whose bread must be earned solely by his labour and who will contribute nothing towards it herself.'[135]

The ideal of a breadwinner wage served two purposes for male workers: it justified demands for higher wages from their employers, and it kept lower-paid women from competing with them for jobs. A number of attempts were made in the early nineteenth century, both by unions and through legislation, formally to exclude or limit women's work, but their impact was relatively small. The most important efforts were made by journeymen's associations and trade unions, especially in the silkweaving, spinning, tailoring, hatmaking, bookbinding, and printing trades. Faced with competition from lower-paid women, which threatened not only their pay packets but also their masculinity (in that their position as primary household provider was threatened), journeymen's associations and trade unions prohibited women from becoming members and attempted to prevent employers from hiring them. The journeymen bookbinders, for example, excluded women from their union in 1779. This did not prevent women from working in the trade, but it did have the effect of confining them to the less skilled tasks of folding and sewing. Another tactic, adopted by the tailors in London, was to

134 Sonya Rose, 'Gender antagonism and class conflict: exclusionary strategies of male trade unionists in nineteenth-century Britain', *Social History* 13 (1988), pp. 202–8; Wally Seccombe, 'Patriarchy stabilized: the construction of the male breadwinner wage norm in nineteenth-century Britain', *Social History* 11 (1986), pp. 53–76; Pat Thane, 'Women and the Poor Law in Victorian and Edwardian England', *History Workshop Journal* 6 (1978), p. 29.

135 *A Present for a Servant Maid* (1743), cited by George, *London Life*, p. 171; Clark, *Struggle for the Breeches*, p. 198.

prohibit work from being done at home, thereby discouraging wives and children from assisting.[136]

Few unions, however, had sufficient power to exclude women from work, unless other factors were in their favour. The brushmakers and the filesmiths attempted to prevent the employment of women in 1829 and 1847 respectively, but census data reveals that the proportions of women in those industries subsequently increased.[137] The tailoring trades in London had lost their battle for exclusion by 1833.[138] As we have seen, the Cotton Spinners' Union, usually credited with the exclusion of women from their industry by the mid-nineteenth century, only succeeded due to other factors: the introduction of 'doubled' mules which required greater strength to operate, and the subsequent lack of trained women when self-acting mules (which could be operated by women) were introduced a decade later.[139] The attack on women's work by the unions reveals an important shift in the attitudes of skilled male workers, which in the long term may have had important repercussions. Nevertheless, it failed in the short run to reduce significantly the number of women working in manufacturing (as we have seen, women accounted for over a third of the workforce in 1851), though in some occupations it kept women out of the more skilled parts of the trade.

Similarly, the legislation passed to control women's employment failed to have much immediate impact, though its symbolic significance was great. The 1842 Mines Act prohibited women and girls and boys under ten from working underground, but its impact was limited since the law was frequently evaded and in any case the number of women working underground had been declining since the late eighteenth century.[140] In 1847, the Factory Act restricted working hours for women and children to ten hours a day. Yet once again the act was evaded: mill owners instituted a relay system, in which women and children were required to spread the ten hours over the twelve-to-fourteen-hour day worked by men in order to keep the mills running as long as possible. At the same time, some male workers attempted to use short time provisions to limit the working hours of men to those worked by women. Despite the fact

136 Berg, 'Women's work', p. 73; Rendall, *Women in an Industrializing Society*, p. 66; Schwarz, *London in the Age of Industrialisation*, p. 190.

137 Jordan, 'Exclusion of women', p. 286.

138 Schwarz, *London in the Age of Industrialisation*, pp. 192–3.

139 Freifeld, 'Technological change'.

140 John, *By the Sweat of their Brow*, chs 1–2.

that these acts often failed to limit women's work, by grouping women's and children's work together they did establish an important precedent: women were now officially classified as no more suitable than children for many types of work.[141]

CONCLUSION

In sum, the constraints on women's employment opportunities imposed by unions and legislation in the second half of our period were less important than broader economic and cultural forces in explaining the limited changes in the sexual division of labour which did occur during this period. As we have seen, the economic pressures of industrialisation led manufacturers to employ more women as a means of obtaining a cheaper, more malleable workforce, and this resulted in a significant increase in the number of women employed in manufacturing, although many of the jobs were low-skilled. This expansion of the female workforce was clearly threatening to many men. Although the restrictions imposed by the unions and parliamentary legislation were largely ineffective, they contributed to the increasing articulation of ideas which sought to define women in terms of domestic duties, and to privilege further men's work through the growing emphasis on occupational identity in male self-definitions and through the concept of the breadwinning wage. Although these ideas were quite influential among the middle classes, they were viewed more sceptically by working-class women, most of whom could not afford to stop working. Nonetheless, they may have encouraged more women to take up employments which incorporated some domestic skills, such as domestic service, nursing, and teaching, and to avoid occupations which involved outdoor work and strenuous physical labour. Moreover, they contributed to a general devaluation of the status of women's work. As a result of these developments, some occupations became more male dominated over the course of this period, in particular a number of tasks within the mining and agricultural sectors, and women lost a number of skilled employments. Concurrently, a number of feminist writers, including Mary Wollstonecraft and Mary Hays, complained about the narrow range of suitable jobs open to

141 Carol Morgan, 'Women, work and consciousness in the mid–nineteenth-century English cotton industry', *Social History* 17 (1992), p. 37; Robert Gray, 'Factory legislation and the gendering of jobs in Britain, 1830–1860', *Gender and History* 5 (1993), pp. 56–80.

women, especially middle- and upper-class women.[142] The increase in women's labour stimulated by industrialisation thus prompted a debate on the nature of women's work, which in 1850 had largely been won by those who wished to prioritise male employments and further limit women's choice of occupation.

142 Jane Rendall, *The Origins of Modern Feminism* (1985), pp. 186, 282, 287; Hill, *Eighteenth Century Women*, pp. 222–8.

CHAPTER SIX

Religion and Politics

The 'public/private' dichotomy is a frequent way of characterising political and social divisions, especially gender differences. We have seen in Chapter 2 that during the second half of our period existing beliefs about gender difference crystallised into an ideology of separate spheres predicated on explicit distinctions between women's domestic responsibilities and the masculine, public world outside the home, though it did not totally discourage female public activity. In actual practice, the public/private distinction did not correspond directly with gender differences. We have seen in Chapter 4 that although women dominated most aspects of family life, including housework and childcare, there was an important masculine presence in the home. Similarly, much paid labour, by men as well as women, still took place in the home, while a significant minority of women worked outside it. This chapter and the next will make a parallel argument about public life: although many aspects of the world outside the family were male dominated, women had a significant if distinctive role to play in religion, politics, social life, and culture. Moreover, despite the increasing articulation of the ideology of separate spheres, these opportunities increased over the course of this period.

RELIGION

Because so much public behaviour was conditioned by religious beliefs, it makes sense to start this discussion with this topic, though it may seem to the modern reader to be an intensely private issue. Much worship in this period did take place in private (including individual and family prayer), yet religious practice had a fundamen-

tal public importance at this time, since the very survival of the state
and society was held to be contingent on the proper Christian behaviour of the people. Consequently, dissent from the established
Church of England was interpreted as politically subversive. Religiosity, in other words, was a matter of immense public, political importance, and its expression was highly visible. Since it was
commonly believed that, as part of their capacity to be more tender
and charitable than men, women were the more pious and devout
of the two sexes, religion gave women an important political voice.

Religious worship in practice was gendered in complex ways,
which occasionally empowered women and subverted gender boundaries. Formally, religious practice was entirely governed by men.
Every office within the Church of England was filled by men, with
the exception of just about the least prestigious office, the parish
churchwarden, in which a few women served. Even within the
home, wives were expected to be subservient to their husbands in
family worship. Women, therefore, had no formal role to play in
governing worship within the Anglican church. Nonetheless, they
could acquire significant informal power. Conceptions of women's
nature which identified them as more receptive to divine signals,
gave women, more than men, the potential to become prophets. By
essentially becoming the voice of God, women could temporarily
transcend the limitations of their gender.

Women were also potentially religiously empowered by the positive use of maternal and other feminine images in Christian
thought, including the image of the church as the bride of Christ
and the use of the relationships of infant to mother and wife to husband to depict close relationships between humans and God. These
images could be used in ways which allowed the sexes to transcend
prescribed gender roles. As Phyllis Mack has argued, men sometimes depicted their intense religious feelings in conventionally
feminine terms, such as when 'as worshippers, they assumed the
role of loving spouse and supplicant before a masculine God'. In
this sense, according to Mack, 'the practice of religion offered the
individual temporary liberation from rigid gender roles.' While this
may have allowed men to adopt traditionally feminine modes of expression, for women the liberation was more limited, in the sense
that such images, although positive, continued to identify them primarily in terms of their maternal and spousal functions. Moreover,
negative feminine images such as depictions of the false church as a
whore and heresy as a form of female sexual deviance were never
far away, and women's supposed suggestibility could just as easily be

seen as leading them to fall victim to the influence of the devil as of God.[1]

Nonetheless, the positive feminine aspects of Christian thought help explain why, although women rarely acquired any formal positions of leadership, they dominated most aspects of religious practice in this period, from day-to-day worship within the Church of England to preaching and prophesying in dissenting sects and even leading some non-institutionalised expressions of religious enthusiasm. Evidence of actual religious belief and everyday religious practice is of course rare, but the limited evidence available suggests women were predominant. The intense piety found in women's diaries and autobiographies, for example, suggests that women may have been more devout practitioners than men. Patricia Crawford has argued that this was the case among seventeenth-century women because faith helped them come to terms with traumatic events like childbirth and the deaths of children; upper- and middle-class women had more time for prayers and devotion than their husbands; and religiosity enabled women to gain control over their own lives: 'denied many other avenues of self-expression, women could express themselves through their religious devotions.' Whether women were more likely to attend church is unclear, but impressionistic evidence suggests that women did outnumber men in many congregations. In 1673, Richard Allestree observed that 'many ladies . . . help to fill our congregations, when Gentlemen desert them.' A century and a half later Sarah Stickney Ellis made a similar point when she wrote that 'women are said to be more easily brought under [religious] influence than men; and we consequently see, in places of public worship, and on all occasions in which a religious object is the motive for exertion, a greater proportion of women than of men.'[2] Women also played a major role in sects outside the established church. Movements of religious enthusiasm throughout this period, notably the sects and prophets of the Civil War and Interregnum, and the Evangelical Revival of the second half of our period, provided considerable opportunities for public

---

1 Phyllis Mack, *Visionary Women: Ecstatic Prophecy in Seventeenth-Century England* (Berkeley, 1992), chs 1 and 2, esp. pp. 39 and 49. See also Patricia Crawford, *Women and Religion in England, 1500–1720* (1993), pp. 10–17.

2 Crawford, *Women and Religion*, ch. 4, quotes at pp. 74 and 78 (see also Sara Mendelsson, 'Stuart women's diaries and occasional memoirs', in *Women in English Society 1500–1800* ed. M. Prior [1985], pp. 185–9); [Richard Allestree], *The Ladies Calling* (Oxford, 1673), p. 130; Sarah Stickney Ellis, *The Women of England, Their Social Duties and Domestic Habits* (10th edn, *c.* 1850), p. 37.

female religious expression and the acquisition by women of positions of responsibility.

Women were very prominent among the separatist sects which flourished during the 1640s and 1650s. In the previous decades puritanism had given those women who were perceived as 'godly' considerable spiritual authority, both within their homes and among the godly community, and following the breakdown of government control over religious practice in the 1640s women were able to play an even greater role among the sects. Believing as they did in the spiritual equality of all their members and, often, in every believer's ability to receive direct inspiration from God, the sects offered women unprecedented opportunities. Encouraged by widespread millenarian expectations, women joined public religious life, engaging in teaching, preaching, prophesying, testifying, leading worship, writing, and missionising. They participated in some aspects of church government, including the choice of ministers and decisions about admitting members. Female prophecy, in which women spoke in a trance, saw visions, and heard voices, was in fact far more common than male, and women prophesied on political as well as religious issues, including the execution of Charles I and social policies.[3]

Yet the spiritual equality of women with men during the Civil War and Interregnum was not complete, nor did it extend to other activities. Gender differences remained, even in the prophets' language: Phyllis Mack has shown that women's pronouncements were more moderate and less self-promoting and arrogant than those of men. Because women needed to project themselves as transcending their normal powerlessness when possessed by the Holy Spirit, they came across as less individualistic and less in control of themselves (and thus, more insane) than their male counterparts. Moreover, virtually all influential female prophets needed male allies, as apologists, editors, or ministers, in order to achieve influence and respectability. Public female preaching (an activity recognisably performed by the woman herself, as opposed to a prophet acting as a vehicle for God's word) was less acceptable, and, despite the fact that women outnumbered men among the membership of sects, women rarely acquired formal positions of leadership. Mack argues that some sects were more receptive to women than others: those which were 'avowedly antiformalist or unprogrammatic', such as the

3 Diane Willen, 'Godly women in early modern England: puritanism and gender', *Journal of Ecclesiastical History* 43 (1992), pp. 561–80; Crawford, *Women and Religion*, pp. 106, 130–6.

Ranters and the Fifth Monarchists, were more receptive, while those 'most concerned with political order' (including the Levellers and the Diggers) preserved exclusive male authority. The contradiction between the theoretical spiritual equality of the sexes and the exclusion of women from most decision-making and many public activities led to a number of female challenges to the male leadership of the sects, but these were largely unsuccessful.[4]

The sect which was most receptive to women was the Quakers. Believing not only in the complete spiritual equality of the sexes, but also that women's subjection to men had been erased by Christ's sacrifice, Quakers accorded women equality in speaking and prophesying, and female Quakers engaged in a number of public activities furthering the Quaker cause, including charity work, missionary work, publishing tracts, and administering funds. In the 1650s, Margaret Fell was one of the most prominent Quakers. A gentlewoman, she engaged in extensive correspondence with Quaker ministers and wrote numerous important pamphlets setting out and defending Quaker doctrines and practices; later she travelled widely, helped to secure the release of many Quaker prisoners, and was instrumental in the development of separate women's meetings. In October 1669, she married the Quaker leader George Fox in a union which symbolised the importance to the Quakers not only of marriage, but also of the role played by both sexes in the movement. Although historians dispute the extent of her theological contributions, her efforts in promoting and defending her faith were unprecedented and vital in sustaining the movement, and arguably her model of 'authoritative female public ministry' set an example which encouraged the active participation of other women.[5]

To a much greater extent than in the other sects, Quaker prophetesses and prophets managed to transcend gender differences. Both adopted the traditional attributes of both sexes, at times rejecting male aggressiveness and egoism and embracing feminine passivity and emotionalism and at other times adopting the public face of aggressive male Old Testament prophets. Still, female

---

4 Keith Thomas, 'Women and the Civil War sects', *Past and Present* 13 (1958), pp. 44–7; Mack, *Visionary Women*, chs 2 and 3, esp. p. 66; Crawford, *Women and Religion*, chs 6 and 7; Anne Laurence, 'A priesthood of she-believers: women and congregations in mid-seventeenth-century England', in *Women in the Church*, ed. W. J. Sheils and D. Wood (Ecclesiastical History Society, Studies in Church History vol. 27, 1990), pp. 351–2.

5 Bonnelyn Kunze, *Margaret Fell and the Rise of Quakerism* (1994).

prophets used somewhat different language from men, and instead of defining a new public image for women their activities were justified in domestic terms, using the biblical archetype of 'Mothers in Israel'. The 'central female symbol of the movement', this was the image of the spiritually active woman who used her caring and domestic skills to further the cause. Even the Quakers tried to limit women's public role, discouraging them at times from speaking in meetings and encouraging modest preaching and prayers. As the controversy over the activities of Martha Simmonds, whose prophecies were rejected by the Quaker leadership in the 1650s, suggests, Quaker leaders soon became wary of female public preaching and attempted to control it. Nonetheless, perhaps the most significant aspect of the Simmonds affair is that it shows how willing some Quaker women were to challenge traditional gender roles.[6]

The restoration of the monarchy and the established Anglican church in 1660 brought a more repressive climate for the sects. Just as the collapse of authority in the 1640s had opened up opportunities for women, its restoration in 1660 narrowed them. Women continued to dominate the membership lists of dissenting groups (accounting for 62% of the members in the surviving Baptist and Congregational membership lists between 1650 and 1700[7]), but they were further excluded from public roles and from any decision-making power. This was the result of the altered political climate, in which spontaneous religious expression became increasingly dangerous. Faced with persecution, non-conformist groups needed to impose greater discipline and tighten their organisational structures, and both changes enhanced the powers of the male leaders and restricted opportunities for the rank-and-file members (the majority of whom were women).

Fearful of negative publicity, even the Quakers attempted to control public speaking and de-emphasise public prophecies (which, by their nature, could not be controlled). Unease about the undisciplined nature of female preachers and prophets, which had already surfaced prior to 1660 and was reinforced by the public ridicule which such women often attracted, was now expressed openly by Quakers. When the system of local, regional, and national meetings was established from the mid-1660s, procedures were developed

6 Thomas, 'Women and the Civil War sects', p. 47; Mack, *Visionary Women*, part 2, esp. p. 290; Crawford, *Women and Religion*, ch. 8.

7 Clive D. Field, 'Adam and Eve: gender in the English Free Church constituency', *Journal of Ecclesiastical History* 44 (1993), p. 66.

which limited women's ability to speak and preach in mixed-sex meetings, and to preach in public. For example, those who wanted to speak in meetings had to ask in advance and those who wanted to preach in public had to obtain a licence. Even though female preaching was still permitted, it unsurprisingly became less common, and by the 1700s there is some evidence that 'women preachers seemed unnatural even to women.'[8] Women were also excluded from most aspects of the running of the movement: they were discouraged from participating in the national governing body, the Yearly Meeting of ministers, and the Women's Yearly Meeting was prohibited from meeting throughout most of the eighteenth century. No women participated in the Second Day Morning Meeting, which from 1672 was given the responsibility for vetting all proposed publications by Quakers. As we shall see, in terms of decision-making power the separate women's meetings established in the Restoration were clearly subordinate to the men's.

Women continued to play an important role in the non-conformist sects, but it was increasingly centred around traditional female tasks. With increasing persecution, family and household worship became the safest means of religious expression and this accentuated women's domestic religious roles such as instructing children and servants and subtly reforming their husbands; such activities were vital to the continuing success of a sect. The only public roles accorded to women were increasingly centred around charity. Among the Baptists, the only formal responsibility given to women was the office of deaconess, who from the late 1650s was given the responsibility for looking after the sick and the poor. Among the Quakers, the separate women's meetings were given the responsibility for poor relief, enquiring into the circumstances of couples proposing to get married, and the enforcement of moral discipline (in all cases, women were thought to know more about the circumstances of those involved).[9]

Historians differ on whether the creation of separate women's meetings (which were established nationally in the early 1670s) was a positive step for Quaker women. They can be seen as a means of marginalising women's participation and of reinforcing their traditional domestic obligations. Certainly women's meetings were inferior to men's, in the sense that the men's meetings had greater authority, and men's responsibilities (the organisation of the minis-

<hr>

8 Crawford, *Women and Religion*, pp. 193–7, quote at 207.
9 Mack, *Visionary Women*, ch. 8; Crawford, *Women and Religion*, pp. 195, 201.

try, financial matters, and debates with people outside the movement) can be seen as more central to the running of the movement
than those accorded to women. On the other hand, Phyllis Mack
has argued that the development of separate women's meetings was
'an extremely radical solution to the problem of reconciling emotion and spirituality with the new political order'. For the first time
in any Protestant religious group, women acquired formal, *public* responsibilities over issues where their expertise was undisputed, and
in this sense the women's meetings opened up a number of new opportunities for women. Their control over the provision of poor relief, for example, gave them authority over the Quakers' most
substantial area of expenditure. Moreover, their responsibilities for
the distribution of charity and cases of discipline gave them power
over some men. Nonetheless, we cannot ignore the fact that this
change was achieved at the cost of a narrowing of women's spiritual
and intellectual horizons, and this can be seen in the content of
their doctrinal writings after 1660. According to Mack, women's theological writings became more personal and inner- directed, they
placed greater emphasis on humility and their own physical weakness, and they paid less attention to public activities. According to
Mack, these changing emphases in Quaker women's writings resulted from 'a recognition of the need to present themselves not
simply as Friends, but as females'.[10]

Changes in the gendered pattern of religious behaviour after
1660 have led Patricia Crawford to suggest that the late seventeenth
and early eighteenth centuries witnessed the 'feminisation of religion in England', as middle- and upper-class men were increasingly
attracted to reason and deism, while 'enthusiastic religion' was confined to women and lower-class men.[11] Much of this argument is un-
provable, given the current state of research concerning actual
religious practice. From what is known, however, perhaps a better
way of characterising these changes is in terms of an increasing bi-
furcation of religious practice by gender, as men kept control of
church leadership and regained their monopoly over public religious responsibilities, and were possibly more likely to be allied to
the established church, while women devoted themselves to household religious practice and to more 'enthusiastic' and emotional approaches (in the early eighteenth century, female prophets once
again emerged, within the French Prophets and the Philadelphian

10 Mack, *Visionary Women*, part 33, quotes at 288 and 319.
11 Crawford, *Women and Religion*, p. 185.

Society). Despite the decline of women's opportunities which followed the institutionalisation of the Interregnum sects, the example set by the prominent women in these sects would be followed, as we shall see, in new groups which emerged in the next century. However, men too would continue to be attracted to enthusiastic religion throughout the remainder of our period, from the French Prophets at the beginning of the century, to Methodism from the 1740s, and the Evangelical Revival within the Church of England and dissenting groups from the 1780s.

The Evangelical Revival
Like Crawford, but for later periods, a number of other historians have argued for the 'feminisation' of religion in the eighteenth and/or nineteenth centuries. Yet an examination of the sexual composition of congregations, the role of women preachers, and the content of religious movements during this period suggests that the picture is far more complicated than the word 'feminisation' suggests. Certainly it appears that women formed the majority of committed worshippers both inside and outside the Church of England. Although the evidence on this point is extremely patchy, a review of the available statistics for the period 1700 to 1850 reveals that women constituted between 45% and 70% of the membership of dissenting sects and of confirmands within the Church of England, figures which still include a significant proportion of men. And if we look at the broader category of who showed up in church (the available evidence pertains to dissenting chapels), we find that men and women participated in roughly equal numbers. Clearly a significant proportion of worshippers were men, and we need to ask why they continued to be attracted to church or chapel if religion was becoming 'feminised'. In fact, with the exception of a group of Moravians in Bristol, the statistics do not show a process of feminisation, but instead a fairly constant surplus of women over men over the whole period. Throughout this period women were *somewhat* more likely to be committed worshippers, and this basic fact was not substantially altered by the Evangelical Revival which changed the face of English religion in the second half of our period.[12]

12 Field, 'Adam and Eve', pp. 66–71; G. J. Barker-Benfield, *The Culture of Sensibility: Sex and Society in Eighteenth-Century Britain* (Chicago, 1992), p. 272; James Obelkevich, *Religion and Rural Society: South Lindsey 1825–1875* (Oxford, 1976), p. 132; Madge Dresser, 'Sisters and brethren: power, propriety and gender among the Bristol Moravians', *Social History* 21 (1996), pp. 304–5.

Early examples of evangelicalism occurred primarily among the lower and lower-middle classes, and the most important manifestation was Methodism. Though a number of elite women were influential (the Countess of Huntington, for example, used her social position to encourage piety and mediate disputes), the movement was very much controlled by John Wesley and his male deputies. Female preaching was not allowed at first (though women were able to lead class and band meetings), but Wesley consented to it in 1761, permitting women with 'an extraordinary call' to preach, but not itinerantly. This change of heart appears to have occurred for pragmatic reasons, since Wesley could see the effectiveness of women preachers in recruiting new members (although women preachers were rejected in some places, their novelty often helped them draw crowds). Indeed, they went on to play an important role in many areas, often travelling to remote regions neglected by male preachers. But as Deborah Valenze points out, such women worked on an *ad hoc* basis and 'never gained official status or respect equal to that of male itinerants'.[13]

The effectiveness of female preachers may have been partly due to the fact that Methodism had a lot to offer women. The emotional rather than doctrinal focus offered women what they were conditioned to desire, 'a heaven of love and soft feeling'. Moreover, the focus on man's sinfulness, and specific criticisms of wife beating and many aspects of male popular culture, offered women the possibility of reforming their husbands. Henry Abelove suggests that attendance at meetings offered wives the opportunity to escape from oppressive domestic obligations. This was also attractive to men, who may have wished 'to turn away emotionally from their families', particularly their fathers. The holding of some separate group meetings for each sex (notably the 'bands'), echoing the even stricter gender segregation of the Moravians (where casual contact between unrelated men and women was banned), promoted same-sex emotional bonds among both men and women. Yet, according to Gail Malmgreen, becoming a Methodist for women involved 'more of an act of independence', since female members were much more likely to be unmarried and less likely than men to be joined in membership by another relative. Thus, although Methodism satisfied the

---

13 Deborah Valenze, *Prophetic Sons and Daughters: Female Preaching and Popular Religion in Industrial England* (Princeton, 1985), p. 51; Barker-Benfield, *Culture of Sensibility*, pp. 270–1.

psychological and emotional needs of many men and women, it may have had more to offer women.[14]

Under the impact of the French Revolution and the death of John Wesley two years later, popular evangelicalism splintered into several groups, which provided contrasting opportunities for men and women. The wave of millenarianism which followed the French Revolution included a number of female prophets, of whom the most popular was Joanna Southcott, a Devon upholstress who went to London in 1802 to publicise her visions. Taking ideas of female spiritual equality further than any of her predecessors, she claimed Christ spoke through her as his spirit in a female form, and that she was 'the woman clothed with the sun' of Revelations, who was sent to redeem mankind after the Fall. In 1814, she even claimed that she was pregnant with Shiloh, the new Messiah. She had an hysterical pregnancy and died in that year, by which time it is claimed she had over 100,000 supporters in London alone.

Southcott's message was particularly attractive to women. Many of her prophecies were explicitly directed at a female audience, and, according to Barbara Taylor, 'her writings abounded in images of male villainy and female defiance.' In her struggle with Satan, the devil was given masculine attributes. In a dramatic reversal of normal procedures, women were given precedence at a religious service at which Southcott was present: the women drank the wine first, 'as I am come to redeem the Fall of women', followed by the ministers, the elders, and then the rest of the men in attendance. It is thus not surprising that her supporters were predominantly female. According to surviving evidence (pertaining to 7000 supporters), 63% were women. Yet this figure is similar to that for many other religious groups at the time. Many men, too, had a 'millenial mentality'; Southcott appears to have attracted men as well as women who shared strong beliefs in the supernatural, the literal interpretation of the scriptures, and a deep dissatisfaction with the world, beliefs which cannot be labelled as customarily feminine or masculine.[15]

---

14 Barker-Benfield, *Culture of Sensibility*, p. 271; Henry Abelove, *The Evangelist of Desire: John Wesley and the Methodists* (Stanford, 1990), pp. 64–7, quote at 65; Dresser, 'Sisters and brethren', pp. 318–19; Gail Malmgreen, 'Domestic discords: women and the family in East Cheshire Methodism, 1750–1830', in *Disciplines of Faith: Studies in Religion, Politics and Patriarchy*, eds J. Obelkevich, L. Roper, and R. Samuel (1987), p. 60.

15 Barbara Taylor, *Eve and the New Jerusalem: Socialism and Feminism in the Nineteenth Century* (New York, 1983), pp. 161–5, quote at 164; J. F. C. Harrison, *The Second Coming: Popular Millenarianism 1780–1850* (New Brunswick, NJ, 1979), pp. 110–35, quotes at 112 and 118.

Following the death of Southcott it proved difficult to continue the movement, for not only could it be said that her prophecies had not come true but the movement lacked any formal institutional structure. As was true with the Civil War sects, women played more important roles in religious movements which were short-lived and were not or were not yet institutionalised. As groups became more respectable and formally organised women were marginalised. Even among the Moravians, where women were involved from early on in a number of aspects of church government, power became increasingly centralised in a male elite in the nineteenth century, although women were allocated primary responsibility for poor relief and they continued to carry out a number of other functions. After Wesleyan Methodism broke with the Church of England and formed a separate organisation following Wesley's death in 1791, female preaching became less acceptable. Increasingly concerned to maintain a respectable image and create a professional ministry (which was threatened on both counts by vigorous and vocal lower-class female preachers), the Wesleyan Methodists banned female preaching in 1803 (except to women-only meetings, and even this died out by the 1830s). Shortly thereafter, a number of small radical Methodist sects were founded, notably the Primitive Methodists and the Bible Christians, which adopted a much less formal ministry and welcomed female preachers.[16]

In the fluid world of popular evangelicalism in the 1790s and early 1800s women preachers were common in the Methodist sects which attracted a working-class following. Valenze has argued that 'more than in any other form of contemporary religion, women assumed an active, public role in sectarian Methodism.' Yet we should not overstate the significance of this role. Claiming to be vessels of divine revelation, it was their own supposed weakness as women which they believed gave them a special call to speak for the oppressed. Moreover, even excluding the virtually all-male Wesleyan Methodists, female preachers were almost certainly outnumbered by men. Most women served very short periods of only a few years, typically giving up their preaching when they got married or fell ill. Despite the 'central, strategic status' of female preachers (according to Valenze), women played no official roles within the limited organisational structures of the Methodist sects. The Primitive Methodists resolved in 1824 that at the circuit quarter-day board 'none of our females [are to] speak or vote unless specifically called upon'.

16 Dresser, 'Sisters and brethren'; Valenze, *Prophetic Sons and Daughters*, pp. 92–4.

On occasion this caused some conflict. When Ann Carr, a successful preacher in Leeds, refused to let her activities be planned by the Primitive Methodist leadership, she formed a breakaway group composed primarily of women, the Female Revivalists. Like the Southcottians, however, the movement did not last beyond her death.[17]

Valenze argues that the 'cottage religion' practised by the Methodist sects appealed especially to women. Since households often served as the location for meetings and as nodal points linking networks of the faithful, women acquired a central, if informal, role in organising worship. Moreover, cottage religion sought to defend the domestic economy of the household, in which women found useful industrial employments. Where that domestic security had been shattered and women were forced to move to the cities and work in the factories, Valenze argues, cottage religion offered young women a sense of familial solidarity and security to compensate for the break-up of their families. Given that the message was in part directed to women, it is not surprising that some societies in Leeds specifically asked for women preachers.[18]

Yet in defending the traditions and economic practices of rural society against the forces of change, cottage religion, like the Civil War sects, clearly appealed to plebeian men as well as women, and indeed cottage religion appears to have brought men and women together rather than divided them, in the sense that the sexes heard similar messages and were not given separate responsibilities. Moreover, the prominent role played by women both in congregations and as preachers was justified by their spiritual equality, not by any reconception of worldly gender roles. Thus, the unusual public presence of sectarian women did not subvert male authority; this can be seen perhaps most clearly in the lack of women among the leadership and in the tendency for women to give up preaching when they got married. Cottage religion provided new public opportunities for women, but it did little to undermine traditional gender roles.

---

17 Valenze, *Prophetic Sons and Daughters*, pp. 36, 72, 97–8; Sheila Wright, 'Quakerism and its implications for Quaker women: the women itinerant ministers of York meeting, 1780–1840', in Sheils and Wood, (eds), *Women in the Church*, p. 413; E. Dorothy Graham, 'Chosen by God: the female travelling preachers of early Primitive Methodism', *Proceedings of the Wesley Historical Society* 49 (3) (1993), p. 89. On Ann Carr, see D. Colin Dews, 'Ann Carr and the Female Revivalists of Leeds', in Gail Malmgreen (ed.), *Religion in the Lives of English Women, 1760–1930* (1986), pp. 68–87.

18 Valenze, *Prophetic Sons and Daughters*, *passim*, esp. 192.

The Evangelical Revival among the middle and upper classes from the 1780s, however, did more to enhance male authority, despite the important role played by elite 'bluestocking' women such as Hannah More. Unlike the enthusiastic religion found in popular Methodism and related sects, evangelicalism within the Church of England and 'old' dissent, was, in the context of threatening revolutionary activities both abroad and at home, far more concerned with propriety and the defence of hierarchical authority. In part in response to the publication of Mary Wollstonecraft's *A Vindication of the Rights of Woman* in 1792, their message sought to reinforce both gender distinctions and women's subordination to men. This is clearly evident when considering their approach to the ministry and office holding, in which even the minor role held by women in dissenting sects in the late eighteenth century was reduced. Except with the Quakers, the only positions of authority held by women in the second half of our period were local offices involving such tasks as the distribution of poor relief (e.g. deaconesses within the Baptist church). With the exception of the Moravians, where women dominated the 'conference of the poor' in the late eighteenth and early nineteenth centuries, even these responsibilities disappeared after the 1780s. Female ministers among the Quakers, who outnumbered men in the early nineteenth century, subsequently became less common. Davidoff and Hall note that 'the social climate of the nineteenth century was increasingly unfavorable to women preaching', as the concept of femininity promoted by the evangelicals deemed most public activity as unsuitable for respectable women. Women still had a role to play in the organisation of church and chapel activities, but it was always secondary and informal; in the words of Davidoff and Hall, women were expected to 'support the initiatives of men rather than independently pursuing separate aims and ventures'.[19]

Whereas working-class men attended church much less often than working-class women, the difference among the middle class was much less noticeable. Nonetheless, middle-class evangelicals believed that men and women expressed their religiosity in different ways. Like cottage religion, the evangelicals placed great value on family worship, but unlike the lower classes, they placed heavy emphasis on the different functions of men and women within the family, beliefs which are clearly evident in their prescriptive model

19 Leonore Davidoff and Catherine Hall, *Family Fortunes: Men and Women of the English Middle Class, 1780–1850* (1987), pp. 130–48, quotes at 139, 145.

of gender roles, the ideology of domesticity. Because of their 'natural' gentleness and tendency to spend less time exposed to the corrupting influence of the wider world, women were seen to be more religiously pure. According to the prominent evangelical William Wilberforce, women are 'the medium of our intercourse with the heavenly world, the faithful repositories of the religious principle'. From their position of moral purity, women's function was therefore to be a good influence over the other members of the household. Not only should they take on much of the responsibility for the spiritual education of their children, but they should also subtly work to reform their husbands: in the words of Reverend Thomas Binney, a popular Congregational minister, women 'are to be the *makers* of men'.[20] This idea was certainly not new, but like other aspects of their ideology the evangelicals gave new importance to this duty, and especially to the idea that women needed to be kept pure. Ideas about women's religious purity and the importance of their domestic moral duties did not necessarily prevent them from having a public role. But these prescriptions did tend to confine such activity to missionary and philanthropic work. Another role which was open to middle-class women was writing and publishing, though even then to avoid being perceived as too publicly ambitious women often wrote anonymously or used pseudonyms. Whether they wrote hymns, advice books, or religious fiction, writing provided evangelical women with a rare means for public religious expression.[21]

Although the evangelicals considered men in some ways to be less spiritual than women, it would be more accurate to say that men were expected to possess a different set of religious virtues. Building on the symbol of the Divine Father and the paternal responsibilities of the clergy, the spiritual and moral authority of men as heads of households was enhanced by the increased emphasis given under evangelicalism to family worship. Responsible for both the material and spiritual welfare of his dependants, the evangelical Christian man demonstrated his importance not only in relation to his wife and family, but also his social superiors. In contrast to the traditional gentry, the evangelical man (often middle class) claimed his importance on the basis of his moral authority, as opposed to physical prowess or financial and political power. Davidoff and Hall note that the qualities he was expected to possess (piety, sensitivity, sweetness) came 'dangerously close to "feminine" qualities'. But vir-

---

20 Wilberforce cited by Taylor, *Eve and the New Jerusalem*, p. 126; Binney cited by Davidoff and Hall, *Family Fortunes*, p. 116. See also above, Chapter 3, pp. 121–2.

21 Davidoff and Hall, *Family Fortunes*, pp. 145–7.

tues such as honour, competence, and probity, and the value placed
on men's work as a 'calling', helped distinguish 'manly sensibility'
from 'effeminate sentimentalism', and contributed to the later development of the ideal of 'Christian manliness' in the Victorian
period.[22] Although this moral masculinity was also adopted by respectable artisans and labourers among the Methodists, Baptists and
Congregationalists, this division of religious virtues by gender was
much less evident among 'cottage religion' and supporters of millenarianism. Thus, Joanna Southcott 'spoke publicly about national
events and the rise and fall of ministers', and her prophecies rarely
addressed issues of domesticity.[23]

In sum, the spiritual authority accorded to women by the sects of
the 1650s provided unprecedented, if ultimately limited, opportunities for women to act publicly, most notably as prophets,
preachers, and organisers of poor relief. Of course, the most empowering of these activities were also the most short-lived; when
movements became institutionalised women were often excluded
from positions of responsibility. Yet the examples of the 1650s,
together with the weakened position of the Church of England after
the Restoration, set the stage for the persistent public evidence of
expressions of women's religiosity throughout this period, especially
as female preachers, who can be found in the French Prophets,
Methodism, and in nineteenth-century cottage religion. While there
is some evidence of a decline in female preaching in the mid-nineteenth century, the growing importance of female missionaries
(who evangelised both sexes) and of good works performed by nuns
and Anglican sisters at mid-century shows that female public religious activity had become a permanent feature of religious life by the
end of our period. Moreover, despite attempts to exclude them,
some women became involved in doctrinal issues. A writer complained in 1846 that 'women, whose part it is to moderate and sustain, have been in too many instances the firebrands of religious
controversy'.[24]

22 Ibid., pp. 88–9, 109–14, quotes at 111–12; Norman Vance, *The Sinews of the Spirit: The Ideal of Christian Manliness in Victorian Literature and Religious Thought* (Cambridge, 1985).

23 Anna Clark, *The Struggle for the Breeches: Gender and the Making of the British Working Class* (Berkeley, 1995), pp. 102–9.

24 Donald M. Lewis, '"Lights in dark places": women evangelists in early Victorian Britain, 1838–1857', in Sheils and Wood (eds), *Women in the Church*, pp. 415–27; Michael Hill, *The Religious Order: A Study of Virtuoso Religion and its Legitimation in the Nineteenth Century Church of England* (1973), ch. 9; Susan O'Brien, 'Terra incognita: the nun in nineteenth-century England', *Past and Present* 121 (1988), pp. 110–40; *The English Matron* (1846), p. 118.

Nonetheless, such activity did not lead to any significant break-down in gender roles. Although women's opportunities for *public* action expanded significantly, in many respects these activities strengthened gender differences. The most enduring public relig-ious activities women engaged in, such as the supervision of poor re-lief in Quaker women's meetings or the informal roles encouraging family worship among cottage religion and in evangelical house-holds, involved what we might call the publicisation of women's traditional domestic obligations. Similarly, as we shall see, although women's participation in dissenting groups often led to their invol-vement in radical politics, such activity was also gendered. Men, too, found their traditional duties enhanced under the Evangelical Revi-val, which reinforced their authority within the home as well as in public even as it subjected them to new moral standards. Paradoxi-cally, while short-lived millenarian movements predicated on the spiritual equality of the sexes often temporarily transcended gender roles, it is probably the more established religious movements which contributed most to changing the lives of women, by providing new, if gender-limited opportunities for public action.

Philanthropy

The important, if limited, extension of women's public religious op-portunities is especially evident in the history of philanthropy in this period. Charity was a quasi-public religious activity engaged in by both sexes, but it was often dominated by women. By nature, they were thought to be the more tender and charitable of the two sexes, and charitable activity was enjoined by scripture, where women were told that a woman should 'stretcheth out her hand to the poor; yea, . . . reacheth forth her hands to the needy' (Proverbs 31: 20). As Frank Prochaska summarises, 'Christianity confirmed what nature decreed: women had a rightful and important place in the charit-able world.'[25] Charity was also of course a duty of men, but women were told that they had particular skills and obligations to help the sick and needy, and they engaged in different types of activities than men.

In the seventeenth century charity was a much more personal and individual activity than it would become. Women, especially the wealthy, frequently aided their neighbours by providing medical treatments, attending childbirths, and providing food, clothing, and alms to the poor. As Felicity Heal has argued, women's traditional

25 Frank Prochaska, *Women and Philanthropy in Nineteenth-Century England* (Oxford, 1980), pp. 13, 17.

role in providing hospitality often involved charity, and such activities provided a unique means for them to enhance their reputations and assert their authority in the neighbourhood.[26] Men were
much less likely to provide such personal services to the needy, and
instead seem to have been more likely to express their generosity
through donations of money, including bequests. Women, too, of
course often gave money through bequests and otherwise, but they
had much less control over financial resources and it is likely,
though more research is needed on this point, that they gave less
than men. (They also gave differently, in the sense that women were
disproportionately the targets of their charity.[27])

During the second half of our period charity was to a significant
extent organised and institutionalised, as a large number of voluntary societies were formed with the aim of helping particular groups
of the sick or needy. Although, as we shall see, women at first played
a restricted role in such enterprises (confined largely to acting as individual subscribers and fund raising), by the nineteenth century
they were playing a major role, while continuing to engage in individual acts of charity. The Evangelical Revival gave women an even
greater impetus to engage in good works, since the evangelicals believed charity helped individuals triumph over sin and, as we have
seen, they argued that women possessed special moral authority and
influence. Reflecting the renewed religious impetus, nineteenth-
century women began to describe charitable activity as their
'mission'.[28]

The key question for the evangelicals, however, was how far
women should engage publicly in good works, given concern that
they should not neglect their domestic duties and the need to defend their modesty and respectability from the corrupting influen-
ces of the world. Traditional personal acts of charity were clearly
acceptable, including visiting the homes of the poor (an activity
which was becoming increasingly popular), but it was a matter of
debate whether women should venture outside the home and visit
criminals who were incarcerated in institutions, and whether
women should participate in the running of voluntary societies, or
even form their own. Although change occurred slowly, the range
of activities in which women participated expanded significantly in
the first half of the nineteenth century, to include not only visiting

26 Felicity Heal, *Hospitality in Early-Modern England* (Oxford, 1990), pp. 178–83
27 Margaret Hunt, *The Middling Sort: Commerce, Gender and the Family in England,
1680–1780* (1996), p. 166.
28 Prochaska, *Women and Philanthropy*, pp. 8–17, esp. p. 11.

institutions and running societies but also such activities as running bazaars, acting as salaried evangelists, visiting brothels, and setting up rescue homes. Men continued to donate money and run many societies, but their role clearly became secondary. The expanding philanthropic activities of women led Prochaska to conclude that through their energy and broad interests 'women fundamentally altered the shape and course of philanthropy' in the nineteenth century, as charitable societies came increasingly to focus on causes involving children and women.[29] Even though opportunities were limited by prevailing conceptions of appropriate gender roles, it is through philanthropy that women's religiosity achieved its most public expression.

FORMAL POLITICS

Like the administration of the Anglican church, the world of 'high' politics was very much male dominated. Women had few formal rights and such informal influence as they had could only be exerted in private and indirectly, often through male relatives. Women rarely made public speeches on political issues or wrote about politics in their diaries and autobiographies.[30] As one historian has commented, 'the single most essential truth about women's political influence and involvement in eighteenth-century England is that their political activity must nearly always be measured through the achievements and failures of men'.[31] As will become clear in the remainder of this chapter, however, the more one looks outside formal political rights and the world of 'high' politics and towards the informal exercise of power in society as a whole, the more evidence there is of participation by both sexes, though like religious practice, the *character* of that participation was significantly gendered.

At the very top of society there was, however, an exception to this general rule. Women could become monarchs, since, unlike most of the rest of Europe which was governed by the Salic law, women could inherit the throne in Britain, but only if they had no living

29 Ibid., p. 223 and *passim*; Davidoff and Hall, *Family Fortunes*, pp. 429–32. See Chapter 5, pp. 246–8.

30 S. H. Mendelsson, 'Stuart women's diaries and occasional memoirs', in Prior (ed.), *Women in English Society 1500–1800*, pp. 199–200; Prochaska, *Women and Philanthropy*, pp. 2, 14.

31 Karl von den Steinen, 'The discovery of women in eighteenth-century political life', in *The Women of England from Anglo-Saxon Times to the Present*, ed. Barbara Kanner (Hamden, Conn., 1979), p. 229.

brothers. The implicit contradiction between normal female political impotence and monarchical power could be difficult to resolve.
In the second half of the sixteenth century Elizabeth I had successfully combined feminine and masculine gender symbolism to assert
authority. The constitutional position of the monarchy changed significantly over the next 250 years, however, and this meant that the
queens who ruled during this period – Queen Mary, who ruled with
her husband William from 1689 to 1694; Queen Anne, who ruled
from 1702 to 1714; and Queen Victoria, who came to the throne in
1837 – faced greater limitations on their powers.

Anne ruled at a time when parliamentary supremacy and the
roles of political parties and a prime minister were still in their infancy, and she was able, despite the developing limitations on the
powers of the monarchy and her own physical infirmity, to play an
active role in day-to-day politics and to influence the outcome of important political events in her reign. She was frequently portrayed,
both at the time and since, as not very bright and easily swayed by
the influence of her closest female advisers. Such opinions, however, largely derive from stereotypes of women's alleged unsuita-
bility for politics. On the surface, Anne accepted prevailing
conceptions of women's mental weakness (she frequently referred
self-deprecatingly to 'my poor opinion'), but in practice she refused
to allow herself to be dominated by either one of the political parties (except during the special circumstances which were in force at
the very end of her reign) and she actively exercised the crown's
prerogatives. According to her biographer, the success of her actions can be seen in the fact that they 'significantly contributed to
the growing stability of British society' in the aftermath of the Civil
War and Revolution of 1688.[32]

In contrast, Victoria ruled at a time when parliamentary supremacy was firmly established, the powers of the monarchy had been
further weakened by the Reform Bill of 1832, and some radicals
were advocating republican ideas. Her room for manoeuvre was
thus much more limited. She too was involved in the day-to-day politics of the time, and her opinions were on occasion influential, but
for both constitutional and ideological reasons she interpreted her
royal role more narrowly than Anne. Unlike Anne, she allowed her
husband, Prince Albert, to be intimately involved in affairs of state
and to act as a close adviser, and on his death she largely retreated

---

32 Edward Gregg, *Queen Anne* (1980), pp. 400–5, esp. p. 400. See also Geoffrey
Holmes, *British Politics in the Age of Anne* (Rev. edn, 1987), pp. 185–210.

from public political life. The image of the monarchy which she promoted was personal and domesticated, giving priority to the domestic concerns of the royal family. At a time of constitutional weakness and radical challenges to monarchies across Europe, this repositioning of the monarchy may be seen as a successful strategy for self-preservation. But it does mean that, outside her encouragement of a domesticated life for women, Victoria's influence on English politics was limited.[33]

Queen Victoria's approach to the monarchy can be seen as part of what Linda Colley has labelled 'the femininisation of the British monarchy', dating from the end of the eighteenth century, in which the women associated with the monarchy focused increasingly on domestic issues. While not only Queen Anne, but also the wives of the early Hanoverians were often involved in factional politics (Queen Caroline, the wife of George II, was an important ally of Robert Walpole), Queen Charlotte, the wife of George III 'deliberately abjured political activity and deplored factional strife'. Instead, she spent her time raising thirteen children and projecting herself as a model of maternity.[34] And when Queen Caroline, the wife of George IV, became the focus of political controversy when George IV tried to divorce her, the issues raised concerning the queen's behaviour centred around domestic virtues such as the sanctity of the marriage contract and the acceptability of adultery, not public policy issues. As the powers of the monarchy declined the responsibilities carved out for female royalty were distinctly gendered.

As noted earlier, with the exception of Queens Mary, Anne and Victoria, women in high places achieved political influence indirectly in this period through the men they were related to. As mothers of nobles and monarchs, they influenced the lives of those in power by raising and educating them and even arranging their marriages. As their wives and even their mistresses, they often collected and disseminated political information and lobbied their male relations to take certain actions. Thus, one of the reasons Robert Walpole was able to remain prime minister following the death of George I was that Caroline, the new queen, pressed George II to choose Walpole over Spencer Compton, whom she disliked. Politicians like Walpole worked hard to cultivate highly placed women, and this

---

33 Dorothy Thompson, *Queen Victoria: The Woman, the Monarchy, and the People* (New York, 1990).

34 Linda Colley, *Britons: Forging the Nation 1707–1837* (1992), pp. 268, 272; von den Steinen, 'The discovery of women', p. 232.

gave such women a significant degree of political influence. Given the combination of socialising and politics in court life, female members of the court possessed some indirect political power. Yet there were clear limits to such power: just because one had the ear of the king or a minister did not mean that advice would be followed. Charles II, for example, was perfectly able to separate business and pleasure: he only followed the wishes of his mistresses when they coincided with his own interests.[35] Moreover, female influence was expected to be exercised behind the scenes, and used only to further family interests. Those who stepped beyond these limits were quickly marginalised, as the examples of the Duchess of Marlborough and the Duchess of Devonshire demonstrate.

As a recent biography has shown, Sarah, Duchess of Marlborough had enormous political ambitions. She was well placed to act, since at the age of thirteen she joined the household of the future Queen Anne, and upon Anne's accession to the crown Sarah was appointed First Lady of the Bedchamber and Groom of the Stole. Moreover, she was the wife of one of Anne's most important ministers, the Duke of Marlborough. But, although she successfully exercised power over her social inferiors, her attempts to further the interests of the whigs at court were unsuccessful and she alienated the queen in the process. She overstepped the boundary between using her influence with the queen to promote her family and friends and attempting to influence policy. As she was to write in retrospect, 'tis a simple [silly] thing for a woman to imagine she can do any good' in politics; more than once she wished she was a man.[36] Georgiana, Duchess of Devonshire (1757–1806) was another aristocratic supporter of the whigs who overstepped the bounds of acceptable behaviour for women. As Colley notes, in acting as a political hostess for the whig party, 'passing letters and rumours between great men and serving as the platonic confidante of both [Charles] Fox and the Prince of Wales . . . Georgiana was doing no more than many other patrician women who were always allowed a certain degree of political influence behind the scenes.' But when she actively campaigned for Fox in the 1784 Westminster parliamentary election she went too far. Canvassing for members of one's own family was common enough among aristocratic women, but working publicly for anyone else was not. Georgiana became the

35 Anne Somerset, *Ladies-in-Waiting: From the Tudors to the Present Day* (1984), p. 151.
36 Frances Harris, *A Passion for Government: The Life of Sarah, Duchess of Marlborough* (Oxford, 1991), esp. p. 171.

butt of scores of satirical prints in which she was accused of being Fox's lover and her activities were depicted as unnatural. Needless to say, at the next election she did not venture into public. The phenomenon of the 'political hostess' exerting political influence behind the scenes continued up to the end of our period. By hosting dinners and parties for leading male politicians, upper-class and aristocratic women such as Emily Pankhurst and Harriet, Duchess of Sutherland provided valuable venues for mobilising support for the political parties.[37]

Interestingly, as Karl von den Steinem has pointed out, the exclusion of women from voting in elections in the eighteenth century 'rested primarily upon social constraints rather than legal prohibitions'. In a 1739 King's Bench case the judges found no legal basis for denying women the vote, but argued that they should not vote since women lacked judgement on public issues. Ironically, the first legal denial of the female franchise only came with the Reform Act of 1832, which in the course of opening up the franchise to a greater number of men actually prohibited women from voting. Although women never voted in parliamentary elections in this period, we have seen that they could play a major role at elections, within limits. They were present at the hustings, canvassed support for family members and lobbied those over whom they had some influence by virtue of family or social ties or through property holdings. In her later years, Sarah, Duchess of Marlborough, exerted considerable electoral influence through the lands she owned as a widow and her control of the behaviour of her sons and grandsons (through the threat of disinheriting them).[38]

Local government was also formally controlled by men, but women did occasionally vote and hold some minor offices. Legally, female ratepayers (usually widows) appear to have been eligible to vote in parish elections, except where local custom prohibited it, but some parishes explicitly prohibited them from voting. When parish officers were appointed on a rota system according to the ownership of particular pieces of land, female landowners were sometimes required to serve as sextons, parish clerks, overseers of the poor, and churchwardens, but not the more important office of constable (such women often hired substitutes). The most common

---

37 Colley, *Britons*, pp. 244–8; K. D. Reynolds, 'Politics without feminism: the Victorian political hostess', in *Wollstonecraft's Daughters: Womanhood in England and France 1780–1920*, ed. C. C. Orr (1996), pp. 94–108.

38 von den Steinem, 'The discovery of women', pp. 240–1; Harris, *A Passion for Government*.

offices held by women were apparently overseer of the poor and sexton: one was an onerous and undesirable parish responsibility involving frequent contact with the poor, and the other a minor church office. The office of sexton was described in a court judgment in 1739, which allowed female ratepayers to vote in elections for it, as 'an office that did not concern the public, or the care and inspection of the morals of the parishioners'. By implication, women could therefore also be allowed to serve.[39] According to Davidoff and Hall, even these limited opportunities disappeared in the early nineteenth century, when female parish officeholders were increasingly viewed as unrespectable by evangelical Christians, and women who were appointed to these offices hired proxies to serve in their place. According to the 1851 census, 865 women in England and Wales held offices in parish or church government, compared to 26,235 men. As no other figures are available, it is impossible to determine whether the situation was any better for women earlier in the period. It would appear, however, that formally women had never played more than a very minor role in local government; what we don't know is the extent of the informal influence that they may have exerted, such as that found higher up the social scale.[40]

In the discussion so far politics has been heavily male dominated, and the possible decline in female local officeholding together with the decline of the royal court as an institution of major political significance suggests that opportunities for women may have decreased over the course of this period. Of course most men, too, were denied the opportunity to participate in this oligarchical system: although a minority of men were able to vote in elections and/or hold local parish offices, that was the extent of formal participation in government for those who were not gentlemen or nobles. But we have seen that many women (as well as men) had significant informal opportunities to wield political influence. And, if we define politics more broadly, to include any public actions intended to change government policy or shape social conditions and economic practices, we find a considerable, and increasing, amount of political activity involving both men and women from a broad social spectrum. Depending on social class, such activity, to which we

---

39 Sidney and Beatrice Webb, *English Local Government from the Revolution to the Municipal Corporations Act: The Parish and the County* (1906 rep. edn 1963), pp. 15, 17, 18, 33, 106, and 169, quote at p. 15.

40 Davidoff and Hall, *Family Fortunes*, p. 137; P. J. Corfield, *Power and the Professions in Britain 1700–1850* (1995), pp. 32, 34.

now turn, included public demonstrations and riots, displays of patriotism, cultivation of and participation in 'public opinion', and the formation of voluntary societies and pressure groups.

EXTRAPARLIAMENTARY POLITICS

At the level of the local community, political activity in preindustrial and early industrial England frequently took the form of crowd protests. Riots and demonstrations were endemic during this period, because they offered ordinary men and women virtually their only opportunity to voice their grievances publicly and to influence public policy. While men played a major role in virtually all types of protest, women were prominent participants in protests involving a narrower range of grievances: over food riots and enclosure, defending jobs, and enforcing sexual and marital norms.

Women were rarely involved in riotous protests concerning political issues at Westminster. Although large groups of women had lobbied parliament during the Civil War, women played a limited role in the Leveller movement and in the political activities of the sects in the 1640s and 1650s. Moreover, there is no evidence of female participation in the political crowds of Restoration London (though women were involved in other types of London rioting), and women are few and far between in eighteenth-century political protests in London, including the Sacheverell riots, rioting on the occasion of the accession of George I, the Wilkes and Liberty riots, and the Gordon riots. The evidence of greatest female participation comes from the Gordon riots of 1780, where 20 of 110 rioters prosecuted were women, though nothing is yet known about the circumstances of their participation.[41] Few women can be found in election riots, or protests against military recruitment.[42] In general, women seem to have been reluctant to take to the streets to express their political views in group protest. This is not to say that they did not voice such views in public: in Restoration London some women authored political pamphlets and others were arrested for individually speaking seditious words, accounting for 11% of the cases of seditious words prosecuted during the reign of Charles II.[43] But with rare exceptions they eschewed collective political protests.

41 Mack, *Visionary Women*, p. 123; George Rudé, *Paris and London in the Eighteenth Century* (1970), pp. 262 and 283.

42 John Bohstedt, 'Gender, household and community politics: women in English riots 1790–1810', *Past and Present* 120 (1988), pp. 114–15, 118.

43 T. J. G. Harris, 'The politics of the London crowd in the reign of Charles II' (PhD dissertation, Emmanuel College, Cambridge, 1984), p. 301.

In contrast, a number of historians have commented on the fact that women played a major role in instigating and carrying out riots which occurred during times of food shortages. One of the most common types of protest during this period, food riots involved women and men forcing grain to be sold at a 'just' price, preventing grain from being exported from the local area, and destroying the mills of millers who were were thought to be charging too much or selling adulterated grain.[44] The extent of female involvement has been questioned, however, by John Bohstedt, who, on the basis of a statistical study of English food riots in the period from 1790 to 1810, found that women participated in less than half of the 156 riots for which sufficient information is available, and dominated only 22% of them. For Bohstedt, 'women typically joined men' in food riots, rather than the reverse. The accuracy of these statistics has been questioned, however, and in any case they only apply to a 20-year period towards the end of the 150-year period in which food riots were common in England. In any case, what is irrefutable is that women did play a prominent role in many riots, and this is the type of popular protest in which female participation was most common. It is not hard to see why: since women played a central role in the purchase and preparation of food, and in looking out for the interests of their children, poor-quality, high-priced, or unavailable grain immediately affected them. And to highlight this point, women used the symbolism of the kitchen and motherhood in such riots, banging pots and pans and making a point of bringing along their children.

Nonetheless men, who may also have been involved in shopping and were expected to act as the public spokesmen for household grievances, also played a major role in these protests, especially, it has been suggested, in 'the more complex and planned forms of protest'.[45] Ultimately whether a husband or wife (or both) participated in a protest must have depended on a number of factors, including whether or not the woman was involved in other extra-familial tasks (such as waged labour), and the distribution of power and responsibilities within the marriage (especially for the household budget), which as we have seen varied significantly from couple to couple.

44 E. P. Thompson, 'The moral economy of the English crowd in the eighteenth century', *Past and Present* 50 (1971); John Stevenson, *Popular Disturbances in England, 1700–1870* (2nd edn, 1992), pp. 125–6.

45 Bohstedt, 'Gender, household and community politics', esp. pp. 88 and 91; W. Thwaites, 'Women in the market place: Oxfordshire 1690–1800', *Midland History* 9 (1984), p. 36.

For the same reason that women joined food riots, to ensure the survival of the family, they participated in two other types of riots, against enclosures and expressing grievances over working conditions. The enclosure of common lands threatened an important source of household income, since the commons were used for tending livestock and collecting firewood, tasks typically performed by women. Men and women pulled down fences and demolished gates in a number of places during the eighteenth century, but Bohstedt argues that such riots were rarely successful and relatively uncommon.[46]

Since most organisations of workers excluded them and women workers often worked in isolation from one another, women did not play an active role in most industrial disputes in this period, though there are important exceptions. In 1675, male and female rioters destroyed engine looms in Spitalfields, London, because the looms threatened to put some weavers out of work. In 1697, women joined a disorderly demonstration in front of parliament in favour of a bill to restrain the wearing of imported silks and calicos (since the purchase of imported rather than domestic goods threatened jobs too). As with some food riots, women's role as carers was emphasised, and they were accompanied by their children. It was alleged that one of the supporters of the 1697 bill said 'that if the bill did not pass, they must send the weavers' wives and children to Parliament, to be taken care of', demonstrating that the families faced destitution. Although this man allegedly said that the weavers would *send* their wives and children, other testimony suggests that it was the women who organised the men: a group of poor women got together, pooled their half-pennies, and paid the bell-woman 'to go about to raise the weavers, and so go to Westminster, and petition parliament'.[47]

Similar protests occurred later in the period: women spinners participated in attacks on new machinery in Lancashire in 1776 and 1779, in Somerset in 1801, and in Lancashire in 1826, and female glovemakers attacked other women who wore newly fashionable silk gloves (rather than leather) in Worcester around 1804. With the exception of an attack on a mill in Lancashire in 1812 (which followed food rioting), however, women appear to have played largely supportive roles in the Luddite attacks on steam looms and other new machinery in 1811–12 and in the Captain Swing attacks on thresh-

46 Bohstedt, 'Gender, household and community politics', pp. 113–14.
47 Harris, 'Politics of the London crowd', pp. 232–3; *Journals of the House of Commons*, 11: 683, 29 January 1696/97.

ing machines in 1830–1 (though in 1830–1 some women were
charged with arson and sending threatening letters). According to
Malcolm Thomis and Jennifer Grimmett, although women often
participated in public demonstrations, 'they do not appear to have
been recruited into the organised parties that planned, plotted, and
carried out secret activities' such as machine breaking.[48] Similarly,
during the 'plug plot' riots of 1842 women marched in demonstrations and participated in crowds which closed down mills (which involved, on at least one occasion, stone throwing), but they did not
actually help remove the plugs from factory boilers (thereby shut-
ting them down) or participate in general workers' meetings during
the unrest.[49] Women clearly shared the economic grievances which
led to these violent protests, but for a variety of reasons, including
their often marginal roles in the workplace and their exclusion
from the meetings in which protests were planned, as well as possibly a hesitation to use violence, these protests were male dominated.

Finally, women were often involved in protests against people
who violated norms of sexual and marital conduct. Given the higher
standards of sexual morality which women were expected to adhere
to, it is perhaps not surprising that they assumed the responsibility
for enforcing such standards. In early-eighteenth-century London,
for example, women in small groups frequently assembled in the
streets and in front of houses and accused their victims of sexual
misconduct, and emphasised their point by throwing mud or excre-
ment or breaking windows. A woman was accused in 1713, for
example, of raising a mob and a tumult about the house of another
woman, 'and calling her whore and bitch and her husband cuckold
and many other opprobrious names, and putting her in bodily fear
of the mob she has so raised'. Such incidents may have been small
in scale, but they were frequent: in a sample of the Middlesex Quarter Sessions records over the period 1670–1739, almost three-quarters of the defendants who were prosecuted for such riots (which
were usually labelled mobs or tumults) were female.[50] Such group

48 Malcolm I. Thomis and Jennifer Grimmett, *Women in Protest 1800–1850* (New
York, 1982), pp. 47–51; Dorothy Thompson, 'Women and nineteenth-century
radical politics: a lost dimension', in *The Rights and Wrongs of Women* (1976), pp.
116–17; Sheila Lewenhak, *Women in the Trade Unions: An Outline History of Women in
the British Trade Union Movement* (New York, 1977), pp. 15–17, 22; Bohstedt,
'Gender, household and community politics', p. 115.

49 Thomis and Grimmett, *Women in Protest*, pp. 83–4.

50 London Metropolitan Archives, MJ/SR/1392–2721, *passim*; quotation from
roll 2202, recognisance no. 8.

protests are only the tip of the iceberg, for as we shall see women were also frequently accused of individual acts of defamation. On the other hand, most of the participants in rural demonstrations involving 'rough music', which shamed neighbours who engaged in anti-social activities, were men. This is not surprising once we note that for much of our period such demonstrations typically attacked infringements of patriarchal authority such as wives who committed adultery, or who beat their husbands (though it was the *husbands* of such women who were actually shamed). Women *were* involved, on the other hand, in incidents of rough music which punished other types of sexual or marital misbehaviour. In the late eighteenth and early nineteenth centuries when rough music started to protest against *wife* beating, rather than husband beating, women joined in: E. P. Thompson provides examples of women leading demonstrations against husbands who mistreated their wives as early as in 1747 (Billinghurst, Sussex) and 1748 (Islington).[51]

Women were thus quite frequently involved in collective and individual public protests, but on a somewhat narrow range of grievances where they were seen to have had particular authority: consumer issues; their ability to support their children; and moral issues. In a sense, women assumed the responsibility for the moral welfare of the community, and their focus in protest was, more than men, limited to issues concerning the local neighborhood and community, as opposed to issues of national importance. Yet because they often protested with men, Bohstedt argues that women 'were nearly equal citizens in the arena of community politics rather than having a distinctly sex-differentiated role'.[52] We cannot accept this conclusion entirely, however, since there were important gender differences. Men were involved in riots protesting a wider range of grievances than women, though in some riots, including some involving questions of sexual morality, they were in a minority or even absent. Moreover, women protested in different ways: more than men, they seem to have preferred individual acts of protest (seditious words, defamation) to joining in riots, and they were less likely to participate in violent protests.

Although there are a number of examples of violence committed by women (on occasion female food rioters threw missiles such as potatoes, and even stones and bricks), in general historians have found that, compared to men, women were more likely to engage

---

51 E. P. Thompson, *Customs in Common* (1991), p. 511.
52 Bohstedt, 'Gender, household and community politics', p. 122.

in fierce rhetoric than actual physical violence. In 1808, a food rioter named Hannah Smith threatened to hang the constable if he did not let the riot proceed. We need to be careful here, since the evidence may be distorted by contemporary prejudices about women being weak in body but strong and passionate in their speech. But the available evidence, concerning both rioting and crime (discussed in the next chapter) is very strong. In a study of London riots in the late seventeenth and early eighteenth century it was found that, while women accounted for 39% of all rioters, only 13% of the participants in riots which were described as involving violence were female. Similarly, Bohstedt found that riots involving women around the turn of the nineteenth century 'were significantly less violent than men's . . . [and] were more likely to involve mere coercion (such as forced sales imposed in the markets) or property damage, rather than physical assault against persons'.[53]

Public Opinion and Voluntary Societies

Over the course of our period a number of new developments led to a considerable expansion in opportunities for participation in politics, and in organised public social and cultural activities more generally, especially, but not exclusively, for the middle classes. Although these changes affected both men and women, the impact on women was greater because they had been so thoroughly denied any formal means of political expression. Men and women acquired the ability to influence events at Westminster through the manipulation of 'public opinion' and the formation of voluntary societies, a type of organisation which came to serve a multitude of social and cultural, as well as political purposes.

As those outside Westminster became able to influence those within through the use of the press and lobbying activities, politicians paid increasing attention to what was called 'public opinion' (though in fact it was primarily middle- and upper-class opinion which counted). Although public opinion was conceived by politicians very much in male terms, in fact women played an important role in the formation of such views; we have already seen their involvement in elections. Building on the theories of Jürgen Habermas, in recent years historians have argued that public political discourse (what Habermas called the 'bourgeois public sphere') among the

---

53 R. B. Shoemaker, 'The London "mob" in the early eighteenth century', *Journal of British Studies* 26 (1987), p. 283; Bohstedt, 'Gender, household and community politics', p. 104. For crime, see below, Chapter 7, pp. 298–300.

educated became increasingly important in eighteenth-century England. This discourse took place both in print (in periodicals such as the *Tatler* and the *Spectator*) and in public discussions in coffee houses, assembly rooms, and private homes. Although Habermas saw this discourse as largely gendered, with women excluded from public political discussion but more active than men in the 'literary public sphere', others have argued that the participation of women was common, not only in print but also in public discussion, notably in coffee houses. Indeed, in 1711 the *Spectator* complained about the 'party rage which of late years is very much crept into their conversation'. Although Joseph Addison tried to characterise this as 'in its nature, a male vice', Lawrence Klein argues that female participation became essential, because this new form of sociability demanded polite and refined conversation on moral and civic concerns, skills which women were thought to possess far more than men. Although in the early nineteenth century public opinion was once again conceived of 'as altogether male', in practice, as we shall see, women continued to be actively involved in exerting informal political pressure.[54]

Public opinion could be used to influence parliament through a variety of means, from informal lobbying and letter writing to publishing books and pamphlets, collecting signatures on petitions, and forming societies. Although the bulk of the authors of political pamphlets were male, publishing offered women an unusual opportunity for political influence, since they did not have to appear physically in public; in some cases women even hid behind male pseudonyms. As Harriet Martineau wrote in 1832, 'I want to be doing something with the pen, since no other means of action in politics are in a woman's power.'[55] Examples of female political writers include: Mary De La Rivière Manley, who wrote a number of Tory political tracts in the early eighteenth century, including attacks on the Duke and Duchess of Marlborough; Lady Mary Wortley Montagu, who wrote a political journal in support of Robert Wal-

---

54 Lawrence E. Klein, 'Gender, conversation and the public sphere in eighteenth-century England', in *Textuality and Sexuality: Reading Theories and Practices*, ed. J. Still and M. Worton (Manchester, 1993), pp. 100–15; Jürgen Habermas, *The Structural Transformation of the Public Sphere* (1962; trans. Thomas Burger with Frederick Lawrence, Cambridge, 1989), pp. 33, 55–6; *Spectator* 57 (5 May 1711); Dror Wahrman, '"Middle class" domesticity goes public: gender, class, and politics from Queen Caroline to Queen Victoria', *Journal of British Studies* 32 (1993), pp. 404, 414.

55 Moira Ferguson, *Subject to Others: British Women Writers and Colonial Slavery, 1670–1834* (1992), p. 300 (quoting Gayle Graham Yates, *Harriet Martineau on Women* [1985], p. 1).

pole in 1737; Catherine Graham Macaulay, who although perhaps best known for her historical writings, wrote pamphlets attacking the political views of Edmund Burke; Hannah More, who wrote several widely circulated anti-slavery poems between 1788 and 1795 and later wrote numerous pamphlets in support of the government during the Napoleonic wars; Mary Wollstonecraft, who wrote polemical tracts in support of the French Revolution and attacking the views of Burke; and Elizabeth Heyrick, who wrote a number of pamphlets against slavery between 1824 and 1828.[56] While some of these writings, such as Manley's vicious attack on Sarah, Duchess of Marlborough in a novel, adopted a recognisably feminine tone, many adopted prevailing male forms of discourse. As Moira Ferguson comments on the female anti-slavery writers: 'both Heyrick and Martineau employed forms of discourse customarily associated with male writers, notably pamphlets and economic treatises. Collectively, the female associationists drew up manifestoes that formally echoed those of their male counterparts in the anti-slavery associations.'[57] More than any other form of political activity, writing, because it was initiated from outside the public limelight, allowed women to participate on similar terms to men.

Petitioning parliament was a common procedure throughout this period, though the scale of the activity increased considerably. Although most petitions in the seventeenth and eighteenth centuries were dominated by men, during the revolutionary decades of the 1640s and 1650s large numbers of women participated in petitioning parliament on a number of issues, including women-only petitions against the decay in trade; for religious change and to remove the bishops from the House of Lords; for peace; for the release of imprisoned Leveller leaders; and for reducing the costs of filing lawsuits and the elimination of imprisonment for debt.[58] During the eighteeenth century, however, there is little evidence of female petitioning, and, as we shall see, the next examples of women's petitions that have come to light are from the early nineteenth century.

The same social and political developments which enabled the growing importance of public opinion and petitioning also facilitated the growth of independent organisations such as clubs and voluntary societies. Such organisations first became common in the

---

56 von den Steinen, 'The discovery of women', pp. 233, 238, 239, 245.
57 Ferguson, *Subject to Others*, p. 305.
58 Patricia Higgens, 'The reactions of women, with special reference to women petitioners', *Politics, Religion and the English Civil War*, ed. Brian Manning (1973), pp. 179–222, *passim.*

beginning of the eighteenth century as a consequence of the relaxation of state controls over religious worship and the press. They became a quintessential part of urban life in the eighteenth century, with over 2000 clubs in London alone, and were organised for a wide variety of purposes. These included dining and conversation; providing insurance against sickness; pooling resources for the purchase of consumer goods; discussing scientific, literary, and philosophical ideas; promoting religious and philanthropic goals; and, by the end of the century, promoting political reform. Even though many were solely concerned with the welfare of their own members, they all provided a means for people to socialise with people like themselves, and in this sense, in the words of Peter Clark, 'organised sociability bridged the divide between the individual and the public domain' in eighteenth-century society.[59] And by providing contexts for public or semi-public discussion of issues of political significance, they contributed to the formation and expression of public opinion more generally.

Initially, few women participated. According to Alice Clark, 'none of the associations which were formed during this period [the seventeenth century] for public purposes, either educational, economic, scientific, or political, include[d] women in their membership.' As Margaret Hunt has suggested, at this time 'there seem to have been very powerful and long-standing taboos against women meeting together in a formal manner.'[60] Three of the most significant late-seventeenth-century organisations, the Religious Societies (founded in 1678), the Societies for the Reformation of Manners (founded in 1690) and the Society for the Promotion of Christian Knowledge (founded in 1698), had few if any female members. There is also little evidence of female membership in other organisations, though women may have *attended* meetings of some musical and philanthropic societies.[61] The exclusion of women from these early societies can be explained by the efforts of middle-class men to affirm gender differences. Hunt argues that Reformation of Manners societies (whose principal concern was moral reform) ex-

59 Peter Clark, *Sociability and Urbanity: Clubs and Societies in the Eighteenth-Century* (Victorian Studies Centre, University of Leicester, 1986), p. 19.
60 Alice Clark, *Working Life of Women in the Seventeenth Century* (1919; repr. edn 1982), p. 286; Hunt, *The Middling Sort*, p. 111.
61 Clark, *Sociability and Urbanity*, p. 15. Only one of the 289 members of the London religious societies according to a 1694 membership list was a woman, a pastry cook: T. C. Curtis and W. A. Speck, 'The societies for the reformation of manners; a case study in the theory and practice of moral reform', *Literature and History* 3 (1976), p. 47.

cluded women out of a desire to control female sexuality, while Marie Mulvey Roberts argues that the all-male Freemasons sought to 'find the female in themselves' through rituals of humiliation and rebirth in order to identify and assert masculine values. More generally, voluntary societies, with their goals of individual improvement and public reform, allowed middle-class men to claim a public, political role for themselves, in contrast to the domestic responsibilities which were assigned to their wives.[62]

From the 1750s, however, there is evidence of a number of women-only societies, as well as of female membership in mixed-sex social and entertainment clubs, part of the flourishing social life of the eighteenth-century 'urban renaissance' which will be discussed in Chapter 7. From 1780, women's participation took on a more serious and public face when they began to participate in debating societies, the one type of society in the eighteenth century where extensive female participation has been documented. Such societies evolved over the course of the century in London from private conversation clubs to commercially organised, publicly advertised debates, and, stimulated by the increasingly radical political climate, they became very fashionable among the middle and upper classes in the 1770s and 1780s.[63]

Until 1780, women were admitted only as spectators, and the very idea of female participation was dismissed out of hand. Mary Thale has traced the process by which, over the course of that year, women were gradually admitted, first as observers in the galleries, then as full-scale participants. On 26 February, the first female debating society, La Belle Assemblée, opened, and by May women were speaking at all but one of the London debating societies, some mixed sex and some all-female. Thale attributes this shift to an increased women's presence in other aspects of social life and to efforts by the proprietors to attract more genteel, but also larger, audiences. A wide range of subjects were debated by women. While most topics were issues with which women were expected to be concerned, such as courtship, marriage, morals, and religion, Thale notes that a number of debates addressed the position of women in society. There were debates about the merits or limitations of the

62 Hunt, *The Middling Sort*, ch. 4; Marie Mulvey Roberts, 'Pleasures engendered by gender: homosociality and the club', in *Pleasure in the Eighteenth Century*, ed. R. Porter and M. M. Roberts (1996), pp. 48–76, quote from p. 75.

63 Donna T. Andrew (ed.), *London Debating Societies, 1776–1799* (London Record Society, vol. 30, 1994), pp. vii–xiii.

existing educational provision for women and even about whether women had a right to participate in politics; Thale describes these as the 'first serious public discussions in England of women's political rights'. Many of these and other debates raised the potentially radical notion that what were thought to be inherent female characteristics were actually the result of cultural conditioning. Perhaps even more radical is the very fact that in these debates women were competing and arguing with men on equal terms, something which very rarely happened in any other context.[64]

The debating societies were, however, a transitory phenomenon. Thale suggests that female participation declined after 1780 even faster than the debating societies as a whole, which became less fashionable and, in the 1790s, suffered from the repressive political climate which stifled public debate. Nonetheless, women's participation in the debates signified that in a political system in which public opinion was increasingly important there were openings for women to participate. Thus, when the reformation of manners movement was revived at the end of the century there were some prominent female participants.[65] In the next century associational opportunities for women would be further exploited, though less often in the mixed-sex context found in the debating societies.

Lower down the social scale in the eighteenth century there is evidence of women joining early forms of trade unions in the textile trades in the west country, London, the midlands and the north. Nonetheless, we can trace a similar decline in mixed-sex societies as occurred later among middle-class organisations. Whereas early in the century workers' 'combinations' were often mixed, the trend was for skilled male workers to exclude women from the unions and for women to form their own organisations, such as the Sisterhood of Leicester wool spinners, active around 1780. In the same decade, William Hutton noted a similar pattern of sexual segregation in clubs formed in Birmingham for the pooling of cash for the purchase of consumer goods. While there were many 'clubs of the feminine gender, some composed of young girls, some of wives, or widows, and some a mixture of all', formed for the purchase of mantuas, stays, and other items of clothing, men formed clubs for

64 Mary Thale, 'Women in London debating societies in 1780', *Gender and History* 7 (1995), pp. 5–24, quote from p. 18.

65 Joanna Innes, 'Politics and morals: the reformation of manners movement in later eighteenth-century England', in *The Transformation of Political Culture: England and Germany in the Late Eighteenth Century*, ed. E. Hellmuth (Oxford, 1990), pp. 110–11.

the purchase of items as diverse as breeches, suits, clocks, and even buildings.[66]

As the pace of industrial and urban growth quickened after 1780, voluntary societies further expanded, particularly among the middle class. Indeed, such societies have been seen as having played an important role in the formation of a distinctive middle-class identity. Or perhaps one should say in the formation of middle-class masculinity, for as Davidoff and Hall have argued, 'middle-class men's claims for new forms of manliness found one of their most powerful expressions in formal associations'. By proving their competence in public affairs, such men, like their eighteenth-century predecessors, asserted their importance not only in relation to aristocratic men, but also in opposition to their wives, since the ways in which these societies were founded and organised 'contributed to the maintenance of existing divisions between men and women'.[67] Although the way membership lists were kept (listing married couples under the husband's name only) sometimes obscures women's participation, it is clear that many clubs and societies excluded female members entirely, except on certain social occasions, or as observers. This applies especially to professional and occupational associations, including farmers' clubs and mechanics' institutes, and the Freemasons. Obviously where women were excluded from a trade, they would also not join the corresponding association. But other factors contributed to their absence from many societies: the lack of separately owned capital with which to purchase shares; the fact that many meetings were held in pubs, where middle-class women rarely ventured; and above all the explicit exclusion of women by men who felt that the conduct of such public business was a masculine activity and not suitable for women. In some types of societies a minority of women participated, often in an auxiliary capacity. Women formed only 6% of the 737 members of societies for the prevention of crime and protection of private property in Essex in the second half of the eighteenth century; presumably these were property-owning widows. Literary, philosophical, and scientific societies were rarely open to women, except as invited guests: the Botanical and Horticultural Society of Birmingham (in which women accounted for less than 3% of the subscribers) allowed shareholders to admit a certain number of women depend-

---

66 Lewenhak, *Women in the Trade Unions*, pp. 15–17, 22; William Hutton, *Courts of Requests: Their Nature, Utility, and Powers Described* (Birmingham, 1787), p. 263; William Hutton, *History of Birmingham* (2nd edn, 1783), pp. 135–40.

67 Davidoff and Hall, *Family Fortunes*, pp. 416, 421.

ing on the number of shares they owned. When the Birmingham Infant School Society was founded in 1825, women were only invited to form a ladies' committee several months later, and only for the purpose of looking after the girls' section; the committee had no power.[68]

As this last example suggests, women's participation was more significant in voluntary societies which adopted religious and charitable goals, concerns on which as we have seen women were thought to have particular authority. The number of societies devoted to these issues expanded dramatically from the late eighteenth century, and women played an important role in this expansion. We should not ignore the role played by women in earlier times (particularly the role played by Quaker women's meetings in poor relief from the late seventeenth century), but, with some notable exceptions, eighteenth-century women were largely excluded from power and their participation often took place behind the scenes. A number of women were involved in the planning, running, and funding of charity schools in the early eighteenth century. Although in most cases these women worked alongside men, often no doubt under their direction, Mary Astell arranged that the school for girls she founded at Chelsea was 'always to be under the direction of women'. Twenty-one gentlewomen petitioned the king in the 1730s, requesting a charter of incorporation for the Foundling Hospital in London, but none donated publicly to the hospital, though eighteen had husbands or other male relatives who were active subscribers. The Lock Hospital for the treatment of venereal disease received donations by women, but they did not want their names to be published in the list of subscribers. Both the Lock and the Foundling Hospitals dealt with 'fallen women', and it may be that respectable women feared the association with immorality. On other mid-eighteenth-century subscription lists women account for between 14% and 43% of the subscribers, but they played no direct role in managing the organisations (though matrons were hired to supervise patients in hospitals). In addition to Astell's School in Chelsea only two other examples of charities run by women have surfaced in the period before 1795: the Ladies of St Sepulchre's, Southwark, founded in 1702 and still going in the early nineteenth century, and a spinning school 'entirely directed and run by

68 Ibid., pp. 416–29.

middle-class women' in York in the 1780s.[69] Although further archi-
val research will no doubt locate other examples, the very obscurity
of women's participation in charitable organisations in the eighteenth century is itself significant.

In the late eighteenth and early nineteenth centuries the number of charitable societies increased dramatically, and female participation increased even faster, fuelled by the Evangelical Revival
(which accentuated women's moral responsibilities) and the increasing prosperity and leisure possessed by a growing number of
middle- and upper-class women. Nonetheless, most charitable organisations continued to be run by men, and much female participation continued to be behind the scenes: acting as patronesses;
serving on subcommittees overseeing the care or visiting of women
and children; working as matrons in institutions; visiting the households of the poor; encouraging the activities of husbands (in whose
names subscriptions were often listed); and hosting social events.

But two new developments greatly increased the role played by
women: the formation of separate women's 'auxiliary societies' attached to societies run by men, and the formation of separate societies run by women only. Pioneered by missionary and Bible
societies, it appears that local auxiliaries (to national societies) were
initially set up to recruit support among men, but from the early
1800s separate women's auxiliaries attached to charities were also
set up, and the idea was frequently copied. By 1819, the Bible Society had 350 female branches involving 10,000 women. By the
1840s, most charities which sought nationwide support set up female branches, and there were thousands of local female auxiliaries. While the national organisations (run by men) dictated the
rules of operation and at first excluded women from their meetings,
women ran these societies at the local level. Their primary purpose
was fund raising, and the women's auxiliaries contributed vast
amounts, both from their own subscriptions and through fund-raising ventures such as bazaars. Separate philanthropic societies run
by women followed a similar trajectory, with a small number
founded in the 1790s and early 1800s, increasing to hundreds by
mid-century.[70]

69 Donna T. Andrew, *Philanthropy and Police: London Charity in the Eighteenth Century* (Princeton, 1989), pp. 63–4, 72, 13.; Craig Rose, 'Evangelical philanthropy and Anglican revival: the charity schools of Augustan London 1698–1740', *London Journal* 16 (1991), pp. 53, 57; Ruth Perry, *The Celebrated Mary Astell* (1986), p. 242; Frank Prochaska, 'Women in English philanthropy, 1790–1830', *International Review of Social History* 19 (1974), p. 430; Hunt, *The Middling Sort*, pp. 168–9.

70 Prochaska, *Women and Philanthropy*, chs 1–2.

Like those dominated by men, the charities in which women participated in significant numbers addressed a wide range of causes, but not surprisingly women focused on causes relating to women and children, such as pregnancy, orphans, servants, and poor or sick elderly women. Many societies were formed for the purpose of visiting the poor in order to tend to their spiritual and material needs; the vast majority of all visitors were female. Despite opposition, women began to visit prisons and other institutions as well. Where women and children were inmates, female visitors acquired a powerful position within the relevant charitable society, even when it was run by men. In the 1830s and 1840s women began to focus on three other causes: temperance, where women were attracted by the prospect of diverting funds away from male vices to the needs of the family; rescuing prostitutes, where the earlier unwillingness of respectable women to be associated with 'fallen women' was slowly overcome; and the conditions of factory women, where bourgeois women supported the predominantly male campaigns for reduced hours for female workers and sought to educate working-class women in domestic virtues.[71]

In this way women's increasing participation in philanthropic societies helped transform the nature of philanthropy itself in the nineteenth century as the issues which concerned women gained increasing prominence. While the dominance of domestic and moral issues among the subjects of women's philanthropic activities can be seen as reinforcing traditional gender roles, the increasingly broad range of essentially public activities engaged in by women, often working with men, in the name of charity stretched the boundaries of acceptable female behaviour. Unlike in the eighteenth century, significant numbers of women in the mid-nineteenth century were running organisations and speaking in smaller public meetings, and this represented an important new public role for women.[72] Just as the male participation in eighteenth-century voluntary societies can be interpreted as an assertion of a masculine claim for greater participation in public life, women's membership in nineteenth-century societies suggests that women were making a similar claim, but the feminine claim to a share of public life rested on the

71 Ibid., Part 2; Jane Rendall, *The Origins of Modern Feminism* (1985), pp. 254–60; J. L. L'Espérance, 'Woman's mission to woman: explorations in the operation of the double standard and female solidarity in nineteenth-century England', *Histoire Sociale – Social History* 12 (1979), pp. 316–38; Theodore Koditschek, *Class Formation and Urban-Industrial Society* (Cambridge, 1990), pp. 550–1.

72 Davidoff and Hall, *Family Fortunes*, p. 436.

assertion of authority over a specific range of philanthropic and moral issues.

REFORM AND PROTEST, 1789–1850

The increased importance in the eighteenth century of public opinion and voluntary societies contributed to the dramatic expansion in extraparliamentary reform movements in the decades after 1789, which addressed a wide range of political and social issues. From the point of view of gender, there is even greater evidence of female participation, but significantly women's activities were increasingly segregated from those of men. Although both the working and middle-classes participated in these movements, the processes of class formation meant that they did so in different ways; therefore the activities of each class need to be discussed separately.

Following a period of quiescence during the Napoleonic wars, middle-class men began to lobby for political reform in the years following Waterloo; their efforts finally achieved a degree of success with the passage of the Reform Act of 1832. Middle-class women played only a minor role in groups lobbying directly for this bill: although they were present in demonstrations and contributed to the petitioning campaigns in 1830 and 1832, a female counterpart to the Birmingham Political Union was only formed in 1838, eight years after the Union was founded and long after the middle-class had largely deserted it following the passage of the 1832 Reform Act.[73]

During the 1820s, however, middle-class women did participate in two significant political campaigns, in support of Queen Caroline and the anti-slavery movement. The nationwide campaign on behalf of Queen Caroline, whom George IV tried to divorce in 1820, was supported by large numbers of both men and women, including tens of thousands of women who signed petitions and collected signatures and money. Submitting petitions to parliament was a frequent activity throughout our period, but this was apparently the first time in which women petitioned on a large scale since the Civil War. Possibly due to hostility from men who thought these were inappropriate activities for women, some of the petitions and collections were undertaken by women on their own. At least seventeen women's petitions were sent in support of the queen, including one with 17,652 signatures from the 'married ladies of the metropolis'.

---

73 Carlos Flick, *The Birmingham Political Union and the Movements for Reform in Britain, 1830–39* (Folkestone, 1978), p. 148; Colley, *Britons*, p. 278.

Beyond the fact that this issue attracted probably more female participants to a political dispute than ever before, the Queen Caroline affair is important, as Anna Clark has argued, because it introduced the 'feminine' issue of marital behaviour into politics and it exposed male sexual promiscuity under the double standard to criticism. It was, in the words of one supporter, 'a woman's cause', with the focus very much on women's traditional responsibilities. The queen was celebrated in the iconography of the time as a wife and mother. Men were mostly attracted to the movement for different reasons: it offered an opportunity to criticise the king. Clark notes that 'the Caroline affair never challenged the fundamental principles of sexual difference, but only expanded the limits of womanhood.'[74]

The next example of large-scale participation by middle-class women in a political campaign came with the anti-slavery movement in the 1820s, a movement which clearly grew out of religious and philanthropic societies. The movement itself dates back to 1783 when groups of Quakers formed committees to promote abolition of the slave trade, but no women were involved. Similarly, the Society for the Abolition of the Slave Trade, founded in 1787, was governed entirely by men, though women's interest in the issue is evident from the fact that 10% of the subscribers were women, and many more interested women presumably are hidden behind their husbands' names on the subscription lists. When the popular movement collapsed in the 1790s due to government repression of extra-parliamentary activity and the focus shifted to politics inside parliament, women were once again largely excluded (along with unenfranchised men). With the exception of some activity by wealthy ladies canvassing in elections and engaging in behind-the-scenes lobbying, women contributed little to the passage of the 1807 act which abolished the slave trade.[75]

When the attention shifted to seeking the abolition of slavery itself with the founding of the Anti-Slavery Society in 1823, women were once again excluded from any prominent role, though they could act as subscribers. In 1825, however, the first women's society, the Birmingham Ladies' Society for the Relief of Negro Slaves, was founded (a year before a men's society was organised in that city), and the Birmingham society actively encouraged the formation of

74 Thompson, *Queen Victoria*, p. 11; Colley, *Britons*, p. 265; Thomis and Grimmett, *Women in Protest*, p. 102; Clark, *Struggle for the Breeches*, pp. 164–73.
75 Clare Midgley, *Women Against Slavery: The British Campaigns, 1780–1870* (1992), ch. 2.

similar societies in other cities. By 1831, one-third of all the anti-slavery societies were run by women. Women went on to play an important, if distinct, role in the movement and, as its focus shifted towards the eradication of slavery in other countries after the passage of the 1833 bill which abolished slavery in the British Empire and the 1838 bill which ended the apprenticeship system for blacks in the West Indies, their role increased: by the 1850s, ladies' societies outnumbered the men's. While the increased importance of women was partly the result of the changing character of the movement as its goals shifted from pressuring for changes in British government policy (an activity in which men were particularly involved) to encouraging anti-slavery movements overseas, it is also a sign of the growing political self-confidence of women which resulted from their experiences in the movement since 1825.[76]

Just as male and female supporters of the anti-slavery movement organised themselves into separate societies (only one ladies' society was directly set up by a men's society),[77] they participated for the most part in different types of activities. Men were of course responsible for lobbying parliament; running the national Anti-Slavery Society and attending its meetings; publicising the cause through the press; and organising public meetings, chairing, and speaking at them. In addition to attending meetings (along with men), women, on the other hand, wrote anti-slavery tracts and fiction, promoted and participated in consumer boycotts of slave-produced goods (notably sugar), engaged in neigbourhood canvassing, and signed and collected signatures on petitions submitted to parliament and the queen.

Although some of these activities were also engaged in by men, women's participation was tailored to take advantage of what were thought to be peculiarly feminine talents and responsibilities. Female authors, for example, criticised slavery through the use of 'poetic sentiment and appeals to the emotions'. Both in fiction and in anti-slavery tracts, women emphasised in particular the brutal treatment of slave women and children, in the hope of motivating their female readers to join the movement.[78] Neighbourhood visiting, involving the distribution of literature, recruiting support, and collecting donations, was engaged in primarily by women, while

76 Ibid., chs 3–6.
77 Ibid., p. 47.
78 Ibid., pp. 29–35; Louis Billington and Rosamund Billington, '"A burning zeal for righteousness": women in the British anti-slavery movement, 1820–1860', in Jane Rendall (ed.), *Equal or Different: Women's Politics 1800–1914* (Oxford, 1987), p. 88.

men recruited support through meetings and the press. Local canvassing was thought to be consonant with women's moral responsibilities, 'without violating that retiring delicacy which constitutes one of . . . [women's] loveliest ornaments'. Delicate or not, such activity occurred on a massive scale: in 1827 the Birmingham society distributed 35,000 items of propaganda, and by 1829 women's societies donated more funds to the central Anti-Slavery Society than did the men's.[79]

Campaigns to boycott slave-produced goods focused on the acts of purchasing and consumption, activities largely controlled by women. In the early years of the movement both men and women were engaged in organising and promoting consumer boycotts, but after the formation of women's societies in the 1820s abstaining appears to have been viewed as naturally a female concern, associated as it was with women's domestic responsibilities as consumers. In the 1820s and 1830s there was a sexual division of labour on this issue with women's associations encouraging the boycott of slave-produced sugar through house-to-house visiting, while men's societies lobbied parliament to remove the higher duties placed on 'free-grown' sugar which discouraged support for the boycott.[80]

Similarly, although women were excluded from the early petitions against the slave trade, by the 1830s they played a major role in organising (and signing) women-only petitions. Midgley has calculated that women accounted for 'nearly a third of all the signatories to anti-slavery petitions in 1833', and by 1837–8 (during the campaign against apprenticeship) they accounted for two-thirds of all signatures. Women were responsible for the only nationwide petitions against slavery: the national female petition in 1833, signed by 187,157 women in ten days; the female address to the queen against apprenticeship in 1838, signed by 700,000 women; and the 'Stafford House Address' sent to American women in support of their campaign against slavery in 1852–3, with around 760,000 signatures. The success of these petitions (in terms of the number of signatures gathered) can be attributed to the use of canvassing to gather signatures (rather than calling a meeting and asking people to sign, which was the approach adopted by men), and to the emphasis in the language of the petitions on the suffering experienced by female slaves and apprentices.[81]

79 Ibid., pp. 85–6; Midgley, *Women Against Slavery*, p. 52.
80 Midgley, *Women Against Slavery*, p. 60.
81 Ibid., pp. 62–70, 148.

In sum, although no public monuments were erected to commemorate women's role in the anti-slavery movement, women played a vital and distinct role. Recent research substantiates the claim made by the activist George Thompson in 1834: women 'formed the cement of the whole Antislavery building – without their aid we should never have been united'. Midgley argues that 'women, despite their exclusion from positions of formal power . . . were an integral part of the movement and played distinctive and at times leading roles in the successive stages of the anti-slavery campaign.'[82] Even more important than their role, already outlined, in securing public support for the movement through petitioning, boycotts, and the distribution of propaganda, is the fact that women can be credited with shaping the goals and strategies of the movement.

In the late 1820s, women changed the direction of the anti-slavery campaign. The strategy first adopted by the (male) Anti-Slavery Society was one of securing the amelioration of conditions under slavery and gradual abolition through lobbying parliament, but it achieved little. In 1831, however, the Society adopted a policy of demanding the immediate abolition of slavery, a goal which was achieved within thirty months when parliament abolished slavery throughout the British Empire in 1833. This change of policy was made by men, but the pressure for change came initially from women, first from Elizabeth Heyrick's anonymous pamphlet, *Immediate, not Gradual Abolition; or, an Inquiry into the Shortest, Safest, and Most Effectual Means of Getting Rid of West-Indian Slavery*, published in 1824, and subsequently from many of the women's societies, which adopted immediate emancipation as their goal in 1827 and 1828. Only later did men's societies switch to this policy, with the national society finally succumbing to public pressure in 1831. Men, who initially supported gradualism due to political pragmatism and their perspective as employers, were thus forced to adopt a policy advocated by women, on the basis of their moral and religious principles, which could not accept slavery in any form.[83]

Midgley characterises women's involvement in the anti-slavery petitions as 'the first large-scale intervention by women in Parliamentary politics'. In explaining women's role in this movement, we need to point to roots in religious dissent and philanthropy. As we have seen, women's important spiritual role within Christianity in

82 Ibid., pp. 3–4, 44.
83 Ibid., pp. 103–17.

general and dissenting groups in particular facilitated female public activism, and a number of the female anti-slavery activists were also active Quakers, Baptists, Independents, and Unitarians, as well as evangelical Anglicans. Many of the founding members of the Birmingham society, for example, were prominent Quakers or evangelical Anglicans. Out of this religious perspective came interest in philanthropy, and the anti-slavery movement clearly benefited from the experience of earlier philanthropic associations in which women were involved. The network of societies affiliated to the Birmingham society seems to have been modelled on the local ladies' branch associations of the British and Foreign Bible Society, which was devoted to printing and distributing the Bible worldwide. Many of the female anti-slavery activists were also involved in philanthropic societies such as those concerned with the education and relief of the poor, missionary work, and relief of suffering of animals.[84]

At a time when all female involvement in politics was condemned, female anti-slavery activists justified their actions in religious and moral terms, and characterised their activities as a form of philanthropy; this is why so much emphasis was placed on the sufferings of the more vulnerable female and young slaves. In *A Vindication of Female Anti-Slavery Associations*, published around 1828, women's activities were characterised as an expression of 'pity for suffering, and a desire to relieve misery', which 'are the natural and allowed feelings of women'.[85] Whether women's ambitions were as limited to the religious and philanthropic realms as their public justifications suggest is impossible to determine, but in any case when combined with the expansion of women's voluntary societies and the opportunities provided by the slavery issue this language provided women with an entrée into the world of extraparliamentary politics and ultimately opened up a new range of possibilities for women, as our discussion of the anti-corn-law movement and the early history of feminist societies will make clear.

The first evidence of the expansion of middle-class women's political opportunities came in the 1840s with the Anti-Corn Law League, when a number of women, including the wives of some prominent members, began to hold meetings, organise tea parties, and collect money and signatures on petitions. Although at least one separate committee, the Manchester Ladies' Committee with

---

84 Ibid., pp. 53, 69, 81, 82; Billington and Billington, 'Women in the British anti-slavery movement', p. 85.

85 Quoted in Midgley, *Women Against Slavery*, p. 94.

200 members, was formed, there were no separate women's anti-corn-law societies.[86] Once again women portrayed their work as a form of charity (helping those who were disadvantaged by the high price of grain), but their role in a movement whose direct object was the repeal of a parliamentary statute is significant nonetheless. Despite their continuing lack of political rights, by 1850 women had forged a political role for themselves which was far more important than any but the most powerful aristocratic or royal women had exercised in previous centuries.

The significance of this new political role for women at the very end of our period is evident in the formation of the first organisations explicitly devoted to feminist causes in the 1850s. As we saw in Chapter 2, arguments for equal treatment of the sexes were circulated in the eighteenth and early nineteenth centuries, but it was not until 1851 that the first woman's suffrage society was formed, the Sheffield Female Reform Association, whose goal was for women to enjoy 'all the political, social and moral rights of man'.[87] Four years later a committee was formed to work for the reform of married women's property law; in 1858, the first avowedly feminist paper, the *English Women's Journal*, began publishing, and a number of related societies were formed; and in 1859 a Society for Promoting the Employment of Women was formed with the purpose of expanding the range of opportunities available to women. The formation of societies devoted to improving the lot of women clearly owed much to the organisational and political skills women acquired in the female religious, philanthropic, and anti-slavery societies formed in the preceding decades, and the impetus for publishing the *English Women's Journal* may well have come in part from the successful use of pamphlets by female abolitionists such as Elizabeth Heyrick.[88] As Midgley argues, women's 'experiences as anti-slavery organisers provided them with the skills, self-confidence, connections, sense of collective identity, and commitment to public and political activism which were essential to the development of organised feminism'; indeed, some leading anti-slavery activists became involved in feminist campaigns.[89]

While it is true that most of the anti-slavery women may be described as 'feminine rather than feminist'[90] and the movement did

86 Thomis and Grimmett, *Women in Protest*, p. 135.

87 Quoted by Rendall, *Origins of Modern Feminism*, p. 309.

88 Ibid., pp. 184–6, 269–70, 307–14; Prochaska, *Women and Philanthropy*, pp. 227–30.

89 Midgley, *Women Against Slavery*, pp. 155, 172, 203.

90 Ibid., p. 154.

much to reinforce existing gender roles, a minority of activists drew links between the condition of slaves and the condition of women, and in this sense the rhetoric of the anti-slavery campaign contributed to the development of feminism. English thinking on this subject was greatly encouraged by the World Anti-Slavery Convention in London in 1840 when the issue of whether to admit female delegates from America (there were none from Britain) was hotly debated. Although the women were not admitted, the Convention introduced more radical American approaches to the subject of women's rights and the abolition of slavery, and English feminists were greatly inspired by these contacts. Eventually, the influence worked the other way and the anti-slavery campaign was influenced by feminist ideas: in the 1850s women in the movement were for the first time allowed to attend conferences, sit on committees, and address mixed-sex public meetings.[91]

In sum, the expansion of middle-class political opportunities outside Westminster which occurred in England in the eighteenth and early nineteenth centuries affected men first, but in the early nineteenth century women also took part. Until the 1780s, public opinion and voluntary societies were predominantly male preserves, but in subsequent decades women increasingly participated in activities and organisations which, although often devoted to philanthropic purposes, sought to influence parliamentary legislation and ultimately raised questions concerning women's rights. Both men and women participated in such movements, but the conventions of gender meant that for the most part women adopted different tactics and used different arguments than their male counterparts.

Working-Class Protest

We can trace a similar expansion in opportunities for women in extraparliamentary activity after 1789 among the working class, but the roles played by women and the outcome of the process are different. In the early nineteenth century riots and demonstrations were increasingly eclipsed by more organised activities as a sense of class consciousness developed among the working class and extraparliamentary politics became more sophisticated. Food riots, neighbourhood shaming demonstrations, and industrial violence became increasingly supplemented, and even supplanted, by strikes, petitions, demonstrations, and consumer boycotts. Unlike their

---

91 Rendall, *Origins of Modern Feminism*, pp. 272, 315, 320; Ferguson, *Subject to Others*, pp. 3, 301–5; Midgley, *Women Against Slavery*, pp. 167–9.

middle-class sisters, working-class women already had a tradition of extensive participation in a wide range of community protest; the challenge for them was how to carry this tradition forward into the more institutionalised world of nineteenth-century working-class politics.

The first voluntary organisations among the lower class were organised, unsurprisingly, around work. From the eighteenth century many workers formed friendly societies, in which members pooled dues for the purpose of providing sickness or burial benefits. Of the societies which included women, some accepted both female and male members, but more appear to have been for women only. Friendly societies were so popular in one Derbyshire factory town that 42% of the female inhabitants in the early nineteenth century were members. There was a much-reduced female presence, however, in the trade unions which evolved out of friendly societies in the first half of the nineteenth century and which campaigned actively for improved wages and working conditions. In part, this is because skilled workers were the first groups to unionise, and fewer women worked in these occupations. But it is also because male trade unions frequently deliberately excluded women, who were seen as potential competitors for men's jobs, which they performed for lower wages.[92]

It was not until the formation of the Grand National Consolidated Trades Union in 1833–4 that significant numbers of women were able to join unions. This is because the GNCTU encouraged groups of unskilled workers to organise and it segregated women into separate unions: its constitution stated that 'lodges of industrious females shall be instituted in every district wherein [it] may be practical.' 'Lodges' were formed of female lace-makers, straw-bonnet-makers, shoebinders, laundresses, milliners, glass-cutters, stockingers, glovemakers, and ladies' maids. The 'Grand Lodge of Miscellaneous Female Operatives' allowed women in smaller trades the opportunity of a union, and it was even proposed that a lodge be formed for non-working wives.[93] All these organisations were short-lived, however, and it was only when women came to dominate the workforce in an important trade, cotton powerloom weaving, that women achieved real power in a trade union. In the

92 Thomis and Grimmett, *Women in Protest,* pp. 70–4; Valenze, *Prophetic Sons and Daughters,* p. 177.
93 Ruth and Edmund Frow (eds), *Political Women 1800–1850* (1989), p. 135; Lewenhak, *Women in the Trade Unions,* pp. 37–40; Taylor, *Eve and the New Jerusalem,* pp. 88–95.

Stockport in 1840, where 58% of the adult powerloom weavers were women, men and women struck together, and some female strikers spoke at the strikers' meetings.[94]

Although women were slow to be admitted to the formal organisations of trade unions, they frequently participated in labour disputes and strikes on an *ad hoc* basis throughout the early nineteenth century. Such activity is often poorly recorded, but the numerous instances of male labour unrest which took place in textile areas in particular, where women formed a major portion of the workforce, could not have been possible without the participation of women. Documented examples of strikes and demonstrations in which women acted along with men include disputes among the Manchester handloom weavers in 1808, the Lancashire cotton spinners in 1818, the Nottingham framework knitters in 1819, cotton workers during the general strike of 1842, and a demonstration of solidarity of all trades in Derby in 1834. In most if not all these cases, the organisers and leaders of the strikes were men. In other cases, however, women workers struck on their own, as with the Loughborough lace runners in 1811, Leeds powerloom stuff manufacturers in 1832, Hartshead wool carders in 1833 (along with some men), washerwomen in London in 1834, powerloom weavers in Bradford and cloth weavers at Elland in 1838, Newcastle plate-glass workers in 1838, Nottingham lace runners and embroiderers in 1840, Kensington washerwomen in 1842, and London female bookbinders in 1844.[95] Concentrations of female workers in these trades enabled concerted action to take place, despite their relative lack of formal organisation.

In addition to strikes, the trade-union movement turned to parliament to seek improved working conditions. The factory reform movement received limited support from women, however, for it was women's as well as children's work that men were seeking to constrain. In campaigning for shorter hours, working men, influenced by domestic ideology, argued that female workers were exploited by the factory system and needed the protection of the state. The suggestion that women should devote more time to domestic tasks, however, did not suit all women, and many female factory workers, such as the powerloom weavers in Lancashire who were worried that shorter hours would mean less pay, refused to support

94 Lewenhak, *Women in the Trade Unions*, pp. 49–50; Clark, *Struggle for the Breeches*, pp. 235, 242.
95 Thomis and Grimmett, *Women in Protest*, ch. 4 *passim*; Lewenhak, *Women in the Trade Unions*, chs 3 and 4 *passim*.

the movement. In areas where the demand for women's labour was high, however, women were able to support it. Following the passage of the 1847 Factory Act which restricted the working hours for women to ten hours a day, however, women did take part in demonstrations which sought to prevent employers from using shift labour in order to allow men to continue working longer hours.[96] Although working-class women often disliked their jobs, many recognised that it was not necessarily in their interest to have their work opportunities further limited without parallel limits being placed on men.

If women's opportunities for formal participation in the expanding trade-union movement were limited, women were even less welcome in the working-class political organisations which, following the French Revolution, sought to reform the political system in order to secure equal representation for 'the people'. Ideologically, the case for securing political rights for *both* sexes was made possible by the publication of Thomas Paine's *The Rights of Man* in 1791–2, which, in contrast to previous political theories, based the claim for equal political rights on the fact that everyone was created equal by God and had access to reason. Although Paine did not argue for women's formal political rights, Mary Wollstonecraft made the obvious connection, even if she did so hesitantly. Yet few radicals followed this path, and in their actions and their arguments most assumed that formal participation in politics was for men only. The London Corresponding Society, the first working-class political organisation in British history, consisted entirely of male members. A proposal to establish a 'society of female patriots' does not appear to have been realised, and the only concrete evidence of female participation in LCS activities is a demonstration organised in 1795 which was attended by large numbers of women and children.[97] As Anna Clark has demonstrated, the male radicals assumed that rationality was a particularly masculine trait (while women were associated with disorder) and they adopted a gendered language in which they opposed their masculine rationality to the alleged effeminacy and homosexuality of their aristocratic opponents.[98] The radicals of the 1790s simply did not believe that women had a significant role to play in politics.

96 Thomis and Grimmett, *Women in Protest*, pp. 80–1; Lewenhak, *Women in the Trade Unions*, p. 54; Clark, *Struggle for the Breeches*, pp. 215–18; 243–4.
97 Clark, *Struggle for the Breeches*, pp. 145–7 Thomis and Grimmett, *Women in Protest*, p. 88.
98 Clark, *Struggle for the Breeches*, pp. 147–56.

After a period of repression, when radical politics were driven underground (and remained a male monopoly), the parliamentary reform movement came to life again after 1815, this time with greater female participation. The radical Samuel Bamford described a meeting in 1818 in which he argued that the women who attended reform meetings should be allowed to vote: 'This was a new idea; and the women who attended numerously on that bleak ridge were mightily pleased with it – and the men being nothing dissentient when the resolution was put, the women held up their hands, amid much laughter; and ever from that time women voted at radical meetings.'[99] Significantly, women were already attending such meetings, but when the idea of formal participation was raised, it was greeted by awkward laughter which must have reflected the novelty of the situation. Shortly thereafter, female reform societies were founded in Blackburn, Manchester, Stockport, and a number of other places. The societies met weekly, and like their male counterparts, heard speeches, passed resolutions, and planned demonstrations. Female reformers played a significant role in the preparations for the massive demonstration at Peterloo in 1819, and women marched at the head of many contingents. When the meeting was violently broken up by soldiers, 100 of the more than 400 wounded demonstrators were female.[100]

There are a number of reasons for this unprecedented female participation in organised radical activity. Working-class women's experiences in other forms of protest such as strikes and food riots, with organisations such as friendly societies, and with dissenting religion (especially 'cottage religion') gave them the confidence to participate in public protest. Moreover, in contrast to London, in the north men were inclined to accept the female presence since a significant portion of the labour force in the industrial districts where the societies were based were women, and men were used to working alongside them. The reform societies were based very much on community networks in which women had always played an important role.[101]

The participation of women, however, did little to undermine traditional gender roles or advance claims for women's political rights. The object of the Blackburn Female Reform Society, founded in 1819, was 'to assist the male population of this country to obtain their rights and liberties'. The role of this and other fe-

---

99 Quoted by Thomis and Grimmett, *Women in Protest*, p. 90.
100 Thomis and Grimmett, *Women in Protest*, pp. 89–93, 100; Colley, *Britons*, p. 264.
101 Clark, *Struggle for the Breeches*, pp. 158–60.

male societies, like so many of the middle-class societies, was very
much to act in an auxiliary capacity; the women it raised money for
the male societies, and the women presented themselves as symbols
of virtue whose role was to inspire men to greater accomplishments.
In demonstrations, the women dressed in white, and they presented
elaborately decorated caps of liberty to prominent male reformers.
Moreover, they justified their participation (in the face of some
criticism from men) in terms of their duties to their families: the
Manchester Female Reformers stated that 'we can no longer bear to
see . . . our husbands and little ones clothed in rags.' And one of
the important duties of female society members, as they saw it, was
by establishing schools 'to instil in the minds of their children a
deep and rooted hatred of our corrupt and tyrannical leaders'.[102]
Nonetheless, women acquired unprecedented political experience
in these societies, experience which was perhaps most valuable
when they acted separately from men. The Stockport society, for
example, explained why it was important for men not to attend
their debates: in case 'in our debates (for it is something new for
women to turn political orators) we should for want of knowledge
make any blunders [and] we should be laughed at, to prevent
which we should prefer being by ourselves'.[103]

Working-class women's participation in the campaign for the reform bill in 1830–2 was somewhat less noticeable than in 1819, but
this may be because their activities were no longer as novel as they
once were. It may also be due to the fact that there were fewer specifically women's issues to latch onto in the debate over the reform
bill, though some women did justify reform on the basis that 'our
children [are] on the brink of starvation owing to profligate government', and they formed organisations to provide assistance to the
families of radicals who were persecuted for their views. More significantly, women were in the forefront of the struggle for a free
press, defending the principle of 'a really free and untaxed press'.
Although much of their work involved supporting husbands and
other relations who were arrested for selling unstamped newspapers, many women were involved in printing, publishing and selling the forbidden publications.[104] On the whole, however, the
campaign for the reform bill was dominated by men.

---

102 Ibid., p. 163; Thomis and Grimmett, *Women in Protest*, pp. 92–9, citing
Annual Register (June 1819), p. 92; Colley, *Britons*, pp. 276–7; Frow and Frow (eds),
Political Women, p. 17.

103 Quoted by Thomis and Grimmett, *Women in Protest*, p. 96.

104 Ibid., pp. 105–7; Frow and Frow (eds), *Political Women*, pp. 34–43.

Women found a lot more to support in the campaign against the New Poor Law following its introduction in 1834. The issue of poor relief was of course central to women's lives, and certain aspects of the new law, especially the provisions which separated families in workhouses and which penalised the mother, but not the father, of a bastard child, were particularly offensive to women. There was some uncertainty at first about the role women should play in the protests. After initially participating in meetings with men, separate women's anti-poor law societies were set up throughout the north. Similarly, it was decided that women should sign separate petitions rather than those which men signed. In a speech at Elland in February 1838 Mrs Susan Fierly exhorted 'the females present to take the question of the repeal of the bill in their own hands, and not to rely on the exertions of others . . . but at once to assert the dignity and equality of the sex'.[105] Shortly thereafter they did just that: a party of women tried to break up a meeting of assistant poor law commissioners and then rolled the poor law guardians in the snow. On another occasion women threw stones at guardians, stole a cart-load of bread meant for paupers (in protest at the withdrawal of outdoor relief to the able-bodied), and threatened a relieving officer.[106]

It has been suggested that women's participation in the anti-poor law movement was transitional, in that it both hearkened back to traditional forms of women's protest such as the food riot and included newer forms of political action. Certainly there are elements of each, but the ideology used to justify women's participation was largely traditional, based as it was on the defence of the family. Thus, one flag carried by women at a radical demonstration in Carlisle depicted a poor law guardian taking a child away from its mother and another guardian separating a man and his wife. And the radical press, attacking the bastardy clause in the new law, portrayed women as 'weaker vessels' who could not be blamed for illegitimacy because they did not have the 'great consideration, reflection, and resistance necessary to resist seduction'. The image of women thus being unable to look after their own interests, as men, reinforced the notion that women were unsuited for political action, except perhaps on issues directly pertaining to the family such as the poor law, and even then in an auxiliary capacity. Clark argues that, as a result of the anti-poor law campaign, working men

---

105 Quoted by Clark, *Struggle for the Breeches*, p. 191. Thomis and Grimmett, *Women in Protest*, p. 63.
106 Thomis and Grimmett, *Women in Protest*, pp. 59–60.

'began to incorporate domesticity into their rhetoric', a strategy
which would further limit women's political involvement in the
future.[107]

An alternative conception of the role of women could be read
into the socialist ideas of Robert Owen, and women were involved
in a number of organisations, both mixed-sex and women only,
which promoted his ideas in the 1830s and 1840s. A number of
women, flouting the constraints of domestic ideology, became public lecturers. Emma Martin (1812–51), for example, was a popular
lecturer on a range of topics including physiology, the condition of
women, socialism, and philosophy of religion, and her lectures attracted mixed-sex audiences of thousands. As suggested by the fact
that such lectures were also the target of violent demonstrations,
these women and the ideas they advocated were very much in the
minority. Even within the Owenite movement, practice did not
match the ideals of gender equality. Although women were theoreti-
cally expected to play an equal role in running the movement, few
became officials.[108]

Out of all these movements grew Chartism, the campaign from
1838 to 1848 for universal male suffrage and other parliamentary
reforms which is often seen as marking the coming of age of working-class politics in England. It also marked a crucial phase in the
history of political activity for women: on the one hand, the scale of
women's participation in the movement was unprecedented, but on
the other, Chartism can be seen as encouraging the subsequent political marginalisation of working-class women. Though outnumbered by men, women supported Chartism on a large scale. After
the publication of the first national petition for the adoption of the
'People's Charter' in 1838, it was reported that 50,000 women
signed it within the first week. Overall, it has been argued that, by a
cautious estimate, there were tens of thousands of active female
Chartists, who were organised into about 150 female Chartist associations, or about one-ninth the number of male associations (women
were also involved in some of the male organisations). In Birmingham alone, there were 1300 enrolled female Chartists. Chartism was
a movement which mobilised whole communities, especially in textile manufacturing areas where there were many female workers,
and therefore women played an important role. Indeed, as Dorothy

---

107 Ibid., pp. 58, 62; Clark, *Struggle for the Breeches*, pp. 187–196, esp. p. 194,
quoting *Poor Man's Guardian* 24 May 1834.
108 Frow and Frow (eds), *Political Women*, ch. 6.

Thompson has argued, 'it is difficult to conceive of Chartism without their participation.'[109]

Chartist women engaged in a wide range of activities. Like the men, they collected and signed petitions, solicited money, attended meetings and demonstrations, and rioted. But women also engaged in activities which were primarily confined to them, such as embroidering caps of liberty, sewing banners, and holding fund-raising tea parties. Two other types of activity may also have been primarily conducted by women: selective shopping (only with traders who supported the charter) and setting up and running Chartist schools. Like earlier movements, women were excluded from any formal role in running the movement: they did not serve on national councils or act as officers, committee members, or (with rare exceptions) as speakers, except in all-female organisations.[110]

In this sense, as in earlier movements, women were auxiliaries in Chartism, providing mass support and fulfilling important functions, but always as followers. This is reflected in the justifications women gave for joining the movement: as the Stockport Chartists declared in 1839,

> we regret that we should be driven by dire necessity to depart from the limits usually prescribed for female duties; but when . . . even with the most rigid economy we are unable to provide for the actual necessities of subsistence . . . we can feel justified in declaring our conviction that nothing less than the adoption of the principles of the People's Charter can effectively remove the existing distress.[111]

Like their activities in the anti-poor law movement, women justified their participation in Chartism by emphasising their moral duty to look out for the welfare of their families and neighbours, and by explaining that they sought to fulfil a supportive role, encouraging the men 'to further exertions' but not in any way attempting to supersede or rival them. Chartist men adopted similar attitudes, seeing their own participation in the movement as enhancing their masculinity and viewing the women as subsidiary supporters: according to Thomis and Grimmett 'the presence of women at political meetings was frequently welcomed for decorative reasons', with speakers

109 Thomis and Grimmett, *Women in Protest*, pp. 123–6; Dorothy Thompson, *The Chartists* (1984), ch. 7, quote from p. 150, and pp. 342–68.
110 Thomis and Grimmett, *Women in Protest*, pp. 124–31; Thompson, *The Chartists*, pp. 142, 147, 148.
111 *Northern Star*, 25 May 1839, quoted by Thomis and Grimmett, *Women in Protest*, pp. 111–12.

commenting on 'the pleasant smiles of the ladies'. As Jutta Schwarz-kopf has argued, 'commitment to Chartism bolstered men's shared identity as men, by promoting their common identification as fam-ily breadwinners who waged a political struggle for conditions in which they would better be able to secure their families' economic survival.'[112]

Chartism did, however, directly raise the question of women's political rights, since in pushing for universal manhood suffrage the issue of the vote for women could hardly be ignored. Dorothy Thompson argues that 'support for the idea of women's votes was always widespread among the Chartists', especially in the 1840s, but the leaders were worried that if they pushed for female suffrage it might retard the achievement of the vote for men. She notes that women were not in the forefront in pushing for female suffrage:

> most of the references and discussion of the question came from men. The women seem much more concerned with immediate issues such as the operation of the Poor Law, the low level of wages, or the threat of the press gang. . . . The women at this stage did not see their interests as being in opposition to those of their husbands – or if they did, they did not see any solution to such conflict in political action.[113]

Thus, when the Chartist R. J. Richardson wrote his book T*he Rights of Women*, he argued that only spinsters and widows needed the vote, since married couples could speak with one (male) voice. Al-though many Chartists welcomed the idea of the vote for women in theory, women's rights did not become a major priority of the movement: there were no public rallies or meetings specifically on the issue, and only a minority of Chartists actively worked for it.[114]

After 1843 women's presence in the Chartist movement declined significantly: there were fewer reports of women's meetings and of women's presence in demonstrations, and fewer women signed pe-titions, though the movement itself continued to be active until 1848. A number of explanations have been advanced for this de-cline. It has been suggested that the improving economic climate and the fact that the New Poor Law did not turn out to be as bad as

---

112 Thomis and Grimmett, *Women in Protest*, pp. 113–15, 120; Thompson, *The Chartists*, pp. 139, 141; Jutta Schwarzkopf, *Women in the Chartist Movement* (1991), pp. 284–5.

113 Thompson, *The Chartists*, pp. 124, 126.

114 Thomis and Grimmett, *Women in Protest*, pp. 132, 134.

expected meant that the issues which stimulated female involvement became less pressing; that fewer women were present in the workforce and more remained at home as housewives who did not concern themselves with political issues (though it is unlikely that such a rapid change in the composition of the workforce occurred over such a short time); that women increasingly shifted their attention to the temperance movement, radical religion, and the Sunday school movement, issues closer to traditional notions of women's interests; and that as Chartism became institutionalised, with the foundation of the National Charter Association in 1840 and the Chartist Land Company in 1845, the types of activities commonly participated in by women, such as mass demonstrations, were replaced by committees, which tended to exclude women.[115] In varying degrees it is likely that all these factors played a role, since they are all part of a general ideological shift which tended to marginalise women politically: the adoption among the working class of middle-class notions of domesticity and respectability.

Anna Clark has argued that Chartist men embraced these values for a number of reasons. By arguing that women even of the lower class should not work outside the home and should devote themselves to domestic duties (while the men should be paid a 'breadwinner's wage'[116]), radicals defused tensions created by competition between men and women for jobs and reestablished the traditional balance of power within the family economy. By emphasising women's moral duties, they defended the morality of working-class women against middle- and upper-class attacks, whether in the form of the assumptions implicit in the New Poor Law, or the allegations of the Chartists' opponents, who questioned the chastity of female activists. And, by arguing that working women had suffered greatly under the factory system, Chartists undermined a central ideological tenet of government policies, laissez-faire economic theory. Clark argues that working women also found domesticity attractive, both because it promised them freedom from factory labour and because they were promised more respectable husbands, who would be transformed 'from drunken louts into responsible breadwinners'. A stress on women's duties as wives and mothers was of course nothing new in working-class politics, for as we have seen women had often justified their participation in protests by emphasising their concerns to protect their families from starvation. Chartist

115 Ibid., pp. 136–7; Thompson, *The Chartists*, pp. 122–32; Clark, *Struggle for the Breeches*, pp. 244–7.
116 Discussed in Chapter 5, pp. 204–5.

women, like those before them, adopted a 'militant' form of domesticity, which, in contrast to middle-class women, called for women to labour and protest outside the home in order to feed their families. In this sense, domesticity and politics were not mutually exclusive. It may also be the case that 'the stress on domesticity was in part simply a rhetorical gesture to answer vitriolic attacks made on [women's] activities by the middle-class press.'[117]

Nonetheless, the importance of domesticity in Chartist rhetoric and especially the emphasis placed on women as victims of the political and economic system, together with the arguments Chartists adopted when making the case for male suffrage, appear to have had the effect of excluding many working-class women from politics. Just as the anti-poor law and factory reform movements depicted women as vulnerable to exploitation (and therefore unable to come to their own defence), Chartists depicted women as defenceless creatures who were being exploited by a corrupt system, which would be reformed by male Chartists acting to aid and protect women.[118] Moreover, in justifying their argument for male (but not female) suffrage, Chartists argued that it was the possession of skills (rather than the possession of property, as in existing practice) which qualifed men for the vote (it was assumed that men had a monopoly on skill). This justified the exclusion of women not only from politics, but also from work, since women's work was thought to be a cause of the deskilling of male workers, since manufacturers often cut costs by simplifying tasks and hiring lower-paid female workers to perform them. In this way men were recast in the role of skilled workers, breadwinners, and politically responsible citizens, while women were confined to domestic activities.

The Chartists' emphasis on domesticity thus contributed, as Anna Clark has argued, to a 'narrow notion of working-class politics', one which effectively excluded not only women, but also many unskilled men, from working-class organisations (especially trade unions) in the decades after 1850. As a consequence, the important advances in feminist political action in the 1850s and 1860s took place largely without working-class participation, despite the major advances working-class women had made as contributors to organised protest movements in the first half of the century.

---

117 Clark, *Struggle for the Breeches*, part 3, quotes from pp. 223, 229; Schwarzkopf, *Women in the Chartist Movement*, chs 4–5.
118 Thomis and Grimmett, *Women in Protest*, p. 120.

CONCLUSION

The dramatic changes in the conduct of British politics over the course of the period 1650 to 1850 allowed men and women of all but the highest social classes increasing scope for political action, but opportunities for women came later than for men, and were more limited. The eighteenth-century growth of public opinion and voluntary societies as influential political forces was largely confined to men. From the late eighteenth century, however, women began to join voluntary societies, often forming their own women-only organisations, though these were often subordinate to men's societies. Through their membership in voluntary societies, women were the driving force behind a number of philanthropic and reform activities in the first half of the nineteenth century which had a direct impact on parliamentary politics, notably the anti-slavery movement. Lower down the social scale, women played an important role in some incidents of labour unrest and in political reform campaigns, especially Chartism.

Yet women's political activities at all levels were constricted, in the sense that they found their greatest opportunities with causes relating to philanthropy, and wherever they could claim an issue affected their 'domestic' concerns. In the early part of our period aristocratic and royal women exercised real political power (often behind the scenes), but this took place primarily within the quasi-domestic environments of the royal court and aristocratic society. When these powers declined (but by no means disappeared) over the course of this period, middle-class women found new, arguably more public, opportunities for action, but the range of issues they were involved in was narrower than those of their aristocratic predecessors. Working-class women were initially less constrained by domesticity (as is clear from their participation in early-nineteenth-century reform movements), but they found their activities curtailed in the 1840s as working-class men and women adopted notions of domesticity which excluded women from politics. Perhaps the reason middle-class women were ultimately more active politically and contributed more to the development of the feminist movement after 1850 is that they were better able to combine domestic concerns with political action. Middle-class women had more experience with domesticity (in the sense that they had been expected to adopt such values throughout this period and they were more able to practise it in their day-to-day lives), and they were better able to use that experience to justify their public political activities. They were also, of course, wealthier, which meant they could afford to hire more servants to perform their domestic duties, leaving more time for politics.

Despite women's growing public role, the political world remained male-dominated throughout this period. In terms of 'high' politics, men benefited from the reduction in the powers exercised by monarchical and aristocratic women, and they gained more influence than women from the increased importance of public opinion and extraparliamentary pressure groups. Yet it is important to note that men's activities were also in some ways constricted during this period, in the sense that some activities, especially where they concerned women and children, were increasingly seen as women's responsibility. Whereas men had previously dominated the running of charities, they were increasingly obliged to defer to the activities of women, even where men retained formal positions of leadership. These constraints even on occasion reached parliament where, when issues affecting women or the needy (including slaves) arose, women could exert significant pressure. Women in public life increasingly concerned themselves with 'domestic' issues, and men were expected to defer to them. Echoing the decline of mixed-sex voluntary societies in favour of distinctly homosocial organisations (both male and female), gender differentiation in the conduct of politics increased during this period.

CHAPTER SEVEN

Social and Cultural Life

Public life involves much more than politics: this chapter broadens the discussion to include the more informal social and cultural experiences of English men and women in a variety of contexts: on the streets, in alehouses and coffeehouses, at fairs and at assemblies and the theatre, and through literature. In some of these contexts one can also speak of an expansion of the 'public sphere' similar to that seen in the world of politics, which opened up new opportunities for both men and women, though not of course on the same terms. The chapter concludes by looking at patterns of crime, to see if the gender patterns we have identified in our examination of public life are any different when we consider behaviour which violated social and legal norms.

SOCIAL LIFE

The most ubiquitous type of public activity was of course walking, loitering, and working on the streets. Evidence of street behaviour is patchy, but surviving sources (which pertain primarily to London) suggest that both men and women were present on the streets in large numbers. Both sexes, for example, participated in the spontaneous riots which so frequently erupted in London. We have seen that both men and women frequently worked as hawkers and pedlers. Both sexes also figure prominently in the street scenes of William Hogarth. In his 'Four Times of the Day' series and 'Beer Street', for example, one can see men and women walking, chatting, working, begging, and kissing. Nor was the presence of women restricted to those of the lower class. As the 'Morning' print illustrates, with a respectable woman walking purposefully towards church, middle-class women could also frequently be found on the

269

streets, though they were less likely to loiter. One of their primary pursuits was shopping, a time-consuming and labour-intensive activity in an age which valued consumption but had not yet made it convenient. Consequently, according to Margaret Hunt, in eighteenth-century London 'many middling women consumers may have spent less time at home than their husbands did'.[1] Although such women were often accompanied by servants or companions, evidence from novels suggests they also travelled alone. As we shall see, some streets were best avoided, but, as Penelope Corfield has commented, 'there was no suggestion of a female curfew, or that city streets were seen as intrinsically male terrain.'[2]

Experiences of street life nonetheless varied considerably by sex, as well as class and age. In rural areas, roads appear to have been dominated by men. Farmers' wives and women employed as domestic servants or servants in husbandry were kept busy in and around farmhouses (and, at certain points during the year, in the fields), while men's work and social life more frequently took them into the fields and villages. Nonetheless, we have seen that there were a significant number of female hawkers and peddlers, who supplied rural areas with consumer goods. Elite women were dependent on the availability of a carriage for travel, since they were rarely able or willing to ride horses, and this severely limited their mobility.[3] In urban areas, although men and women were both physically present on the streets, the spatial experiences and perceptions of each sex could be very different. For one thing, men and women behaved differently towards each other: men were expected to 'surrender the wall' (the cleanest part of the pavement away from the gutter, an open sewer which ran down the middle of the street) to women. While men acknowledged respectable passersby by doffing their hats, women curtsied, though both practices waned during the period.[4]

1 See above, Chapter 3, pp. 116–20; R. B. Shoemaker, 'The London "mob" in the early eighteenth century', *Journal of British Studies* 26 (1987), pp. 285–6; Margaret Hunt, 'Wife beating, domesticity, and women's independence in eighteenth-century London', *Gender and History* 4 (1992), p. 12.

2 P. Corfield, 'Walking the city streets in the eighteenth century', *Journal of Urban History* 16 (1990), p. 134.

3 John Beattie, 'The criminality of women in eighteenth-century England', *Journal of Social History* 8 (1975), pp. 98–9; Joyce Ellis, ' "On the town": women in Augustan England', *History Today* (Dec. 1995), pp. 21–2; Karl Westhauser, 'Friendship and family in early modern England: the sociability of Adam Eyre and Samuel Pepys', *Journal of Social History* 27 (1994), p. 521; above, Chapter 5, p. 172.

4 Corfield, 'Walking the city streets', pp. 154, 156.

More importantly, women seem to have spent more time loitering on city streets, especially in that liminal area between public and private spaces, the doorstep. Much of this time was spent talking, which could lead to public accusations against friends and neighbours suspected of behaving improperly. Prosecutions for defamation show that women frequently called into question the sexual reputation of other women in public: 63% of the defendants accused of defamation in the London church courts between 1700–10 and 1735–45 were women, and the insults they were accused of making were invariably sexual, most commonly involving the use of the term 'whore'.[5] By making such accusations, defamers called attention to their own sexual virtue. The church court evidence is potentially misleading, however, in suggesting that women's insults were virtually always sexual. Evidence from other sources shows that women also made public insults for other reasons, such as to accuse men and women of theft or unfair business practices. Men, too, used the streets to make public insults on both sexual and other issues, but court evidence suggests they did so less frequently than women. In the early eighteenth century, however, conduct-book writers expressed concern about an apparent outbreak of male defamation, as men increasingly preferred non-violent methods of pursuing conflicts and attacking the honour of their antagonists.[6]

The victims of public insults concerning sexual behaviour were overwhelmingly women, and this raises another important way in which women's experiences of street life differed from those of men: in certain circumstances, especially in urban areas, they were liable to suspicion, attack, or arrest as prostitutes. We have seen that prostitution was a constant feature of urban life during this period; that, as a consequence of the double standard of sexual morality, it was frequently seen as a necessary evil which could only be controlled, not abolished; and that virtually all efforts to contain the problem were addressed at the prostitutes, not their clients.[7] Even if there had been a consensus among the authorities against prostitution (and there was not), the limitations of the law and the limited powers of local officials meant that it could not be eliminated. In-

5 Tim Meldrum, 'A women's court in London: defamation at the Bishop of London's Consistory Court, 1700–1745', *London Journal* 19 (1994), p. 6.

6 Garthine Walker, 'Expanding the boundaries of female honour in early modern England', *Transactions of the Royal Historical Society*, 6th series, 6 (1996), pp. 239–45; R. B. Shoemaker, 'Reforming male manners: public insult and the decline of violence in London', 1660–1740', in *English Masculinities, 1660–1800*, ed. T. Hitchcock and M. Cohen (forthcoming).

7 Above, Chapter 3, pp. 75–9.

stead, accommodations were reached between constables and the night watch on the one hand and prostitutes on the other in which the latter were allowed, in exchange for bribes and/or accepting certain limitations on their behaviour, to solicit on the streets in certain parts of town, notably around Covent Garden in London.[8] On such streets, which were well known for the trade, prostitutes could act quite openly, using aggressive tactics such as tugging at men's sleeves and making obscene comments in order to recruit clients.

The fact that prostitution flourished in this manner had important consequences for women on the streets, whether or not they were prostitutes. The fragile accommodation with the authorities often broke down, leaving prostitutes and others vulnerable to harassment and arrest. Although prostitution was not technically illegal, parish officials and magistrates possessed sufficient powers of arrest and punishment, when they chose to use them, to cause considerable hardship. The considerable powers of discretion possessed by officers could be used arbitrarily to arrest poor or deviant women regardless of whether the fact of prostitution could be proved against them. Through the use of search warrants to arrest anyone suspected of acting disorderly and/or not having a visible and legal means of support, officers arrested large numbers of women on the basis of weak and circumstantial evidence, such as the fact that their dress was outlandish or tatty or they were out late at night unaccompanied by men on streets where prostitutes were known to solicit. Although men, too, were victims of similar arrests, though on suspicion of theft or vagrancy rather than prostitution, this happened far less frequently, as is evident in the fact that women account for 65% of the commitments to the Middlesex and Westminster houses of correction in the early eighteenth century for loose, idle, and disorderly conduct or vagrancy.[9] With the introduction of the new police in stages from 1829, and the passage of acts against vagrancy in 1822, 1834, and 1844, official surveillance of the streets was increased for working-class men as well as women, leading to increased arrests for petty public-order offences such as drunkenness, begging, vagrancy, illegal street trading, and suspicious loitering, as well as prostitution.[10]

8 A. R. Henderson, 'Female prostitution in London, 1730–1830' (University of London, PhD thesis, 1992), ch. 5.

9 R. B. Shoemaker, *Prosecution and Punishment: Petty Crime and the Law in London and Rural Middlesex, c. 1660–1725* (Cambridge, 1991), pp. 178–82 and table 7.3, p. 185.

10 Clive Emsley, *Crime and Society in England, 1750–1900* (2nd edn, 1996), p. 235; R. D. Storch, 'The policeman as domestic missionary: urban discipline and popular culture in Northern England, 1850–1880', *Journal of Social History* 9 (1976), pp. 481–509.

In terms of prostitution, the problem for women was that, even though prostitutes tried to attract attention by wearing distinctive clothes, any woman could be suspected of prostitution if she dressed inappropriately or travelled on the wrong streets, especially if she was unaccompanied by a man and out late at night. Daniel Defoe commented in 1726 that since even ordinary ladies had acquired 'gay dress and jaunty airs', it was impossible to be certain who was and who was not a prostitute. In addition to the danger of being propositioned by a lecherous man, women were in danger of being mistreated by the watch or even ordinary citizens who felt that suspected prostitutes could be abused and assaulted with impunity: in 1727 Defoe complained that under the pretence of punishing prostitutes 'many honest women are mobbed, and oftentimes robbed in the very face of the world ... For if anyone makes a struggle or an outcry, these villains swear they are whores, and so are left at liberty to rob or abuse them at pleasure.' In addition, prostitutes sometimes attacked women who entered their streets, thinking that they were other prostitutes infringing on their territory.[11] When venturing into public, women clearly needed to regulate their appearance and behaviour so as not to be susceptible to being labelled a prostitute.

A further and related factor limiting women's freedom of movement in public was the fear of rape. This was a real possibility, given the sexual attitudes of the time, but these fears were exacerbated, particularly in the nineteenth century, by the reporting of incidents in newspapers. According to Anna Clark, 'by the 1820s the notion that sexual violence made the streets unsafe for respectable women was rarely questioned.' The way women chose to travel in public, the routes taken and the times travelled must inevitably have been influenced by these considerations, probably more so in the nineteenth century than earlier. In certain limited contexts men, too, needed to be careful about their attire and street behaviour, lest they be harrassed and/or arrested for suspected homosexual behaviour. This problem was restricted, however, largely to London and to certain periods of public panic.[12]

Beyond work, travel, and gossip, men and women frequently

---

11 [Daniel Defoe], *Some Considerations Upon Street-Walkers* [1726], p. 4; Andrew Moreton, Esq. [Daniel Defoe], *Parochial Tyranny: or, the Housekeeper's Complaint Against the Insupportable Exactions, and Partial Assessments of Street Vestries, etc.* (1727), p. 21; Henderson, 'Female prostitution in London', pp. 217–18.

12 Above, Chapter 3, pp. 80–4; Anna Clark, *Women's Silence, Men's Violence: Sexual Assault in England, 1770–1845* (1987), p. 116.

used the streets and other public places for leisure. Although not all leisure took place outside the home, much did. Plebeian houses were too small and crowded to permit much recreation, and in any case leisure activities served a number of public functions in this period, in some cases enhancing communal solidarity and in other ways serving as an arena of social competition, as people with social aspirations displayed their wealth and status. Historians and anthropologists dispute whether leisure activities tend to mirror existing social structures and hierarchies, or whether when stepping outside normal patterns of life people are able to transcend or reverse such structures. For the historian of gender, the question thus poses itself: were normal gender roles transcended or subverted in leisure activities? This discussion will start with the most common form of leisure throughout this period, drinking at an alehouse, and then examine other forms of relaxation and recreation, starting with the lower class and then moving up the social scale.

The alehouse in the early modern period is normally seen as a male-dominated social environment, a place where husbands could escape from their families to enjoy drinking and chatting with their friends and fellow workers. Women, however, were present throughout this period, not only running alehouses but also increasingly as clients. Lists of licensed victuallers from four areas in the early eighteenth century include between 10% and 17% women, most of whom were probably widows. And although men held the vast majority of alehouse licences, their wives commonly took the responsibility for the day-to-day running of the house, aided by a number of female as well as male servants, while the husband carried on with his craft. As customers, however, women were far less common than men. For most of our period women could only go to an alehouse in certain circumstances, lest they be suspected of offering sexual favours. They could go with their husbands or boyfriends, especially during times of family celebration or communal festivities, or they could go with groups of other women. Nonetheless, they did not go anywhere near as often as did men, and when they did Peter Clark suggests 'it is likely the two sexes sat apart when drinking.'[13]

In the first half of the nineteenth century women seem to have become more common in pubs, encouraged by the fact that female friendly societies often met there and that women were attracted to

13 Peter Clark, *The English Alehouse: A Social History, 1200–1830* (1983), pp. 203, 225, 236, 311, quotation at p. 311.

the growing availability of spirits, especially gin, and music and dancing. A witness before the 1834 parliamentary committee on drunkenness testified that women made up 43% of the customers in a number of gin shops in the east end of London. Nonetheless, patterns of use still varied significantly by sex and drinking in mixed-sex groups seems to have been relatively rare. Anna Clark suggests that 'plebeian men seem to have reserved specific times for drinking with their wives and to have kept others sacrosanct to their workmates.' Although women had always been present (seventeenth-century ballads depict women frequently meeting in alehouses to gossip), women seem to have become increasingly present in the quasi-public space of the drinking house over the course of our period. At other times and places, however (particularly perhaps outside London), the pub remained very much a 'masculine republic', where men met to smoke, exchange news, and socialise in an environment where the only women present were there to serve them. Although middle-class men in the nineteenth century increasingly abandoned the alehouse for the more respectable private club, they valued such homosocial environments perhaps even more than in earlier periods, due to the opportunity they provided to escape from the 'constraining femininity' of domestic life.[14]

Although the alehouse and gin shop were the most common venues for popular recreation, plebeian men and women also attended a wide range of organised leisure activities, including fairs, feasts, and festivals. Many of these were community celebrations which were open to both sexes, and indeed some, such as wakes, provided opportunities for young men and women to court. When traditional customs fell into decline in the second half of our period, new commercialised forms of recreation, such as pleasure gardens and singing saloons, were also open to both sexes.[15] Yet opportunities did differ by sex, and it may be true to say that in

14 Anna Clark, *The Struggle for the Breeches: Gender and the Making of the British Working Class* (Berkeley, 1995), pp. 29–30, 35, 39, quotation at p. 29; *Parliamentary Papers* 1834, vol. 8, Report of the Select Committee on Drunkenness, p. 3; J. A. Sharpe, 'Plebeian marriage in Stuart England: some evidence from popular literature', *Transactions of the Royal Historical Society* 5th series, 36 (1986), p. 80; Brian Harrison, *Drink and the Victorians* (1971), pp. 46–7; Leonore Davidoff and Catherine Hall, *Family Fortunes: Men and Women of the English Middle Class, 1780–1850* (1987), pp. 427–8; John Tosh, *Men at Home: Domesticity and the Victorian Middle Class* (forthcoming), ch. 6.

15 H. Cunningham, 'Leisure and culture', in F. M. L. Thompson (ed.), *The Cambridge Social History of Britain 1750–1950* (3 vols, 1990), p. 310; P. Bailey, *Leisure and Class in Victorian England* (1978), p. 31.

general men had more active roles in popular recreations than women. Some traditional holidays, such as Guy Fawkes Day and Shrove Tuesday, were particularly associated with men, and men seem to have carried out the processions which occurred at wakes or on Rogation Day. Most popular sports (football, cricket, boxing, and wrestling) 'assumed that women would attend only as spectators, or not at all'. Where female spectators were present, there was an element in sports of male competition for women's attentions.[16] Nonetheless, there is some evidence of women playing cricket, competing in running races, and boxing and fighting, often in front of spectators, in early-eighteenth-century London.[17]

Some holidays offered gender-specific roles for men and women. Traditional Mayday celebrations contrasted rural masculine and feminine symbols: 'the male working world . . . of the woodland and hedgerow . . . [in opposition to] the tamer "domesticated nature" of the cow-pasture and the dairy'. Although this ritual assumed a new form in eighteenth-century London, gender differences remained in the form of a contrast between female milkmaids, who symbolised 'chastity, modesty, and clean, but hard *country*-living', and rival processions of young male chimney-sweeps who forced their attentions on the better off with 'ritualised aggression'.[18] At wakes at Hollinwood, near Oldham in the early nineteenth century 'there was something for everyone': athletic races for the young men, 'tea drinking matches' for old women, and sack races and other comic races for women, old men, people with wooden legs, and specific tradesmen (butchers and carters).[19] In general, holidays and leisure activities either confirmed existing gender roles or, at most, they provided times when men and women could interact informally in public, though the normal rules governing courtship and sexual encounters were only marginally relaxed.

The middle and upper classes obviously had different leisure pursuits, opportunities which not only expanded significantly over

16 Robert W. Malcolmson, *Popular Recreations in English Society, 1700–1850* (Cambridge, 1973), pp. 54–8, quote at p. 56; Robert Poole, 'Oldham wakes', in J. Walton and J. Walvin (eds), *Leisure in Britain 1780–1989* (Manchester, 1983), p. 75.

17 Daniel Lysons, *Collectanea: or, A Collection of Advertisements and Paragraphs from the Newspapers, Relating to Various Subjects* (5 vols, 1840), 1, f. 147; 4, ff. 130, 231, 252, 253 (I am indebted to Tim Hitchcock for these references); Z. C. von Uffenbach, *London in 1710* (trans. and ed. W. H. Quarrel and M. Mare, 1934), p. 90; Peter Earle, *The Making of the English Middle Class* (1989), p. 58.

18 Charles Pythian-Adams, 'Milk and soot: the changing vocabulary of a popular ritual in Stuart and Hanoverian London', in D. Fraser and A. Sutcliffe (eds), *The Pursuit of Urban History* (1983), pp. 83–104, quotes at pp. 99–100.

19 Poole, 'Oldham wakes', pp. 78–9.

the course of this period but also performed different social functions. Leisure provided these classes with a chance to display their wealth and advertise their status. There is a significant urban/rural contrast in the activities of these classes, in that rural entertainments were largely male and the new urban activities involved both sexes, in some cases giving greater prominence to women. The leisure pursuits of the rural gentry, riding, hunting, shooting, and fishing, were open primarily to men, while middle- and upper-class women were apparently for the most part confined to their homes. Though walking was a popular pastime, opportunities for visiting friends or alehouses were rare, if the activities of Adam and Susan Eyre, a Yorkshire yeoman and his wife who lived in the mid-seventeenth century, are typical. According to Adam's diary, his wife was rarely able to join him when travelling to social occasions due to the fact that they only had one horse and his neighbours were unwilling to lend theirs to women.[20] In contrast, we have seen that urban women were able to travel relatively freely around the city and therefore had a much wider range of opportunities to socialise.

Opportunities for urban leisure increased dramatically during the eighteenth century due to the 'urban renaissance', a flourishing of social and cultural activities including clubs, societies, coffeehouses, assemblies, musical events, walks and gardens, and the theatre. Peter Borsay has argued that these activities were characterised by public display, and were attended by the middle classes and gentry (both urban and rural) who were competing for social status in an increasingly fluid social structure.[21] Since such public display frequently involved women, they played a key role in the urban renaissance, though one which was clearly gendered. We have already seen that voluntary societies and clubs, which were as much institutions of leisure and entertainment as they were agents of social and political reform, became open to women later than men and were often sex-segregated; what of the other institutions of the urban renaissance?

The earliest was the coffeehouse, which first appeared in the 1650s and quickly spread to cities and towns across the country. According to one calculation London had 2000 by 1700. Evidence of the early coffeehouses suggests that women were frequent patrons. Steve Pincus argues that in late-seventeenth-century London '"city

---

20 Ellis, 'Women in Augustan England', p. 21; Westhauser, 'Friendship and family in early modern England', p. 521.

21 Peter Borsay, *The English Urban Renaissance: Culture and Society in the Provincial Town, 1660–1760* (Oxford, 1989).

ladies and citizens' wives" were said to relish the opportunity for
political discussion the coffee houses provided.' Owing to the
presence of so many women and the lack of traditional masculine
recreations (such as heavy drinking), these new public spaces were
perceived to erase distinctions between the sexes and they threatened to make men 'effeminate'. Moreover, there is evidence (from
Bath in 1725) of women taking up male pastimes such as gamb-
ling.[22] Later manifestations of the urban renaissance did more to reinforce existing gender roles, and it would be interesting to see
whether the apparently gender-neutral environment of the early
coffeehouses changed in any way over the course of the eighteenth
century.

One of the main characteristics of the urban renaissance was the
organisation of specific events promoting display and social interaction, notably assemblies and, especially in the early nineteenth
century, concerts. These were attended by men and women in equal
numbers and offered the chance for the sexes to intermingle. In
the case of masquerades, which were especially popular in London
in the eighteenth century and which women could attend unes-
corted, men and women had the opportunity to cross-dress and
adopt the behavioural traits of the opposite sex, and thereby experiment with their sexual and gender identity.[23] Whether such activity
ultimately subverted or confirmed gender roles is an open question,
but it is likely that established gender differences were confirmed in
other social events which took place in the assembly rooms. Although the primary activity was dancing, venues such as the York
Assembly Room had a 'retiring place for the ladies', as well as a card
room possibly monopolised by the men. In Bath, women appear to
have sat separately on the dance floor. Moreover, men and women
did not have equal roles in organising and running these events.
The York assemblies were governed by a board of male directors,
though 'the ladies' clearly played an important role in initiating
events, organising their conduct, and drumming up interest. On 6
November 1747, for example, the directors responded to the problem of declining attendance by asking 'the ladies' to 'severally take
upon themselves the title of Queen of the Assemblies, [so that] the
management thereof will flourish again'. It is not clear what this
role involved, though it appears to have been largely informal, as

22 Steve Pincus, ' "Coffee politicians does create": coffeehouses and Restoration
political culture', *Journal of Modern History* 67 (1995), pp. 807–34, quote at p. 816;
Borsay, *English Urban Renaissance*, pp. 249–50.

23 Terry Castle, *The Female Thermometer: Eighteenth-Century Culture and the Invention
of the Uncanny* (Oxford, 1995, ch. 6).

the directors retained the power to 'rectify' any problems arising with the music or servants. The successful Birmingham music festivals were run by men. Generally, at balls, concerts, assemblies and race meetings men acted in the socially prestigious role of stewards, responsible for determining who would be admitted and where they would be seated, and acting as masters of ceremony.[24] Although the presence of women was crucial to the social function of these events as arenas of sociability and display, they rarely had more than an informal role in their management.

Social display also took place on the planned urban walks (such as the 'New Walk' or 'Long Walk' at York) and at the commercial pleasure gardens (notably London's Vauxhall and Ranelagh gardens) which became popular in the eighteenth century. These were more public and less exclusive than the assemblies and concerts, but through the price of admission to the gardens and other measures attempts were made to maintain social respectability. Men and women frequently promenaded together, though in the gardens men might be attracted to bowls while women took tea. As on the public streets, women's experiences of walks and gardens were limited somewhat by the possibility that they would be suspected of immorality. There were constant concerns that these venues were used for amorous assignations and that, in the words of Joseph Addison, there were more 'strumpets' than 'nightingales' present.[25] Women's role in these activities was also limited by the fact that arguably their most important function was as a means of displaying their families' social status, through their dress, jewellery, coiffure, and demeanour. Nonetheless, like the assemblies and concerts these walks and gardens offered women a degree of freedom and visibility in public life.

Another venue for entertainment and display was the theatre. Although, as in walks and gardens, prostitutes were present, the audiences were primarily from the middle classes and above, and of both sexes. That great lover of the Restoration theatre and observer of audiences, Samuel Pepys, went mostly with his wife (when she was in town), and she also attended the theatre without him. Mixed-sex audiences seem to have been the norm throughout this period.

24 Borsay, *English Urban Renaissance*, p. 246; Ellis, 'Women in Augustan England', p. 22; York City Archives, M. 23:1, York Assembly Rooms, Directors' Minute Book (I am indebted to Peter Borsay for this reference); Davidoff and Hall, *Family Fortunes*, p. 441.

25 T. J. Edelstein, 'Vauxhall Gardens', in Boris Ford (ed.), *The Cambridge Cultural History of Britain, volume 5: Eighteenth-Century Britain* (Cambridge, 1992), p. 203, quoting the *Spectator*, no. 383, 1712.

Perhaps the most significant aspect of the introduction of a significant female presence in theatre audiences after the Restoration is
that by the early eighteenth century they arguably influenced the
content and choice of the plays performed. It has been suggested
that women's objections to the obscenity and insulting images of
women in Restoration plays encouraged the subsequent movement
towards sentiment and moral reform, though it should be noted
that this trend was part of a broader cultural change. According to
Jacqueline Pearson, 'after 1703 it became a regular feature to present stock plays which were specially requested by "Ladies" '. Analysis
of such requests shows that women preferred tragedies of pathos,
comedies with sentimental elements, and Shakespeare, disregarding
almost totally comedies of wit and sex. A 'Shakespeare Ladies Club'
was founded in 1736 for the purpose of persuading theatres to put
on more of Shakespeare's plays, and it was successful in achieving
this goal.[26]

Not only were women in the audience, but for the first time they
were on the stage as well. With the return of the theatre after the Interregnum actresses as well as actors were allowed to perform in
public, an aspect of the Restoration theatre which has been called
'arguably, [its] most popular single element'. More than any other
women in public, however, actresses faced difficulty in protecting
their moral reputations. The whole idea of women performing for
pay in public smacked of prostitution, and the association of actresses with sexual promiscuity was enhanced by the bawdy content
of so much Restoration drama. Actresses were immensely popular
with audiences, who seemed to enjoy their titillating behaviour on
stage, both in female parts and when disguised as men. Audience
enjoyment was furthered by the fact that they were encouraged to
see a correspondence between the sexual adventures of actresses on
the stage and in their real lives. This assumption that actresses led
immoral lives led them to be sexually harassed and exploited off
stage. A study of eighty Restoration actresses found that twelve were
courtesans and another twelve left the theatre to become kept
women or prostitutes; only a quarter led respectable lives. Although
the possibility of acquiring an immoral reputation haunted actresses
throughout our period, the growing respectability of drama over
the course of the eighteenth century made the problem less acute.
While actresses faced other disadvantages – notably low pay and low

26 Jacqueline Pearson, *The Prostituted Muse: Images of Women and Women
Dramatists 1642–1737* (1988), pp. 33–41, quote at p. 39.

status within their companies – they represent yet another aspect of the expanding female presence within the 'public sphere' in this period.[27]

Scholars dispute the nature of the impact the use of actresses had on the way women were portrayed in English drama. On the one hand, stereotypes of women as deceptive and lustful were arguably confirmed in the roles actresses played, and however assertive female characters were, in the end they continued to be defined by the moral requirements of the double standard and a need to obtain male affection. Tragedies, moreover, included scenes of violence against female victims, who were depicted as passive and helpless. On the other hand, the very fact that women were speaking and acting on the stage 'brought about the stronger expression of an exclusively female viewpoint in comedy', in which women expressed their own needs and, for example, drew explicit attention to the pitfalls of marriage for women.[28]

The sexuality of actors was also a concern in the eighteenth century, but here the worry concerned homosexuality. The seventeenth-century concern that the use of boys to play women's parts encouraged sodomy was no longer an issue once boys were replaced by actresses, but in the next century actors were still frequently perceived as 'sexually suspect', given that their job involved the 'feminine' task of seeking to please their audience. With the increasing intolerance of male homosexuality during the century, actors needed to defend themselves against suspicions of effeminacy and sodomy. Concurrently, cross-dressing actresses were increasingly condemned. In this sense, the theatre probably became more confining in its depiction of gender roles over the period, as the heterosexual man and the modest woman became dominant.[29]

In sum, the changing pattern of middle-class sociability enhanced women's physical presence in public life in this period, to the extent that one observer, John Gregory, wrote in 1774 that women are 'always in our eye at public places, . . . conversing with us with the same unreserved freedom as we do with one another . . .

27 Antonia Fraser, *The Weaker Vessel: Woman's Lot in Seventeenth-Century England* (1989 edn), pp. 474–80, citing esp. the work of J. H. Wilson: *All the King's Ladies, Actresses of the Restoration* (1958); Elizabeth Howe, *The First English Actresses: Women and Drama 1660–1700* (Cambridge, 1992).

28 Howe, *First English Actresses*, esp. pp. 173–6; Eric A. Nicholson, 'The theater', in N. Z. Davis and A. Farge (eds), *A History of Women in the West, III: Renaissance and Enlightenment Paradoxes* (1993), pp. 296–305, 314.

29 Kristina Straub, *Sexual Suspects: Eighteenth-Century Players and Sexual Ideology* (Princeton, NJ, 1992), chs 2–3.

resembling us as nearly as they possibly can'.[30] While Gregory exaggerates the degree to which gender distinctions had dissolved, his point about the public visibility of women is an important one. This will become even more apparent when we consider what might be called the literary public sphere, the body of published works which, although created in private, were made available for consumption by large numbers of people unknown to the creators. As with other aspects of the public sphere, this area of activity expanded considerably over the course of the period for both sexes, but particularly for women.

CULTURAL LIFE

A number of developments within the world of publishing in this period greatly enhanced opportunities for authors and increased the impact of what they wrote. Government controls over printing, which had lapsed during the Civil War and Interregnum, disappeared for good with the expiration of the Press Licensing Act in 1695, and books came to be marketed for a much wider audience. Concurrently, dramatic improvements in literacy rates and, for the middle class, prosperity, greatly increased the number of potential consumers. Publishers and other businessmen cultivated this new market with new types of publications such as the periodical and new methods of dissemination with reduced prices through subscription, publication by installments, and circulating libraries. Both male and female authors benefited from these changes, but the impact on women was greater, both because the system of publishing by subscription allowed publishers to risk lesser-known authors, and more importantly due to the dramatic growth in female readership. This was encouraged by the growth of the middle class (which increased the number of women with leisure time), the availability of cheaper publications, and improvements in literacy. Literacy rates for both sexes (as measured by the ability to sign one's name) increased substantially over the course of our period, but proportionally the increase for women was greater because they started from such a low base. David Cressy estimates that male literacy more than doubled, from just over 30% in 1650 to 70% in 1850, while female literacy increased even more dramatically, from just 15% to 55%. Interestingly, the gap between male and female literacy was fairly constant throughout the period at around 15%, which suggests that

30 John Gregory, *A Father's Legacy to His Daughters* (1774), p. 41.

throughout this period women remained at a similar disadvantage relative to men. These statistics, of course, hide considerable variations by social class: more upper-class women could read than lower-class men.[31] They also fail to indicate what proportions of men and women actually devoted a significant amount of time to reading. For much of our period women seem to have been more prone to read, so that despite lower rates of literacy women dominated the reading public. By the nineteenth century, the issue of 'the woman reader' was the subject of considerable comment.[32]

Nonetheless, women who wished to publish faced considerable obstacles. They had fewer educational opportunities, and the act of going into print was seen as disreputable for a woman in the first half of our period. While the act of writing for private consumption was acceptable (as with a spiritual diary, or private correspondence), going public was not. To publish was to draw attention to and to expose oneself, almost literally: it suggested immodesty and what inevitably followed, immorality. Women who did venture into print were liable to be vilified with charges of sexual promiscuity or even madness. Alternatively, they were accused of plagiarising men's work. For these reasons, female authors frequently published anonymously or pseudonymously (even on occasion referring to themselves as men in the preface). Those who admitted their sex often felt the need to apologise for it: according to one study, half of the prefaces to published poetry written by women between 1667 and 1750 included apologies for the author's sex, statements that the poet did not take her writing seriously, and/or statements that it was not initially intended for publication.[33]

These attitudes changed over the course of this period. By the end of the eighteenth century female authorship on a narrow range of subjects which were accepted as within women's domain (religious devotional works, fiction, childcare manuals, and cookery books and herbals) was for the most part respectable, as long as the motives for publication were acceptable: authors could claim they were following the command of God, or their writings served a moral didactic purpose, or they were suffering from financial necessity due to the absence or inability (due to death, desertion, or

31 David Cressy, *Literacy and the Social Order: Reading and Writing in Tudor and Stuart England* (Cambridge, 1980), p. 177; R. Schofield, 'Dimensions of illiteracy, 1750–1850', *Explorations in Economic History* 10 (1973), pp. 437–54.

32 Kate Flint, *The Woman Reader 1837–1914* (Oxford, 1993), p. 10.

33 R. G. Gibson, ' "My want of skill": apologies of British women poets, 1660–1800', in F. M. Keener and S. E. Lorsch (eds), *Eighteenth-Century Women and the Arts* (1988), pp. 79–81.

illness) of a male breadwinner to provide for them. By this time
public sympathy for female authors was such that some novels written by men were actually given fictitious female authors or simply
entitled 'By a Lady' because they were more marketable, and in
their prefaces women felt less need to apologise for venturing into
print. Whereas most of the female authors of the late seventeenth
century were either unmarried or widows, by 1800 married women
frequently wrote for publication as part of middle-class family businesses. Nonetheless, antagonism to women writers remained. The
poet Richard Polwhele, for example, wrote a poem in 1798 against
women writers in which he described them as unnatural and having
allowed pride and vengeance to smooth 'their softer charms'. Even
in 1837, when female authorship was well established, the Poet
Laureate Robert Southey wrote (to Charlotte Brontë) that 'literature cannot be the business of a woman's life and it ought not to
be.'[34]

Although it is impossible to determine the precise proportion of
works published by women (given the large number of works published anonymously or pseudonymously), the evidence of the
growth in the number and proportion of writers who were female is
impressive. In the first four decades of the seventeenth century new
publications by women averaged only about one per year, and accounted for just 0.5% of all the works published. Most of the female
authors were aristocratic, and many of the limited number of works
they wrote were circulated in manuscript. The breakdown of control over printing and the social and political turmoil during the
Civil War and Interregnum led to an increase to an average of
about a dozen new published works by women each year, which
now accounted for about 1% of all publications. Although the number of publications declined during the Restoration, the proportion
written by women remained constant. By 1700 women still accounted for only a tiny proportion of the works published.[35]

With the publishing explosion in the eighteenth century, however, the expansion of female authorship speeded up, as women

34 Olwen Hufton, *The Prospect Before Her: A History of Women in Western Europe
1500–1800* (1995), pp. 425–6; J. Raven, *British Fiction 1750–1770: A Chronological
Checklist* (1987), p. 18; Pearson, *The Prostituted Muse*, p. 21; Davidoff and Hall, *Family
Fortunes*, p. 162; Richard Polwhele, *The Unsex'd Females* (1798), cited by Bridget Hill,
The Republican Virago: The Life and Times of Catharine Macaulay, Historian (Oxford,
1992), p. 132; Southey quoted by Elaine Showalter, *A Literature of Their Own: British
Women Novelists from Brontë to Lessing* (rev. edn, 1982), p. 55.

35 P. Crawford, 'Women's published writings 1600–1700', in M. Prior (ed.),
Women in English Society 1500–1800 (1985), pp. 265–7.

played a major role in new genres such as periodicals and the novel. Between 1750 and 1769 women accounted for at least 7% of all the novels published, but the real figure is no doubt higher since the sex of more than a third of novel authors is unknown. Between 300 and 400 women published during the decade of the 1790s alone, and ten of the twelve most popular novelists between 1780 and 1830 were women. Between 1800 and 1835 women accounted for 21% of the writers of literature. Even these figures do not fully portray the extent of women's role, since as a result of the low status of their works many have been lost. Moreover, women wrote a disproportionate number of the manuscripts which publishers rejected. Contemporaries, of course, had less access to statistics and came to more impressionistic conclusions: based on the unprecedented popularity of female novelists there were claims from the 1770s onwards that female authors accounted for the majority of the fiction published. This was not true, of course, but the fact that people thought it was shows how extensively women had entered the literary marketplace by the end of our period.[36]

By the mid-nineteenth century writing had become a largely acceptable occupation for middle-class women and some were able to make a living through their writing. Although aristocratic women, with their secure social position and good connections, continued to play a significant role in publication well into the nineteenth century, the expansion of women's publication could not have occurred without more middle-class women taking up the pen, many of whom depended on the income for their livelihood. The first women to make their livings through published writings lived in the late seventeenth century: Sarah Jinner and Hannah Wolley, who used their advice books to advertise their medical and cooking skills; and the playwright Aphra Behn. These individuals were highly unusual, and it was not until the late eighteenth century that female professional writers became more respectable and commonplace, though even then, given the low levels of remuneration, most would have had to publish several books a year in order to support their families.[37]

The growth of female authorship was accompanied by a change

36 Raven, *British Fiction 1750–1770*, pp. 18–19; Janet Todd, *The Sign of Angellica: Women, Writing and Fiction, 1660–1800* (1989), p. 218; Richard Altick, 'The sociology of authorship', *Bulletin of the New York Public Library* 66 (1962), p. 392; Showalter, *A Literature of Their Own*, pp. 38–9; Anne K. Mellor, *Romanticism and Gender* (1993), p. 7.

37 Elaine Hobby, *Virtue of Necessity: English Women's Writing 1649–1688* (1988), p. 114; Todd, *Sign of Angellica*, p. 220.

in the types of works published. More than half of women's writings in the period between 1649 and 1688 were religious prophecies, and there were many other religious works including prayers, meditations, spiritual autobiographies, and godly advice. A similar tabulation of works by subject matter for men would also no doubt identify a large number of religious works, but there would be more works on politics, economic issues, law, and science. Nonetheless, women did write on a wider range of issues than it first appears: we have noted that female prophecies during the Interregnum, which outnumbered men's, often addressed the social and political issues of the day. The other main types of female writing in the late seventeenth century were poetry, romances, and books on housewifery, medicine, and midwifery.

Over the ensuing century women branched out into other types of literature. In the 1660s the first plays written by women, notably by Katherine Philips (a translation) and Frances Boothby (*Mercelia*, a tragi-comedy) were performed, and in the next two decades Aphra Behn published a number of plays. Behn's success, of course, was predicated on adopting the prevailing racy style of the Restoration stage. Female authorship was suspicious enough without addressing such topics, and Behn's reputation, already damaged by her irregular sexual life, suffered accordingly. This, combined with a more prudish cultural climate in the early 1700s, dissuaded many respectable women from writing for the theatre, and women were increasingly attracted to other genres.

One of the most important of these was the periodical. The expansion of the periodical press in England in the late seventeenth century is one of the early facets of the expanding availability of printed literature in this period. Periodicals were cheap and sought to attract a wide audience, including women, through a combination of articles of instruction and entertainment. The *Athenian Mercury*, published between 1691 and 1697, for example, not only sought female as well as male readers but published monthly 'ladies' issues' and frequently printed and responded to letters purportedly from women. The latter have been characterised as 'among the earliest instances of the representation of women articulating their own experiences in print'.[38] As we shall see, however, the *Athenian Mercury* and subsequent periodicals, while appealing to women readers and writers, clearly differentiated women's concerns

---

38 Kathryn Shevelow, *Women and Print Culture: The Construction of Femininity in the Early Periodical* (1989), p. 60.

from those of men. It is thus not surprising that by the third decade of the eighteenth century separate periodicals were written for women, and women began to write primarily for them: Eliza Haywood's *Female Spectator* (which was published between 1744 and 1746) was the first periodical explicitly written by women for women; others followed. By the end of the century women were not only writing for women's magazines but also for magazines and reviews targeted at both sexes.[39]

The other important genre taken up by women was the novel. We can see the roots of the novel, a genre which was not part of the classical tradition and therefore could be written by those who had not received a classical education, in earlier women's writings. The variety of points of view in the novel and its informality of expression derived from its origins in correspondence, and the transition into print was aided by the publication of women's letters in the early periodicals. Private letter-writing had always been an acceptable activity for women, and this formed the basis for early works of prose fiction such as Aphra Behn's *Love Letters Between a Nobleman and His Sister* (first published 1684). Indeed, women accounted for a substantial proportion of the epistolary fiction published in the first half of the eighteenth century, at a time when the genre was considered inferior and unskilled. As the form and content of the novel evolved and became more respectable, especially under the influence (and the successes) of Samuel Richardson, the number and output of female novelists increased; women wrote at least 30% of the novels published in the eighteenth century and it has been estimated that over half the novelists in the century were women.[40]

In the second half of the eighteenth century women published proportionally fewer works of letters, autobiography, and religious works as fiction became more popular. Nonetheless, other forms of writing, notably poetry and didactic material (which was closely related to the approach of most novels), continued to be more acceptable from women, and women writers, including those who wrote novels, also wrote other types of fiction (poetry and plays) and non-fiction (social commentaries, religious works, treatises on education, and advice books). In the 1780s, according to Roger Lonsdale, women 'virtually took over', as the writers and readers of fashionable poetry. It has been estimated that there were over 400 women poets publishing in England between 1760 and 1830. Other important new developments include the publication of cheap didactic literature for children and the lower class (notably by Sarah Trimmer and Hannah More), and the eight-volume history of seventeenth-century England written by Catherine Macaulay, who also wrote a number of political and philosophical pamphlets (mostly published anonymously). Although her works were widely respected, Macaulay was rewarded for departing from the acceptable subject matter for female authors with defamatory reports to the effect that she was 'deformed' and 'ugly'; any merit in her works was allegedly the result of her having a 'masculine mind' and/or having been helped by a man.[41]

In sum, by the end of our period women authors had acquired a significant presence in the world of publication, particularly in novels and poetry. In addition, women had authored a number of important advice books and religious and moral tracts. Yet there remained many subject areas where women were present in very small numbers, if at all: history, philosophy, classical studies, theology, politics, law, medicine, and the sciences.[42] Moreover, we should not forget that men still accounted for over three-quarters of the fiction published, and hostility to female authors remained. Women had achieved a significant presence in the world of print, but it was still largely a man's world.

Did women's growing presence as authors lead to the development of a distinctively feminine type of writing?[43] It is possible to detect some important changes in the content of women's writings, though historians and literary critics differ over the significance of these changes, both in terms of their implications for women and in terms of the difference between men's and women's writings. Although the early periodicals and novels have been seen as having 'domesticated' women's writing, this did not prevent comment on political issues. Ros Ballaster has argued that the early novels of Mary De La Rivière Manley sought, through satiric depictions of the

41 J. Stanton, 'Statistical profile of women writing in English from 1660–1800', in *Eighteenth-Century Women and the Arts,* ed. F. M. Keener and S. E. Lorsch (New York, 1988), p. 250; Cheryl Turner, *Living by the Pen: Women Writers in the Eighteenth Century* (1992), pp. 111, 125–6; Roger Lonsdale (ed.), *Eighteenth-Century Women Poets: An Oxford Anthology* (Oxford, 1990), p. xxxv; Mellor, *Romanticism and Gender,* p. 7; Hill, *Republican Virago,* esp. pp. 133–4, 138–9.

42 Hufton, *The Prospect Before Her,* pp. 420–1.

43 See also the discussion of representations of gender in literature above, in Chapter 2, pp. 36–44.

sexual duplicity of politicians, to 'privilege the woman as commentator upon and actor in the political realm'. In the 1730s, however, women writers did begin to focus exclusively on domestic and moral issues. Although this new, morally serious cultural climate affected men as well as women, it had a much more marked effect on female writers, thereby creating a more gender-divided pattern of publishing. Describing the transformation between the bawdy late-seventeenth-century plays and novels written by Manley and Behn and the more sentimental novels and poetry of the eighteenth century, Janet Todd argues that a separate style of 'feminine writing' developed which was modest, sensitive, and didactic and usually addressed issues surrounding the preservation of female chastity. Paradoxically, this tradition was encapsulated in (and stimulated by) the writings of a male author, Samuel Richardson, but Richardson claimed initially that in his epistolary novels he was only editing letters written by women. In contrast, Todd suggests, there persisted a male tradition of fictional writing centred around the writings of Henry Fielding, Tobias Smollett, and Laurence Sterne, which was often based on classical models and involved the use of wit, satire, and the heroic, and which was far less subjective and personal than women's writings.[44]

Nonetheless, in the second half of the century the focus on feeling and morality in the sentimental novel became common among both male and female authors. Although in this sense all writing was accustoming itself to 'feminine' standards, female authors were still expected to write in a more natural and modest style than their male counterparts. When at the end of the century the sentimental movement was attacked as self-indulgent and escapist, both male and female writers became more concerned with contemporary moral and political issues. Under the influence of the French Revolution women's writings were divided between those who embraced radical politics (in the 'Jacobin' novels) and those who rejected a directly 'political' approach, but who nonetheless used their writings to urge moral reform. Most female writers adopted the second approach, and in the process elevated women to a dominant position among novelists. In contrast, according to Todd, at the end of the century 'the most imaginative male writers tended to turn towards poetry for self expression . . . [moving] from direct political expression into a realm of the aesthetic.' Romantic poetry in some senses

---

44 Todd, *Sign of Angellica*, part 2; Ros Ballaster et al., *Women's Worlds: Ideology, Femininity and the Woman's Magazine* (1991), pp. 48–9; *idem, Seductive Forms: Women's Amatory Fiction from 1684 to 1740* (Oxford, 1992), p. 131.

constituted a masculine rejection of the prevailing female style: William Wordsworth, a primary exponent, argued that poets should adopt a 'manly' style, using 'the real language of men', as opposed to what he termed 'the gaudy and inane phraseology' of current (female-dominated) fashionable poetry.[45] As Anne Mellor has argued, a significant amount of romantic poetry was also written by women, but from a very different perspective. Masculine romanticism tended to derive from classical models, take the form of epics, tragic verse drama, prophetic elegies, and satire, and be concerned with 'the capacities of the creative imagination, with the limitations of language, with the possibility of transcendence or "unity of being", with the development of the autonomous self, with political (as opposed to social) revolution, [and] with the role of the creative writer as political leader or religious saviour'. In contrast, female romantic writers sought moral reform 'not by utopian imaginative vision, but by the communal exercise of reason, moderation, tolerance and the domestic affections . . . [and] this ideology found its appropriate mode of linguistic expression in specific genres': odes, romances, ballads, shorter verse narratives, sonnets, 'occasional verse', and nursery rhymes, as well as the novel.[46]

As Mellor notes, however, not all male and female authors fit this model: since gender roles are constructed, 'any writer, male or female, could occupy the "masculine" or the "feminine" ideological or subject position, even within the same work.'[47] But with respect to the novel, it is significant that in the early nineteenth century more male authors seem to have adopted 'feminine' approaches than the reverse. As Susan Morgan has argued, just as Samuel Richardson's approach to the sentimental novel built on and influenced the work of female novelists in the eighteenth century, nineteenth-century novelists, whether male or female, developed a 'feminine heroic tradition'. Yet as novels became more prestigious, there is evidence at the end of our period that the serious (as opposed to popular) novel was once again beginning to be defined as a male preserve, with a new emphasis on realism.[48]

By the first half of the nineteenth century, therefore, not only were women frequently involved in the creation of an important

---

45 Todd, *Sign of Angellica*, part 3; Lonsdale, *Eighteenth-Century Women Poets*, p. xl.
46 Mellor, *Romanticism and Gender*, pp. 2–3, 10, 209–10.
47 Ibid., p. 4.
48 Susan Morgan, *Sisters in Time: Imagining Gender in Nineteenth-Century British Fiction* (Oxford, 1989), p. 11; Gaye Tuchman with N. E. Fortin, *Edging Women Out: Victorian Novelists, Publishers and Social Change* (1989), pp. 1–18.

part of the public sphere, printed literature which was publicly available and discussed, but their writings shaped literary trends. Not coincidentally, we saw in Chapter 2 that women were also often represented in this literature as a sex which could play an important public role in society. In this sense although it is true that female authorship frequently propagated and reinforced traditional 'feminine' values, both women's authorship and the representations of women in their works gave such values greater influence over public life than they had had in the seventeenth century. Much the same could be said about the growing public presence of women in most aspects of social and cultural life in this period. The expanded public sphere opened up significant opportunities for women, but these proved to be largely gender-limited along the lines of existing definitions of appropriate feminine behaviour in the family and at work.

CRIME AND THE LAW

Up to this point we have examined activities which were, for the most part, socially and legally acceptable. In this final section we will discuss the gendered dimensions of antisocial activity, by considering gender differences both in the commission of crime and in how the sexes used the legal system to attempt to right wrongs and further their interests. Here the story up to 1850 is not one of an increased public presence of women as we have discussed above; rather it is men who increasingly dominate criminal and legal activity. But neither is this a story of female absence. Because patterns of criminality (especially recorded criminality) are shaped by the law, and by plaintiffs' access to the law, it is helpful to start our discussion by examining men's and women's use of the law.

As in many other areas of public life, women faced a number of disincentives to litigating. Most importantly, married women were prevented by the common-law principle of 'coverture' from initiating lawsuits in property cases. Married women were unable to sue or be sued, except jointly with their husbands. According to an anonymous female author in 1785, men 'have taken upon themselves to be the whole, insomuch that they have voted us dead in law, except in criminal causes'. Even single women and widows faced disincentives to prosecution: not only would they have been disadvantaged by the costs, since they were typically poorer than their male equivalents, but the courts were male dominated (judges, justices, and jurors were all male) and there is the possibility that women's testimony in the courts was less likely to be taken seriously than men's. Harriet Taylor Mill and John Stuart Mill argued in 1846 that women 'in the lower ranks of life' were reluctant to initiate prosecutions because they 'do not expect justice from a bench or jury of the male sex'.[49]

Although women, regardless of marital status, did use the criminal courts (where the rules of coverture did not apply), these factors help explain why female litigants were vastly outnumbered by men in criminal cases, and why women were most likely to use the less formal legal procedures, which were not only cheaper but also less off-putting. Available statistics on female participation at quarter sessions range from 6% (the proportion of single women and widows prosecuting property cases in Surrey between 1743 and 1790) to 18% (the proportion of women of all marital statuses prosecuting indictments in Middlesex between 1660 and 1725). Yet at the inferior borough courts and with prosecutions by recognisance, summary conviction, and informal mediation by justices of the peace, female participation was much higher: female litigants prosecuted 44% of the indictments for assault in Bath, 48% of the recognisances to attend the Middlesex quarter sessions, and around a third of the cases informally settled by two justices of the peace in the mid-eighteenth century, one in rural Wiltshire and the other in Hackney, on the urban periphery of London. Proportionally, women were more likely to be involved with the criminal law in urban areas, where justice was more accessible, women led more independent lives, and informal methods of dispute resolution by respected members of the community may have been less available.[50]

Far less research has been done on women's use of the civil-law courts, but it is clear that, given the principle of coverture, their greatest opportunities lay outside the common law. Amy Erickson reports that 'substantial numbers of the litigants coming before the manorial and borough courts were women' in the seventeenth century, but the only evidence to support this claim for the period of this study comes from the borough court of King's Lynn in the late seventeenth century, where women account for 9% of the litigants

49 *The Hardships of the English Laws in Relation to Wives* (1785), p. 51; *Morning Chronicle*, 28 August 1851, cited by Anna Clark, 'Humanity or justice? Wifebeating and the law in the eighteenth and nineteenth centuries', in *Regulating Womanhood: Historical Essays on Marriage, Motherhood and Sexuality*, ed. C. Smart (1992), p. 202.

50 John Beattie, *Crime and the Courts in England 1660–1800* (Princeton, 1986), p. 193; Shoemaker, *Prosecution and Punishment*, p. 208; R. S. Neale, *Bath 1680–1850: A Social History* (1981), pp. 88–9; Norma Landau, *The Justices of the Peace 1679–1760* (Berkeley, 1984), p. 197.

for debt. However, almost all of those who appeared on their own were widows or spinsters. Married women's opportunities were greatest under the laws of equity, since under these laws they could acquire rights to certain categories of property, known as their separate estate, and they could, through the trustees of that property, sue and be sued on issues relating to that property. Thus married women participated in over half of the 26% of the cases litigated by women at the Court of Chancery between 1613 and 1714. Such women never acted alone, however: they litigated with their husbands or other men.[51]

Because at any given time only a minority of adult women were married, women acting on their own formed a small but significant minority of the litigants in every civil court. And because widows were more likely to own property, they far outnumber spinsters among female litigants. Widows used a number of courts to defend or secure their financial interests. At Chancery in the seventeenth century they accounted for a third of the cases involving female plaintiffs. In the second half of the century war widows were also adept at petitioning for county pensions, even though the funds were intended primarily for maimed soldiers. Widows also frequently used courts of request: according to William Hutton, writing in the late eighteenth century, these courts, which dealt primarily with cases of debt, 'could not live without the widows'.[52]

Another type of court outside the common law where women frequently litigated was the ecclesiastical courts. We have seen that female defendants frequently came before these courts accused of sexual defamation; women also frequently prosecuted such cases. In early-eighteenth-century London women prosecuted an average of between two and three dozen defamation cases at the Consistory Court each year, accounting for 95% of the cases. Two-thirds of these women were married. Women were also involved in other major areas of the church courts' activities. They prosecuted over half the matrimonial cases which came before the London consistory court, filing suit for breach of contract (often the woman had

51 Craig Muldrew, 'Credit and the courts: debt litigation in a seventeenth-century urban community', *Economic History Review* 46 (1993), pp. 28–9; Amy Erickson, *Women and Property in Early Modern England* (1993), pp. 30, 115; Lee Holcombe, *Wives and Property: Reform of the Married Women's Property Law in Nineteenth-Century England* (Oxford, 1983), ch. 3.

52 Geoffrey L. Hudson, 'Negotiating for blood money: war widows and the courts in seventeenth-century England', in J. Kermode and G. Walker, *Women, Crime and the Courts in Early Modern England* (1994), pp. 146–69; William Hutton, *Courts of Requests: Their Nature, Utility and Powers Described* (1787), p. 294.

been abandoned and was pregnant) or seeking legal separations (though these suits were more often initiated by men). They also brought a considerable amount of administrative business to the courts: as widows, they proved wills, exhibited inventories, and filed accounts, accounting for three-quarters of the people appearing on probate matters. Such business was more routine than litigation, but also more common.

Thus, although on the whole they did so less than men, women appeared before courts routinely during this period for a number of reasons, many of which arose out of their distinctive experiences as women: defending their sexual reputation, establishing and protecting separate property rights within marriage, defending marriage contracts or seeking separation, and securing widows' property rights. The nature of these cases meant that women were more likely to use the ecclesiastical courts (where they accounted for the majority of the business), courts of equity (frequently acting jointly with men), and informal criminal procedures, while men dominated the common-law courts and formal criminal proceedings. To cater for the large number of female litigants, a few advice books on the law were specifically addressed to women.[53]

Changes in the Law
Women's opportunities at civil and ecclesiastical law declined somewhat over the course of the period 1650–1850. The growing ascendancy of the common-law courts over other jurisdictions was disadvantageous for women, given the common-law principle that married women had no separate legal identity. Both the manorial courts and the ecclesiastical courts declined in reputation and in the amount of business conducted. By the 1820s the number of defamation cases prosecuted by women at the London Consistory Court (by this point none were prosecuted by men) had declined to about one per year. Though men and women continued to litigate over matrimonial issues at Consistory Courts and at the Court of Arches, high legal costs meant that the litigants were increasingly confined to the middle and upper classes. In principle, the increase in the number of marriage settlements and bequests involving separate property for married women enhanced their opportunities to control and defend property through courts of equity, but Susan Staves has shown that in some ways the judges retreated from the

---

53 Meldrum, 'A woman's court', p. 6; Lawrence Stone, *Road to Divorce: England 1530–1987* (Oxford, 1995), p. 428; Erickson, *Women and Property*, p. 32. On the last point see, for example, *A Treatise of Feme Coverts; or, The Lady's Law* (1732).

radical implications of this in the mid-eighteenth century and circumscribed those rights. By the end of our period women's opportunities for using the civil law were increasingly confined to the common-law courts, where married women were constrained by coverture. It was in the context of complaints over these issues that the first campaign for the reform of married women's property law began in the 1850s.[54]

Much less is known about the distribution by sex of plaintiffs at the criminal courts in the second half of this period, but the available figures on the proportion of litigants who were female (between 6 and 10%) are not widely different from those for the century before 1750.[55] However, the increasing proportion of criminal accusations settled by summary jurisdiction may have opened up opportunities for women, since they tended to favour less formal methods of prosecution. In the early nineteenth century, for example, the London police courts acquired jurisdiction over a number of types of crime previously tried at quarter sessions, including disputes between husbands and wives. Although there are no studies of these courts before 1850, Jennifer Davis's work on the use of the courts by the working class in the second half of the nineteenth century has demonstrated that women as well as men frequently brought both civil and criminal complaints to the court on a wide range of issues, including requests from the elderly for poor relief, from mothers for support for their illegitimate children, and from deserted wives for protection of their property from their husbands. In addition, women prosecuted a number of cases of petty theft and assault, including 'daily' requests for protection from violent husbands. Although abused wives often did not seek formal convictions, they appeared before the court in the hope that judicial persuasion and the threat of punishment would suffice to reform their husbands' behaviour. These women were reluctant to discuss their personal lives in public, but the public nature of the court did not dissuade them from doing so.[56] In sum, although women's opportunities outside the male-dominated common law contracted

54 Erickson, *Women and Property*, pp. 230–1; Report of the Royal Commission to Enquire into the Practice and Jurisdiction of the Ecclesiastical Courts, *Parliamentary Papers* (1832), p. xxiv; Stone, *Road to Divorce*, pp. 35–40; Susan Staves, *Married Women's Separate Property in England, 1660–1833* (1990); Holcombe, *Wives and Property*.

55 David Philips, *Crime and Authority in Victorian England* (1977), pp. 100, 124; George Rudé, *Criminal and Victim: Crime and Society in Early Nineteenth-Century England* (Oxford, 1984), ch. 4.

56 Jennifer Davis, 'A poor man's system of justice: the London police courts in the second half of the nineteenth century', *Historical Journal* 27 (1984), pp. 309–35.

during this period, women continued to have the opportunity to make both civil and criminal complaints in less formal venues, and such opportunities increased with the expansion of summary justice towards the end of the period.

Crime

Finally, what about behaviour that contravened legal and social norms? Here we face considerable limitations of evidence, for in studying criminal activity we are largely confined to looking at judicial records, despite the fact that the vast majority of criminal activities never led to prosecution. And, as in many other areas of life, women's criminality may have been less well recorded than men's. The best that can be done in addressing this problem is to look at a wide range of judicial activity: just as women disproportionately preferred to prosecute using less formal legal methods such as summary jurisdiction, it is also likely that female defendants were more likely to be prosecuted in this manner.

The quarter sessions and assizes records indicate that, as has been true in virtually all societies in which records have been kept, women were accused of committing far fewer crimes than men, and the pattern of crimes they were accused of was different. The most comprehensive study of crime in this period to date is that of John Beattie, who studied the counties of Surrey and Sussex between 1660 and 1800. Beattie found that women account for 13% of the accused in property offences in Sussex, and 24% of the accused in Surrey, a county with a large urban population bordering on London. Similarly, women accounted for only 18.5% of those accused of offences against the person in Surrey. Within these broad categories there are often wide variations according to type of offence, but this broad pattern of female defendants rarely accounting for more than a third of all criminal prosecutions (and often much less) is found in other court records, with the important exception of summary convictions (discussed below).[57]

A number of explanations can be advanced to account for this basic pattern. It has been suggested that prosecutors were reluctant to prosecute women, either because they were seen as less legally responsible for their actions or because female criminality was less conceivable, or less threatening, than male criminality. Although these factors are important, they can provide only a partial explana-

---

57 Beattie, *Crime and the Courts*, p. 239; Beattie, 'Criminality of women', p. 81; Malcolm Feeley and Deborah Little, 'The vanishing female: the decline of women in the criminal process, 1687–1912', *Law and Society Review* 25 (1991), pp. 719–57.

tion of the low level of prosecuted female criminality. Legally, through the principle of *feme covert*, married women were not deemed responsible for most types of crime if their husbands were present when it was committed, since, as William Blackstone argued, the husband's presence was equivalent to a command, which a wife must be expected to follow.[58] Although this could have led to fewer prosecutions of married women, it did not in practice, since married women were frequently indicted. Instead, this principle seems to have resulted in women being discharged without punishment or receiving milder punishments than men, rather than their not being prosecuted or punished at all.[59]

Women were often seen as less prone to criminality than men, and therefore it is possible, at a time when only a small proportion of crimes were actually prosecuted, that prosecutors and the courts were less concerned to prosecute crimes committed by women than those committed by men. With the exception of prostitution, women were simply not suspected as potential criminals; participation in crime involved the opposite of expected feminine virtues (subordination, passivity, moral superiority), whereas male crime could much more easily be seen as an outgrowth of natural masculine assertiveness, courage, and physical agility. In the words of Lucia Zedner, 'the low level of recorded female crime may, therefore, be at least partly attributable to the pervasive designation of women as non-criminal.'[60] This helps explain why those women who were prosecuted were treated more leniently by the judicial system and why those who were convicted typically received more lenient punishments: since punishments were meant to deter others and women were not thought to be prone to commit crime, it made much less sense to punish female convicts as examples. Such attitudes, however, were predicated on the existence of a relatively low level of actual female criminality: if experiences of crime suggested otherwise judicial authorities and others would eventually have been forced to revise their attitudes.

In the eighteenth and nineteenth centuries female criminals came increasingly to be seen as the victims of social forces beyond their control, and particularly of male sexual seduction, as evi-

58 William Blackstone, *Commentaries on the Laws of England* (4 vols, Oxford, 1765–69), 4, p. 28.
59 Beattie, 'Criminality of women', pp. 95–6; Shoemaker, *Prosecution and Punishment*, p. 159.
60 Lucia Zedner, *Women, Crime and Custody in Victorian England* (Oxford, 1991), p. 27.

denced by the increased institutional and legislative efforts to protect 'fallen' and disadvantaged women. Thus criminal activity by
women came to be treated as essentially a sexual rather than a
criminal offence. At the same time, the small number of women
who were specifically identified as criminals were treated more
harshly, since their behaviour so clearly undermined the essential
definition of femininity: these women were socially ostracised as
well as legally punished. Unsurprisingly, such women found it even
more difficult than usual to reintegrate into normal life and as a
consequence rates of recidivism among female convicts in the Victorian period were much higher than those for men.[61]

Thus, the lower prosecution rates of women were clearly shaped
by the different ways of thinking about male and female criminality.
Other explanations for men's domination of recorded crime accept
that women did commit fewer crimes, and explain that this was due
to differences between male and female socialisation or the different circumstances of men's and women's lives, which meant there
were fewer pressures and fewer opportunities for women to commit
crimes. It has even been suggested that the low level of women's
criminality is indicative of women's limited participation in public
life. We can best assess the merit of these arguments through an
examination of gender differences in the types of crimes men and
women were accused of committing.

We have seen, for example, that women accounted for a small
proportion of the diverse category of 'offences against the person'.
When this category is broken up into its constituent parts, however,
the story is more complicated. Except in cases of suspected infanticide, which was almost by definition committed only by women
since the charge typically centred around the concealment of a
birth, women were less frequently accused of offences which involved violence. Men, for example, were far more likely to be accused of committing all other forms of murder, accounting for 91%
of the accused in eighteenth-century Surrey. Women were also
much less likely to be involved in assaults and thefts which were aggravated by violence, injury, or death. Legally, the offence of assault
was defined broadly, to include everything from threatening behaviour to serious violence, and women were disproportionately

---

61 Feeley and Little, 'The vanishing female', pp. 749–50; Zedner, *Women, Crime
and Custody*, pp. 40–6; Martin Wiener, 'The Victorian criminalization of men', in
*Violent Men: Male Culture, Honor Codes, and Violence in Europe and America from the
Seventeenth to the Twentieth Centuries* (Ohio State University Press, forthcoming). I am
grateful to Professor Wiener for allowing me to see this article prior to publication.

charged with the less physical aspects of the offence. In late-seventeenth and early-eighteenth-century London, they accounted for 26% of the indictments for assault. An examination of these cases reveals that the offending behaviour frequently involved verbal rather than physical violence, and as we have seen defamation is an offence for which women were a majority of the accused in this period.[62] It could be argued that this evidence that women, more than men, preferred verbal over physical violence simply reflects contemporary stereotypes, and violent women were less likely to be prosecuted than violent men. It seems more plausible, however, that women whose violent actions violated contemporary expectations were *more* likely to be brought before justices of the peace.

Of course one explanation for this pattern is the fact that women were socialised not to be violent. Whereas men, as household heads, could legitimately inflict violence on their wives, children, and servants, women were much less likely to learn violent behaviour since there were fewer socially acceptable situations in which they could be physically aggressive (though women could discipline their children and servants). Yet on occasion women were violent, assaulting men and women, and even parish officers, in the streets, fields, and other public spaces. From her study of wife beating in London Margaret Hunt has remarked that 'the frequency with which women engaged in violent acts in public is particularly striking. Women may not have assaulted their husbands in large numbers, but they seem to have had few compunctions about assaulting anyone else.'[63] In contrast to the stereotype that women committed murders by stealth or deception (such as by using poison), women did on occasion commit vicious murders, involving the use of weapons and physical violence. The relatively small number of such incidents may be explained not so much by patterns of upbringing as by the distinctive circumstances of women's lives. Beattie notes that women were less likely to carry weapons or tools which could, if a dispute erupted, inflict serious wounds. They probably also drank less alcohol, in part because they spent less time in alehouses; among men drinking often led to violence. Moreover, because

62 Beattie, *Crime and the Courts*, p. 97; Shoemaker, *Prosecution and Punishment*, p. 213; Robert B. Shoemaker, 'Crime, courts and community: the prosecution of misdemeanors in Middlesex county, 1663–1723' (PhD diss., Stanford University, 1986), p. 291; above, p. 271.

63 Hunt, 'Wife beating, domesticity, and women's independence', p. 22. See also Beattie, 'Criminality of women', p. 88.

women spent more time in and around the home the disputes they were involved in typically involved family and neighbours, and it seems likely that in the normal course of events such disputes were less likely to result in serious violence than disputes with strangers. (Of course this was not always the case: more women than men were accused of murdering members of their own family.) The relative absence of violence in female criminality should perhaps therefore be ascribed less to their socialisation than to their distinctive pattern of private and public sociability.[64]

A similar pattern of significant female participation, but in a somewhat different range of specific offences, is evident with property crime. Although on average women accounted for a distinct minority of such offences, in some jurisdictions in urban areas more than half the offenders prosecuted were female. John Beattie has shown that more women than men were prosecuted for property crime at the Old Bailey in most years between 1700 and 1713, and a sample of commitments to houses of correction in London over the period from 1670 to 1721 found that women accounted for 56% of the commitments for theft and fraud.[65] But a number of studies have shown that women were typically accused of different types of theft than men: women were disproportionately accused of shoplifting, theft from masters or mistresses, pickpocketing (including thefts by prostitutes from their clients), and receiving and selling stolen goods. In general, women were disproportionately more often accused of petty theft, and they stole different types of goods, notably clothes and household linens. In contrast, men accounted for higher proportions of those accused of robbery; theft from ships, warehouses, docks, and places of manufacture; and the theft of horses, sheep, and cattle.[66]

It has been suggested that women's property crime was 'rather less direct, less open, risking less of a confrontation with the victim' than men's. While this mirrors the general low level of female violence, we must note that women were involved in a significant number of cases of burglary and housebreaking. Clearly, a large

---

64 Beattie, 'Criminality of women', pp. 83, 102; Beattie, *Crime and the Courts*, pp. 97, 105.

65 Shoemaker, *Prosecution and Punishment*, p. 185; John Beattie, 'The prosecution of crime in London, 1670–1714', seminar paper given at the University of Durham, 12 May 1993. I am grateful to Professor Beattie for allowing me to cite from his unpublished research.

66 Beattie, 'Criminality of women', pp. 89–96; Garthine Walker, 'Women, theft and the world of stolen goods', in Kermode and Walker, *Women, Crime and the Courts*, pp. 81–105; Emsley, *Crime and Society*, p. 155.

part of the explanation for the gendered pattern of property offences reflects the different opportunities for theft encountered by men and women: men stole from their places of work (whether in agriculture, manufacture, or commerce) while women stole from theirs, whether as servants, prostitutes, or shoppers providing for their household. Women's important role in the disposal of stolen goods can thus be explained as reflecting their experience with marketing and their network of social contacts. As Garthine Walker has commented, we should interpret women's role in property crime in the context of 'their own economic activities [and] interactive social position within the community'.[67]

Similarly, it is the contrasting nature of women's lives in urban and rural areas which explains the dramatic differences in patterns of female criminality identified by historians. Beattie found that, proportionally, women accounted for twice as many crimes in urban as in rural parishes of Surrey, and similar differences are evident in misdemeanour prosecutions in Middlesex. That this pattern is not restricted to the London area is evident from the large number of women prosecuted in the borough courts of Colchester and Bridgwater in the eighteenth century. Beattie suggests that these patterns of prosecuted crime may actually reflect real differences in criminality: that urban women committed more offences, both because they faced greater economic hardship and they were more independent than rural women. Urban women were more often unmarried and/or recent immigrants, cut off from networks of support provided by family and friends, and they were often employed in insecure and poorly paid jobs; if turned out of work, they had few options besides crime or prostitution. Because such women were less restrained by family and community norms and lived more public lives, Beattie argues, they were more likely to get involved in disputes and antisocial behaviour than their rural counterparts.[68]

Yet it is also likely that women's crime was dealt with differently in urban areas: whereas suspected female criminals in rural areas were often dealt with informally, in towns they faced greater distrust. In part, this pattern resulted from the greater ease of prosecuting women in towns; not only were quarter sessions courts more accessible, but less formal means of prosecution were more available. Given the general reluctance to prosecute women, prosecutors were more likely to pursue cases where methods of prosecution

67 Beattie, 'Criminality of women', p. 95; Walker, 'Women, theft and the world of stolen goods', p. 92.
68 Beattie, 'Criminality of women', p. 97.

were more accessible and lenient.[69] However, urban women were also seen as less trustworthy. In particular, those who were unmarried and not under the control of men were viewed suspiciously in eighteenth-century London, out of fear that they might become prostitutes, have bastard children, become dependent on poor relief, and/or commit crime. It is these concerns which arguably explain why so many women were committed to houses of correction (twice as many women as men were committed to the Middlesex and Westminster houses between 1670 and 1721).[70] The significantly higher proportion of accused female criminals in urban areas was thus due to a combination of factors which include not only greater hardship and greater independence, but also greater suspicion, but the common denominator is the very different, and more public, circumstances of women's lives in towns than in the countryside, especially when they were unmarried.

The Masculinisation of Crime?

Paradoxically, despite the growing urbanisation of English society, the proportion of defendants accused of serious crime who were female declined dramatically over the course of this period. Most of the evidence so far presented in this section pertains to the first half of the eighteenth century, when women accounted for approximately 35% of the felony indictments filed at London's Old Bailey sessions. This proportion steadily declined over the next century, so that by 1850 only 15% of the accused were women; this basic trend is also found in studies for other parts of the country. To date, not enough research has been done to allow a convincing explanation of this striking phenomenon to emerge. The authors of the study which documents these findings, Malcolm Feeley and Deborah Little, suggest that the decline resulted from a combination of changes in female behaviour and shifting prosecutorial attitudes, in which 'new conceptions of the roles of women may have led those in a position to bring criminal charges to eschew public prosecutions for other more private responses.' As noted earlier, criminality came increasingly to be seen as a 'male' problem, and female criminality was interpreted as a consequence and aspect of sexual immor-

---

69 Shoemaker, *Prosecution and Punishment*, pp. 213–14, 286; Peter King, 'Crime, law and society in Essex, 1740–1820' (PhD diss., Cambridge University, 1984), ch. 3.
70 Beattie, *Crime and the Courts*, pp. 241–3; Shoemaker, *Prosecution and Punishment*, pp. 185–6, 213–14, 284–6.

ality, and was addressed through other agencies of protection and control. At the same time, Feeley and Little suggest, decreasing work opportunities for women, new institutional attempts to protect and control them, and the growing influence of domestic ideology led to women having fewer opportunities to commit crimes.[71]

At present this is little more than a hypothesis, and one which is based in part on a narrative of social and economic change (decreasing work opportunities for women, increasing confinement of women to the home) which previous sections of this book have shown to be problematic. Much more research needs to be done on how victims and the police responded to female crime in the nineteenth century. In particular, as with plaintiffs, we need to look at the number of women prosecuted in the inferior courts and by the increasingly important powers of summary jurisdiction; it may be that suspected female criminals were increasingly tried using less formal methods, though that in itself would be a significant development. Davis found that women accounted for 34% of the shoplifters prosecuted in the police courts of Middlesex in 1856; if this example is typical for this type of jurisdiction, then the decline documented by Feeley and Little may be little more than a consequence of changing methods of prosecution.[72]

Nonetheless, the data assembled by Feeley and Little demonstrate unquestionably that attitudes towards female criminality changed significantly over the course of this period, towards a situation where female criminals were much more rarely prosecuted formally in the higher courts. This suggests that while women continued to lead public lives and, undoubtedly, to commit crimes, society came to conceive of female criminality as a problem which should be addressed in different ways. Though, reflecting different opportunities, it took different forms from men's crime, women's crime did not disappear. It was just, together with a significant proportion of male crime, probably prosecuted less formally: in the lower courts, in front of individual magistrates, or outside the judicial system entirely. While much of this activity took place in private, we should note that the police courts were conducted very much in public: they were crowded with spectators and their proceedings were covered by local and national newspapers. By most accounts women maintained a public criminal presence up to the end of our

---

71 Feeley and Little, 'The vanishing female', pp. 743–50.

72 Jennifer Davis, 'Prosecutions and their context: the use of the criminal law in later nineteenth-century London', in D. Hay and F. Snyder (eds), *Policing and Prosecution in Britain 1750–1850* (Oxford, 1989), p. 403.

period, but their antisocial activity became much less likely than men's to be formally defined as criminal.

Crime, therefore, came to be interpreted as almost entirely a male phenomenon in the nineteenth century, but the character of male crime also changed. Although we have seen that men were the more violent sex, the amount of violent crime they committed appears to have declined considerably over the course of this period.[73] In this sense, the efforts of conduct-book writers and others to reform men's 'manners' were partly successful. Even more than in previous centuries, theft and other property crimes became the principal crimes for which men were prosecuted in the nineteenth century, a development in patterns of antisocial behaviour which nicely echoes the political arguments of the time that men should be the principal breadwinners for their families. What is impossible to say is whether patterns of male and female crime actually changed, or whether changing conceptions of proper public behaviour for men and women simply led to a redefinition of crime, which increasingly meant property crime, as a quintessentially male activity.

73 Lawrence Stone, 'Interpersonal violence in English society, 1300–1980', *Past and Present* 101 (1983), pp. 22–33; J. S. Cockburn, 'Patterns of violence in English society: homicide in Kent, 1560–1985', *Past and Present* 130 (1991), pp. 70–106; Beattie, *Crime and the Courts*, pp. 132–9.

CHAPTER EIGHT

Conclusion:
The Emergence of Separate Spheres?

The chapters in this book have been organised around an implicit distinction between private and public spheres of activity. This distinction, fundamental in western political thought, has become conceptually important to historians of gender in recent years. As an anthropologist, Michele Rosaldo, argued in an early and influential essay, 'characteristic aspects of male and female roles in social, cultural, and economic systems can all be related to a universal, structural opposition between domestic and public domains of activity'.[1] The distinction has been seen as particularly appropriate to the history of gender in the late eighteenth and early nineteenth centuries, and it is clearly fundamental to the argument that an ideology of 'separate spheres' emerged at this time, and was embedded in practice, in which home life turned into a female-dominated space and public life was dominated by men. More recently, the public/private distinction has acquired new prominence in the writings of English historians as a result of the translation of the theories of the German philosopher Jürgen Habermas, who argued that a new 'public sphere' of influential political discourse was constructed in the eighteenth century, which was distinct from the private spheres of market transactions and family life on the one hand and the formal public authority of the state on the other. While Habermas's theory is not dependent on gender difference (men dominated not only the new public sphere and formal public authority, but also the economic aspects of the private sphere, as he

---

1 Michele Zimbalist Rosaldo, 'Women, culture and society: a theoretical overview', in M. Rosaldo and L. Lamphere (eds), *Women, Culture and Society* (Stanford, 1974), p. 35.

defined it), his theories have injected new life into the arguments of gender historians based on public/private dichotomies.[2]

Clearly there are important problems of definition here: Rosaldo defined the 'domestic' sphere as 'those minimal institutions and modes of activity that are organised immediately around one or more mothers and their children', while she used the term 'public' to refer to 'activities, institutions, and forms of association that link, rank, organize, or subsume particular mother-child groups'. In contrast, Habermas's private sphere included not only family life but also all economic activity. Yet whether defined in terms of the distinction between public opinion and non-political activity, or in terms of the contrast between domestic responsibilities and those activities which link domestic groups, or even in terms of physical space between the home and the world outside it, this book has demonstrated that such contrasts correlate very imperfectly with actual gender-role differences.[3]

In Chapter 4, for example, we have seen that although women dominated certain aspects of family and household life, including housework and childcare, this was not a male-free zone: men often spent significant amounts of time in the home. Not only did much of men's (as well as women's) paid labour take place at home, but men performed some household tasks (though they were often peripheral) and they were responsible for aspects of child raising, especially with older sons. Women may have dominated the 'domestic' or 'private' sphere, but men retained considerable emotional investment, authority, and physical presence in the home, and they had distinctive roles to play. Similarly, even the ideology of domesticity allowed women some public activities, and we saw in Chapters 6 and 7 that life outside the home included a substantial, and in many ways growing, feminine presence during this period. In religion, women acted as prophets, preachers, and organisers of charity; in politics, women participated in the formation of public opinion and in the growth of pressure groups; and in social and cultural life, women were present in pubs, leisure activities, and as authors. In Chapter 5, it was evident that women worked in a number of different types of employment outside the home, even if their

2 Jürgen Habermas, *The Structural Transformation of the Public Sphere* (1962; trans. Thomas Burger with Frederick Lawrence, Cambridge, 1989).

3 Rosaldo, 'Women, culture and society', p. 23. For an insightful account of the variable meanings of public and private in the eighteenth century, and their lack of direct correspondence with gender differences, see Lawrence E. Klein, 'Gender and the public/private distinction in the eighteenth century: some questions about evidence and analytic procedure', *Eighteenth-Century Studies* 29 (1995) pp. 97–109.

opportunities were more limited than those of men. In all these ways, the public sphere was not a woman-free zone.

Nonetheless, the public/private distinction was incorporated into contemporary perceptions of gender difference, in the sense that women's activities outside the home were often described at the time as private, or as occurring in 'society', rather than in public. While 'public women' were seen as anomalous (and the term reserved for prostitutes), the expression 'public man' was clearly redundant and not used at all. Eliza Haywood argued that her *Female Spectator*, as a periodical targeted at women, did not need to cover news of wars, for accounts of this sort 'are every day to be found in the public papers'. Implicitly newspapers were defined as masculine and public, while magazines for women were characterised as private and feminine even though, like newspapers, they were clearly publicly available.[4] In 1846, an anonymous female author justified women's lack of political rights with the comment that women are 'required to perform duties so various, and to act in so important a part in society, [that] she has little reason to murmur that she is . . . precluded from any participation in the busy and anxious career of public life'.[5] As Denise Riley has argued, the nineteenth century witnessed the construction of a 'social' sphere, an 'arena for domesticated intervention' which 'blurred the ground between the public and the private', in which women could work outside the home to improve society.[6] The refusal to use the term 'public' to describe women's activities outside the home clearly served to marginalise women and attach greater importance to what men did. But we should not allow this normative statement to obscure the very significant, if distinctive, role which women played in political, cultural, and social life throughout this period. Moreover, it is important to note that aspects of the male 'public' sphere, as defined by contemporaries, only applied to a minority of adult men: most men, for example, did not have the right to vote. Indeed, the term 'private man' was sometimes used in this period to refer to those who were not in a position to participate in parliamentary politics or other aspects of elite 'public' life.

Despite the long history of the public/private distinction in the West, many historians have identified the second half of our period as a time when this distinction was exacerbated. Philippe Ariès, for

---

4 *The Female Spectator* (1744–6), 2, p. 123, cited in Ros Ballaster et al., *Women's Worlds: Ideology, Femininity and the Woman's Magazine* (1991), p. 61.

5 *The English Matron* (1846), p. 129.

6 Denise Riley, *'Am I that Name?' Feminism and the Category of 'Women' in History* (1988), pp. 44–51.

example, has argued that from the beginning of the eighteenth century in Europe the public realm became 'deprivatised', as private interests such as the preservation of individual and family honour were removed from public consideration. Hence the practices of duelling and defamation, where insults to the reputations of private citizens were settled in public, declined. Public life thus became less communal, and more institutionalised: new forms of semi-public clubs and societies were founded, and new institutions for regulating public behaviour such as the police were created.[7] At the same time we have seen that the period witnessed an intensification of the ideology of separate spheres, with its attempt to map gender differences onto this growing distinction between public and private life. We must now consider, in conclusion, whether, despite the obvious overlaps in male and female behaviour between the spheres, such an intensification of gender difference actually occurred.

CONTINUITIES

Unquestionably, this period did witness important changes in gender roles. But before discussing such changes we must come to terms with the substantial continuities documented in this volume. Whether in courtship, family life, work, or in many aspects of public life, gender differences evident in the nineteenth century were already present two centuries earlier. In courtship, although the decline of arranged marriages among the upper and middle classes and the growing importance of prenuptial sex among the lower classes gave women as well as men a greater role in the choice of their spouse, men were still expected to take the initiative and women could only reject or accept as their inclinations and circumstances dictated. Within marriage, although we still do not know enough about the dynamics of power relations between spouses, the limited evidence available suggests that, while much depended on personalities, men dominated the decision-making in most marriages throughout the period. Arguments (from Lawrence Stone and others) that the period witnessed a transition from patriarchal to companionate marriages founder on the fact that evidence of both types of marriages can be found throughout this period, and in any case companionship was not incompatible with patriarchy. The basic division of household labour between spouses also appears to have changed remarkably little: men were the primary wage

7 Phillipè Ariès, 'Introduction', in Roger Chartier (ed.), *A History of Private Life, III: Passions of the Renaissance* (trans. A Goldhammer, 1989), pp. 1–11.

earners, with women combining housework and childcare with a variety of lower-paid activities which contributed to the family income. And we have seen that the phenomenon of the 'idle' middle-class wife who did not work for wages was not the creation of separate-spheres ideology: such women can be found throughout our period.

Continuities are even more evident in the world of paid labour. Despite the massive changes in work patterns brought about by agricultural change and industrialisation in terms of the organisation of units of production and the nature of the actual tasks men and women performed, there is little evidence of a long-term shift in the sexual division of labour. There are strong continuities not only in terms of the low status of women's work, but also its restriction to a limited number of sectors of the economy which could be linked directly with women's domestic responsibilities, notably domestic service, the textile trades, and the food and drink trades. While there are plenty of examples of new opportunities opening up to women, such as in factory work, these often proved to be temporary or of limited significance, in the sense that women were still excluded from more skilled and managerial tasks. It is in public life that we have identified the greatest changes in the gendered pattern of opportunities, but significant continuities should be noted here as well. Despite arguments for the 'feminisation' of religion in this period, the proportion of the religiously active who were female remained constant at around 55–65% of committed members and, while women frequently dominated eruptions of religious enthusiasm, they were inevitably sidelined if a movement lasted long enough to become institutionalised. In political life, women remained without the right of formal participation throughout this period, and we have seen that their opportunities in extra parliamentary politics, while significant, tended to be confined to issues where they were thought to have particular expertise.

Why did these fundamental gender differences persist over this 200-year period, despite the major economic, social, and political upheavals of the time? Like much historical work on gender, this study has sought primarily to document differences rather than explain them, but historians are now turning to study the processes of creating and maintaining distinct gender roles. While research on this subject is still in its infancy, we can make some important preliminary comments. Most obviously, as we have seen in Chapter 4, from an early age boys and girls learned gender differences, both by witnessing the contrasting behaviour of their mothers and fathers and by being subjected to different expectations and training. Boys and girls played with different toys and, as they got older, they read different books, were expected to perform different chores, experienced contrasting relationships with their mothers and fathers, and received educations which prepared them for very different adult lives. As we saw in Chapter 5, boys went to school earlier and for longer periods, they learned different skills, and different personality traits were encouraged. While boys' education, at school or in an apprenticeship, was often vocational, girls were primarily taught domestic skills, religion and morality, and, in the higher social classes, 'finishing' skills which would enhance their social standing and marriageability.

For those men and women entering adulthood who had not fully internalised the gender differences they had experienced as children, other aspects of society reinforced them. Those who attended church, regardless of denomination, were exposed to the gendered precepts of Christian ideology. For the literate, advice books and literature portrayed distinct patterns of expected male and female behaviour. We do not know how influential prescriptive literature was in shaping actual behaviour, but the frequent repetition of the expected virtues of women (chastity, modesty, compassion, piety) and men (intelligence, strength, courage, determination) and of the sexual division of labour that was derived from them cannot but have had some impact on the men and women who read such books. Many of the points made in the advice literature were used, selectively, in letters written by mothers and fathers to their sons and daughters.[8] Since the basic content of Christian doctrine and the advice books did not change over the course of the period, they provided a strong force for continuity. Probably more influential, because they were less overtly prescriptive and were more widely read, were the new genres of the novel and periodicals, both of which have been described as conduct books in different forms. Like advice books, these new genres depicted women largely in domestic contexts and those written for women focused on issues of love (concentrating particularly on the preservation of female chastity), marriage, and the family. The female and male virtues portrayed would not have been out of place in the conduct books, though it is important to note that women were increasingly portrayed as having the capacity and willpower to play a significant pub-

8 Linda Pollock, ' "Teach her to live under obedience": the making of women in the upper ranks of early modern England', *Continuity and Change* 4 (1989), pp. 231–58.

lic role. Yet it was through the exercise of moral and domestic virtues that female characters exerted influence over the wider society. While men, too, were expected to lead more virtuous lives by the early nineteenth century, they were expected to remain strong and courageous.

We should not, however, exaggerate the impact of literary representations of gender. For one thing, there were some important variations in how men and women were portrayed, both within and between genres, as the discussions of popular literature and the novel in Chapter 2 will have made clear. For another, it would be wrong to assume that readers consistently followed the role models they encountered in what they read: the evidence presented in Chapters 6 and 7, for example, shows that many women did not follow the domestic prescriptions of separate-spheres ideology in the early nineteenth century. But it would be absurd to argue that such images had no influence whatsoever. Kate Flint, in a study of the woman reader between 1837 and 1914, argues that through common reading patterns women shared 'both subjectivity and socialisation', but she also notes that individual women were able to rebel against expectations and assert their individuality through their reading.[9] Further research on how readers responded to literature is clearly needed. In documenting the intellectual constraints which sustained the status quo, we should also note that, despite the important developments in feminist thought which occurred during this period, comprehensive challenges to existing gender roles were rarely voiced until the very end of this period, and even then they reached only a narrow audience.

Perhaps an even more important factor in encouraging conformity to expected gender roles is the informal social pressure, arising out of the power of gossip, neighbourly observation, and collective action, to which deviants were subjected. In the early part of our period men and women resorted to public defamation as well as the courts to attempt to control people whose sexual and marital behaviour did not conform to community norms, focusing, following the double standard, on unchaste women. Men too, could be subject to community (and legal) punishment if their sexual misdeeds involved the wrong women or extended to fathering bastard children or homosexuality. Although evidence of public defamation declines over the course of the period, nineteenth-century evidence especially among the working class suggests that gossip continued to

9 Kate Flint, *The Woman Reader 1837–1914* (Oxford, 1993), quote from p. 249.

serve as an effective enforcer of community norms among women.[10] Perhaps men, who were not accustomed to being told what to do, were less susceptible to this kind of action: certainly they were the victims in a relatively small number of the prosecutions for defamation. Men who committed egregious violations of accepted gender roles were, however, on occasion subjected to public demonstrations: we have seen that rough music punished husbands who allowed their wives to beat them or commit adultery in the eighteenth century. Although in the nineteenth century the focus of such demonstrations changed to punishing husbands who beat their wives too severely, it was still the husband's behaviour that was subject to scrutiny. In addition, men who showed signs of effeminacy and/or homosexuality were subject to adverse comment, crowd action, or legal prosecution throughout this period. In these ways, gender roles were policed by community pressures.

Finally, we should note the legal constraints which prevented or discouraged women from engaging in certain male activities. In addition to the absence of political rights, women were seriously disadvantaged by the property laws. As we saw in Chapter 5, women's chances of owning land were severely limited by the laws of male primogeniture (even though daughters were often compensated in the distribution of movable goods), and the ability of married women to enter business was limited by the legal principle of coverture, which made it difficult for them to control property independently of their husbands. Moreover, the guild system of regulating trades discriminated against women. The guilds lost power in the second half of this period, but they were replaced by trade unions which largely excluded women, and in the 1840s new legislation controlling women's employment in factories and mines was passed. Although it was argued in Chapter 5 that informal discrimination contributed most to shaping the sexual division of labour, these formal constraints were also important in preventing access to forms of employment monopolised or dominated by men. While there was little change in this legal framework before 1850, the power of these legal constraints in limiting women's opportunities and preventing change is demonstrated by the fact that the repeal of many during the subsequent seventy years was accompanied by a reduction in gender differences at work and in politics.

---

10 J. Walkowitz, 'Male vice and feminist virtue: feminism and the politics of prostitution in nineteenth-century Britain', *History Workshop Journal* 13 (1982), p. 86.

It is important to note, however, that these forces promoting gender difference were not always successful. At many points in this book we have noted instances where in practice men and women engaged in the same activities. Although this was true of some aspects of housework and child rearing, the best examples come from the world of work, where both sexes contributed to the family income and, in some sectors of the economy, engaged in similar tasks, notably in hawking, shopkeeping, and weaving. In literature, especially the novel, we have seen that authors of each sex were capable of using styles and approaches normally thought to be characteristic of the other. And in the most dramatic, but also probably least common, examples of crossing gender boundaries in this period, some men and women chose to cross-dress, notably in the eighteenth-century entertainment form, the masquerade. Opportunities to adopt unconventional lifestyles were probably greatest for the significant number of men and women who were not married, though we have seen that women in this position faced considerable disadvantages.

CHANGE

Because historians are accustomed to looking for change, they have failed to pay sufficient attention to the significant continuities in gender roles outlined in the previous section. Rather, as outlined in the Introduction, historians have frequently identified this period (typically, but not exclusively, focusing on the period after 1750) as a time when gender roles became more rigidly defined into 'separate spheres'. In a sense, separate spheres existed throughout this period: we have seen that a rough division of labour in which women's responsibilities were primarily domestic and men dominated activities outside the home was not new in the second half of our period. Yet this is not to say that changes in belief and practice regarding gender roles did not occur. Ideologically, largely as a result of the Evangelical Revival, we have seen that the value of domesticity was articulated with increasing intensity in the second half of our period, as greater moral value was accorded to the maintenance of gender differences and particularly to women's activities within the home, and there is evidence of the adoption of such beliefs by the working as well as the middle classes. This phenomenon was reinforced by the confining, if newly positive, representations of women in the increasingly popular genre of the novel, and by changing ideas about the body and sexuality. The shift from the one-sex to the two-sex model of understanding physical difference; the growing belief that men, rather than women, were the lustful sex; and the increasing importance that was placed on heterosexual, vaginal penetrative sex to the exclusion of other sexual practices, all accentuated and contributed to the growing emphasis on women's maternal functions.

We can also identify some important changes in behaviour, though in most cases they cannot be directly related to specific ideological changes. As we have seen, problems of evidence make it difficult to document changes in sexual practices and family life, but we have seen that over the course of this period middle-class husbands and fathers performed somewhat fewer household tasks and in some cases distanced themselves emotionally from their families out of a growing concern to prepare their sons for the harshness of the real world. Nonetheless, it is important to note the considerable variation to be found in gender roles within family life.

In general, there is less evidence of change in these aspects of private life than in the public sphere which was increasingly differentiated from private life during this period. In the world of work (which crossed the public/private divide), women's domestic skills were increasingly emphasised. Despite the essential continuities in the sexual division of labour discussed above, some changes did occur in the types of work women performed, in which women were excluded from work deemed more appropriate for men due to the strength or 'scientific' skills involved, and they found increased opportunities in other employments requiring traditionally feminine skills. In agriculture, the introduction of the scythe in harvesting, which was thought to be too heavy for women to operate, pushed women out of what had been a mixed-sex activity, though women still performed less skilled tasks. Similarly, the mechanisation of spinning through the introduction of spinning mules (particularly long or doubled mules) which required more strength to operate than the traditional spinning wheel resulted (for complicated reasons) in the exclusion of women from a task they had previously dominated. Men took over other trades, such as managing dairies and midwifery, due to the alleged superiority of their 'scientific' methods and business practices. Many of the occupations in which the number of women significantly increased in this period, on the other hand, such as domestic service, teaching, and nursing, were jobs which exploited the types of skills women were expected to have as mothers and housewives. While men's occupations were more diverse (and included feminine-dominated trades such as textile work), men increasingly promoted the idea of the 'bread-winner' to emphasise their superior position in the world of work.

Perhaps the most significant changes in gender roles in this period, however, came with the growing opportunities for public action which resulted from the weakening of traditional authority in church and state. With the consequent growth of a pluralist society, new religious sects, voluntary societies, and political pressure groups flourished. While arguably men benefited first from these changes, it was not long before women also became involved. We have seen the important role women played in religious dissent (where their involvement at the very start of the period was a significant new departure), even if their greatest opportunities were as prophets who subordinated individual identity in order to allow the voice of God to speak through them; and in popular protest and pressure groups, especially on issues such as slavery and philanthropy which were seen to have important religious and moral dimensions. On the other hand, the most influential religious movement, the upper- and middle-class Evangelical Revival among the Church of England and 'old dissent', gave women fewer public opportunities, both in the movement and in their prescriptions for day-to-day life. Women's participation in movements which sought fundamental parliamentary reform, such as Chartism, while initially significant, was transitory, and women rarely participated in the leadership of religious groups (although in some cases they were given explicit responsibility for poor relief) or political organisations. At the very top of society, female royalty focused on domestic issues in the second half of the period.

The new form of public space created by the proliferation of printed literature, a kind of eighteenth- and nineteenth-century virtual reality in which works created in private could be distributed throughout society, also provided significant new opportunities for women. We have seen how the vast increase in female readership and authorship influenced the development of new genres such as the periodical and the novel. Yet we have also seen how the subjects of their writing remained largely confined to a fairly narrow range of subjects: rather than trespass on the traditional male subjects of history, philosophy, classical studies, theology, politics, law, medicine, and the sciences, women were primarily involved (along with many men) in the production of works of fiction, as well as advice books and religious and moral tracts. We have seen that female dominance in the production and consumption of fiction in the second half of our period gave public prominence to what were essentially traditional feminine values, though they were presented in a more positive form.

In sum, women's opportunities increased, but the subjects of their concerns seem to have narrowed. At the end of our period women's greatest public opportunities lay in areas where they could take advantage of the traditional feminine strengths of maternity, morality, religiosity, and philanthropy, while men continued to dominate 'high' politics, institutional management, and most forms of paid employment which did not involve domestic skills. This cultural limiting was indeed confining for women, but it did not confine them to the home. Instead, in the second half of our period women acquired new opportunities to fight publicly for their interests, and this led as we have seen to the formation of groups explicitly fighting to improve conditions for women in the 1850s.

It is important to note that men's opportunities were also confined by changes in gender roles. Men, too, were limited by the new moral climate. As the double standard came under attack in the nineteenth century they were expected to be less promiscuous and lead more virtuous, 'manly', and heterosexual lives than their predecessors. The sharpening of gender roles pushed men out of some activities where women were increasingly active and placed greater emphasis on men's core activity of breadwinning. In the public sphere, as philanthropic activities, especially where they concerned women and children, came to be seen as women's responsibility men were obliged to defer to the activities of women, even though men often retained formal positions of leadership. This contributed to what Denise Riley has labelled a 'dislocation of the political', as the male world of politics was constricted and took on 'an intensified air of privacy and invulnerability, of "high politics" associated with juridical and governmental power in a restricted manner'. In addition, with the growing importance of occupational identity and the idea of the 'breadwinning wage' for men in the nineteenth century, work became a more serious and more important part of masculine identity than it had been previously.[11] The fact that crime was now seen to be an essentially masculine activity, with illegal actions committed by women increasingly redefined as sexual rather than criminal offences, exemplifies these changes: antisocial men, but not women, would fulfil their breadwinning functions by committing thefts, and be confronted by the state and punished.

11 Riley, *'Am I that Name?'*, p. 51; J. Tosh, book review, *History Workshop Journal* 29 (1990), p. 187.

The public sphere thus expanded in gendered ways, in the sense that older ideas of the respective duties and virtues of men and women were used to determine how new public activities would be gendered. These expectations were not new, but as a result of the growing importance of public life they did become more manifest. As Amanda Vickery has suggested, the accentuation of separate-spheres ideas in this context may have been a response to, and an attempt to constrain, this growth in opportunities for women.[12] Although this ideology did not succeed in halting that growth, it may have contributed to the channelling of men's and women's activities into more definably masculine and feminine channels (as exemplified in the development, after the initial mixed societies, of separate male and female voluntary societies). In contrast, in the early modern period individual men and women were freer, within limits, to adopt both male and female attributes, as is evident for example in the prevalence of cross-dressing, both in real life and in masquerades, and the qualified acceptance of hermaphrodites and same-sex sexual activity. For the most part, such activity could not be allowed to obscure a man's or woman's fundamental gender identity, and it could only be superficial and temporary. Yet to a greater extent than at the end of our period, such transgressions were possible. By the end of the eighteenth century virtually all of these activities were either in decline or subject to increasing disapproval: masquerades 'virtually disappeared' after 1789, and homosexuality was subject to greater persecution. Concurrently, cross-dressing played a much less important role in novels and popular ballads.[13] In this sense, early modern gender roles were less internalised and less confining than they were to become in the Victorian period.[14]

With the advent of a pluralist society in the nineteenth century, however, alternative conceptions of gender roles to the prevailing concept of separate spheres were not silenced. As we saw in Chapter 2, in the 1840s some socialist and feminist writers questioned the very foundations of gender difference, in some cases even promoting the idea of an androgynous personality. Shortly after the end of this period feminist groups began to work for the reform of some of

12 Amanda Vickery, 'Golden age to separate spheres? A review of the categories and chronology of English women's history', *Historical Journal* 36 (1993), p. 400.

13 Dianne Dugaw, *Warrior Women and Popular Balladry, 1650–1850* (Cambridge, 1989), p. 1; Terry Castle, *The Female Thermometer: Eighteenth-Century Culture and the Invention of the Uncanny* (Oxford, 1995), pp. 104–17.

14 Phyllis Mack, *Visionary Women: Ecstatic Prophecy in Seventeenth-Century England* (Berkeley, 1992), p. 6; Pollock, ' "Teach her to live under obedience" ', p. 233.

the laws and social prejudices which limited women's opportunities. Subcultures adopting alternative gender roles developed, notably among utopian socialists and homosexuals. Such sustained opposition to accepted social norms would not have been possible in the early modern period, but given the greater flexibility individuals had at that time to adopt male and female attributes, it was also perhaps far less necessary.

In conclusion, the concept of separate spheres may be useful if we define it as a loose division of responsibilities between men and women within both public life and private life, and we recognise that the impact of ideological prescriptions on day-to-day practice was limited: the spheres were never truly separate, certainly not physically. In contradistinction to the mechanical boundaries implied by this metaphor, we should recognise that significant areas of overlap and possibilities for dissent remained.[15] And while recognising that gender differences existed throughout this period, it is true that they acquired greater moral importance and public prominence in the second half of our period due to a combination of ideological change and the vast expansion of opportunities for both sexes which developed within public life; this constitutes an accentuation, rather than the emergence, of separate spheres. The continuities in gender roles across this long period remain striking: basic divisions of responsibilities persisted, without ever, even at the end of our period, becoming watertight.

---

15 For the suggestion that the polyrhythms of jazz offer more suitable metaphors for understanding women's history, see Elsa Barkley Brown, 'Polyrhythms and Improvization: Lessons for Women's History', *History Workshop Journal* 31 (1991), pp. 85–90.

Select Bibliography

Place of publication is London unless otherwise stated.

CHAPTER 1: INTRODUCTION

H. BARKER and E. CHALUS, eds, *Gender in Eighteenth-Century England. Roles, Representations and Responsibilities* (1997).

L. DAVIDOFF and C. HALL, *Family Fortunes: Men and Women of the English Middle Class, 1780–1850* (1987).

ANTHONY FLETCHER, *Gender, Sex and Subordination in England 1500–1800* (1995).

OLWEN HUFTON, *The Prospect Before Her: A History of Women in Western Europe, Volume 1* (1995).

MARGARET HUNT, *The Middling Sort: Commerce, Gender and Family in England, 1680–1780* (1996).

M. ROPER and J. TOSH (eds), *Manful Assertions: Masculinities in Britain since 1800* (1991).

JOAN SCOTT, 'Gender: a useful category of historical analysis', *American Historical Review* 91 (5) (Dec. 1986), pp. 1053–75.

AMANDA VICKERY, 'Golden age to separate spheres? A review of the categories and chronology of English women's history', *Historical Journal* 36 (1993), pp. 383–414.

CHAPTER 2: IDEAS ABOUT GENDER

ANNE DIGBY, 'Women's biological straitjacket', *Sexuality and Subordination: Interdisciplinary Studies of Gender in the Nineteenth Century*, ed. S. MENDUS and J. RENDALL (1989), pp. 192–220.

CATHERINE HALL, 'The early formation of Victorian domestic

ideology', in her *White, Male and Middle Class: Explorations in Feminism and History* (1992), pp. 75–93.

SUSAN MORGAN, *Sisters in Time: Imagining Gender in Nineteenth-Century British Fiction* (Oxford, 1989).

RUTH PERRY, 'Colonizing the breast: sexuality and maternity in eighteenth-century England', *Journal of the History of Sexuality* 2 (1991), pp. 204–34.

KATHARINE ROGERS, *Feminism in Eighteenth-Century England* (Brighton, 1982).

JANE RENDALL, *The Origins of Modern Feminism* (Basingstoke, 1985).

KATHRYN SHEVELOW, *Women and Print Culture: The Construction of Femininity in the Early Periodical* (1989).

CHAPTER 3: SEXUALITY

G. J. BARKER-BENFIELD, *The Culture of Sensibility: Sex and Society in Eighteenth-Century Britain* (1992).

EMMA DONOGHUE, *Passions Between Women: British Lesbian Culture 1668–1801* (1993).

TIM HITCHCOCK, *English Sexualities, 1700–1800* (1997).

THOMAS LAQUEUR, *Making Sex: The Body and Gender from the Greeks to Freud* (1990).

R. PORTER and M. TEICH, *Sexual Knowledge, Sexual Science: The History of Attitudes Towards Sexuality* (Cambridge, 1994).

KEITH THOMAS, 'The double standard', *Journal of the History of Ideas* 20 (1959) pp. 195–216.

RANDOLPH TRUMBACH, 'Sex, gender and sexual identity in modern culture: male sodomy and female prostitution in enlightenment London', *Journal of the History of Sexuality* 2 (1991), pp. 186–203.

CHAPTER 4: FAMILY AND HOUSEHOLD LIFE

VALERIE FILDES (ed.), *Women as Mothers in Pre-Industrial England* (1990).

JOHN R. GILLIS, *For Better, For Worse: British Marriages 1600 to the Present* (Oxford, 1985).

A. JAMES HAMMERTON, *Cruelty and Companionship: Conflict in Nineteenth-Century Married Life* (1992).

ROSEMARY O'DAY, *The Family and Family Relationships, 1500–1900: England, France and the United States of America* (1994).

LINDA POLLOCK, ' "Teach her to live under obedience": the making of women in the upper ranks of early modern England', *Continuity and Change* 4 (1989), pp. 231–58.

LAWRENCE STONE, *The Family, Sex and Marriage in England 1500–1800* (1977).

JOHN TOSH, 'Authority and nurture in middle-class fatherhood: the case of early and mid-Victorian England', *Gender and History* 8 (1996), pp. 48–64.

RANDOLPH TRUMBACH, *The Rise of the Egalitarian Family: Aristocratic Kinship and Domestic Relations in Eighteenth-Century England* (1978).

CHAPTER 5: WORK

MAXINE BERG, 'What difference did women's work make to the Industrial Revolution?', *History Workshop Journal* 35 (1993), pp. 22–44.

MAXINE BERG, 'Women's work, mechanisation, and the early phases of industrialization in England', in P. JOYCE (ed.), *Historical Meanings of Work* (1987), pp. 64–98.

PETER EARLE, *A City Full of People: Men and Women of London 1650–1750* (1994).

BRIDGET HILL, *Women, Work and Sexual Politics in Eighteenth-Century England* (Oxford, 1989).

JANE RENDALL, *Women in an Industrializing Society: England 1750–1880* (1990).

M. ROBERTS, 'Images of work and gender in early-modern England', in L. CHARLES and L. DUFFIN (eds), *Women and Work in Pre-industrial England* (1985), pp. 122–80.

WALLY SECCOMBE, 'Patriarchy stabilized: the construction of the male breadwinner wage norm in nineteenth-century Britain', *Social History* 11 (1986), pp. 53–76.

PAMELA SHARPE, *Adapting to Capitalism: Working Women in the English Economy, 1700–1850* (1996).

DEBORAH VALENZE, *The First Industrial Woman* (Oxford, 1995).

CHAPTER 6: RELIGION AND POLITICS

ANNA CLARK, *The Struggle for the Breeches: Gender and the Making of the British Working Class* (1995).

PATRICIA CRAWFORD, *Women and Religion in England, 1500–1720* (1993).

RUTH FROW and EDMUND FROW (eds), *Political Women 1800–1850* (1989).

PHYLLIS MACK, *Visionary Women: Ecstatic Prophecy in Seventeenth-Century England* (Berkeley, 1992).

CLARE MIDGLEY, *Women Against Slavery: The British Campaigns, 1780–1870* (1992).

FRANK PROCHASKA, *Women and Philanthropy in Nineteenth Century England* (Oxford, 1980).

W. J. SHEILS and D. WOOD (eds), *Women in the Church* (Ecclesiastical History Society, Studies in Church History vol. 27, 1990).

KARL VON DEN STEINEN, 'The discovery of women in eighteenth-century political life', in *The Women of England from Anglo-Saxon Times to the Present*, ed. BARBARA KANNER (Hamden, Conn., 1979), pp. 229–58.

MALCOLM I. THOMIS and JENNIFER GRIMMETT, *Women in Protest 1800–1850* (New York, 1982).

DEBORAH VALENZE, *Prophetic Sons and Daughters: Female Preaching and Popular Religion in Industrial England* (Princeton, 1985).

CHAPTER 7: SOCIAL AND CULTURAL LIFE

JOHN BEATTIE, 'The criminality of women in eighteenth-century England', *Journal of Social History* 8 (1975), pp. 80–116.

AMY LOUISE ERICKSON, *Women and Property in Early Modern England* (1993).

MALCOLM FEELEY and DEBORAH LITTLE, 'The vanishing female: the decline of women in the criminal process, 1687–1912', *Law and Society Review* 25 (1991), pp. 719–57.

ELAINE HOBBY, *Virtue of Necessity: English Women's Writing 1649–1688* (1988).

J. KERMODE and G. WALKER, (eds) *Women, Crime and the Courts in Early Modern England* (1994).

TIM MELDRUM, 'A women's court in London: defamation at the Bishop of London's Consistory Court, 1700–1745', *London Journal* 19 (1994), pp. 1–20.

JANET TODD, *The Sign of Angellica: Women, Writing and Fiction, 1660–1800* (1989).

CHERYL TURNER, *Living by the Pen: Women Writers in the Eighteenth Century* (1992).

KARL WESTHAUSER, 'Friendship and family in early modern England: the sociability of Adam Eyre and Samuel Pepys', *Journal of Social History* 27 (1994), pp. 517–36.

Index